Designing, Engineering, and Analyzing Reliable and Efficient Software

Hardeep Singh
Guru Nanak Dev University, India

Kulwant Kaur
Apeejay Institute of Management, India

Information Science
REFERENCE

Managing Director:	Lindsay Johnston
Editorial Director:	Joel Gamon
Book Production Manager:	Jennifer Yoder
Publishing Systems Analyst:	Adrienne Freeland
Development Editor:	Myla Merkel
Assistant Acquisitions Editor:	Kayla Wolfe
Typesetter:	Henry Ulrich
Cover Design:	Jason Mull

Published in the United States of America by
Information Science Reference (an imprint of IGI Global)
701 E. Chocolate Avenue
Hershey PA 17033
Tel: 717-533-8845
Fax: 717-533-8661
E-mail: cust@igi-global.com
Web site: http://www.igi-global.com

Library of Congress Cataloging-in-Publication Data

Designing, engineering, and analyzing reliable and efficient software / Hardeep Singh and Kulwant Kaur, editors.
    pages cm
 Includes bibliographical references and index.
 Summary: "This book discusses and analyzes various designs, systems, and advancements in software engineering, concenntrating on the integration of mathematics, computer science, and practices in engineering"--Provided by publisher.
 ISBN 978-1-4666-2958-5 (hardcover) -- ISBN 978-1-4666-2959-2 (ebook) -- ISBN 978-1-4666-2960-8 (print & perpetual access) 1. Software engineering. 2. Computer software--Development. I. Singh, Hardeep, 1963- II. Kaur, Kulwant, 1968-
 QA76.758.D474 2013
 005.1--dc23

2012037376

British Cataloguing in Publication Data
A Cataloguing in Publication record for this book is available from the British Library.

All work contributed to this book is new, previously-unpublished material. The views expressed in this book are those of the authors, but not necessarily of the publisher.

Table of Contents

Section 1
Advanced Software Engineering

Section 2
Systems Analysis, Software Design, and Design Patterns

Section 4
Case Studies and Emerging Technologies

Detailed Table of Contents

Section 1
Advanced Software Engineering

Chapter 1
Fathi Taibi, University of Management and Technology, Malaysia

In order to support the collaborative development of software specifications, there is a need to automate the extraction and integration of the parallel changes or revisions that are made to a shared specification. These revisions are aimed at reaching a specification that satisfies the needs of all the stakeholders. Hence, merging conflicts are inevitable and must be detected and resolved in order to commit the changes made properly to the shared specification leading to a consistent result. A framework is proposed in this chapter to extract and integrate the parallel changes made to Object-Oriented formal specifications in a collaborative development environment. A formal foundation is proposed to uniformly define the specifications, the revisions made to them and the possible merging conflicts. The proposed framework allows extracting and integrating the parallel changes made while addressing a wide range of merging conflicts at the same time. Evaluating the developed algorithms has shown good signs in terms of accuracy and scalability.

Chapter 2
Parminder Kaur, Guru Nanak Dev University, India
Hardeep Singh, Guru Nanak Dev University, India

Component-based technology deals with the process of assembling existing software components in an application such that they interact to satisfy a predefined functionality. The success of component-based software depends on system integrator's ability to select the most suitable software components for their intended application (Leavens and Sitaraman, 2000; Voas and Payne, 2000; Crnkovic et al., 2001). One persistent and largely unaddressed challenge is how the consumers of software components can obtain a meaningful level of trust in the runtime behaviour of software components. The most frequently cited concerns are centered on issues of security and component behaviour (Wallnau, 2004). Certification is a practical, proven means of establishing trust in various sorts of things in other disciplines and is, therefore a natural contender for developing trust in software components. This is only possible if component suppliers have clear and reliable information about their component's functional and non-functional properties. The component attributes allow system integrator to better classify the components. The reliability of a component-based software system is dependant on the reliability of the components that is made of. Proper search, selection, and evaluation process of components is considered as cornerstone for the development of any effective component-based system (Alexandre, 2010).This chapter defines certain properties of a component, which are helpful during their classification process along with component certification/accreditation process, which further helps component suppliers to issue the guarantee of claimed functional properties and quality attributes. Component certification framework is also discussed to evaluate the quality of software components with the help of component quality model and measurement mechanism.

Chapter 3

Reusable software components are the software modules that can be (re)used across a number of applications in a particular domain. Component users prefer to use those components which can be adapted easily for their changing requirements. So components have to evolve continuously in order to attract users. This chapter focuses on the evolutionary aspects of software components. It mentions various techniques for monitoring software evolution. It uses metrics based analysis as the technique to show software evolution of 15 reusable components from the point of view of their size, complexity, and functionality. The evolution analysis is motivated by laws of software evolution which suggest that as software ages, it increases in size and complexity (unless it is managed) and it has to offer increased functionality to please its users. The findings of the study indicate that the size of the software components (in this data set) grows at a linear rate, and complexity is well managed. However, increase in functionality is sub linear for almost all the components. It remains almost constant for some of them.

Chapter 4

Recommender systems are widely used intelligent applications which assist users in a decision-making process to choose one item amongst a potentially overwhelming set of alternative products or services. Recommender systems use the opinions of members of a community to help individuals in that community by identifying information most likely to be interesting to them or relevant to their needs. Recommender systems have various core design crosscutting issues such as: user preference learning, security, mobility, visualization, interaction etc that are required to be handled properly in order to implement an efficient, good quality and maintainable recommender system. Implementation of these crosscutting design issues of the recommender systems using conventional agent-oriented approach creates the problem of code scattering and code tangling. An Aspect-Oriented Recommender System is a multi agent system that handles core design issues of the recommender system in a better modular way by using the concepts of aspect oriented programming, which in turn improves the system reusability, maintainability, and removes the scattering and tangling problems from the recommender system.

The chapter focuses on a graph – semantic based conceptual data model for semi-structured data, called Graph Object Oriented Semi-Structured Data Model (GOOSSDM), to conceptualize the different facets of such system in object oriented paradigm. The model defines a set of graph based formal constructs, varieties of relationship types with participation constraints. It is accompanied with a rich set of graphical notations and those are used to specify the conceptual level design of semi-structured database system. The approach facilitates modeling of irregular, heterogeneous, hierarchical, and non-hierarchical semi-structured data at the conceptual level. The GOOSSDM is also able to represent the mixed content in semi-structured data. Moreover, the approach is capable to model XML document at conceptual level with the facility of document-centric design, ordering and disjunction characteristic. The chapter also includes a rule based transformation mechanism for GOOSSDM schema into the equivalent XML Schema Definition (XSD). Moreover, the chapter also provides comparative study of several similar kinds of proposals for semi-structured data models based on the properties of semi-structured data and future research scope in this area.

Maintainability is one of the important characteristics of quality of software. It is the measure of efforts needed to modify the software. Large number of subjective techniques has been developed in industry to deal with assessment or prediction of this characteristic. But these techniques generally fail due to their inability to break down maintainability to a level of actual evaluation. They also lack homogeneity in the models thus developed and so fail to take into account the cost factor associated with maintainability. Activity based quality model is found to decompose maintainability to an actual analyzable level. It manages maintainability in terms of software maintenance efforts but it lacks quantitative evaluation of this characteristic. Bayesian approach to deal with this model added quantitative feature but also added crispness to the system developed. In this chapter, the authors propose the use of fuzzy approach to correct the existing Bayesian approach to deal with activity based quality model. A comprehensive comparative study is presented to show the effectiveness of proposed technique.

In the present time, software plays a vital role in business, governance, and society in general, so a continuous improvement of software productivity and quality such as reliability, robustness, etc. is an important goal of software engineering. During software development, a large amount of data is produced, such as software attribute repositories and program execution trace, which may help in future development and project management activities. Effective software development needs quantification, measurement, and modelling of previous software artefacts. The development of large and complex software systems is a formidable challenge which requires some additional activities to support software development and project management processes. In this scenario, data mining can provide a helpful hand in the software development process. This chapter discusses the application of data mining in software engineering and includes static and dynamic defect detection, clone detection, maintenance, etc. It provides a way to understand the software artifacts and processes to assist in software engineering tasks.

Chapter 8

G. Sreedhar, Rashtriya Sanskrit Vidyapeetha (Deemed University), India

Today, the web is not only an information resource, but also it is becoming an automated tool in various applications. Due to the increasing popularity of WWW, one can be very cautious in designing the website. Poor and careless web design leads to hardship to public utility and does not serve the purpose. If the website is not designed properly, the user may face many difficulties in using the website. In last few years a set of website metrics were defined and specified based on the data collection point of view. Among hundred and fifty automated web metrics catalogued up to now, metrics for link and page faults, metrics for navigation, metrics for information, metrics for media, metrics for size and performance, and metrics for accessibility are important categories for evaluation of quality of web site. The website structure and navigation depicts the structure of the website. The navigation of website is dependent on structure of the web site. The present chapter is an attempt to develop a comprehensive quality assurance mechanism towards quality web design process. In this chapter, various measures and metrics for the quality of website structure are investigated as a part of quality assurance process.

Chapter 9

Lakhwinder Kaur, Apeejay Institute of Management Technical Campus, India
Kuljit Kaur, Guru Nanak Dev University, India
Ashu Gupta, Apeejay Institute of Management Technical Campus, India

Refactoring is a process that attempts to enhance software code quality by using small transforming functions and modifying the structure of the program through slightly different algorithm. It is important to analyze the design pattern of the software code as well as the impact and possibility of the application of some conflicting refactorings on it. The objective of this chapter is to present an approach for analyzing software design patterns in order to avoid the conflict in application of available refactoring techniques. This chapter discusses the mechanism to study software code or design patterns to automate the process of applying available refactorings while addressing the problem of conflict in their application.

Section 3
Advancements in Engineering of Systems

Chapter 10

Ayda Saidane, University of Luxembourg, Luxembourg

Nicolas Guelfi, University of Luxembourg, Luxembourg

The quality of software systems depends strongly on their architecture. For this reason, taking into account non-functional requirements at architecture level is crucial for the success of the software development process. Early architecture model validation facilitates the detection and correction of design errors. In this research, the authors are interested in security critical systems, which require a reliable validation process. So far, they are missing security-testing approaches providing an appropriate compromise between software quality and development cost while satisfying certification and audit procedures requirements through automated and documented validation activities. In this chapter, the authors propose a novel test-driven and architecture model-based security engineering approach for resilient systems. It consists of a test-driven security modeling framework and a test based validation approach. The assessment of the security requirement satisfaction is based on the test traces analysis. Throughout this study, the authors illustrate the approach using a client server architecture case study.

Chapter 11

Neeraj Sharma, Punjabi University, India

Kawaljeet Singh, Punjabi University, India

D.P. Goyal, Management Development Institute, India

Chapter 12

Amandeep Kaur, Apeejay Institute of Management Technical Campus, India

Usability engineering is a field that focus on the human-computer interaction and exclusively in making the GUI's with high usability. A Usability Engineer validates the usability of an interface and recommending methods to improve its purview. This chapter elaborates various techniques to improve usability of websites: software graphical user interfaces (GUIs). It includes details on assessing and making recommendations to improve usability than it does on design, though Usability Engineers may still engage in design to some extent, particularly design of wire-frames or other prototypes. They conduct usability evaluations of existing or proposed user-interfaces and their findings are fed back to the designer.

Chapter 13

Punam Bedi, University of Delhi, India

Vandana Gandotra, University of Delhi, India

Archana Singhal, University of Delhi, India

This chapter discusses adoption of some proactive strategies in threat management for security of software systems. Security requirements play an important role for secure software systems which arise due to threats to the assets from malicious users. It is therefore imperative to develop realistic and meaningful security requirements. A hybrid technique has been presented in this chapter evolved by overlapping the strengths of misuse cases and attack trees for elicitation of flawless security requirements. This chapter also discusses an innovative technique using fuzzy logic as a proactive step to break the jinx of brittleness of present day security measures based on binary principle. In this mechanism, partially secure state evolved between safe state and failed state using fuzzy logic provides an alert signal to take appropriate additional preventive measures to save the system from entering into the failed state to the extent possible.

Section 4
Case Studies and Emerging Technologies

Chapter 14

Daljit Kaur, Lyallpur Khalsa College, India
Parminder Kaur, Guru Nanak Dev University, India

This chapter is an effort to develop secure web applications based on known vulnerabilities. It has been seen that in the rapid race of developing web applications in minimum time and budget, security is given the least importance, and a consequence of which is that web applications are developed and hosted with a number of vulnerabilities in them. In this race, one thing is constant that attackers take advantage of weaknesses existing in technology for financial gain and theft of intellectual property. In this proposed method of secure web development, most common vulnerabilities and their occurrence in development process is discussed. Mapping vulnerabilities to the actions needed to take during development process may help developers to understand vulnerability and avoid vulnerabilities in application.

Chapter 15

Aggelos Liapis, European Dynamics SA, Greece
Evangelos Argyzoudis, European Dynamics SA, Greece

The Concurrent Design Facility (CDF) of the European Space Agency (ESA) allows a team of experts from several disciplines to apply concurrent engineering for the design of future space missions. It facilitates faster and effective interaction of all disciplines involved, ensuring consistent and high-quality results. It is primarily used to assess the technical and financial feasibility of future space missions and new spacecraft concepts, though for some projects, the facilities and the data exchange model are used during later phases. This chapter focuses on the field of computer supported collaborative work (CSCW) and its supporting areas whose mission is to support interaction between people, using computers as the enabling technology. Its aim is to present the design and implementation framework of a semantically driven, collaborative working environment (CWE) that allows ESA's CDF to be used by projects more extensively and effectively during project meetings, task forces, and reviews.

Chapter 16

Nisha Ratti, Rayat Institute of Engineering and Technology, India
Parminder Kaur, Guru Nanak Dev University, India

As software is developed and deployed, it is extremely common for multiple versions of the same software to be deployed in different sites, and for the software's developers to be working privately on updates.

Bugs and other issues with software are often only present in certain versions (because of the fixing of some problems and the introduction of others the program evolves). Therefore, for the purposes of locating and fixing bugs, it is vitally important for the debugger to be able to retrieve and run different versions of the software to determine in which version(s) the problem occurs. All these tasks are related with version control. This case study makes an attempt to show that how Subversion, an open source version control tool, is helpful in tracing the changes processed at different time. This case study also shows the comparison between open source and commercial version control tools.

Foreword

It is refreshing to see a book that addresses current issues and topics in the field of software engineering, which has the potential to make significant contribution to the analysis and design of reliable and efficient software.

Modern day software systems are highly complex and their design are exponentially challenging task. Several strategies and techniques have been proposed and applied to develop good quality software - may be in the realm of real-time, parallel and distributed, autonomic, web-space, and so on. Variety of models and architectures, such as, object-, aspect-, component-, agent-oriented, agile approach, and a few others, exist and are being developed. Assuring quality of software systems is a daunting task and is drawing the attention of the leading software specialists in the field.

Prof. Hardeep Singh, himself a renowned teacher and researcher, and Ms. Kulwant Kaur, a senior faculty and one of the prominent contributors in the area of Software Engineering, have assembled a team of leading experts to present the best of current scenario and practices in the field of software engineering. The contents of the book are divided into four sections: (1) Advanced Software Engineering, (2) Systems Analysis, Software Design and Patterns, (3) Advancements in Engineering of Systems, and (4) Case Studies and Emerging Technologies. The various topics covered in these sections, such as, change management, component certification and standards, aspect-oriented multi-agent system, quality assurance of website structure, test-driven architectures, development of secure software systems, usability engineering, and others, are comprehensive and presented in lucid style. The chapters in the book are filled with proven methods, illustrative examples, tools and representative results from working systems in the field. The relevant subject matter is treated with fair details that are of quite significance for an emerging field.

The section on "Case Studies and Emerging Technologies" will prove of immense value to the students of software engineering and researchers.

This book is a must read for all software engineers interested in acquainting themselves with the current developments in the field.

P. S. Grover
Guru Tegh Bahadur Institute of Technology, GGS Indraprastha University, India

P. S. Grover *has been Dean and Head of Computer Science Department and Director of Computing Services at University of Delhi, Delhi, India. He has been among the pioneers of computer education, training, development and research in the country. He has widely published research papers (over 125) in international/national journals/conferences (referred), including*

ACM, IEEE, Journal of Object Technology, Journal of Software and Knowledge Engineering, Journal of Software: Practice and Experience, Physical Review, and Physics Letters. He has written nine books in the field of computer science. He was also the Guest Editor of the special issue of Journal of Computer Science and Informatics on Software Engineering, published by Computer Society of India. He is on the Editorial Board of three international journals. His area of work is: software engineering, computer modeling & simulation, emotion and opinion mining, multimedia and information systems, quality assurance in higher education, and outcome-based teaching/learning methodology.

Preface

This book presents recent developments and discoveries in the vital areas of software engineering to stimulate further research, and to rapidly pass such discoveries to our community. Software engineering (SE) is concerned with developing and maintaining software systems that behave reliably and efficiently, are affordable to develop and maintain, and that satisfy all the requirements that customers have defined for them. This is important because of the impact of large, expensive software systems and the role of software in safety-critical applications. It integrates significant mathematics, computer science, and practices whose origins are in engineering.

The materials presented in this book include: advanced software engineering, systems analysis, software design and design patterns, advancements in engineering of systems, and case studies and emerging technologies.

OBJECTIVE OF THE BOOK

- To promote awareness of software engineering methodologies.
- To identify quality oriented software architecture (design and Support).
- To highlight educational establishment in information systems analysis and specification.
- To analyze advancements in engineering of systems.
- To analyze various approaches to software engineering.
- How software engineering helps for performance enhancement and appraisal.
- To analyze university-industry collaborations which may result in benefits to universities as well as industry, through complementary, as well as differing goals of each party?

The editors believe that the edited book presents the recent developments and discoveries in field of software engineering and offers important information for students and scientists in the community.

The book divided into four sections that reveal the main concepts examined in the book.

Section 1 throws light on aspects related to advanced software engineering which includes change management in shared software specifications; component certification process and standards; analyzing growth trends of reusable software components; and aspect-oriented recommender system.

Section 2 provides insight in to systems analysis, software design, and design patterns. This section includes chapters on design of semi-structured database system: conceptual model to logical representation; a comparative study of Bayesian and fuzzy inference approach to assess quality of the software using activity-based quality model; data mining techniques for software quality prediction; quality assurance of website structure; and resolving conflict in code refactoring.

Section 3 provides details related to advancements in engineering of systems and includes chapters such as Towards Test - Driven and Architecture Model Based Security and Resilience Engineering; Software Engineering, Process Improvement & Experience Management: Is the Nexus Productive? Clues from the Indian Giants; Usability engineering methods and tools; and Innovative Strategies for Secure Software Development.

Section 4 deals with how software engineering techniques can be used in case studies and emerging technologies. Case studies include secure web development; Galileo case study for collaborative design environment for the European Space Agency's concurrent design facility; and version control in component-based systems.

The intended audience of this book is primarily researchers, research students and practitioners interested in the advances of software engineering. The book presents in a clear and accessible language a coherent integration of the different quality research papers ranging from conceptual to applied research. The resulting synthesis of experience and concepts will be of significant value to the academicians and researchers working in this emerging field. Thanks go to all those who provided constructive and comprehensive reviews.

We wish to thank all of the authors for their insights and excellent contributions to this edited book. We trust that this book will extend the thinking in software engineering and more broadly be of benefit to those who read it.

Hardeep Singh
Guru Nanak Dev University, India

Kulwant Kaur
Apeejay Institute of Management, India

Acknowledgment

Looking back over this year – long work, we feel a sense of deep satisfaction that we managed to achieve so much. In this brief section, the editors wish to acknowledge with thanks to all those involved in the process of this book, without whose support it could not have been completed successfully.

We have benefited from the help of many people during the evolution of this book. We express our thanks to Erika Carter, Kristin M. Klinger, and Myla Harty, IGI Global, USA.

Many persons have contributed time, energy, ideas, and suggestions for realization of this project. The strength of this book is largely attributed to collective wisdom, work, and experiences of academia, researchers, students, and practitioners. The book would not have been possible without the unflinching dedication of one and all.

The editors wish to acknowledge with thanks their families as they always supported us throughout editing this book and we really appreciate it.

We would also like to express thanks to the management and staff of Guru Nanak Dev University, Amritsar and Apeejay Institute of Management Technical Campus, Jalandhar, India for always providing us necessary support when we needed the most.

Section 1
Advanced Software Engineering

Chapter 1
Change Management in Shared Software Specifications

Fathi Taibi
University of Management and Technology, Malaysia

ABSTRACT

In order to support the collaborative development of software specifications, there is a need to automate the extraction and integration of the parallel changes or revisions that are made to a shared specification. These revisions are aimed at reaching a specification that satisfies the needs of all the stakeholders. Hence, merging conflicts are inevitable and must be detected and resolved in order to commit the changes made properly to the shared specification leading to a consistent result. A framework is proposed in this chapter to extract and integrate the parallel changes made to Object-Oriented formal specifications in a collaborative development environment. A formal foundation is proposed to uniformly define the specifications, the revisions made to them and the possible merging conflicts. The proposed framework allows extracting and integrating the parallel changes made while addressing a wide range of merging conflicts at the same time. Evaluating the developed algorithms has shown good signs in terms of accuracy and scalability.

INTRODUCTION

Collaborative development has been identified as one of the most important keys to the success of a software project (Frost, 2007). This is especially true in the case of the requirements specification phase since the latter involves several people specifying the requirements of various stakeholders. The degree to which a software system satisfies its requirements is the primary measure of a software project's success (Nuseibeh & Easterbrook, 2000), which makes specifying software requirements even more critical.

DOI: 10.4018/978-1-4666-2958-5.ch001

Formal methods in general (Ciapessoni et al., 1999; Hinchey, 2008; Woodcock et al., 2009) and Object-Oriented (OO) formal methods in particular (Smith, 2000) allow specifying software requirements in a precise, well-structured and unambiguous manner compared to informal or even semi-formal specifications. Whenever used in industrial software projects, they have always been the driving factor to success. For example, the options and tax exemption subsystems of the TradeOne project have been developed using an OO formal method where 41.96% reduction in the number of defects detected per Kilo Lines Of Code (KLOC) was observed in the components developed using the formal method (Fitzgerald et al., 2008; Fitzgerald & Larsen, 2006). Even a partial or gradual use of OO formal methods (or formal methods in general) could make reliability and dependability in today's large and complex software systems achievable, and could lead to a considerable reduction or prevention of software defects. Moreover, supporting the collaborative development of OO formal specification could allow widening the usage of formal methods in software development, which should improve software quality.

The objective of this chapter is to give an overview of a framework intended for the systematic extraction and integration of the parallel changes made to shared OO formal specifications in a collaborative development environment. A formal foundation is proposed to model the manipulated specifications, the changes made to them and any resulting merging conflicts. Additionally, three algorithms are proposed for extracting and integrating the parallel changes while maintaining consistency through the detection and resolution of merging conflicts. The developed algorithms are empirically evaluated using well defined case studies and experiments. The experimental results are carefully analyzed to assess the ability of the proposed framework in dealing with larger and more complex specifications.

THE CHANGE MANAGEMENT PROBLEM

Software merging (Altmanninger et al., 2009; Boronat et al., 2007) is the process of combining n (usually n=2) alternative versions of a software document into a consolidated version. Supporting collaborative development of OO formal specifications requires merging the parallel revisions made to a shared specification located at shared repository. It also requires the detection and resolution of any conflicts caused by the various revisions made. Hence, the main problem here is how the parallel changes made to a shared OO formal specification can be systematically combined while ensuring the consistency of the resulting specification.

The copy-modify-merge paradigm (Ignat & Norrie, 2006) allows optimistic collaborative editing (Penichet et al., 2007) to be performed on documents located in a shared repository. The latter contains some shared documents undergoing revisions and is accessed by multiple users working in a distributed and asynchronous fashion. In the shared repository, only the last version of a particular document is saved. However, the revisions made over the collaboration time to each one of the documents are saved as well. This version management style allows saving a substantial amount of disk space since not all versions of a particular document are maintained and the revisions made (differences) are generally much smaller than the documents themselves. Figure 1 shows a graphical illustration of this paradigm.

In Figure 1, collaborative editing according to the copy-modify-merge paradigm is described using five operations encompassing various activities. The *Checkout* operation is used to create a local copy of a shared document (base version) in a particular local workspace. The operation *Modify* represents the modifications made to the shared document by some user in the local workspace. Once the modifications are completed, this user can save the changes made into the shared

Figure 1. A graphical illustration of the copy-modify-merge paradigm

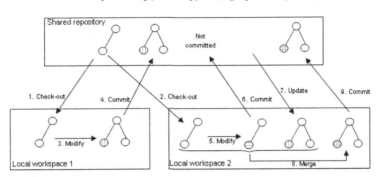

repository through the *Commit* operation. This is possible only if the version of the document being modified has not evolved in the meantime. Otherwise, the revisions made cannot be committed into the repository and the user at the local workspace needs to get the current version of the document in question through the *Update* operation. Hence, using the base, the local and the current versions of the shared document, a *Merge* operation is performed to combine the modifications made. Merging involves also detecting and resolving any conflicts resulting because of the parallel modifications made. The version obtained through merging can then be committed into the repository.

Accurate extraction of the parallel changes made in the versions is a pre-requisite to integrating them properly to the shared version. Change extraction itself requires accurate matching of the elements of the compared specifications. This is probably the most challenging problem since matching has to be tool-independent (i.e. it should not depend on the tools used to create or edit the specifications) and has to consider all the features of the elements while maintaining a good balance between the accuracy of the results and the efficiency of the matching process.

The information available in the versions alone is not enough to perform an accurate merging. The revisions made must also be carefully analyzed in order to perform a more precise and accurate merging compared to when only the information

available in the versions is used. Moreover, dealing with merging conflicts is crucial in order to ensure the consistency of its results. Conflicts arise because of the diversity of views and perspectives of the developers who make the parallel changes. Handling them is a tedious and complex process due to the diversity of the changes and conflicts that can occur. However, when conflicts are dealt with properly, a consistent and complete specification that consolidates the views of all the revisions made is obtained. Furthermore, locking mechanisms (Sun & Chen, 2002) can prevent conflicts from occurring by not allowing parallel changes to the same elements. However, such mechanisms are not suitable to environments where development tasks are carried out in an asynchronous and distributed manner such as during requirements specification. Additionally, locking often hinders collaboration rather than supports it.

An operation-based approach (Mens, 2002) should enable producing precise and accurate results since the exact modifications made in the versions are used during merging. It should also provide a good support for conflicts detection since comparing the differences between the versions is more effective than comparing the elements of the versions themselves (state-based merging). However, this requires an effective modeling of the changes made during collaboration and also the extraction of highly accurate edit scripts representing them. Moreover, it requires defining conflicts precisely and the development of systematic resolutions to handle them, which should increase the effectiveness and productivity of the collaboration. Finally, transformation techniques are needed in order to enable integrating the parallel changes made so that they can be committed properly to the shared specification while ensuring redundancy-free results.

FORMAL FOUNDATION

Modeling the Manipulated Specifications

A graph-based meta-model is proposed for representing OO formal specifications where elements are represented as nodes and their relationships as edges. A typing hierarchy separates the various elements and relationships. A specification is modeled as a set of heterogeneous elements interconnected through several types of relationships. Figure 2 shows the proposed meta-model.

The elements of specifications are categorized into four main groups. Attributes of classes, inputs and outputs of operations are modeled using the meta-class *Variable*. The *Predicate* meta-class is used to model invariants of classes, initialization predicates, and pre/post conditions of operations. Finally, the *Class* and *Operation* meta-classes are used to model classes and their operations. Fur-

thermore, the relationships between the elements of specifications are categorized into six groups. The *DeclaredIn*, *AccessedBy*, and *ChangedBy* meta-classes are used to model the relationships between the elements of a class. For example, an attribute or an operation is declared in a class, and an attribute is accessed by or changed by an operation. The meta-classes *Aggregates*, *AssociatedWith* and *Extends* are used to model the main types of relationships that exist between the classes of specifications namely aggregation, association and inheritance.

A *Node* has a *name* and a *visibility* attributes. The latter attribute is used to specify whether an element is accessible outside the class in which it is declared (i.e. public) or not. An *Edge* has a *label*, a *source* node and a *target* node while a *Variable* node has a *data_type* attribute that can be a basic data type provided by the formal language, a predefined type or a class name. Finally, a *value* attribute is used to represent the content of a *Predicate* node, which is a set of strings (i.e. the conjunction of several predicate lines).

Modeling the Changes Made to Specifications

The changes made to a shared specification during collaborative development are modeled as a set of primitive edit operations (*delta*). Each operation

Figure 2. The proposed meta-model for representing specifications

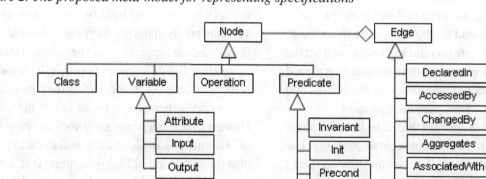

deals with one element at a time, and contains all the necessary details that facilitate committing them properly to the shared specification. Table 1 summarizes the details of the proposed change operations and the effect of each one of them.

The operations are classified into five categories dealing with all possible changes that need to be detected when comparing two versions of a shared specification. The first category is concerned about *insertions* and includes the operations *insertNode* and *insertLink*. The second category deals with *deletions* and includes the operations *deleteLink*, *deleteAllLink* and *deleteNode*. The third and fourth categories are concerned about *renames* and *modifications* and include the operations *Rename*, *setNodeProperty* and *Modify* while the fifth category is concerned about *moves* and includes the operation *Move*.

Modeling Merging Conflicts

Given a graph G representing a specification located in a shared repository and two sets of change operations D_{Last} and D_{Local} representing some parallel modifications made to it. Let D_{Last} be the modifications made by a user and have already been committed to the shared specification whose current state is G' and let D_{Local} be the modifications made by another user to G and cannot be committed since the latter has changed. Two classes of conflicts can be defined:

- **Evolution Conflicts:** Happen when the modifications made in D_{Last} to G forbid committing those in D_{Local} (i.e. lost updates). For example, if a class' operation is renamed differently in D_{Last} and D_{Local}.
- **Structural Conflicts:** Happen when the modifications made in D_{Local} or D_{Last} and D_{Local} lead to structural conflicts in G. For example, if the insertion of an inheritance link between two classes leads to an inheritance cycle.

A more detailed description of change operations and how they lead to evolution and structural conflicts is proposed using a formal specification. The data types *OperationType*, *ARGUMENT*, and *StructuralConsistencyRule* are used to allow defining change operations by assigning their types (*insertNode*, *setNodeProperty*, etc) and arguments (i.e. the nodes and edges they manipulate and their associated properties and values) as well as defining conflicts. *ARGUMENT* represents a *Node* reference, an *Edge* reference or a *PHRASE*. *StructuralConsistencyRule* represents a structural consistency rule that should be satisfied by a specification S in order to ensure its well-formedness. A formal specification (in Object-Z) of evolution and structural conflicts is shown in Figure 3.

A change operation is specified as a class *COperation* with attributes representing the operation's type (*opType*) and a non-empty set of arguments (*opArgs*). The operations *setDetails*,

Table 1. The proposed change operations

Operation	Effect
insertNode(n, t)	Inserts a new node n where t is the node's type.
setNodeProperty(n, p, v)	Assigns for the 1st time a value v to the property p of a node n
insertLink(k, n_1, n_2, t)	Inserts a new link k between the nodes n_1 and n_2 where t is the link's type
deleteLink(k)	Removes a link k.
deleteAllLink(n)	Removes all *links* associated with a node n.
deleteNode(n)	Removes a node n.
Rename(n, oldname, newname)	Renames a node n named *oldname* with *newname*.
Modify(e, p, v_1, v_2)	Modifies an element e by changing the value of its property p (other than name) whose value is v_1 with a new value v_2.
Move(n, A, B, t)	Moves a node n by deleting its existing link (of type t) with a class A and creating a new link of the same type with another class B.

Figure 3. A formal specification of merging conflicts

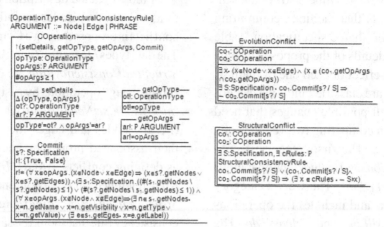

getOpType and *getOpArgs* are specified to allow assigning values to the class' attributes as well as getting them. *Commit* is used to specify the pre and post conditions of integrating a change operation to a shared specification *s?*. These conditions ensure that the changed node(s) or edge(s) exist in *s?*, the existence of a new version s_1 of the shared specification whose nodes differ from those of *s?* by one node at most and the existence of a *Node n* or an *Edge e* in s_1 whose properties have been set/changed by the arguments of the change operation. Moreover, an evolution conflict is specified as a class *EvolutionConflict* with two change operations (co_1 and co_2) as attributes and an invariant indicating that co_1 and co_2 manipulate the same *Node* or *Edge* and that committing co_2 to a specification *S* is not possible after co_1 is committed. Similarly, a structural conflict is specified as a class *StructuralConflict* with two change operations (co_1 and co_2) as attributes and an invariant indicating that committing co_1 or co_2 after co_1 to a specification *S* makes it break some structural consistency rule.

A balanced set of 26 conflicts were defined and used to evaluate the proposed framework (Table 2). Evolution conflicts are cause by two operations while structural conflicts are caused by either one operation (R17-R23) or two (R15-R16 and R24-R26). For example, a *cyclic-inheritance-link*

is caused by one *insertLink* operation while a *link-without-source* conflict is caused by an *insertLink* operation whose source node has been removed by a *deleteNode* operation that has already been committed to the shared specification.

CHANGE EXTRACTION

Similarity Detection and Matching

The proposed matching algorithm compares the elements of two specifications in order to produce a set of their matched elements according to a chosen similarity threshold. It uses an overall similarity metric that is calculated based on name and structural similarity. Comparing inputs, outputs, and predicates is prevented if the operations or classes in which they are declared have not been matched, which reduces the number of comparisons during matching. This should translate into a gain in terms of accuracy and efficiency in the proposed algorithm. The choice of the similarity threshold is crucial since low thresholds may increase the number of false positives (i.e. incorrectly matched elements), while high thresholds may increase the number of false negatives (i.e. undetected real matches). These mismatches lead to inaccurate and highly sub-optimal change extraction results.

Table 2. Merging conflicts and their causes

Evolution Conflict	Cause		Structural Conflict	Cause	
	Operation 1	Operation 2		Operation 1	Operation 2
modify-deleted-element (R1)	deleteNode	Modify	link-without-source (R15) link-without-target (R16)	deleteNode	insertLink
rename-deleted-element (R2)	deleteNode	Rename	double-containment (R17)	insertLink	-
move-deleted-element (R3)	deleteNode	Move	symmetric-link (R18)	insertLink	-
modify-deleted-link (R4)	deleteLink	Modify	cyclic-inheritance-link (R19)	insertLink	-
concurrent-update (R5)	Modify	Modify	redundant-link (R20)	insertLink	-
concurrent-renaming (R6)	Rename	Rename	redundant-declaration (R21)	insertLink	-
concurrent-moving (R7)	Move	Move	redundant-element (R22)	insertNode	-
concurrent-deletion (R8)	deleteNode	deleteNode	double-definition (R23)	Rename	-
	deleteLink	deleteLink	unwanted-reachability (R24)	insertLink	insertLink
modify-renamed-element (R9)	Rename	Modify	modify-source-class (R25) modify-target-class (R26)	Modify	insertLink
move-renamed-element (R10)	Rename	Move			
delete-renamed-element (R11)	Rename	deleteNode			
modify-moved-element (R12)	Move	Modify			
rename-moved-element (R13)	Move	Rename			
delete-moved-element (R14)	Move	deleteNode			

The proposed name similarity between any two given elements of specifications A and B is a value between 0 and 1 that measures how close their names are. Measurements using three practically proven string similarity metrics were used in the calculation. They include similarity metrics using the Longest Common Substring (SIM_{LCS}), Bi-Gram measure (SIM_{BG}), and Levenstein distance (SIM_{Lev}) (Navarro, 2002). Rather than calculating the name similarity using the three metrics and then taking the maximum result obtained, which reduces the efficiency of the matching algorithm. Analyzing the results obtained from the experiments conducted has made it possible to derive a simple rule based on which the best similarity result is obtained using only one or two calculated

metrics at most. Additionally, four normalization techniques have been used (*stringNormalization* procedure) to improve the precision of name similarity. They include converting the compared strings to uppercase before comparison, replacing link characters (i.e. "-" and "_") with one space, separating digits from other characters with one space, and reducing the space between words to one space only.

The proposed rule used to calculate name similarity (SIM_{Name}) of two strings S and T (representing the names or values in case of predicates) is shown below in Box 1.

SIM_{Name} is calculated using SIM_{BG} in case it is bigger or equal to a similarity threshold α. In case the result obtained is below α, a decision is made

Box 1.

$$
\mathrm{SIM}_{\mathrm{Name}}(S, T) = \begin{cases} \mathrm{SIM}_{\mathrm{BG}}(S', T') \ \mathit{if\ SIM_{BG}(S',\ T') \geq \alpha} \\ \mathit{max}(\mathrm{SIM}_{\mathrm{BG}}(S', T'), \mathrm{SIM}_{\mathrm{Lev}}(S', T')) \ \mathit{if\ SIM_{BG}(S',\ T') < \alpha\ AND\ |S|\text{-}|T| \leq \beta} \\ \mathit{max}(\mathrm{SIM}_{\mathrm{BG}}(S', T'), \mathrm{SIM}_{\mathrm{LCS}}(S', T')) \ \mathit{else} \end{cases} \quad (1)
$$

Where: S'=stringNormalization(S) and T'=stringNormalization(T)

on which one of the other metrics to calculate. If S and T have similar lengths (i.e. the distance between them is equal to or below a distance threshold β) then SIM_{Lev} is calculated otherwise SIM_{LCS} is calculated. This is due to the fact that SIM_{Lev} has produced better results when the compared strings have similar lengths. The maximum of the two calculated similarity values is taken in both cases. The proposed metric has been tested extensively, and the results obtained were compared to the maximum of the similarity values obtained using SIM_{BG}, SIM_{Lev}, and SIM_{LCS}. In 85.96% of the cases, SIM_{Name} was able to produce the best result using $\alpha=0.9$ and $\beta=2$.

The proposed structural similarity between two specification elements A and B is a number between 0 and 1 measuring the similarity of their structures. Comparing structures involves comparing the adjacent elements of A and B. Hence, the more similar their adjacent elements are, the better their structural similarity should be. Additionally, only compatibly typed and compatibly linked adjacent elements are compared. For example, in the case of two classes A and B, their adjacent classes are compared only if they are linked to A and B using the same type of relationships, which makes the proposed algorithm more efficient. Furthermore, comparing adjacent elements based on name similarity only does not lead to very accurate results since the names chosen for the inputs and outputs of an operation as well as the attributes of a class are often different (i.e. renamed elements). Hence, data types were compared instead of names for *Variable* nodes and names of variables were replaced with their types for *Predicate* nodes

(*typeNormalization* procedure). This have led to a more precise calculation of structural similarity for elements that are structurally similar even if they have undergone a considerable amount of renames and modifications. The proposed structural similarity (SIM_{str}) between two elements A and B is calculated using the following formula.

$$
SIM_{Str}(A, B) = \frac{2 \times \sum SIM_{\mathrm{Name}}(x_i', y_i')}{n + \sum SIM_{\mathrm{Name}}(x_i', y_i')} \quad (2)
$$

where: (x_i, y_i) are the pairs of adjacent elements of (A, B) that are compatibly typed and compatibly linked to A and B respectively. n is the number of comparisons. $x'_i = $ typeNormalization(x_i) and $y'_i = $ typeNormalization(y_i)

Given two specification elements A and B, their adjacent elements that are compatibly typed and compatibly linked are compared and their similarities are accumulated after applying the normalization techniques discussed previously. The accumulated values and the number of comparisons performed are used to calculate a normalized value that has given far better results in comparison to a simple average.

The proposed overall similarity between two specification elements A and B is a normalized value between 0 and 1 which combines their structural similarity SIM_{Str} and their name similarity SIM_{Name}. Rather than calculating the average of SIM_{Str} and SIM_{Name}, a metric that is driven by SIM_{Str} is used where the impact of SIM_{Name} is reduced for structurally similar elements. Let $S_1 = SIM_{Name}(A, B)$ and $S_2 = SIM_{Str}(A, B)$. The overall similarity between *A* and *B*, *SIM(A, B)*, is calculated using the following formula:

$$SIM(A,B) = \frac{S_1 + S_2}{1 + S_1} \qquad (3)$$

The formula used has been chosen in such way that even if the name similarity of two elements is zero they will be matched if they are structurally similar (i.e. case of renamed elements). Additionally, elements with strong name similarity that have undergone a moderate amount of changes to their structures can still be matched to a certain extend. Hence, a metric driven by structural similarity is created since it contains more significant similarity weight.

The proposed matching algorithm accepts two versions of a shared specification represented as graphs (G_1 and G_2), compares their elements using the overall similarity *SIM* and a similarity threshold *T*, and produces a set *Match* storing their confirmed matches (the best match is taken). In order to increase the algorithm's efficiency, the graphs are traversed first to produce four sets of different types of nodes (i.e. *Class*, *Operation*, *Variable* and *Predicate*) before comparison. After completing the matching of *Class* elements, the algorithm processes *Operation*, *Variable*, and *Predicate* elements in this order. The aim is to prevent comparing and matching invariants and initialization predicates if their classes have not been matched as well as to prevent comparing and matching inputs, outputs, pre and post conditions if their operations have not been matched. However, *Operation* and *Attribute* elements can still be matched even if their respective classes have not been matched since they indicate moved elements. Hence, the proposed matching algorithm employs a top-down approach in order to deal with these constraints and at the end of the matching process, the matching results will be ordered according to the types of the elements of specifications.

CHANGE EXTRACTION

The proposed change extraction algorithm compares two versions of a shared specification using the results of the matching algorithm in order to produce a set of edit operations representing precisely the exact differences between them. The algorithm accepts two graphs G_1 and G_2 (the compared specifications), their matching set *Match*, and produces a set *delta* containing the edit operations transforming G_1 into G_2. A pseudo-code representation of the proposed algorithm is given below in Box 2.

The algorithm starts by processing the unmatched nodes of G_1 (lines 2-4). For each one of them, a *deleteNode* operation is added to *delta* (line 3) to indicate that they have been removed in G_2. Similarly, the unmatched nodes of G_2 are treated as newly inserted (lines 5-7). Hence, for each one of them, *insertNode*, *setNodeProperty*, and *insertLink* operations are added to *delta* (line 6) according to their properties and links in G_2. The matched nodes of G_1 and G_2 are processed as follow (lines 8-18). Firstly, if the matched elements have different names (if applicable), a *Rename* operation is added to *delta* in that case (lines 9-11). After that, all the properties (other than names) of the matched elements with different values are addressed by adding a *Modify* operation to *delta* for each one of them (lines 12-13). Moreover, the adjacent nodes of the matched elements are checked to detect any differences between them in terms of relationships and this is addressed by adding *insertLink* and *deleteLink* operations to *delta* (lines 14-17). Furthermore, because of the *insertLink* and *deleteLink* operations added to *delta*, cases of redundant operations could arise. Hence, a procedure *removeRedundantOperation* is called (line 19), which is in charge of removing any duplicated operation in *delta*. Finally, the operations contained in *delta* are analyzed in the last step of the algorithm to detect any moved elements and update *delta* accordingly. This is shown as a call to a procedure

Box 2.

```
Input: 2 graphs G₁, G₂ and their Match set
Output: A set of operations 'delta' differencing G₂ from G₁
  1.  delta=0
  2.  for all nodes n of G₁ not in the domain of Match do
  3.    add 'deleteNode' operation to delta for the node n
  4.  end for
  5.  for all nodes m of G₂ not in the domain of Match do
  6.    add 'insertNode', 'setNodeProperty' and 'insertLink' operations to delta
        for the node m
  7.  end for
  8.  for all elements x=(n₁, n₂) in the domain of Match do
  9.    if (n₁.name ë n₂.name) then
 10.      add 'Rename' operation to delta to rename n₁ with n₂.name
 11.    end if
 12.    select all properties p≠name of n₂ with values different from n₁:
 13.      add 'Modify' operation to delta for each p
 14.    select all elements n in Adjacent(n₂) not in Adjacent(n₁):
 15.      add 'insertLink' operation to delta for each n
 16.    select all elements n in Adjacent(n₁) not in Adjacent(n₂):
 17.      add 'deleteLink' operation to delta for each n
 18.  end for
 19.  removeRedundantOperation(delta)
 20.  updateMoving(delta)
 21.  return delta
```

updateMoving (line 20). The process involves analyzing *delta* for any element *n* (or its matched element *n'*) that is the source node of an *insertLink* operation as well as the source node of an edge removed by a *deleteLink* operation and the link type is the same in both operations but the target class is different. Hence, the element *n* is confirmed as being moved, the *insertLink* and *deleteLink* operations are removed from *delta* and a new operation *Move* is added to it with the moved element, the old class, the new target class, and the link's type as arguments. This allows a precise representation of the changes made while reducing the size of *delta* at the same time.

CONSISTENCY-PRESERVING CHANGE INTEGRATION

Merging in the context of this work is the process of combining the effects of two sets of change operations representing the parallel modifications made to a shared specification (locally and remotely). The aim is to produce a consolidated set of local change operations that takes into consideration the effect of the parallel modifications made remotely and committed while maintaining the consistency of the shared specification when the operations produced are committed.

Detecting and Resolving Conflicts

Given a shared specification represented by a graph G and two parallel sets of modifications made to it where D_{Last} represents the set of operations that have already been committed to the version of the shared specification that is modified concurrently by D_{Local}. Conflicts are detected by comparing the operations of D_{Last} and D_{Local} according to the defined conflict rules. When one of the operations in D_{Local} or both of the compared operations cause a conflict then a new conflict object is created and added to a conflict list C. The latter object contains the details of the conflicting operation(s) and a conflict type (R1-R26).

A Conflict resolution is a set of transformations that need to be made to the conflicting change operations as well as any other operation affected by the change so that a conflict is resolved. A set of systematic conflict resolutions is proposed to deal with most of the conflicts. However, some conflicts cannot be resolved systematically since they require some form of user interaction. The proposed algorithm employs two techniques namely *alignment* and *cancellation* in order to address conflicts systematically. An alignment (*alignOperations* procedure) consists of updating the set D_{Local} in regards with the effect of an operation O_i conflicting with one of its operations O_j. For example, if O_j attempts to delete an element that is renamed by O_i then the name reference made in O_j as well as all the operation of D_{Local} dealing with the renamed element are updated with the new reference name. A cancellation consists of removing/aborting a local change operation if its effect is the one causing the conflict. For example, in case of a conflict originating because of the insertion of a link, a possible resolution consists of cancelling the operation causing it. However, some changes may have greater degrees of relevance (i.e. priorities) compared to other changes. Hence, in case of a conflict involving two operations, a cancellation should be based on the priorities associated with the sites (i.e.

users) where the changes were performed. This may require inversing the effect of an operation O_i that has already been committed to the shared specification (*inverseOperation* procedure), which consists of identifying the inverse of O_i and then adding it to D_{Local}.

The proposed algorithm shown below in Box 3 accepts a graph G representing the shared specification, the list C of conflicts detected and the sets of change operations D_{Last} and D_{Local} representing the parallel modifications made to the shared specification and returns C and D_{Local} after performing the transformations necessary to resolve the conflicts detected.

The algorithm processes all the elements of the conflict list C and attempts to resolve them using the two techniques discussed previously. Conflicts are removed from C once they are resolved (line 14). All the conflicts are resolved using the same reasoning except for those which cannot be resolved systematically (line 2) since they require user intervention (e.g. rules R24, R25 and R26). Firstly, if the conflict type is the same as rules R1 to R16 (line 3) and the first conflicting operation is a deletion, then the resolution consists of removing the conflicting operation from D_{Local} if the priority associated with the changes made in D_{Last} is greater than the one of the changes made in D_{Local} (line 5). Otherwise, the inverse operation of the first conflicting operation (O_i) is added to D_{Local} (line 6). In case O_i is not a deletion, the operations of D_{Local} are aligned with the effect of this operation (line 8). Secondly, if the conflict type is the same as rules R17 to R23 then the resolution consists of removing the conflicting operation from D_{Local} (lines 10-12). The proposed algorithm could be easily adapted to similar domains. The idea is to define any additional conflicts using the proposed change operations and then to consider them as members of the following four groups of conflicts: those caused by two operations including a deletion, those caused by two operations excluding deletion, those caused by one operation only, and those that

Box 3.

```
Input: G, D_Last, D_Local, and C
Output: D_Local and C after resolving the conflicts
 1.  for all elements x=(O_i, O_j, ConflictType) in C do
 2.    if (ConflictType Not same as {R24, R25, R26}) then
 3.      if (ConflictType same as {R1, ..., R16}) then
 4.        if (O_i same as {deleteNode, deleteLink}) then
 5.          if getPriority(D_Last) ≥ getPriority(D_Local) then remove O_j from D_Local
 6.          else add inverseOperation(O_i, D_Last) to D_Local
 7.          end if
 8.        else alignOperations(O_i, D_Local)
 9.        end if
10.      else if (ConflictType same as {R17, ..., R23}) then
11.            remove O_j from D_Local
12.          end if
13.    end if
14.    remove x from C
15.    end if
16.  end for
17.  return D_Local, C
```

require user interaction. Alignment and cancellation should be sufficient in resolving any additional conflicts. However, the alignment procedure may need to be extended in order to handle the new conflicts included.

Integration of Parallel Changes

The proposed change integration algorithm consists of finalizing the results of the conflicts detection and resolution algorithm (i.e. the list C and the set D_{Local}) by applying additional modifications to D_{Local} that are needed in order to commit them to the shared specification. This is achieved by resolving the remaining conflicts (if any), injecting additional operations to D_{Local} (if needed), removing all forms of redundancy from it, and applying the necessary precedence rules that enable committing the operations of D_{Local} to the shared specification.

In case the conflicts list C is not empty, there is a need for user intervention in order to resolve the remaining conflicts. This process (i.e. *getResolutionOperation*) involves displaying the remaining conflicts and letting the user choose the necessary changes to the operations of D_{Local} involved in these conflicts in order to resolve them. Currently, this part is not supported in the developed tool. The injection of new operations is intended to allow the revision made by an operation to take effect. The injected operations as well as conflict resolutions could lead to some redundancy. Hence, a procedure *removeRedundancy* checks for all cases of redundancy in D_{Local} and removes them. Additionally, another procedure (*applyPrecedence*) rearranges the final set of operations in D_{Local} so that a change operation is always applied after any other operation preceding it (i.e. based on proposed precedence relationships between change operations). During this process, operations dealing with the same element of specification are

Box 4.

```
Input: G, D_Local and C
Output: The finalized D_Local
  1.  for all elements x in C do
  2.    getResolutionOperation(x) and then update D_Local accordingly
  3.    remove x from C
  4.  end for
  5.  for all operations O_j in D_Local do
  6.    injectOperation(O_j, D_Local)
  7.  end for
  8.  removeRedundancy(D_Local)
  9.  applyPrecedence(D_Local)
  10. return D_Local
```

grouped together. This is needed in order to allow committing the operations produced to the shared specification properly. The proposed algorithm accepts G, C and D_{Local} and returns the finalized D_{Local} after performing the necessary additional modifications, as presented in Box 4.

The algorithm starts by handling the remaining conflicts in C (if any) through user interaction, resulting in possible changes made to the operations of D_{Local} (lines 1-4). For example, in case of conflicts involving rules R24, R25, and R26, the most effective resolution is to abort the conflicting operation of D_{Local}. Moreover, the algorithm injects new operations to handle the effect of renames, modifications and deletions (lines 5-7). For example, in case of a *Modify* operation involving a class attribute, the arguments of all the operations accessing or changing the modified attribute are updated with this change, i.e. the new data type in this case. Similarly, in case of a *deleteNode* operation, a *deleteAllLink* operation is added to D_{Local} for the deleted node and then a new *Modify* or *deleteNode* (and *deleteAllLink*) operation is added to D_{Local} for all the predicate nodes of the classes or operations linked to the deleted element. However, an operation is injected if and only if it is not included in D_{Local}.

This process can be seen as a form of change mentoring. In the final stage of the algorithm, any possible redundant operations are removed from D_{Local} (line 8) and precedence relationships are enforced by rearranging the operations of D_{Local} (line 9).

Dealing with Redundancy and Enforcing Precedence

The proposed algorithm allows dealing with five different forms of redundancy (*removeRedundancy* procedure). They include duplication, redundant effect, reverse effect, void effect and finally inapplicable effect. Cases of redundant effect should arise more often due to the operations injected during merging. For example, given an element n who is the source or target node of a link k, in case $O_1=deleteAllLink(n)$ and $O_2=deleteLink(k)$ then O_2 is redundant since its effect is already handled by O_1, which deletes all the links associated with n including k. Reverse cases and cases of void (and inapplicable) effect can also arise. For example, if an operation O_1 inserts a node n while another operation O_2 deletes the same node then both O_1 and O_2 are removed. Similarly, if the element manipulated by an operation O_1 is deleted by another operation O_2 deletes n then O_1 is removed. Additionally, if an operation O_1 deals with an element or a link that does not exist in the current version of the shared specification and has no matching equivalent in it then O_1 is removed since its effect is inapplicable.

Precedence relationships among the operations of D_{Local} that deal with the same element or link are enforced using four proposed rules (*apply-Precendence* procedure). The first rule ensures that a rename operation is always applied after any other operation dealing with the renamed element, while the second rule ensures that an operation inserting a new node n (or a link k) is applied before any other operation dealing with n or k. The third rule ensures that modification and move operations are applied before deletion operations. The fourth rule ensures that any change made to a specification' element is applied before any change dealing with the element in which it is declared (i.e. its ancestor).

An Illustrative Example

As an illustrative example, consider the class *PItem* that is part of a specification of an online purchasing system and two parallel revisions made to it as presented in Figure 4.

The class *PItem* specifies two operations. The first one allows setting the purchased quantity of a product (must be greater than zero) and the second one allowing a purchase to be made by updating the quantity of the product in stock and returning the purchasing price. The modifications made in the first version of the class (D_1) include renames and deletions. It consisted of renaming the class as *PurchasedItem* and its two operations as *setQuantity* and *chargeItem* respectively as well as deleting the class' invariant and the precondition of the operation *Set_Quantity*. The changes made in the second version (D_2) include a rename and a modification. The class name has been changed to *Item* and its invariant has been updated. Table 3 summarizes the main parallel

Figure 4. An illustrative example

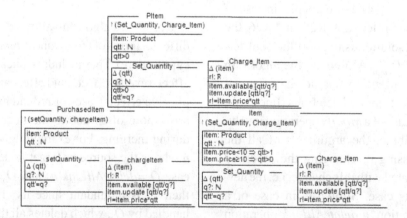

Table 3. Operations representing the changes made

D_1	D_2
(1) Rename(PItem, "PItem", "PurchasedItem") (2) deleteNode(PItem\Invariant) (3) Rename(PItem\Set_Quantity, "Set_Quantity", "setQuantity") (4) deleteNode(PItem\ Set_Quantity\Precond) (5) Rename(PItem\Charge_Item, "Charge_Item", "chargeItem")	(1) Rename(PItem, "PItem", "Item") (2) Modify(PItem\Invariant, "value", "qtt>0", "item.price<10 ⇒ qtt>1 ∧ item.price≥10 ⇒ qtt>0")

Figure 5. Preview of the resulting conflicts from the developed tool

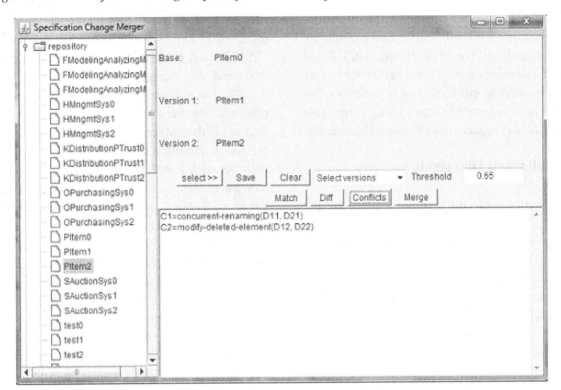

changes made (insertion and deletion of links have been omitted for the sake of simplicity) and Figure 5 gives a preview of the resulting conflicts from the developed tool.

The first conflict is resolved by aligning the operations of D_2. The second conflict is resolved either by removing the operation $(D_{2(2)})$ or by inversing the effect of the operation $(D_{1(2)})$ depending on the priorities of the changes made in D_1 and D_2. This makes it possible to commit the finalized operations of D_2 leading to a consistent version of the class *PItem* whose final name is *Item*.

PERFORMANCE EVALUATION

Experimental Setup

A Java prototype tool has been developed to help evaluating the proposed approach. The evaluation involved comparing the results obtained automatically to reference results that were manually recorded from the developed benchmark and calculating *precision, recall*, and *f-measure* metrics. Additionally, a similarity threshold (0.5 to 0.95) was used to run a wide range of tests using specifications with various structures and sizes that deal with different types of systems. This was intended to make the experimental results obtained to be significant. The amount of changes performed on them in the tests as well as the type of these changes and their distribution varied considerably, which allowed evaluating the robustness of the approach in regards to all these aspects.

The developed benchmark contained modifications that allowed creating two versions (S_1 and S_2) from the original (shared) specification S. The modifications made to the shared specification S in the versions were manually recorded. These modifications included controlled experiments that were aimed at stress testing the proposed approach as well as uncontrolled experiments allowing the incorporation of random modifications in order to ensure that the performance results are more significant. The three versions (i.e. S, S_1 and S_2) of each specification were hard-coded using Java in order to eliminate any noise/errors that could have originated from parsing them. This made the performance results more representative.

Results and Discussion

The accuracy of edit scripts produced by the change extraction approach depends largely on the accuracy of the matching results. For example, similar elements of the compared specifications that are not matched are added to the edit scripts as several incorrect insertion and deletion operations. However, if these elements were properly matched, only one correct *Rename* or *Modify* operation will be able to represent their difference. Similarly, mistakenly matched elements lead to even more incorrect operations. Hence, inaccurate matching results affect the accuracy of the differences produced and their size. This makes any approaches using these scripts inefficient and inaccurate. Figure 6 shows the overall accuracy (%) of the edit scripts produced by the change extraction algorithm in terms of their *F-Measure* and *Sub-Optimality* for matching thresholds ranging from 0.5 to 0.95.

The results obtained indicated a good *f-measure* between 68.47% and 80.64% for thresholds ranging from 0.5 to 0.9. A relatively lower *f-measure* (55.17%) was obtained for a large threshold of 0.95, and the average *f-measure* obtained was 73.38%. The performance was sensibly better for thresholds between 0.65 and 0.8. Additionally, the sizes of the edit scripts produced by the change extraction algorithm were only slightly sub-optimal (between 2.49% and 16.83%). The average increase in size in comparison with optimal differences was 9.04%. Furthermore, the algorithm's ability to detect renames and modifications was slightly better than the other types of changes. This is due to the fact that the matching algorithm is driven by structural similarity.

In order to study the effectiveness of the conflict detection and resolution algorithm in dealing with various types of conflicts, the results obtained automatically were compared to the conflicts that were injected through the concurrent modifications made in the benchmark. Table 4 summarizes the overall results obtained.

The results showed an overall *f-measure* of 71.25%. The latter was good (71.26% to 72.98%) for some conflicts (e.g. R5, R6, R8, and R9) and slightly less good for the other types of conflicts. This small variation in the performance results obtained is attributed to two main factors. Firstly, the ability of the change extraction algorithm to

Figure 6. Performance of the change extraction algorithm

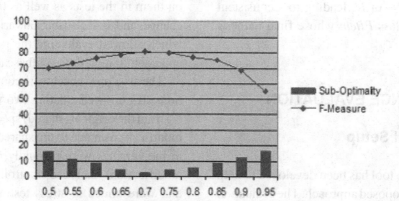

Table 4. Performance of conflicts detection and resolution algorithm

Conflict Type	Number of conflicts	F-Measure (%)
R1	3	69.84
R2	6	70.68
R5	12	71.26
R6	16	72.98
R8	3	72.97
R9	1	71.43
R10	2	68.29
R11	4	68.24
R16	1	66.67
R21	1	66.67
Overall	49	71.25

deal better with the some change operations (renames and updates) that are causing the conflicts in comparison with the other types of changes. Secondly, some of the elements causing these conflicts are hard to match elements (i.e. elements with little structural information).

The change integration algorithm was evaluated by comparing the final consolidated set of change operations D_{Local} that was produced automatically to a reference set derived manually from the benchmark used. Figure 7 shows the *F-Measure* (%) and the *Sub-Optimality* (%) of the

merging scripts obtained for similarity thresholds ranging from 0.5 to 0.95.

The average *f-measure* and sub-optimality obtained were 70.06% and 11.24% respectively. For similarity thresholds ranging from 0.5 up to 0.85, f-measure was between 67.34% and 77.39%. However, *f-measure* deteriorated slightly for high thresholds (0.9 and 0.95) leading to results between 50.69% and 64.04%. This decrease in performance is the result of two factors. Firstly, a considerable decrease in the number of correct operations in D_{Local}, which is due to an increase in the number of undetected change operations in the differences produced. Secondly, a slight increase in the number of operations mistakenly injected due to a small increase in the number of inaccurate conflicts detected (false negatives during matching).

Merging scripts were sub-optimal by 7.13% to 17% for low similarity thresholds (0.5 to 0.65). This is due to an increase in the number of false positives during matching. For similarity thresholds between 0.7 and 0.75, a considerable reduction in the number of incorrect change operations in the merging scripts produced was obtained where the sub optimality of the resulting scripts was between 4.38% and 6.5%. For high similarity thresholds of 0.8 to 0.95, the sub optimality increased slightly, it was between 8.86% and 17.66%. This deterioration is mainly due to an increase in the number

Figure 7. Performance of the change integration algorithm

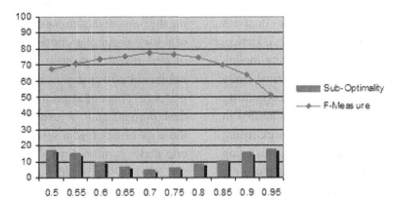

of incorrect change operations produced because of the false negatives obtained during matching.

The proposed algorithms outperformed several similar approaches in terms of accuracy and sub-optimality of the results. For example, the average sub-optimality of the differences produced in (Abi-Antoun et al., 2008) was 16.88%, while it was around 50% in (Cobena et al., 2002). The average accuracy of the differences produced in (Fluri et al., 2007) was 66% and the results were 26.22% sub-optimal. Moreover, a reduction in the number of comparisons during conflicts detection and merging was achieved by exploiting the order in the operations of D_{Last} and D_{Local}, which are clustered according to their types (i.e. insertions, deletions, etc) and the type of elements they manipulate (i.e., classes, operations, etc). Additionally, some change operations are not considered during comparison since they do not cause any conflicts (i.e. *setNodeProperty* and *deleteAllLink*). This reduced the complexity of the proposed algorithms from a quadratic to an almost linear complexity.

FUTURE RESEARCH DIRECTIONS

New heuristics could be proposed and evaluated to make matching the elements of specifications more effective while producing accurate results by attempting to reduce both the number of false positives and the number of false negatives. This could be the subject of an empirical study aimed at developing and evaluating new matching algorithms handling various classes or styles of specifications (not just the OO ones). Hence, this requires extending the proposed meta-model. The tests performed during this empirical study should allow evaluating the proposed similarity metrics and determining their applicability in matching the elements of specifications according to their respective styles. Additionally, clustering specifications could be exploited to enhance the effectiveness of the developed algorithms.

A direct extension of the framework's formal foundation consists of developing new meta-models to handle more types of formal specifications rather than just the OO ones. This could benefit the widely used model-based formal specification languages such as Z and VDM. Moreover, extending the types of specifications that are handled by the framework requires extending the set of conflicts that need to be detected and resolved. Both the priorities of the change operations and those of the users performing the changes could be considered during conflicts resolution. Furthermore, the cost or impact of resolving conflicts could be analyzed and a possible set of transformations together with their associated costs could be generated for user selection. Prevention or reduction of conflicts could also be explored.

The approaches of the developed framework could be adapted to address some of the main problems faced in two related software engineering fields. Firstly, the change extraction approach could be adapted to perform model-differencing for the benefit of change management in Model Driven Development (MDD). Similarly, the conflict detection and resolution approach could be adapted for the same benefit. Secondly, the developed framework provides a natural support for reusing the developed specifications and the changes made to them during collaborative development. However, it needs to be extended to provide some support to Component-Based Software Engineering (CBSE) in aspects such as component specification and integration.

Finally, the development of tools implementing the proposed framework or any new extension of it for a particular domain could be the subject of new research projects. These tools could be implemented as plug-ins in existing open-source projects. This could promote both collaborative development and the use of formal methods at the same time, especially if parsing specifications encoded in commonly used formats such as LaTeX and XML is supported.

CONCLUSION

In this chapter, a framework for merging OO formal specifications was proposed and evaluated. It incorporated a formal foundation aimed at representing the manipulated specifications, the changes made to them and the possible merging conflicts. Additionally, a set of algorithms were developed to extract, integrate the parallel changes made while addressing a wide set of merging conflicts at the same time. A graph-based meta-model was used to represent the manipulated specifications. It generality should allow using the proposed algorithms for other similar software artifacts. Additionally, a set of primitive change operations were proposed to represent the parallel changes made to shared specifications, which allowed a precise definition of merging conflicts. A wide range of conflicts were defined and used during evaluation.

The proposed change detection employed several similarity metrics and heuristics with an emphasis on structural similarity, which allowed matching the elements of the compared specification more accurately since it lowers the impact of renamed and updated elements on similarity calculation. Change extraction was performed based on the highly accurate matching sets obtained. Moreover, the proposed change integration relied on a conflicts detection and resolution algorithm to address any possible merging conflicts by comparing the parallel changes made and then applying systematic resolutions. Additionally, operations were injected to allow certain changes to take effect. Furthermore, the set produced by the change integration algorithm was redundancy-free and ordered. This allows committing the change operations properly to the shared specification.

The proposed framework was empirically evaluated and the evaluation results showed good signs in terms of accuracy and scalability. The accuracy was measured through f-measure, which combines both precision (quality) and recall (coverage). Hence, it is more representative.

Additionally, all developed algorithms produced highly accurate results while having an almost linear complexity at the same time. This provides us with a good confidence that the proposed framework should scale up well with the increase in sizes of the manipulated specifications and the changes made to them.

REFERENCES

Abi-Antoun, M., Aldrich, J., Nahas, N., Schmerl, B., & Garlan, D. (2008). Differencing and merging of architectural views. *Automated Software Engineering Journal*, *15*(1), 35–74. doi:10.1007/s10515-007-0023-3

Altmanninger, K., Seidl, M., & Wimmer, M. (2009). A survey on model versioning approaches. *International Journal of Web Information Systems*, *5*(3), 271–304. doi:10.1108/17440080910983556

Boronat, A., Carsi, J. A., Ramos, I., & Letelier, P. (2007). Formal model merging applied to class diagram integration. *Electronic Notes in Theoretical Computer Science*, *166*(1), 5–26. doi:10.1016/j.entcs.2006.06.013

Ciapessoni, E., Mirandola, P., Coen-Porisini, A., Mandrioli, D., & Morzenti, A. (1999). From formal models to formally based methods: An industrial experience. *ACM Transactions on Software Engineering and Methodology*, *8*(1), 79–113. doi:10.1145/295558.295566

Cobena, G., Abiteboul, S., & Marian, A. (2002). Detecting changes in XML documents. *Proceedings of 18th International Conferenceon Data Engineering*, San Jose, USA, (pp. 41-52).

Fitzgerald, J., & Larsen, P. G. (2006). Triumphs and challenges for model-oriented formal methods: The VDM++ experience. *Proceedings of the 2nd International Symposium on Leveraging Applications of Formal Methods, Verification and Validation*, Paphos, Cyprus, (pp. 1-4).

Fitzgerald, J., Larsen, P. G., & Sahara, S. (2008). VDMTools: Advances in support for formal modeling in VDM. *ACM SIGPLAN Notices, 43*(2), 3–11.

Fluri, B., Wursch, M., Pinzger, M., & Gall, H. C. (2007). Change distilling: Tree differencing for fine-grained source code change extraction. *IEEE Transactions on Software Engineering, 33*(11), 725–743. doi:10.1109/TSE.2007.70731

Frost, R. (2007). Jazz and the eclipse way of collaboration. *IEEE Software, 24*(6), 114–117. doi:10.1109/MS.2007.170

Hinchey, M. G. (2008). *Industrial-strength formal methods in practice*. Springer.

Ignat, C. L., & Norrie, M. C. (2006). Customizable collaborative editing supporting the work processes of organizations. *Computers in Industry, 57*(8), 758–767. doi:10.1016/j.compind.2006.04.005

Mens, T. (2002). A state of the art survey on software merging. *IEEE Transactions on Software Engineering, 28*(5), 449–462. doi:10.1109/TSE.2002.1000449

Navarro, G. (2001). A guided tour to approximate string matching. *ACM Computing Surveys, 33*(1), 31–88. doi:10.1145/375360.375365

Nuseibeh, B., & Easterbrook, S. (2000). Requirements engineering: A roadmap. *Proceedings of the Conference on the Future of Software Engineering*, Limerick, Ireland, (pp. 35-46).

Penichet, V. M. R., Marin, I., Gallud, J. A., Lozano, M. D., & Tesoriero, R. (2007). A classification method for CSCW systems. *Electronic Notes in Theoretical Computer Science, 168*(1), 237–247. doi:10.1016/j.entcs.2006.12.007

Smith, G. (2000). *The object-Z specification language*. Kluwer Academic Publishers. doi:10.1007/978-1-4615-5265-9

Sun, C., & Chen, D. (2002). Consistency maintenance in real-time collaborative graphics editing systems. *ACM Transactions on Computer-Human Interaction, 9*(1), 1–41. doi:10.1145/505151.505152

Woodcock, J., Larsen, P. G., Bicarregui, J., & Fitzgerald, J. (2009). Formal methods: Practice and experience. *ACM Computing Surveys, 41*(4), 1–36. doi:10.1145/1592434.1592436

ADDITIONAL READING

Apiwattanapong, P., Orso, N., & Harrold, M. J. (2007). JDiff: A differencing technique and tool for object-oriented programs. *Automated Software Engineering, 14*(1), 3–36. doi:10.1007/s10515-006-0002-0

Bagheri, E., & Ghorbani, A. A. (2008). A belief-theoretic framework for the collaborative development and integration of para-consistent conceptual models. *Journal of Systems and Software, 82*(4), 707–729. doi:10.1016/j.jss.2008.10.012

Canfora, G., Cerulo, L., & Di Penta, M. (2009). Tracking your changes: A language-independent approach. *IEEE Software, 26*(1), 50–57. doi:10.1109/MS.2009.26

Dig, D., Manzoor, K., Johnson, R., & Nguyen, T. N. (2008). Effective software merging in the presence of object-oriented refactorings. *IEEE Transactions on Software Engineering, 34*(3), 321–334. doi:10.1109/TSE.2008.29

Flesca, S., Manco, G., Masciari, E., Pontieri, L., & Pugliese, A. (2005). Fast detection of XML structural similarity. *IEEE Transactions on Knowledge and Data Engineering, 17*(2), 160–175. doi:10.1109/TKDE.2005.27

German, D. M., Hassan, A. E., & Robles, G. (2009). Change impact graphs: Determining the impact of prior code changes. *Information and Software Technology, 51*(10), 1394–1408. doi:10.1016/j.infsof.2009.04.018

Godfrey, M. W., & Zou, L. (2005). Using origin analysis to detect merging and splitting of source code entities. *IEEE Transactions on Software Engineering*, *31*(2), 166–181. doi:10.1109/TSE.2005.28

Lian, W., Cheung, D., & Mamoulis, N. (2004). An efficient and scalable algorithm for clustering XML documents by structure. *IEEE Transactions on Knowledge and Data Engineering*, *16*(1), 82–96. doi:10.1109/TKDE.2004.1264824

Lin, L., Prowell, S. J., & Poore, J. H. (2009). The impact of requirements changes on specifications and state machines. *Software, Practice & Experience*, *39*(6), 573–610. doi:10.1002/spe.907

Lucas, F. J., Molina, F., & Toval, A. (2009). A systematic review of UML model consistency management. *Information and Software Technology*, *51*(12), 1631–1645. doi:10.1016/j.infsof.2009.04.009

Maqbool, O., & Babri, H. A. (2007). Hierarchical clustering for software architecture recovery. *IEEE Transactions on Software Engineering*, *33*(11), 759–780. doi:10.1109/TSE.2007.70732

Martinez, A. B. B., Aria, J. J. P., Vilas, A. F., Duque, J. G., Nores, M. L., Redondo, R. P. D., & Fernandez, Y. B. (2008). Composing requirements specifications from multiple prioritized sources. *Requirements Engineering*, *13*(3), 187–206. doi:10.1007/s00766-008-0064-6

Paige, R. F., Brooke, P. J., & Ostroff, J. S. (2007). Metamodel-based model conformance and multiview consistency checking. *ACM Transactions on Software Engineering and Methodology*, *16*(3), 11. doi:10.1145/1243987.1243989

Sabetzadeh, M., & Easterbrook, S. (2006). View merging in the presence of incompleteness and inconsistency. *Requirements Engineering Journal*, *11*(3), 174–193. doi:10.1007/s00766-006-0032-y

Tsantalis, N., Chatzigeorgiou, A., Stephanides, G., & Halkidis, S. T. (2006). Design pattern detection using similarity scoring. *IEEE Transactions on Software Engineering*, *32*(11), 896–909. doi:10.1109/TSE.2006.112

Wang, Y., DeWitt, D. J., & Cai, J. Y. (2003). X-Diff: An efficient change detection algorithm for XML documents. *Proceeding of 19th International Conference on Data Engineering*, Bangalor, India, (pp. 519-530).

Xing, Z., & Stroulia, E. (2007). Differencing logical UML models. *Automated Software Engineering*, *14*(2), 215–259. doi:10.1007/s10515-007-0007-3

KEY TERMS AND DEFINITIONS

Change Management: Concerned with the control of the evolution of software artifacts.

Collaborative Development: A style of software development that involves developers working in an asynchronous and distributed way.

Conflict Resolution: A set of transformations that are made to the conflicting change operations so that a merging conflict is resolved.

Formal Specification: The specification of various aspects of a system such as requirements in a language defined by mathematical logic.

Merging Conflicts: The inconsistencies resulting from the diversity of views in the parallel changes made to some software artifact.

Object-Oriented Methods: The software engineering methods whose fundamental unit is a class encapsulating the data and the behavior of a set of objects. They promote several qualities such as modularity and reuse.

Software Merging: The process of combining *n* alternative versions of a software document into a consolidated version.

Chapter 2
Component Certification Process and Standards

Parminder Kaur
Guru Nanak Dev University, India

Hardeep Singh
Guru Nanak Dev University, India

ABSTRACT

Component-based technology deals with the process of assembling existing software components in an application such that they interact to satisfy a predefined functionality. The success of component-based software depends on system integrator's ability to select the most suitable software components for their intended application (Leavens and Sitaraman, 2000; Voas and Payne, 2000; Crnkovic et al., 2001). One persistent and largely unaddressed challenge is how the consumers of software components can obtain a meaningful level of trust in the runtime behaviour of software components. The most frequently cited concerns are centered on issues of security and component behaviour (Wallnau, 2004). Certification is a practical, proven means of establishing trust in various sorts of things in other disciplines and is, therefore a natural contender for developing trust in software components. This is only possible if component suppliers have clear and reliable information about their component's functional and non-functional properties. The component attributes allow system integrator to better classify the components. The reliability of a component-based software system is dependant on the reliability of the components that is made of. Proper search, selection, and evaluation process of components is considered as cornerstone for the development of any effective component-based system (Alexandre, 2010).This chapter defines certain properties of a component, which are helpful during their classification process along with component certification/accreditation process, which further helps component suppliers to issue the guarantee of claimed functional properties and quality attributes. Component certification framework is also discussed to evaluate the quality of software components with the help of component quality model and measurement mechanism.

DOI: 10.4018/978-1-4666-2958-5.ch002

INTRODUCTION

Component-based technologies simplify functional decomposition of complex systems and support building of re-configurable compositions and tuning of component compositions for the particular context they are used in. Various component models like CORBA from Object Management Group, COM/ COM+/DCOM/.NET from Microsoft, and Enterprise JavaBeans from Sun Microsystems and OpenDoc from Apple (John, 1994), [App] focus on functional features of the components and entire component systems and are unable to estimate the non-functional properties of the components and their compositions.

One of the most compelling reasons for adopting component –based technology is the principle of reuse. The idea is to build software from existing components for reduced development time and improved product quality. The top objective is to avoid reinvention, redesign and reimplementation when building a new product, capitalizing on previously done work that can be immediately deployed in new contexts (Jacobson et al, 1997).

Reliable and high - quality software systems can build only by using components of high quality and reliability. Reused components must be free of design and implementation flaws. Usually components benefit from multiple reuses in that they are thoroughly tested. The idea behind the certification of components is to guarantee that a specific set of quality guidelines has been met (Michael and John, 1993). Traditional quality certification standards e. g. ISO/IEC 12207, Capability Maturity Model – CMM and Capability Maturity Model Integrated – CMMI are focused on the software development process. However, the certification of components for safety and business critical application must consider both the development process and the product intrinsic quality. Several ISO standards like ISO/IEC 12119, ISO/IEC 9126, ISO/IEC 25051 are now focusing on component certification.

RELATED WORK

Certification has the goal to offer a general scheme that indicates the quality or compatibility of a component in respect to certain properties. (Wohlin and Runeson,1994) has presented a usage modeling technique, which can be used to formulate usage models for components. This technique will make it possible not only to certify the components, but also to certify the system containing the components. The usage model describes the usage from a structural point of view, which is complemented with a profile describing the expected usage in figures. The failure statistics from the usage test form the input of a hypothesis certification model, which makes it possible to certify a specific reliability level with a given degree of confidence. This certification model becomes the basis for deciding whether the component can be accepted, either for storage as a reusable component or for reuse.

In early years, software products were based on related monolithic building blocks whereas now Component-Based Development (CBD) appeared as a new perspective for software development, aiming at breaking monolithic blocks into interoperable pre-tested components with the promise of reduced development complexity as well as its cost (Sametinger, 1997).

(Voas, 1998, 1999) suggested that independent agencies such as software certification laboratories should assume the role of software product certification and suggests that the only approach that consumers can trust is the certification provided by agencies that are completely independent from the software product providers. A certification methodology using automated technologies, such as black-box testing and fault injection to determine whether the component fits into a specific scenario is defined. This methodology uses three quality assessment techniques to determine the suitability of a candidate COTS component. Black-box component testing is used to determine whether the component quality is high enough.

System-level fault injection is used to determine how well a system will tolerate a faulty component. Operational system testing is used to determine how well the system will tolerate a properly functioning component. The methodology can help developers decide whether a component is right for their system, showing how much of someone else's mistakes the components can tolerate.

The work presented by (Rodriguez, 1999) focuses on safety certification using the notion of risk assessment of software systems, including systems that use COTS. The proposal includes an iterative process for safety certification focusing on the software product development process. According to that proposal, the safety verifications are done in parallel with software development. The work emphasizes the relevance of both static and dynamic characteristics of software evaluation but does not specify how to deal with them.

Most current methods for certifying software are process-based and requirement according to (Voas, 2000) that software publishers "take oaths concerning which development standards and processes they will use." Voas, among others, has suggested that independent agencies like software certification laboratories (SCLs) should take on a product certification role. He believes that "completely independent product certification offers the only approach that consumers can trust." In Voas's scheme, SCLs would accept instrumented software from developers, pass the instrumented software along to prequalified users, gather information from user sites, use data gathered from several sites to generate statistics on use and performance in the field, and provide limited warranties for the software based on these statistics. Thus, the SCLs assume the role of independent auditors that monitor the processes developers follow and provide statistics about how their clients' products perform.

The Carnegie Mellon University's Software Engineering Institute (CMU/SEI) had studied industry trends in the use of software components (Bass et al, 2000). This study examined software components from both technical and business perspectives. The conclusion consist facts like lack of available components, lack of stable standards for component technology, lack of certified components and lack of an engineering method to produce quality systems from components.

(Trass & Hillegersberg, 2000) has discussed conditions for the growth component markets related to intrinsic characteristics of certification processes, such as the documentation, component quality and well-defined services. (Wallnau, 2003; Heineman et al, 2000,2001; Crnkovic, 2001) also pointed certification as the key precondition for Component-Based Software Engineering (CBSE) to be successfully adopted in the large. Moreover, certified components used during development will have predetermined and well-established criteria in order to reduce the risks of system failure.

(Council, 2001) established a satisfactory definition about what software component certification is: "Third-party certification is a method to ensure that software components conform to well-defined standards; based on this certification, trusted assemblies of components can be constructed". The certification process must provide a certificate that evidences that it fulfills a given set of requirements. A set of requirements is also presented to guarantee software component quality. This work emphasizes the importance of estimated risk and the identification, in early software life cycle, the correct implementation of specified requirements among others suggestions to improve software quality.

(Morris et al., 2001) proposed an entirely different model for software component certification. The model was based on the tests that developers supply in a standard portable form. So, the purchasers can determine the quality and suitability of purchased software. This model is divided in four steps: Test Specification, which uses XML (eXtensible Markup Language) files to define some structured elements that represent the test specifications, Specification Document Format, which describes how the document can be used or specified by a tester; Specified Results, which are directly derived from a component's specification. These results can contain an exact value or a method for computing the value, and are stored in the test specifications of the XML elements and Verificator, which evaluates a component. The limitation of this model is the additional cost for generating the tests and developer resources to build these tests.

The work presented by (Stafford and Wallnau, 2001) proposes a model in which several actors participate in software component development and receive the responsibilities on the software component development rather than vesting trust in third-party certification authority. Different actors with distinct roles to play in a component-based development paradigm may interact in a variety of ways to achieve trust.

The (ISO/IEC 9126, 2001) standard defines a software quality model which has been used as a reference for the evaluation of software quality. This standard is composed by the ISO/IEC 9126-1 quality model, the ISO/IEC 9126-2 external metrics, the ISO/IEC 9126-3 internal metrics, and the the ISO/IEC 9126-4 quality in use metrics. The main objective of this standard is the identification of software quality attributes that can be described by suppliers aimed at evaluation/selection of COTS.

According to (Szyperski, 2002), a software component is "a unit of composition with contractually specified interfaces and explicit context dependencies only. A software component can be independently deployed and is subject to third-party composition". The contractually specified interfaces are required to form a common layer between the client and the component developer. The explicit context dependencies refer to the deployment environment for proper functioning of components. Independently deployable component needs separation from its environment and other components. Finally, for a component to be composed with other component by a third-party it must be sufficiently self-contained, i.e. the func-

tion that the component performs must be fully performed within itself.

(Hissam et al., 2003) introduced Prediction-Enabled Component Technology (PECT) as a means of packaging predictable assembly as a deployable product. PECT is meant to be the integration of a given component technology with one or more analysis technologies that support the prediction of assembly properties and the identification required component properties and their possible certifiable descriptions.

(Meyer, 2003) highlighted the main concepts behind a trusted component along two complementary directions: a low road, leading to certification of existing components (e.g. defining a component quality model), and a high road, aimed at the production of components with fully proved correctness properties. In the first direction, Meyer's major concern was to establish the main requirements that the component must have. Meyer's intention is to define a component quality model, in order to provide a certification service for existing components – COM, EJB, .NET, OO libraries. This model - still under development - has five categories. Once all properties in one category are achieved, the component has the corresponding quality level.

(Wallnau, 2004) has defined one persistent and largely unaddressed challenge i.e. how the consumers of software components can obtain a meaningful level of trust in the runtime behaviour of software components. The most frequently cited concerns are centered on issues of security; for example, trust that a component does not contain malicious code or exhibit vulnerabilities that can be exploited by malicious code. There are, however, other concerns about software component behaviour that can be just as important. For example, in an embedded system, it may be crucial to trust that a component will always execute a function within a particular time bound or never introduce unbounded priority inversion.

ISO/IEC 25000 (2005), an International Standards provides guidance for the use of the new series of International Standards named Software product Quality Requirements and Evaluation (SQuaRE). The purpose of this Guide is to provide a general overview of SQuaRE contents, common reference models and definitions, as well as the relationship among the documents, allowing users of the Guide a good understanding of those series of standards, according to their purpose of use. SQuaRE series of standards is intended for, but not limited to, developers, acquirers and independent evaluators of software products, particularly those responsible for defining software quality requirements and for software product evaluation. It is recommended that users of the SQuaRE as well as ISO/IEC 14598 and 9126 series of standards also use this International Standard as a guide to execute their tasks.

(Roshanak et al, 2006) has proposed a framework for reliability estimation of software components at the level of software architecture. The proposed reliability estimation framework attempted to bridge the gap between architectural modeling and analyses, and software reliability measurement. This framework also tied to state of the practice techniques in architectural specification, and leverages a defect quantification and cost framework to quantify failure behavior of a component.

The (ISO/IEC 25051, 2006) standard focuses on COTS software products and specifies quality requirements which address test documentation, test cases and test reporting. It provides the instructions to evaluate the conformity to the standard. It also includes recommendations for the safety of business critical COTS software products. The main objective of this standard is to provide the user with confidence that the COTS software product performs as offered and delivered. This standard does not address the development process quality of the COTS software supplier.

(Siraj and Antonio, 2007) presented an early exposition towards a quality model for open source software (OSS). This research work described some basic notions of quality i.e. quality by access, quality by development and quality by design for OSS and presented a basic model, where quality notions consist of various factors like understanding of goals and requirements, Use of recognized design and engineering techniques, Correctness, Formal analysis and verification, Frequently updated documentation, effective communication, coordination and management.

(Yoonjung et al, 2008) introduced an in-house Component Quality Model which includes metrics for component quality evaluation, tailoring guidelines for evaluations, and reporting formats of evaluations. To formalize and visualize the quality of S/W components in a quantitative way, Component Quality Model has been applied to embedded system development projects so that component developers can control component quality to build reusable and quality components while enabling cost reduction and quality improvement.

(Carvalho, 2009), has proposed a quality verification framework to evaluate the quality of embedded software components in an efficient way. This model was based on component characteristics, sub-characteristics, quality attributes and metrics. As assessment and evaluation of software components has become a compulsory and crucial part of any CBSE lifecycle, therefore quality evaluation has become an increasingly essential activity in order to bring reliability in (re)using software components.

(Alexandre, 2010) highlighted one of the major problems with Component-Based Software Engineering (CBSE) is the quality of the components used in a system. The reliability of a component-based software system is dependant on the reliability of the components that is made of. Proper search, selection and evaluation process of components is considered as cornerstone for the development of any effective component-based system. A software component quality framework, validated with the help of metrics, was proposed to evaluate the quality of software components in a very efficient way.

(Nitin et al, 2011) presented a software component quality model (SCQM) by overcoming shortcomings of existing quality models. Based upon this model, end user can take decision upon selection, evaluation and ranking of potential component candidates and wherever possible attain improvements in the component design and development. To build complete software solution, the main focus is to create high quality parts and later join them together. Quality model is thus very essential to make component selection process smooth.

COMPONENT ATTRIBUTES

A component can be defined with the help of certain attributes. Some attributes are generic apply to all components, but others are domain specific and apply only to certain components. Attributes may also be specific to certain platforms and specific to components on other platforms. The identification of attributes (Sametinger, 1997), (Brereton et al., 2002) can be done on the basis of the following:

- Functionality
- Interactivity
- Interaction
- Concurrency
- Interoperability
- Adaptation
- Reliability
- Security
- Performance Standards
- Conceptual Clarity
- Coupling and Cohesion

Functionality

The functionality of a component refers to its reusability in a certain context. A component designed for binary search is useless to sort items. Components with higher level of abstraction like classes and applications provide behavioural interfaces that include several operations. Component applicability, generality and completeness are three major parameters which are essential for its reusability. The applicability of a component is its likelihood to be a reuse candidate in the range of software systems for which it as designed to be reused. It can be high, low or zero according to a certain domain. The generality of a component increases its reusability. High generality of a component means high applicability of the component. But excessive generality leads to complex components and unnecessary overhead in both execution time and resource consumption. Completeness of a component is difficult to achieve yet important for reuse. A component is complete only when it offers the functionality expected by the re-users in its intended reuse process.

Interactivity

Components are categorized as interactive, non-interactive, proactive and reactive components. Macros and Functions are non-interactive components where as Objects and applications are interactive components. Function-oriented systems transform an initial state to a final state where as object-oriented systems work according to messages they receive from other objects by doing some computation. Reactive components become active only when they get request from another component. Proactive components become active on their own. For example: a timer component might become active whenever a certain amount of time has passed, and can cause reactive components to become active.

Interaction

A component can interact with other component through component interaction or through user interaction. Component interaction in the form of reusable components, deals with high cohesion and low coupling. For example: classes can easily be reused in their programming language domain if they have no dependencies on other classes. User interaction needs some sort of window or textual input/output facilities to interact with component. For example: editors can be integrated in programming environments.

Concurrency

The execution of concurrent components can overlap in time and deliver different results when run with same input data. The reasons, why concurrency is included in running components are (Alan Burns and Geoff Davies, 1993):

- Gains in execution speed by assigning physical processors to different processes.
- Elimination of potential processor idle time by sharing the processors among a number of components running as concurrent processes.

Concurrent components have their own thread of control and do not require call for completion. Synchronization becomes necessary when two components share any kind of resource. Concurrency in components can be distinguished as intra-concurrency and inter-concurrency. In some cases concurrency may happen within components but not among components. For example: tools may be implemented concurrently in a concurrent programming language. Concurrent components can also be interconnected for sequential processing. On the other hand, sequential components may run concurrently and communicate on different processors like client/server programs.

Interoperability

For reusability, components are required to be executable on variety of platforms. Thus components should be able to communicate and exchange data among distributed platforms. Independent components can be implemented in different

programming languages and paradigms using language-independent mechanisms for communication. The main reasons for the popularity of distribution are not only cost considerations but increased capabilities, greater flexibility of incremental expansion and choice of vendors (John and Susanne, 1993). One common form of distributed system architecture is client/server organization.

Adaptation

Adaptability enables the component to be reused and become a part of software system. It refers to customization and modification. An example of customization is UNIX tools, used as filters, which enhance their potential to reuse. Object-oriented technology is a good example of inherent adaptation means for components. The inheritance mechanism allows modifications that have not necessarily been foreseen by the developers of a class to be reused. However, widely used programming languages still lack features at the source code level of abstraction.

Reliability

High-quality reliable components are essential to build high-quality software systems. The objective of reliable software is to make sure that a software system does not fail even when it contains some faulty components. Techniques like recovery block approach and N- version programming (Pankaj Jalote, 1994) are used to organize diverse designs in order to build fault-tolerant software. The idea behind these approaches is to use multiple components for the same functionality.

Security

Security vulnerability posed by third-party software components is a serious obstruction to their adoption in areas that offer great economic potentials such as embedded software and large-scale enterprise software. The lack of security in component-based systems (CBS) results in breach of its own integrity and confidentiality. The work of (Lindqvist and Jonsson, 1998) and (Kumar, 2002) provides taxonomy of security risks in off-the-shelf components along with other vulnerabilities such as component mismatch, errors encountered during their adaptation, malicious security threats and security mechanisms applicable to component-based development. A framework based on logic programming is proposed in (Khan and Han, 2002) for characterizing and analyzing compositional security properties.

Performance Standards

A component should comply with certain performance standards like memory utilization and numeric accuracy. A variety of efficient implementations are also desired to check performance standards.

Conceptual Clarity

A component should be clear and understandable. The interface should contain only what is necessary to reuse the component. The component should be general enough to be applicable in various contexts.

Coupling and Cohesion

A component should have high cohesiveness and low coupling. Any dependencies on operating systems, compilers, hardware etc. should be isolated and clearly documented.

ATTRIBUTE CERTIFICATION MODEL

Certification is a process through which a third party gives written assurance that a product or process confirms to specified requirements (Wallnau, 2004). Figure 1 shows the general model of certification of component (Brereton et al., 2002), (Boegh, 2006) attributes using an entity-relationship diagram. The European Clear and Reliable Information for Integration (CLARIFI) model assumes that an attribute possesses simple attributes, which can be derived from standard requirements. Component suppliers claim values of

Figure 1. The CLARIFI component certification model (Boegh, 2006)

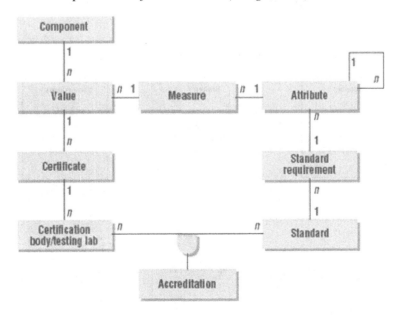

attributes which are certified by applying specified measures in a testing lab or by certification body. An accreditation body ensures the component trustworthiness against these specified standards.

The flow of information according to this model consists of four parts:

- Broker administration
- Component classification
- Component selection
- Component certification

The broker registers component suppliers, system integrators, and certifiers and manages access rights and other administrative tasks. Component suppliers enter descriptions of their components according to their attributes and the component integrator makes use of integrator contexts to embody specific preferences or constraints that are imposed on the selection processes. The broker uses the integrator's preferences and nonfunctional requirements to rank components. After component selection, certifiers certify attribute-value pairs of components using a scheme based on cryptographic techniques that ensures a unique correspondence between a certificate and a specific version of the component under certification. This whole process is shown in Figure 2.

The above said four prototypes allow testing of software components with their realistic size and complexity. The success of this approach depends on the measures used for certification of components, which can be considered as its limitation. Measures cannot be applied directly as they are imprecise. Formalized approach with counting rules helps in careful examination of component standards.

COMPONENT CERTIFICATION STANDARDS

The component properties can be formalized using software measures. Measurable quality properties are called attributes. When a component supplier offers a component to the broker, the supplier must decide which attributes are necessary to describe the component and which claim values are required for describing attributes. These claim values must formalize with measures for each attribute. The claimed values represent the component supplier's expression of the degree to which the component possesses the attributes. Therefore, the trustworthiness of claimed values depends on the component supplier's trustworthiness.

Figure 2. Information flow from component suppliers to system integrators

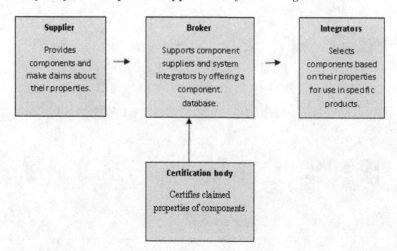

ISO/IEC 9126 standard (ISO/IEC 9126-1, 2001) indicates how to measure attributes and provides the measures in accompanying technical reports. ISO/IEC 14598-3:2000 standard (Chirinos et al., 2005) formalize quality measures by specifying a counting rule, unit, and scale type. The counting rule specifies the measurement procedure, the conditions under which measurements can be taken which involve calculations and logical operations. These operations help in reproducing the relations between attributes.

Component certification assures that a component possesses defined properties, standards and specifications. Certification process of components includes test and evaluation methods. In the other words, a certification system has its own rules, procedures, and management system for carrying out certification of conformity. In principle, anybody can issue a certificate, but to ensure the certificate's credibility, an accreditation system must be established. Accreditation is a procedure by which an authoritative body gives formal recognition that an organization or person is competent to carry out specific tasks. Examples of accreditation system standards are the ISO/IEC 17011 and ISO/IEC 17025 standards (ISO/IEC 17011, 2004), ISO/IEC 17025, 1999).

Generally, certification is used to certify the functional requirements standards, security standards and ISO/IEC 25051 standard (ISO/IEC 25051, 2006). An important aim is to make certification as objective as possible. Currently, most software evaluation and certification done in practice is qualitative and, to some extent, subjective. The European Clear and Reliable Information for Integration (CLARIFI) (Brereton P. et al., 2003), (Boegh J, 2006) scheme suggest methods of making practical software certification more quantitative and more objective. To achieve this aim, the attributes of component are categorizes as:

- Simple attributes
- Complex attributes

Simple attributes refer to the quality attributes of the component. ISO/IEC 9126 standard (ISO/IEC 9126-1, 2001) provides a software product quality model, which is hierarchical and identifies six high-level quality characteristics i.e. functionality, reliability, usability, efficiency, maintainability and portability. These six quality characteristics along with 27 sub-characteristics are considered as a good starting point for identifying attributes describing relevant quality properties.

In the ISO/IEC 9126 quality model, security appears as a sub characteristic of functionality, defined as the software product's ability to protect information and data so that unauthorized persons or systems can't read or modify them and authorized persons or systems can access them. Components intended for security - critical applications known as complex attributes, usually require detailed information about the security attributes. In this case, a specialized security standard such as the ISO/IEC 15408 (ISO/IEC 15408, 1999) can be considered. This standard provides requirements for assuring software security at seven increasingly higher levels:

- Functionally tested
- Structural tested
- Methodically tested and checked
- Methodically designed, tested, and reviewed
- Semiformal designed and tested
- Semiformal verified design and tested
- Formally verified design and tested

This security standard provides an extensive set of requirements for compliance at the different levels of assurance. The only thing is to identify relevant requirements and formulate these requirements as the software's attributes. For example:

Is the reference for the component unique to each version of the component?

Or

Is the component labelled with its references?

Or

Does the CM system uniquely identify all configuration items?

The set of attributes for the ISO/IEC 15408 standard is large, but understood aspects of the component. A similar standard (IEC 61508, 1998) defines compliance at four different safety integrity levels (SIL) expressed in terms of the probability of failure. The (ISO WD-12199-V4 standard, 2001) defines guidelines, which are directly applicable on quality of components. It gives instructions for testing, in particular for third party component testing.

COMPONENT CERTIFICATION PROCEDURE

Software components are often delivered as black boxes or as executable objects. To determine the quality of a component, the following three key questions (Voas, 1998) are to be taken care of:

- Does the component fulfil the developer's needs?
- Is the quality of the component high enough?
- What impact will the component have on system?

The five basic scenarios which could provide an answer to these questions and may lead to the successful development and certification of a software system are listed in the Table 1.

A component can be described and classified with different methods. Without a proper description and classification scheme, it is difficult to select the most appropriate component for a spe-cific purpose. The component description must reflect the component's functional abilities like its environmental needs such as operating system and interfaces to other software. The range of required information depends on the actual component and the intended application area. The independent certification methodology (Jeffrey M. Voas, 1998) shown in Figure 3 could be helpful in taking a decision that whether a new component should be adoptable to existing system or not.

Three pivotal decision points: functional compatible, function quality and adoptability in existing system help in selecting the appropriate component. The first step is to decide whether the component has the functionality needed. Any component that does not meet the developers need can be ignored. The three pivotal decision points help developers in taking the decision with respect to following aspects:

- Whether the component is functionally compatible?
- Whether the component's quality is sufficient?
- Whether the system is ready to adopt the component?

Component certification techniques like black-box testing of executable software components

Table 1. Key questions concerning the use of component in system (Voas, 1998)

Scenario Classifications	Is the component a required component?	Is the component of high quality?	Does component has positive impact on system?
1	Yes	Yes	Yes
2	Yes	Yes	No
3	Yes	No	Yes
4	Yes	No	No
5	No	No	No

Figure 3. Component certification process

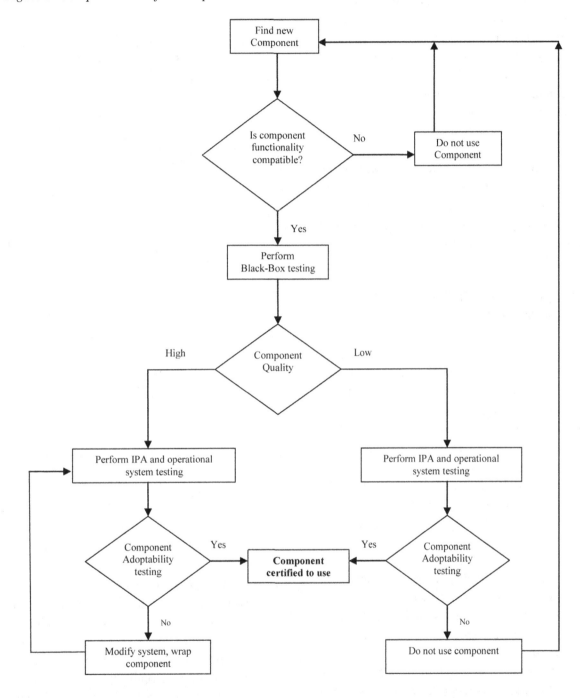

(Musa and Okumoto, 1987), system-level fault injection analysis also called as Interface Propagation Analysis (IPA) (Clark and Pradhan, 1995), (Arlat J. et al., 1990) and operational system testing (Arlat J. et al., 1990) contribute a lot in satisfying the above said decision points. Black-box component testing is used to determine whether the component is of high enough quality. It refers to a family of software testing techniques that selects test cases without regard for software's syntax.

System-level fault injection is used to determine how well a system will tolerate or adopt a failing component. It does not explicitly state how reliable the system is, but rather provides worst-case predictions for how badly the system might behave in the future if components that the system depends on were to fail. Operational system testing is used to determine how well the system will tolerate or adopt a properly functioning component. Even these components can create system wide problems. it executes the full system with system test cases. System-level fault injection and operational system testing are used for checking component adoptability in the existing system.

COMPONENT CERTIFICATION FRAMEWORK

(Alexandre et al, 2007) has proposed a certification framework to evaluate the quality of software components in an efficient way to demonstrate that component certification is not only possible and practically viable, but also directly applicable in the software industry. Through component certification, some benefits can be achieved, such as: higher quality levels, reduced maintenance time, investment return, reduced time-to-market, among others. The process of certifying components consists of:

- Component quality model to should consider Component-Based Development (CBD) characteristics, and describe attributes that are specific to the promotion of reuse (Table 2).
- A series of techniques consist of Documentation analysis, Suitability analysis, Component use-guide analysis, Accuracy analysis, Customizability analysis, Extensibility analysis, Component execution in specific environments analysis, Cohesion, Coupling, Modularity and Simplicity analyses, Cohesion of the docu-

Table 2. A component quality model (Alexandre et al, 2007)

Characteristics	Sub-Characteristics (Runtime)	Sub-Characteristics (Life cycle)
Functionality	Accuracy Security	Suitability Interoperability Compliance Self-contained
Reliability	Fault Tolerance Recoverability	Maturity
Usability	Configurability	Understandability Learnability Operability
Efficiency	Time Behavior Resource Behavior Scalability	
Maintainability	Stability	Changeability Testability
Portability	Deployability	Replaceability Adaptability Reusability
Marketability	Development time Cost Time to market Targeted market Affordability	

mentation with the source code analysis are required. With the help of these techniques, one can evaluate if a component conforms to the model or not. The correct usage of these techniques should follow a well-defined and controllable certification process.

- A certification process (as shown in Figure 4) in order to guide the evaluator during the evaluation activities like evaluation of requirement specifications, guidelines for selecting evaluation level, product documentation, development tools, personnel, expertise requirement, evaluation costs and reporting methods. Figure 4 describes the software component procedure that should be investigated in order to provide the level of confidence required by component markets.

Figure 4. Software component certification process (Alexandre et al, 2007)

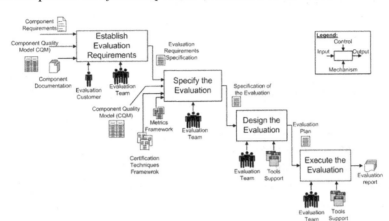

Table 3. A measurement mechanism for quality attribute

Functionality	
Sub-Characteristic	Accuracy
Quality Attribute	Correctness
Goal	Evaluates the percentage of the results that were obtained with precision.
Question	Based on the amount of tests executed, how much test results return with precision?
Metric	Amount of Test / precision
Interpretation	$0 <= x <= 1$; which closer to 1 is better.

- A set of metrics, a measurement mechanism for feedback and evaluation are needed, in order to track the components properties and the performance of the certification process (Table 3).

These above said four modules complement each other in order to achieve a well-defined software component evaluation process.

SUMMARY

Reliable and high - quality software systems can build only by using components of high quality and reliability. Reused components must be free of design and implementation flaws. This chapter summarizes the attributes of components. The attributes like functionality, component interaction and user interaction are component specific where as attributes like adaptation, concurrency and distribution are platform specific. Quality control lies somewhere in the middle because platforms can provide great help for it (e.g. tests, verification, compiler checks) but quality still is a component specific matter which, for example, requires thorough testing of a component. Component quality and its adoptability in the existing system help the developers in selecting one component over the other. The three decision-point methodology can help the developer to decide whether the component is fit to adopt or not.

Certification involves two separate and distinct tasks. The first is to establish facts or attributes about the component being certified, and the second is to establish trust in the validity of these facts or attributes. The first task has consequence on the engineering discipline where application developers can work with known quantities and second has consequence on the development of consumer trust (Wallnau, 2000). Certification process provides advantages for both component suppliers and system integrators. With certification, component suppliers can offer customers an independently issued guarantee of claimed functional properties and quality attributes. For system integrators, certification offers a guarantee against unexpected surprises when building software from components. Certification is a practical, proven means of establishing trust in various sorts of things in other disciplines and is, therefore, a natural contender for developing trust in software components.

It is not fully claimed that certification of software components solve all problems, still there are many open issues. There is an ongoing research related to which attributes of a software architecture are the most important. The certification provides an efficient approach to software systems based on certified components.

REFERENCES

Alvaro, A., Santana de Almeida, E., & Lemos Meira, S. (2007). Towards a software component certification framework. In *Proceedings of Seventh International Conference on Quality Software* (QSIC 2007). ISBN 0-7695-3035-4/07

Alvaro, A., Santana de Almeida, E., & Romero de Lemos Meira, E. (2010). A software component quality framework. *SIGSOFT Software Engineering Notes, 35*, 1-18. DOI=10.1145/1668862.1668863

Apple Computer Inc. (1995). *Open doc: User manual*. Retrieved from http://opendoc.apple.com

Arlat, J. (1990). Fault injection for dependability validation: A methodology and some applications. *IEEE Transactions on Software Engineering, 16*(2), 166–182. doi:10.1109/32.44380

Bass, L., Buhman, C., Dorda, S., Long, F., Robert, J., Seacord, R., & Wallnau, K. (2000). *Market assessment of component-based software engineering*. Software Engineering Institute (SEI). *Technical Report, I*, 2000.

Boegh, J. (2006). Certifying software component attributes. *IEEE Software, 23*(3), 74–81. doi:10.1109/MS.2006.69

Brereton, P., Linkman, S., Thomas, N., Begh, J., & Panfilis, S. D. (2002). Software components—Enabling a mass market. *Proceedings of the International Workshop Software Technology, & Engineering Practice* (STEP) 2002, (p. 169). IEEE CS Press.

Burns, A., & Davies, G. (1993). *Concurrent programming*. Reading, MA: Addison Wesley.

Carvalho, F. (2009). Towards an embedded software component quality verification framework. In *Proceedings of 14th IEEE International Conference on Engineering of Complex Computer Systems*, (pp 248-257).

Chirinos, L., Losavio, L., & Boegh, J. (2005). Characterizing a data model for software measurement. *Journal of Systems and Software, 74*(2), 207–226. doi:10.1016/j.jss.2004.01.019

Choi, Y., Lee, S., Song, H., Park, J., & Kim, S. (2008). Practical S/W component quality evaluation model. *International Conference on Advanced Computer Technology*, (pp. 259-264).

Clark, A., & Pradhan, D. K. (1995). Fault injection: A method for validating computer-system dependability. *Computer, 28*(6), 47–56. doi:10.1109/2.386985

Councill, B. (2001). Third-party certification and its required elements. In *Proceedings of the 4th Workshop on Component-Based Software Engineering* (CBSE), Canada, May, 2001.

Crnkovic, I. (2001). Component-based software engineering – New challenges in software development. *Software Focus, 2*(4), 27–33. doi:10.1002/swf.45

Crnkovic, I., et al. (Eds.). (2001). 4th ICSE Workshop on Component-Based Software Engineering: Component Certification and System Prediction. *Software Engineering Notes, 26*(6).

Demillo, R. A., Lipton, R. J., & Sayward, F. G. (1978). Hints on test data selection: Help for the practicing programmer. *Computer, 11*(4), 34–41. doi:10.1109/C-M.1978.218136

Dong, X., Hua, W., Qiming, T., & Xiangqun, C. (2007). *Towards a software framework for building highly flexible component-based embedded operating systems.* In IFIP International Federation For Information Processing (2007).

Dunn, M. F., & Knight, J. C. (1993). *Certification of reusable software parts.* Technical Report CS-93-41, University of Virginia, August 31, 1993.

Heineman, G. T., & Councill, W. T. (2001). *Component-based software engineering: Putting the pieces together.* Reading, MA: Addison-Wesley.

Heineman, G. T., Councill, W. T., et al. (2000). Component-based software engineering and the issue of trust. In *Proceedings of the 22nd International Conference on Software Engineering* (ICSE), Canada, 2000, (pp. 661-664).

Hissam, S. A., Moreno, G. A., Stafford, J., & Wallnau, K. C. (2003). Enabling predictable assembly. *Journal of Systems and Software, 65,* 185–198. doi:10.1016/S0164-1212(02)00038-9

IEC 61508. (1998). Functional Safety of Electrical/Electronic/ Programmable Electronic Safety Related Systems, Int'l Electrotechnical Commission, 1998.

ISO. IEC 12119. (1994). International Organization for Standardization ISO/IEC 12119, Information Technology – Software Packages – Quality Requirements and Testing, p. 16, Geneve ISO.

ISO. IEC 17025. (1999). *General requirements for the competence of testing and calibration laboratories.* Geneva, Switzerland: ISO.

ISO. IEC 15408. (1999). *Information technology—Security techniques—Evaluation criteria for IT security.* Geneva, Switzerland: ISO.

ISO. IEC 14598-1. (1999). *International organization for standardization ISO/IEC 14598-1 Information technology- Software product evaluation- Part 1: General overview.* Geneva, Switzerland: ISO.

ISO. IEC 9126-1. (2001). *Software engineering—Software product quality—Part 1: Quality model.* Geneva, Switzerland: ISO.

ISO. IEC 17011. (2004). *Conformity assessment—General requirements for accreditation bodies accrediting conformity assessment bodies.* Geneva, Switzerland: ISO.

ISO. IEC 25000. (2005). *Software engineering – Software product quality requirements and evaluation (SQuaRE): Guide to SQuaRE.* Geneva, Switzerland: ISO.

ISO. IEC 25051. (2006). *Software engineering—Software product quality requirements and evaluation (SQUARE) — Requirements for quality of commercial off-the-shelf (COTS) software product and instructions for testing.* Geneva, Switzerland: ISO.

ISO International Standard ISO/WD121199. ISO/WD121199-V4. (2001). *Software engineering –Software product evaluation- Requirements for quality of commercial off-the shelf software products (COTS) and instructions for testing.* Geneva, Switzerland: ISO.

Jacobson, I., Griss, M., & Jonsson, P. (1997). *Software reuse: Architecture, process and organization for business success.* Reading, MA: Addison-Wesley, Longman.

Jalote, P. (1994). *Fault tolerance in distributed systems.* Englewood Cliffs, NJ: Prentice Hall.

John, R. (1994). OpenDoc, IBM and Apple's pitfall for mega-applications. *Scientific American,* 130–131.

Khan, K. M., & Han, J. (2002). Composing security-aware software. *IEEE Software, 19*(1). doi:10.1109/52.976939

Kumar, B. (2002). *Component security*. White paper.

Leavens, G. T., & Sitaraman, M. (2000). *Foundations of component-based systems*. Cambridge, UK: Cambridge University Press.

Lindqvist, U., & Jonsson, E. (1998). A map of security risks associated with using COTS. *IEEE Computer, 31*(6).

Meyer, B. (2003). The grand challenge of trusted components. In *Proceedings of 25th International Conference on Software Engineering* (ICSE), USA, (pp. 660–667).

Morris, J., Lee, G., Parker, K., Bundell, G. A., & Lam, C. P. (2001). Software component certification. *IEEE Computer, 34*.

Musa, J. D., Iannino, A., & Okumoto, K. (1987). *Software reliability measurement prediction application*. New York, NY: McGraw- Hill.

Patel, S., Stein, A., Cohen, P., Baxter, R., & Sherman, S. (1992). *Certification of reusable software components*. In WISR 5 [WIS92].

Quarterman, J. S., & Wilhelm, S. (1993). *UNIX, POSIX, and open system*. Reading, MA: Addison-Wesley.

Rodriguez-Dapena, P. (1999). Software safety certification: A multidomain problem. *IEEE Software, 16*(4), 31–38. doi:10.1109/52.776946

Roshanak, R., Somo, B., Leslie, C., Nenad, M., & Leana, G. (2006). *Estimating software component reliability by leveraging architectural models*. ICSE'06. Retrieved from http://www.irisa.fr/lande/lande/icse-proceedings/icse/p853.pdf

Sametinger, J. (1997). *Software engineering with reusable components*. New York, NY: Springer-Verlag.

Shaikh, S. A., & Cerone, A. (2007). *Towards a quality model for open source software (OSS)*. Elsevier Science B.V.

Stafford, J., & Wallnau, K. (2001). Is third-party certification necessary? In *Proceedings of the 4th ICSE Workshop on Component-Based Software Engineering*, Toronto, Canada, (pp. 13-17).

Szyperski, C. (2002). *Component software: Beyond object-oriented programming*. Reading, MA: Addison-Wesley.

Trass, V., & Hillegersberg, J. (2000). The software component market on the Internet, current status and conditions for growth. *ACM Sigsoft Software Engineering Notes, 25*(1), 114–117. doi:10.1145/340855.341145

Upadhyay, N., Despande, B. M., & Agrawal, V. P. (2011). Towards a software component quality model. *Journal of Advances in Computer Science and Information Technology. Communications in Computer and Information Science, 131*(3), 398–412. doi:10.1007/978-3-642-17857-3_40

Voas, J., & Payne, J. (2000). Dependability certification of software components. *Journal of Software Systems, 52*, 165–172. doi:10.1016/S0164-1212(99)00143-0

Voas, M. J. (1998). Certifying off-the-shelf software components. *IEEE Computer, 31*(6), 53–59. doi:10.1109/2.683008

Voas, M. J. (1999). Certifying software for high-assurance environments. *IEEE Software, 16*(4), 48–54. doi:10.1109/52.776948

Voas, M. J. (2000). Developing a usage-based software certification process. *Computer, 33*(8), 32–37. doi:10.1109/2.863965

Wallnau, K. (2004). *Software component certification: 10 useful distinctions* (CMU/SEI-2004-TN-031). Retrieved May 2, 2012, from the http://www.sei.cmu.edu/library/abstracts/reports/04tn031.cfm

Wallnau, K. C. (2003). *Volume III: A technology for predictable assembly from certifiable components.* Software Engineering Institute (SEI), Technical Report, Vol. 03.

Wallnau, W. (2000). *Technical concepts of component-based software engineering*, 2nd ed. (Technical Report CMU/SEI-2000-TR-008, ESC-TR-2000-007).

Wohlin, C., & Runeson, P. (1994). Certification of software components. *IEEE Transactions on Software Engineering, 20*(6), 494–499. doi:10.1109/32.295896

ADDITIONAL READING

Brown, A. W. (Ed.). (1996). *Component-based software engineering: Selected papers from the Software Engineering Institute.* Los Alamitos, CA: IEEE Computer Society Press.

Kaur, P., & Singh, H. (2008). Certification process of software components. *SIGSOFT Software Engineering Notes, 33*(4), 1–6. doi:10.1145/1384139.1384142

Lau, K. K. (2003). Some ingredients of trusted components. In *Proceedings of Workshop on Trusted Components*, (pp. 1-5). January 2003, Prato, Italy.

Lau, K. K., & Ornaghi, M. (2001). A formal approach to software component specification. In D. Giannakopoulou, G. T. Leavens, & M. Sitaraman (Eds.), *Proceedings of Specification and Verification of Component-based Systems Workshop at OOPSLA2001*, (pp. 88-96). Tampa, USA.

Lüders, F., Lau, K. K., & Ho, S. M. (2002). Specification of software components. In Crnkovic, I., & Larsson, M. (Eds.), *Building reliable component-based software systems* (pp. 23–38). Artech House.

KEY TERMS AND DEFINITIONS

Software Component: A software component is a unit of composition with contractually specified interfaces and explicit context dependencies only. A software component can be deployed independently and is subject to composition by third party.

Component-Based Software Engineering (CBSE): It refers to a process that emphasizes the design and construction of computer-based systems using reusable software component.

Component-Based System: A systematic approach for the effective reuse of already developed concepts.

Component Certification: Certification is a process through which a third party gives written assurance that a product or process confirms to specified requirements.

Component Attributes: A component can be defined with the help of certain attributes like functionality, Interactivity, Interaction, Concurrency, Interoperability, Adaptation, Reliability, Security, Performance Standards, Conceptual Clarity, Coupling and Cohesion.

Component Quality: the conformance of the component to the requirements and standards.

Chapter 3
Analyzing Growth Trends of Reusable Software Components

Kuljit Kaur
Guru Nanak Dev University, India

ABSTRACT

Reusable software components are the software modules that can be (re)used across a number of applications in a particular domain. Component users prefer to use those components which can be adapted easily for their changing requirements. So components have to evolve continuously in order to attract users. This chapter focuses on the evolutionary aspects of software components. It mentions various techniques for monitoring software evolution. It uses metrics based analysis as the technique to show software evolution of 15 reusable components from the point of view of their size, complexity, and functionality. The evolution analysis is motivated by laws of software evolution which suggest that as software ages, it increases in size and complexity (unless it is managed) and it has to offer increased functionality to please its users. The findings of the study indicate that the size of the software components (in this data set) grows at a linear rate, and complexity is well managed. However, increase in functionality is sub linear for almost all the components. It remains almost constant for some of them.

INTRODUCTION

Software crisis is characterized by two major phenomena: Lack of ability to produce software within budget and time constraints, and lack of quality in produced software (Kim & Blodyreff, 1996). In 1968, Mcllroy suggested software reuse as a means for overcoming software crisis (Mcll-roy, 1968). He pointed towards the effective use of reusable software components to build large reliable software systems in a controlled and cost effective way. It has been observed in several studies (Melo et al., 1995; Mohagheghi et al., 2004; Mohagheghi & Conradi, 2007) that using reusable software components can improve the reliability of a system as they generally contain fewer bugs.

DOI: 10.4018/978-1-4666-2958-5.ch003

Component developers develop software components keeping in mind their reuse value across product lines and organizations. These reusable components are reused as is or are adapted to meet the requirements of a different project in a context other than the one anticipated during their development (Ravichandran & Rothenberger, 2003; Yu et al., 2009). They need to satisfy not only the initial demands of their stakeholders, but also need to offer support for future, changing requirements. This study focuses on the evolutionary aspects of software components. It considers the software components modeled using the object oriented approach.

Software evolution is concerned with the aging process of source code. Lehman et al.(1997) established the laws of software evolution, which suggest that as software ages, it increases in size and complexity (unless it is managed) and it has to offer increased functionality to please its users (Godfrey & German, 2008; Lehman, 1980; Lehman et al., 1997). Several studies have been done to prove or refute these laws (Godfrey and Tu, 2000; Xie et al., 2009). Godfrey and Tu (2000) found in an experiment that the Linux source code grows super-linearly in size and complexity. This research analyzes evolution of reusable software components in terms of their size, complexity, and functionality to understand their growth as they evolve. Reuse based software systems follow a different kind of development model. As they are subject to different kinds of evolutionary pressures in comparison to monolithic single use system, they are expected to have a different kind of evolutionary behaviour.

REUSABLE SOFTWARE COMPONENTS

Component Based Development (CBD) has emerged as an important paradigm for software development. In this paradigm, a software system is developed as a composite of sub-parts, rather than a monolithic entity. These sub-parts are pre-built software units, or components. A new software system for a specific domain is just assembled using the domain-specific pre-built components. This approach reduces production cost, gives a shorter time-to-market, and results in a high quality product (Mohagheghi & Conradi, 2007), the sought after goals of the software industry since long.

Reusable components are just modules that have been designed to be useful in solving all the problems including the ones which are not anticipated beforehand. Software development organizations can reuse software components which are built in-house or acquired from third parties. Third party components fall in two categories – Open Source Software (OSS) Components and Commercial Off the Shelf (COTS) components.

A widely accepted definition of a software component is given by Szyperski [3]:

A software component is a unit of composition with contractually specified interfaces and explicit context dependencies only. A software component can be deployed independently and is subject to composition by third parties.

The definition covers the characteristic properties of components. It has a technical part with aspects such as independence, contractual interfaces, and composition. Explicit context dependencies refer to the component needs that it has to mention explicitly in the context of its composition and deployment. Interfaces are the means by which components connect. Each component implements two interfaces: a required interface, and a provided interface. A provided interface is a set of operations that clients can invoke. A required interface is a set of operations that a component, as a client, invokes from the provided interfaces of its servers. The definition refers to the market aspects such as composition of components by third parties.

In the context of object oriented paradigm, Valerio *et al.* (2001) define a component as:

A homogeneous set of objects that collaborate to perform a feature or functionality and exposing a component interface that allows to integrate it in a system and make available to the external environment a set of services.

The 3 C's model of reuse design says that there are three aspects of a reusable component--the concept, the content, and the context (Latour *et al.*, 1991). The concept corresponds to the abstract functionality of a component. Its purpose is to focus on the essence of the component, and ignore other details e.g. implementation details. The content is the implementation of the component which includes selection of a programming language and a design. The transition from concept to content involves moving from the problem, or domain, space to the solution space. The context is the environment in which a component is deployed. It includes the required machine, operating systems, compiler version, and so on.

There are different ways in which existing components can be reused: black box reuse or white box reuse. In black box reuse, component users can use the components without making any changes to its source code. This kind of reuse is encouraged. It does not compromise a reuser's confidence in the component's properties such as its correctness as it is assumed that making changes to the source code may introduce some defects as well. In white box reuse, the component users study the source code to understand the implementation. They may be using features of the component through its interfaces only, but sometimes, inadvertently, end up in writing application code which depends upon the source code of the component. So whenever implementation details of the reusable component change, the application code also has to change.

Frameworks and Libraries are considered as components, in that they are sold as products and that an application can use various frameworks. They are the systems that provide generic/reusable abstractions with a well defined API (Application Programming Interface).

MONITORING SOFTWARE EVOLUTION

Metrics Based Analysis

This approach makes use of software metrics in order to understand the evolution of software systems. In order to better understand the evolution of a software system, a set of metrics, from each release of a software system, are extracted and changes in these metrics, over time, are observed. A major aspect of the FEAST (Feedback, Evolution And Software Technology) program of research into long-term software evolution processes has been the collection of metrics for evolving software products, and the examination of trends over time in these metrics. Applying metrics over the evolution of the software can aid a developer to understand how a system has evolved over time (Lee *et al.*, 2007).

Several metrics have been proposed in this regard such as the System Design Instability (SDI) metric. It indicates the progress of an object oriented (OO) project once the project is put in use (Alshayeb *et al.*, 2008). The SDI metric is based on the belief that if the domain abstraction and design are stable, the number of classes, class names, and the inheritance hierarchy in an application are likely to stay stable as well. Therefore, a measure of the system design stability/instability at the abstraction/system level is obtained by measuring the changes in these factors during development. Lee *et al.* (2007) provide an overview of open source software evolution with software metrics, and present that the size, *fan-in/out* coupling and cohesion metrics can be used during the software evolution process to understand the evolution behavior. Lines of source code (LOC), function points (FP) or other change related metrics may also be used to monitor software evolution activity.

Visualization Based Analysis

Due to a large amount of information, which need to processed and understood during the software evolution, software evolution analysis gets very complex. Visualization has proven to be a key technique to depict the structural evolution of large software systems both at a coarse-grained and a fine-grained level (Lanza, 2001; Ratzinger *et al.*, 2005; Fischer & Gall, 2006, Langelier *et al.*, 2005). Evolution of classes, represented as rectangles, is depicted in terms of a set of metrics mapped on the dimensions of the rectangles. Evolution of a software system is represented with the help of large evolving graphs, using colors to depict the changes. Information extracted from a systems' release history has been used to produce 2D visual representations of the evolution of its structural dependencies. 3D visualizations have also been used to display structural information, by representing classes as boxes with metrics mapped on height, color and twist, and packages as borders around the classes, using a tree layout or a sunburst layout. Several tools have been developed for visualization of software evolution. D'Ambros et al. (2009) proposed Evolution Radar, a visualization-based approach that integrates both file-level and module-level logical coupling information. Lanza (2001) proposed an Evolution Matrix to visualize the software evolution. Wu, Holt and Hassan (2004) used spectrographs to explore software evolution. It has been felt that visualizations oversimplify the representation of the evolution (Wettel & Lanza, 2008) as visual displays allow the human brain to study multiple aspects of complex problems in parallel (Girba, 2005).

Qualitative Simulation Techniques

Qualitative reasoning is an approach that helps to create models at an abstract level when there is a lack of complete or precise knowledge. It requires fewer assumptions during model building than do quantitative techniques. This lack of precise knowledge is tackled through reasoning at a more abstract level than it could be done in quantitative modeled. Qualitative simulation is believed to

lead to more solid findings and conclusions than conventional quantitative methods. In qualitative simulation, a system is modeled as a set of ordinary differential equations. The output of the simulation is qualitative. It is expressed in terms of shapes and direction. A qualitative simulation system predicts multiple possible behaviors given certain sets of qualitative constraints and initial conditions. For example, a qualitative simulation may be able to tell us under which conditions an important attribute, such as functional growth rate, displays sustained increase (linearly, sub-linearly or super-linearly), steadiness or decrease (again, linearly, sub-linearly or superlinearly). Smith *et al.* (2005) applied qualitative simulation methods to the study of software evolution of five proprietary software systems.

Design Rule Theory and Design Structure Matrices

A Design Structure Matrix (DSM) is a square matrix, in which each design variable corresponds both to a row and a column of the matrix. A cell is checked if and only if the design decision corresponding to its row depends on the design decision corresponding to the column. A DSM represents modules as blocks along the diagonal. They provide positive evidence that the model and theory have the power to formally explain phenomena related to the evolution of large-scale software systems. The concept of design structure matrix (DSM) was initially conceived by Steward (1981), and later developed by Eppinger *et al.* (1991) as means of modeling interactions between design variables of engineered systems. Lemantia *et al.* (2007) present two case studies which apply the model and theory to real-world large-scale software designs, studying the evolution of two complex software systems through the lens of DSMs and DR theory. This approach enabled the team to discover poorly-modularized design structures and refactor the design prior to coding, and to ensure a well modularized implementation.

Measuring Software Evolution

Software systems exhibit two broad quantitative aspects that are captured by a range of software metrics: *size* and *structural complexity*. A number of different software related metrics have been proposed such as size-oriented measures like the number of lines of code (LOC) or function-oriented measures to analyze process aspects like costs and productivity. These metrics are useful for analyzing the product quality as well (Fenton and Pfleeger, 1996). When these metrics are collected and analyzed over time, they reveal valuable information such as evolutionary jumps in the architecture and complexity of the software system under observation (Godfrey and Tu, 2001). Size measures provide an indication of the volume of implementation provided by a software system. Since it takes usually more effort to create a larger-sized system than a smaller one (Fenton & Neil, 1999), size metrics are considered to be a broad indicator of effort required to build and maintain a software system. An example of a size metric within the context of object oriented systems is the metric Number of Classes.

An important aspect of the studies, which analyzed the growth patterns, has been the choice of the size metric. Lehman suggests using the number of modules to quantify program size. He argues that this metric is more consistent than considering source lines of code (LOC). However, there are different interpretations of a module in studies of software evolution. There are instances of treating a file or a directory as a module. The definition of LOC also varies depending on the tools used for analysis and available data sources. In addition, several other metrics such as number of packages, number of functions, and total size in kilobytes have also been used for analyzing evolution.

Lehman (1980) and Lehman et al. (1997) discuss the laws of program evolution. Based on the patterns observed in proprietary software, they find that source code tends to grow in size and complexity, while its growth rate and quality decrease. Lehman *et al.* used module count for software growth estimation. They empirically studied IBM OS360/370 and found that the software growth rate is linear. Godfrey *et al.* (2001) used SLOC, global functions and variables for (Linux Kernel) growth estimation. They concluded that Linux Kernel is growing at super linear rate.

Izurieta and Bieman (2006) used SLOC, number of directories, total size in bytes, and SLOC of header files for software evolution estimation. They also drilled down their analysis and applied Module Count for subsystems. In their conclusion, they said that no evidence was found to support that open source software grows faster than traditional software systems. Open source and commercial projects have a similar growth rate over time with respect to the total functions, the total size, and the total complexity of the release. Deshpande and Reinkle (2004) quantitatively analyze the growth of more than 5000 active and popular open source software projects. They show that the total amount of source code as well as the total number of open source projects is growing at an exponential rate. The total amount of source code and the total number of projects double about every 14 months.

Mens and Demeyer (2002) explore how and where software metrics have been used during the software evolution process and to identify avenues of future research. They are of the opinion that software metrics can be used to analyze the software, with the aim (a) to assess which parts *need* to be evolved (evolution-critical), (b) which parts are *likely* to be evolved (evolution-prone), and (c) which parts can *suffer* from evolution (evolution-sensitive).

Robles *et al.* (2006) argue that software artifacts other than source code also exhibit interesting maintenance and evolution patterns. In their paper, they present a study of the evolution of build systems, a software artifact that co-evolves with project source code. Adams *et al.* (2008) consider that not only do build systems evolve but also that they co-evolve with the program source code.

Xie et al. (2009) analyze long spans in the life time of seven open source projects to better understand the process of software evolution. They verify Lehman's laws of software evolution and confirm application of four of them. They found that interface changes are much less than the implementation changes, and tend to occur towards the initial phases of software evolution.

Experimental Analysis

Motivation for this research stems from Lehman's laws especially the 2nd and the 6th, increased complexity and continuing growth, which stipulate that programs usually grow in size and complexity over their lifetime to accommodate pressures of change and increase in functionality. The research in the past started to verify these with some studies of the proprietary systems. Later on, with the onset of the open source software development paradigm, a number of studies have examined the open source systems to verify the law. The develop-

ment scenario is further changing with the use of components, frameworks, and powerful libraries becoming commonplace. So, research is needed to understand the evolutionary behaviour of these reusable components, which form major portion of the present and the future software systems.

Case Studies

The reusable software components, for analysis, are taken from the Helix data repository (Vasa *et al.*, 2010). The repository provides a number of programs but in the current study, the programs that are reusable are selected i.e. a program listed either as a component, framework, or library is selected for analysis. Table 1 presents a view of the components selected for analysis in this study. It gives information about their names, number of releases, dates and sizes of the first and last releases. The components listed in the table are put into two categories for an analysis of their growth trends in size, complexity, and functional-

Table 1. Basic information regarding the software components

S. No.	Name	Num. of Releases	First Release		Last Release	
			Date	Size	Date	Size
1.	Acegi	30	29-April-2004	135	19-February-2010	525
2.	Axis	25	15-August-2001	166	19-October-2009	1273
3.	Castor	27	28-March-2001	483	03-January-2010	1309
4.	Cacoon	15	24-February-2000	105	19-March-2008	692
5.	iBatis	27	18-February-2004	208	17-April-2010	346
6.	Jena	25	28-September-2001	328	01-June-2010	915
7.	Jung	25	03-November-2003	117	24-January-2010	358
8.	Stripes	27	31-August-2005	108	16-December-2009	229
9.	Struts	18	22-September-2000	106	23-Sep-2009	910
10.	WebWork	14	18-November-2003	148	26-January-2008	505
11.	Hybernate	60	19-January-2002	120	16-June-2010	1893
12.	Spring	55	26-June-2003	384	15-June-2010	2593
13.	Tapestry	33	11-October-2002	308	23-April-2009	791
14.	Wicket	39	17-September-2004	181	19-May-2010	803
15.	ActiveMQ	34	26-April-2004	205	26-April-2010	1382

ity. The first category contains the components with less than or equal to 30 version releases, and the second category contains components with more than 30 versions. The choice of the number 30 is just random. It has been done to study the growth trends of older components (in terms of the number of releases) separately.

Metrics Selection

The main objective of this study is to analyze the growth in size, complexity, and functionality of the reusable software components over their life time. In the past research, different metrics such as LOC, and number of modules have been used for measuring growth in size of the software systems. This study uses number of classes as the metric for measuring size of the object oriented reusable components. It also analyzes the size growth rate which is calculated by taking difference of the number of classes in the current and the first of a component, dividing it by the number of classes in its first release, and multiplying the value thus obtained by 100. Complexity is measured by calculating the number of methods per class. As an interface defines a standard and public way of specifying the behavior of a class, the number of interfaces of a release are used to measure the set of functions supported by the software component at one point of time.

Growth Trends

Figure 1 shows the trend in size of the reusable software components whose more than 30 versions have been released. The size data has been plotted against the Release Sequence Number (RSN), a pseudo unit of time, rather than the natural time such as the release dates. This has been done to keep the presentation of data simple, as different release dates for different components would have complicated the presentation. All of the curves in the figure, except for the components ActiveMQ and Tapestry, are showing almost ever increasing trend in the number of classes. There are some instances, as in case of ActiveMQ, when the software size has decreased in a subsequent release (such as RSN 19 and 30). The growth trend of ActiveMQ is going topsy-turvy in its latest releases. A look at the change logs of its project reveals that developers have handled a large number of issues, more than 200 in each release, during these releases (from RSN 29 to 32). So shift in the trend may be the result of cleanup tasks performed by the developers. However, more detailed analysis of the change logs is required to understand the exact type of issues taken up in this period.

For the components in the second category, some of them have more than doubled in size in the period, and their growth was relatively steady, as presented in Figure 2. There are occasional drops in their number of classes. Only Castor and Stripes, and Acegi show an ever increasing trend

Figure 1. Growth trends of reusable software components (with more than 30 releases)

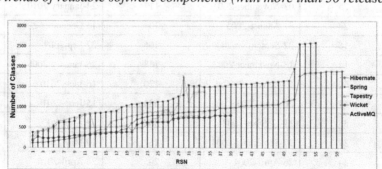

Figure 2. Growth trends for reusable components (with less than 30 releases)

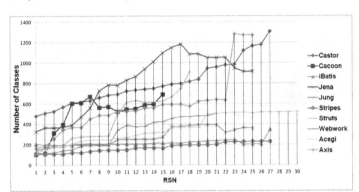

in their size growth. However, growth of some of the components such as Cacoon, Struts, and Jena has been confusing. They have grown exponentially in the beginning, and later on followed a downward trend. It will be interesting to see the factors behind their change in size. It may be related to the cleanup/restructuring drives. But it is hard to believe that cleanup/restructuring may not have been done for the other components which show sub linear growth.

Size Growth Rate

Growth rate is calculated by taking difference of the number of classes in the current and the first of a component, dividing it by the number of classes in its first release, and multiplying the value thus obtained by 100. This information is then put on the graph against the release sequence number of each release. Figure 3 shows the growth rate for the components with more than 30 releases. It can be seen that all the curves show a few jumps and slumps in the period. But in all the cases, growth rate has not shown much variation. Increase or decrease in the number of classes has always been less than 100%. Tapestry and ActiveMQ see positive as well as negative corrections in their size. However, the other set of components (with less than 30 releases in Figure 4) show much larger jumps/slumps in their size in terms of number of classes (e.g. Cacoon and Axis). It could be observed in most of the cases that changes in size occur periodically (Jung is the perfect example). There is a period of stillness after a major jump or slump. It further establishes the fact that software evolution is a case of punctuated equilibrium instead of a gradual change (Antón & Potts, 2003). Evolution occurs in discrete bursts. But Castor, iBatis, and Stripes show negligible growth in their size. It is important to study these systems in de-

Figure 3. Growth rate of reusable components (with more than 30 releases)

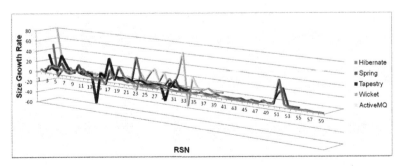

Figure 4. Growth rate of reusable software components (with less than 30 releases)

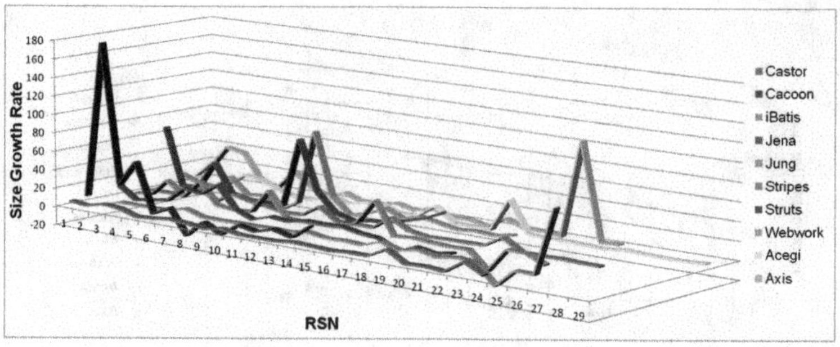

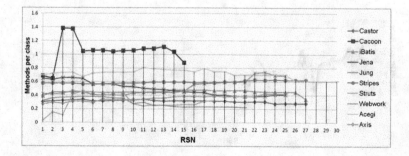

tail to understand their evolution. There could be several reasons that resist change such as market saturation or complexity of the software itself (Godfrey and German, 2008).

Complexity Trends

In the previous research, Weighted Methods per Class (WMC) metric has been used for measuring complexity at class level, and average WMC for measuring complexity at system level. In this study, Complexity is measured by using the same approach i.e. the average number of methods per class. Figure 5 and 6 show the trends in complexity of the reusable components. In the first category of components (with less than 30 releases), majority of them (7/10) have a sub linear increase in their complexity over the period of time. It is almost constant for two components: iBatis and Stripes. Cacoon has super linear growth in complexity in the beginning, but it reduces substantially after the

4th release. Similarly, Jena has a negligible growth in the beginning which further shows a decreasing trend in the recent releases (after the 5th release). Jung has been following a sub linear growth in complexity with a sudden rise in its 22nd release. It could be observed that complexity has been well managed in majority of the cases. There is need to explore the reasons behind it so as to understand the mechanisms used in managing the complexity. For the second category of components, growth in complexity has almost been constant (Figure 6) except the ActiveMQ component which shows a drastic decline in complexity since its first release. The growth rate (in Figure 3) of the component has also shown a number of corrections in size over its life period. The reasons may include an active developer community.

Figure 5. Complexity trends of reusable components (with less than 30 releases)

Figure 6. Complexity trends of reusable components (with more than 30 releases)

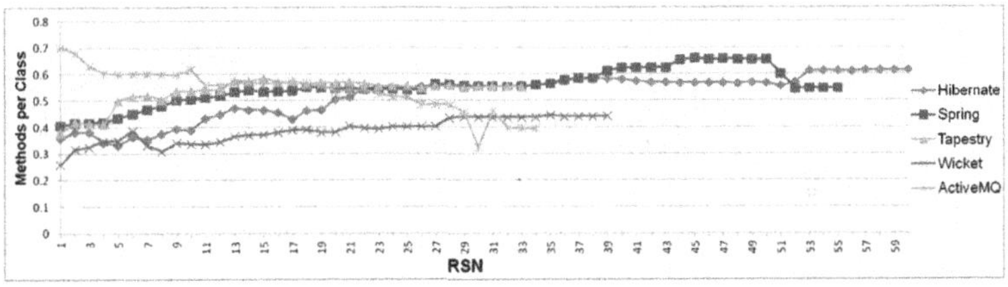

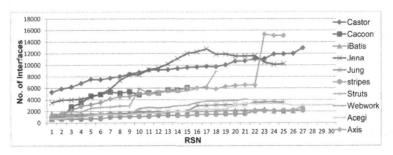

Functionality Trends

An interface in Java defines a standard and public way of specifying the behavior of classes. Interfaces declare contracts that are meant to be implemented through classes. In this study, we measure the number of interfaces of a release as the set of functions supported by the software component at one point of time. Increase/decrease in number of interfaces over a period of time can help in analyzing the trends in software component's functionality. Figure 7 shows the trends for the software components in the first category i.e. components with less than 30 releases. All the components have a sub linear growth in their functionality. Jena has a linear growth till its 17th release, after that it shows a downward trend. Cacoon also shows a similar trend. In the second category of components (with more than 30 releases), Hibernate and Spring show almost a similar trend (Figure 8). Tapestry shows a downward trend in its functionality. ActiveMQ shows a neglegible growth in its functionality in its initial 19 releases, but a linear trend after that.

CORRELATION ANALYSIS

This part of the analysis involves calculating the correlation for each metric across all software components. Correlation measures the relationship between two data sets that are scaled to be independent of the unit of measurement. The population correlation calculation returns the covariance of two data sets divided by the product of their standard deviations. Correlation can be used to determine whether two ranges of data move together. Positive correlation indicates that large values of one set are associated with large values of the other set. Negative correlation indicates that small values of one set are associated with large values of the other. If both data sets are unrelated, then the correlation is near zero. Table 2 shows the data regarding the correlation analysis. The rank of correlation is calculated for size (Number of classes), complexity (Number of methods per class), and functionality (Number of Interfaces). Table cells with value of the rank of correlation r, in the interval $-0.5 <= r >= 0.5$, are bolded. It could be observed that size and functionality are

Figure 7. Functionality trends of reusable components (with less than 30 releases)

Figure 8. Functionality trends of reusable components (with more than 30 releases)

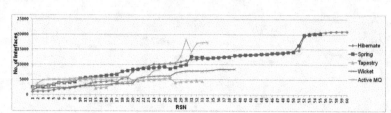

highly related with one another in all the cases. There is high correlation in complexity and size for all the cases except for two software components: Cacoon and Struts. Cacoon shows super linear growth in size and complexity in the initial releases, but subsides in the later releases. On the other side, Struts shows a super linear growth towards the later releases. Size and functionality are highly correlated for all the 15 reusable software components. It indicates that as functionality increases, size also increases which is intuitive as well. Another fact that can easily believe is that as functionality increases complexity may also increase. But the analysis of data in this experiment proves it wrong. Increase in functionality in some of the components is not followed by increase in complexity (rather it follows a reverse trend). It could be observed that complexity is controlled in many of the components such as Castor, Jena, Webwork, Acegi, and ActiveMQ. It is important to see the mechanisms used to reduce/stabilize the complexity. There is further need to study other project information to understand the nature of evolution.

CONCLUSION

This chapter presents an analysis of the evolutionary behaviour of reusable components from the point of view of changes in their size, complexity, and functionality from their first release to the final release (available in the data set). The software evolution data of the components is obtained from a publicly available source. The data set has been divided into two categories: category 1 includes component with more than 30 releases, and category 2 includes components with less than and equal to 30 releases. This study is motivated by Lehman's laws that as a program evolves, its size increases and its complexity also increases unless it is managed. In continuation another law is that a program has to provide increased functionality to stay popular amongst its users. The metrics used for measuring size, complexity, and functionality of a release are number of classes, number of methods per class, and number of interfaces available in a release respectively. It is found that though size and functionality of almost all the

Table 2. The correlation matrix

Software Component	Size X Complexity	Size X Functionality	Functionality X Complexity
Castor	-0.793	0.967	-0.651
Cacoon	0.355	0.976	0.382
iBatis	-0.530	0.868	-0.175
Jena	-0.927	0.998	-0.936
Jung	0.775	0.942	0.932
Stripes	0.907	0.985	0.942
Struts	0.001	0.980	0.036
Webwork	-0.941	0.990	-0.921
Acegi	-0.551	0.993	-0.471
Axis	0.872	0.998	0.851
Hibernate	0.874	0.990	0.924
Spring	0.657	0.994	0.716
Tapestry	0.592	0.944	0.348
Wicket	0.915	0.998	0.921
ActiveMQ	-0.938	0.992	-0.934

components are growing, their complexity remains almost constant or follows a downward trend. The present study will be extended in future to understand the mechanism used to stabilize or reduce the complexity. For some of the components, there is negligible change in their functionality throughout their lifetime (20+ releases). It has found to be decreased for a component called Tapestry (with more than 30 releases). This study emphasizes the fact that there is need to study the project information in order to understand better the evolution of these software.

FUTURE RESEARCH DIRECTIONS

Lehman's second law states that as a program grows its complexity increases. However, it does not hold true for the current set of programs subject to analysis in this study. In future, it is important to see the reason behind this stabilization or reduction in complexity. There is also need to extend the study choosing different complexity metrics. In this study, some of the programs show negligible growth from all aspect of the analysis i.e. size, complexity, and functionality. It will be interesting to see the reasons behind this. Future research in this field should focus on the project characteristics of the open source reusable software components. It can help us to understand the evolutionary pressures on them.

ADDITIONAL READING

Nowadays, software evolution has become a very active area of research. Meir M. Lehman, the pioneer in software evolution studies, identified the phenomenon as early as 1969. The whole story on how software evolution was identified may be found in the seminal book on software evolution (Lehman & Belady, 1985). A discussion on some of the important research themes in software evolution is given in the book by Mens and De-

meyer (2008) and (BENEVOL 2008). With the availability of open source software in which the code base, history of releases and change logs of the software programs are open in public domain, the researchers have explored their evolutionary behaviour. Breivold *et al.* (2010) give a survey of open source software evolution studies.

REFERENCES

Adams, B., Schutter, K., Tromp, H., & Meuter, W. (2007). The evolution of the Linux build system. *ERCIM Symposium on Software Evolution*, Vol. 8.

Alshayeb, M., & Li, W. (2005). An empirical study of system design instability metric and design evolution in an agile software process. *Journal of Systems and Software*, *74*(3). doi:10.1016/j.jss.2004.02.002

Antón, A., & Potts, C. (2003). Functional paleontology: The evolution of user-visible system services. *IEEE Transactions on Software Engineering*, *29*(2), 151–166. doi:10.1109/TSE.2003.1178053

BENEVOL. (2008). *The 7th Belgian- Netherlands Software Evolution Workshop*, Eindhoven, December 11-12, 2008.

Breivold, H. P., Chauhan, M. A., & Ali Babar, M. (2010). A systematic review of studies of open source software evolution. *Asia-Pacific Software Engineering Conference*, (pp. 356-365). 2010 Asia Pacific Software Engineering Conference, 2010.

D'Ambros, M., Lanza, M., & Lungu, M. (2009). Visualizing co-change information with the evolution radar. *IEEE Transactions on Software Engineering*, *35*(5), 720–735. doi:10.1109/TSE.2009.17

Deshpande, A., & Riehle, D. (2004). The total growth of open source. *Proceedings of the Fourth conference on Open Source Systems*, (pp. 197–209). Springer Verlag.

Eppinger, S. D. (1991). Model-based approaches to managing concurrent engineering. *Journal of Engineering Design, 2*(4), 283–290. doi:10.1080/09544829108901686

Fenton, N., & Neil, M. (1999). A critique of software defect prediction models. *IEEE Transactions on Software Engineering, 25*(5), 675–689. doi:10.1109/32.815326

Fenton, N., & Pfleeger, S. L. (1996). *Software metrics: A rigorous and practical approach* (2nd ed.). London, UK: International Thomson Computer Press.

Fischer, M., & Gall, H. C. (2006). Evograph: A lightweight approach to evolutionary and structural analysis of large software systems. In *Proceedings of the 13th Working Conference on Reverse Engineering* (WCRE), (pp. 179–188). IEEE Computer Society.

Girba, T. (2005). *Modeling history to understand software evolution.* PhD thesis, University of Berne.

Godfrey, M., & Tu, Q. (2000). Evolution in open source software: A case study. *Proceedings of the International Conference on Software Maintenance*, (pp. 131–142).

Godfrey, M., & Tu, Q. (2001). Growth, evolution, and structural change in open source software. In *Proceedings of the 4th International Workshop on Principles of Software Evolution* (IWPSE '01), (pp. 103–106). Vienna, Austria: ACM Press.

Godfrey, M. W., & German, D. M. (2008). The past, present, and future of software evolution. *Proceedings of Frontiers of Software Maintenance*, (pp. 129-138). Beijing.

Izurieta, C., & Bieman, J. (2006). The evolution of FreeBSD and Linux. *Proceedings of International Symposium on Empirical Software Engineering* (pp. 204–211).

Kim, H., & Boldyreff, C. (1996). Lecture Notes in Computer Science: *Vol. 1088. An approach to increasing software component reusability in Ada. Reliable Software Technologies –Ada-Europe'96* (pp. 89–100). Berlin, Germany: Springer.

Langelier, G., Sahraoui, H. A., & Poulin, P. (2005). Visualization based analysis of quality for large-scale software systems. In *Proceedings of 20th IEEE/ACM International Conference on Automated Software Engineering* (ASE 2005), (pp. 214–223). ACM Press.

Lanza, M. (2001). The evolution matrix: Recovering software evolution using software visualization techniques. In *Proceedings of IWPSE 2001, 4th International Workshop on Principles of Software Evolution*, (pp. 37–42). ACM Press.

Lanza, M., & Ducasse, S. (2002). Understanding software evolution using a combination of software visualization and software metrics. In *Proceedings of Langages et Modèles à Objets* (LMO'02), (pp. 135–149). Paris, France: Lavoisier.

Latour, L., Wheeler, T., & Frakes, B. (1991). Descriptive and Prescriptive Aspects of the 3 C's Model: SETA1 Working Group Summary. *Ada Letters, XI*(3), 9–17. doi:10.1145/112630.112632

Lee, Y., Yang, J., & Chang, K. (2007). Metrics and Evolution in Open Source Software, Proceedings of Seventh International Conference on Quality Software (QSIC 2007), pp 191-197.

Lehman, M. (1980). On understanding laws, evolution and conservation in the large program life cycle. *Journal of Systems and Software, 1*(3), 213–221.

Lehman, M., & Belady, L. A. (1985). *Program evolution. Processes of software change.* San Diego, CA, USA: Academic Press Professional, Inc.

Lehman, M., Ramil, J., Wernick, P., Perry, D., & Turski, W. (1997) Metrics and laws of software evolution—The nineties view. In *Proceedings of the 4th International Software Metrics Symposium* (METRICS).

Lemantia, M., Cai, Y., & MacCormack, A. (2007). Analyzing the evolution of large-scale software systems using design structure matrices and design rule theory: Two Exploratory Cases. *WICSA '08: Proceedings of the Seventh Working IEEE/IFIP Conference on Software Architecture* (WICSA 2008).

Mcllroy, D. (1968). Mass-produced software components. *Proceedings of the 1st International Conference on Software Engineering,* (pp. 138–155). Garmisch, Germany.

Melo, W. L., Briand, L., & Basili, V. R. (1995). Measuring the impact of reuse on quality and productivity in object-oriented systems. Technical Report CS-TR-3395, University of Maryland, 1995.

Mens, T., & Demeyer, S. (2001). *Future trends in software evolution metrics.* Vienna, Austria: IWPSE.

Mens, T., & Demeyer, S. (Eds.). (2008). *Software evolution.* Springer Verlag.

Mohagheghi, P., & Conradi, R. (2007). Quality, productivity and economic benefits of software reuse: A review of industrial studies. *Empirical Software Engineering, 12,* 471–516. doi:10.1007/s10664-007-9040-x

Mohagheghi, P., Conradi, R., Killi, M., & Schwarz, H. (2004). An empirical study of software reuse vs. defect-density and stability. In *ICSE '04: Proceedings of the 26th International Conference on Software Engineering,* (pp. 282–292). Washington, DC: IEEE Computer Society.

Ratzinger, J., Fischer, M., & Gall, H. (2005). Evolens: Lens-view visualizations of evolution data. In *Eighth International Workshop on Principles of Software Evolution,* (pp. 103–112).

Ravichandran, T., & Rothenberger, M. (2003). Software reuse strategies and component markets. *Communications of the ACM, 46*(8), 109–114. doi:10.1145/859670.859678

Robles, G., Gonzalez-Barahona, J., & Merelo, J. (2006). Beyond source code: The importance of other artifacts in software development (A case study). *Journal of Systems and Software, 79*(9), 1233–1248. doi:10.1016/j.jss.2006.02.048

Smith, N., Capiluppi, A., & Ramil, J. (2005). A study of open source software evolution data using qualitative simulation. *Software Process Improvement and Practice, 10,* 287–300. doi:10.1002/spip.230

Steward, D. V. (1981). The design structure system: A method for managing the design of complex systems. *IEEE Transactions on Engineering Management, 28*(3), 71–74.

Szyperski, C. (1999). *Component software - Beyond object-oriented programming* (2nd ed.). Addison-Wesley.

Valerio, A., Cardino, G., & Leo, V. (2001). Improving software development practices through components. *Proceedings of the 27th Euromicro Conference 2001: A Net Odyssey* (Euromicro01), (pp. 97-103). Warsaw, Poland.

Vasa, R., Lumpe, M., & Jones, A. (2001). *Helix - Software evolution data set.* Swinburne University of Technology, 2010.

Wettel, R., & Lanza, M. (2008). *Visual exploration of large-scale system evolution.* 2008 15th Working Conference on Reverse Engineering, IEEE Computer Society Press.

Wu, J., Holt, R. C., & Hassan, A. E. (2004). Exploring software evolution using spectrographs. In *Proceedings of the 11th WCRE,* (pp. 80-89).

Xie, G., Chen, J., & Neamtiu, I. (2009). Towards a better understanding of software evolution: An empirical study on software evolution. *Proceedings of the International Conference on Software Maintenance.* Edmonton, Canada: IEEE Computer Society Press.

Yu, L., Chen, K., & Ramaswamy, S. (2009). Multiple-parameter coupling metrics for layered component-based software. [Springer.]. *Software Quality Journal, 17,* 5–24. doi:10.1007/s11219-008-9052-9

Chapter 4
Aspect–Oriented Recommender Systems

Punam Bedi
University of Delhi, India

Sumit Kr Agarwal
University of Delhi, India

ABSTRACT

Recommender systems are widely used intelligent applications which assist users in a decision-making process to choose one item amongst a potentially overwhelming set of alternative products or services. Recommender systems use the opinions of members of a community to help individuals in that community by identifying information most likely to be interesting to them or relevant to their needs. Recommender systems have various core design crosscutting issues such as: user preference learning, security, mobility, visualization, interaction etc that are required to be handled properly in order to implement an efficient, good quality and maintainable recommender system. Implementation of these crosscutting design issues of the recommender systems using conventional agent-oriented approach creates the problem of code scattering and code tangling. An Aspect-Oriented Recommender System is a multi agent system that handles core design issues of the recommender system in a better modular way by using the concepts of aspect oriented programming, which in turn improves the system reusability, maintainability, and removes the scattering and tangling problems from the recommender system.

1 INTRODUCTION

People are often overwhelmed with the number of options available to them. The sheer number of available options often makes a wise choice impossible without some intelligent computational assistance. Recommender systems or the concept of automatic recommendation generation is one of the possible solutions to this information overload problem. Recommender Systems attempt to reduce information overload and retain customers by selecting a subset of items from a universal set

DOI: 10.4018/978-1-4666-2958-5.ch004

based on user preferences. A recommender system recommends items to users by predicting items relevant to the user, based on user profile which contains various kinds of information including items, user information and interactions between users and items (Adomavicius & Tuzhilin, 2005). Some of the core design issues in Recommender systems are as follows:

- **User Preference Learning:** Recommender systems acquire information about user preferences in an explicit (e.g., letting users express their opinion about items) or implicit (e.g., observing some behavioral features) way which is required to generate a list of recommended items (Bedi & Agarwal, 2011b).
- **Security:** Recommender systems are highly vulnerable to profiles injection attacks. Therefore, security mechanisms are needed for protecting the recommender systems against these attacks (Bedi & Agarwal, 2011c).
- **Mobility:** Recommender systems use the demographic information of the user i.e., the knowledge of the user's location at a particular time for generating the more relevant recommendations for him (Bedi & Agarwal, 2011a).
- **Visualization:** Recommender systems use effective visualization interfaces in order to provide more effective and persuasive recommendations (Vashisth et al., 2011).
- **Interaction:** Recommender systems use various interactive interfaces in order to gather information about user preferences with minimum user interaction with the system (Zhang et al., 2008).

These core design issues of the recommender systems are crosscutting concerns. Crosscutting concerns usually refer to non functional properties of system such as learning, security, trans-

action management, synchronization, mobility, interaction, visualization and error handling etc that are used across the scope of a piece of the system. Implementation of these crosscutting concerns using conventional agent-oriented approach creates the problem of code scattering and code tangling. Scattering in agent-oriented models is the manifestation of design elements that belong to one specific concern, over several modeling units referred to other multi-agent system concerns. Tangling in agent-oriented models is the mix of multiple concerns together in the same modeling elements. Aspect-Oriented Recommender Systems (AORS) is the solution of these crosscutting design issues of the recommender system. Aspect-oriented recommender systems are multi agent systems that handle the core design issues of the recommender system in a better modular way by using the concept of aspect oriented programming to remove the scattering and tangling problems from the recommender system.

This chapter describes the brief introduction of an Aspect-oriented programming (AOP) and its constructs along with the various aspects of recommender system. Beginning with the description of various constructs of AOP and crosscutting issues of recommender system, this chapter introduces the inherent problems and their consequences of not having explicit support for the modularization of crosscutting concerns in the recommender systems. This chapter also provides a solution of these inherent problems to support crosscutting issues in design of multi-agent recommender system along with its advantages.

The chapter is organized as follows. Section 2 reviews the related work in this area. Concepts used in the proposed approach are discussed in section 3. Section 4 describes the proposed approach to deal with crosscutting concerns in the recommender system. Experimental details and results are shown in section 5 and finally conclusion and future work are discussed in section 6.

2 RELATED WORK

There is a lot of work available on core design issues of the recommender systems in literature. (Kass & Finin, 1988) introduced implicit (observing behavior of the user and inferring facts) and explicit (let the users express his opinion about items) preference learning methods in recommender systems. (Montaner et al., 2003) presented a comparative analysis between these explicit and implicit learning techniques. (Rojanavasu et al., 2005) presented a general framework for recommendation system based on reinforcement learning. (Lam & Riedl, 2004) have explored the problem of shilling attacks and also discussed the difficulty of dealing with these attacks against collaborative recommender systems. (O'Mahony et al., 2004) developed several techniques such as stability of prediction, power of attack etc to defend against the attacks described by (Lam & Riedl, 2004). (Chirita et al., 2005) proposed several metrics such as Number of Prediction-Differences (NPD), Standard Deviation in User's Ratings, Degree of Agreement with Other Users, and Degree of Similarity with Top Neighbors for analyzing rating patterns of malicious users and evaluated these metrics for detecting profile injection attacks. (Burke et al., 2005; Burke et al., 2006) explored attack models for secure recommendation and used model based approach to detect attribute generation. (Burigat et al., 2005) introduced decision support functions with a map interface to generate recommendations for visitors. (Tumas & Ricci, 2009) developed personalized mobile city transport advisory system using knowledge-based approach for providing best route between two arbitrary points in the city. (Good et al., 1999) in their work have explored the cold-start problem of recommender systems. (Kim & Li, 2004) proposed a probabilistic model to address the cold start problem, in which items are classified into groups and predictions are made for users considering the Gaussian distribution of user ratings. (Hussein, 2010) presented the enhanced K-means algorithm to minimize the validity (intra-cluster/inter-cluster) to get optimum number of clusters for generating most suitable recommendations. (Kiczales et al., 1997) proposed the new program development methodology AOP to generate more efficient, modularize and better understandable code. They shown that program written in AOP is more easily maintainable. (Mehmood et. al., 2005) presented a framework that separates the performance aspects from other agent hood, functional and non-functional aspects to improve modularity of multi-agent system using AOP.

Although the considerable amount of work is done in literature on learning, security, mobility and core design issues of recommender systems with some research work focusing on these crosscutting issues of the recommender system, the problem of tangling and scattering in the recommender system has not been resolved as per our knowledge. This chapter presents Aspect-oriented recommender systems, a novel approach to handle learning, security and mobility crosscutting concerns in a better modular way to reduce the cognitive complexity of the recommender systems by using the concepts of AOP.

3 BACKGROUND

This section briefly describes basic concepts of recommender systems along with the introduction of Aspect-oriented programming (AOP) and its constructs.

3.1 Recommender Systems

Recommender Systems are technological proxy for the support provided by the friends, reviews in magazines, newspapers, etc. to filter the set of possible options to a more manageable subset and act like electronic assistants to sort out relevant information for the user (Schafer et al, 1999). Typically, recommender systems analyze data about items' or about interactions between users and items to find the associations amongst them (Figure 1). The results obtained are used to predict relevant and interesting items for the user. The research on recommender systems uses the results of a wide variety of fields like Information Retrieval, Artificial Intelligence, Cognitive Science, Approximation Theory, Forecasting Theories, Statistics, etc. (Adomavicius & Tuzhilin, 2005). The principal mode of operation of the recommender systems can be broken down into three major steps (Burke, 2002) as:

- Acquisition of the background information which is in the form of the explicit ratings given by the users to the products or preferences of the users learnt by the system through the history of purchase transactions, usage records, etc.
- Determination of the pattern of associations among the users or items, from the background information.
- Generation of the predicted ratings or the recommendations for the target user from the patterns found in the background information.

Recommender systems use a specific type of information filtering technique that attempts to present information items such as movies, music,

Figure 1. Working of recommender system

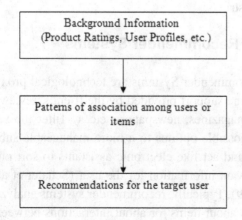

books, news, images, web pages, that are likely to be of interest to the user. These systems are very powerful cognitive decision-makers in the context of distributed online information processing in real time networked scenarios (Adomavicius & Tuzhilin, 2005). Recommender Systems can be classified mainly into content based, collaborative filtering based, knowledge based, context-aware and hybrid recommender systems.

- Content based recommender systems use the ratings of the items the target user liked in the past to predict items the target user would also like in future. These systems assume that taste of the target user does not be change.
- Collaborative filtering based recommender systems use the ratings of the users having taste similar to the target user and predict items of interest for the target user based on liking of users of similar taste.
- Knowledge based recommender systems use a knowledge structure to make inferences about the user needs and preferences.
- Context-aware recommender systems recommend items based on user preferences that are influenced by contextual conditions, such as the time of the day, mood, or current activity, but this type of information is not exploited by standard models (Adomavicius et al., 2005).
- Hybrid recommender systems use a combination of at least two of the above mentioned approaches.

3.2 Aspect Oriented Programming (AOP)

In software engineering the basic desire is to produce engineering methods that allow for the efficient creation and maintenance of system. To that end, there are several key quality issues that need to be improved: modularity, reusability, readability, understandability, correctness and testability of the system. Aspect Oriented Programming (AOP) complements Object-Oriented Programming (OOP) by providing another way of thinking about program structure to produce system that is efficient to run, without sacrificing these quality issues. AOP claims to address those issues that object-oriented programming don't completely or directly solve. AOP is not a replacement for object-oriented analysis and design. It builds upon the object-oriented paradigm by addressing situations where the object-oriented approach does not adequately provide the most desirable solution (Tarr et al., 1999).

AOP is a programming paradigm which aims to improve modularity of the software systems by allowing separation of crosscutting concerns (Garcia et al., 2004; Garcia et al., 2005). Crosscutting concern is a behavior, and often data, that is used across the scope of a piece of system. It may be a constraint that is a characteristic of the system or simply a behavior that every class must perform. AOP has various set of semantics and syntactical constructs such as: aspect, advice, join point and point cut (Tarr et al., 1999) etc.

- An aspect is a basic unit of modularization for crosscutting concern in AOP that cuts across multiple objects. An aspect provides a mechanism by which a cross-cutting concern can be specified in a modular way. An aspect can affect, or crosscut, one or more classes and/or objects in different ways. An aspect can change the static structure (static crosscutting) or the dynamics (dynamic crosscutting) of classes and objects. An aspect is composed of internal attributes and methods, pointcuts, advices, and inter-type declarations.
- Join points are the elements that specify how classes and aspects are related. A join point is a well-defined point in the code at which the concerns crosscut the application such as method call, object construction, object initialization or field access etc.

- An advice is the code that is executed when an aspect is invoked. Advice contains its own set of rules as to when it is to be invoked in relation to the join point that has been triggered. In other words we can say that an advice is a code fragment that is executed when join points satisfying its point cut are reached. This execution can be done before, after, or around a specific join point. There are different kinds of advices: (i) before advices - run whenever a join point is reached and before the actual computation proceeds; (ii) after advices - run after the computation "under the join point" finishes; (iii) around advices run whenever a join point is reached, and has explicit control whether the computation under the join point is allowed to run at all.
- A point cut is a concept that classifies join points in the same way a type classifies values. The point cut provides a mechanism for declaring an interest in a join point to initiate a piece of advice. It encapsulates the decision-making logic that is evaluated to decide if a particular piece of advice should be invoked when a join point is encountered.

The concept of a point cut is very crucial to the aspect-oriented approach because it provides an abstract mechanism by which to specify an interest in a selection of join points without having to tie to the specifics of what joint points are in a particular application. Figure 2 shows the relationships among joinpoints, aspects, pointcuts, and advice with application class.

AOP is generally used for those applications that have lack of support to handle crosscutting concerns in a proper way for implementing good quality and maintainable system. Recommender system is one of the applications that contain various crosscutting concerns such as: security, mobility, interaction, visualization and preference learning etc.

Figure 2. The relationships between joint points, aspects, point cuts, and advice

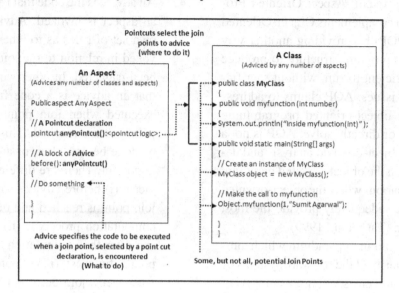

4 Aspect Oriented Recommender Systems (AORS)

This section describes crosscutting concerns in multi-agent recommender system using agent-oriented approach with aspect of AOP. Section 4.1 presents functional description of multi-agent recommender system. Section 4.2 shows the consequences of not having explicit support for the modularization of crosscutting concerns in the recommender system. Section 4.3 illustrates our approach to support these crosscutting concerns in recommender system using agent oriented design enhanced with aspect oriented approach.

4.1 Functional Description of Multi-Agent Recommender System

A multi-agent recommender system (MARS) automates the process of finding the appropriate places for the user to visit according to his demographic information such as location, time and need etc. for example in a tourism recommender system (Bedi & Agarwal, 2011a). Every human user of this system is represented through a software agent. MARS is a trust based multi agent recommender system, which means that every software agent within this system communicates only with its trustworthy software agents (Bedi et al., 2010). The MARS encompasses 3 types of software agents: (i) user agents (UA), (ii) recommender agents (RA) and (iii) information agent (IA). The basic functionality of UAs is to infer and keep information about the corresponding users who want the recommendations from the system. RAs represent the other users who share their knowledge with the system. UA collects the query from the user using web-based GUI. UA passes this query to its trustworthy RAs for recommendations generation. The RA receives a query request from UA and then RA generates the recommendations for the UA using trust based recommendation algorithm. Once, UA receives the recommendations from all trustworthy RAs in its neighborhood, it generates the final recommendation list after taking into account the degree of trust on each of the RA. UA stores trust values for each interacting RA known to it and prioritize the RAs according to their trust value. UA also updates the degree of trust on each RA after evaluating the recommendations given by them. RA also updates the degree of trust on other

RAs implicitly within the system. IA's goals are managing the system information that is mainly stored in a database, and providing information to the other system agents and users as requested. IA stores the profiles of all registered users and their preferences with the system in his local database. IA controls the local database and is able to query for the profile. However, if the information is not available in the database, IA needs to move and try to find out the missing profile in remote environments. Although this mobility concern is separated from collaborative activities (roles), it is mixed with agent classes and methods that implement the agent's basic functionality. So if an agent has multiple roles and mobility actions, then the code of that agent will be more complex. Figure 3 represents the functional diagram of MARS.

We decompose the complex goals of the MARS into more granular goals to distribute them among the agents. The goal view diagrams represent the identification of hierarchy that describes the system goals in terms of software agent's goals of the system. Figure 4, 5 and 6 represents the goal view diagrams of UA, RA and the IA.

4.2 Inherent Problems to Support Crosscutting Concerns in Design of Multi-Agent Recommender System

Existing agent-oriented modeling abstractions and composition mechanisms do not provide adequate support to isolate crosscutting concerns of multi-agent recommender systems as exemplified in Figures 4, 5 and 6. This brings several major design pitfalls, as described below.

- **Repetition of Agent-Oriented Design Elements:** In the agent-oriented design, replication of goals of system agents and their actions are the side effects of tangling and scattering problems. Replication consecutively decreases the system usability and understandability etc. For instance, learning specific goal "Connect DB" (connect with database) is duplicated in the goal view diagram of recommender agent (Figure 5) due to its crosscutting relationships with the goals "Update DB" and "Generate Recommendations" and a

Figure 3. The functional diagram of multi-agent recommender system

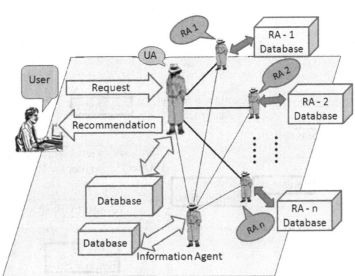

Figure 4. The goal view diagram of user agent

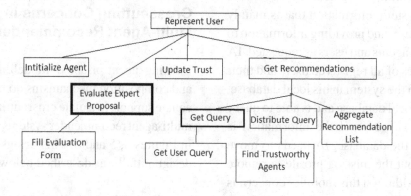

Figure 5. The goal view diagram of recommender agent

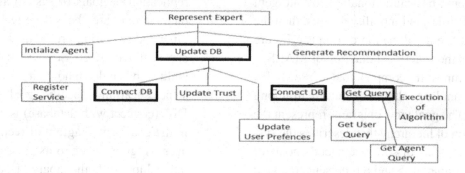

Figure 6. The goal view diagram of information agent

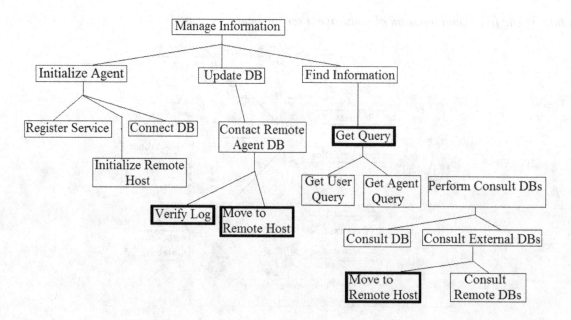

mobility specific goal "Move to Remote Host" is also duplicated in the goal view diagram of information agent (Figure 6) due to same reason with the goals "Contact Remote Agent DB" and "Consult External DBs".

- **Necessary Information Missing:** Recommender system developers cannot locally represent the structural and behavioral implications of the crosscutting concerns without suitable abstractions and composition for crosscutting concerns in conventional agent-oriented design. The consequence of this problem is that design information is not recoverable because of lack of support for specifying them. For example, the learning concern in recommender system would clearly have a goal "Learn User Preferences", which influences at least two sub goals: "Get Query" of RA (Figure 5) and "Evaluate Expert Proposal" of UA (Figure 4) and similarly security concern in recommender system also, would have an obvious goal "Deletion of malicious user attacks", which influences at least two sub goals: "Update DB" of RA (Figure 5) and "Verify Log" of IA (Figure 6). Since designer does not have sufficient support to describe this crosscutting impact of learning-specific and security-specific goals, hence such important design information has been lost and such goals are not appeared in the goal view diagrams.

- **Hindering of Modular and Compositional Reasoning:** Tangling and scattering of MAS concerns hinder both modular and compositional reasoning at the design stage. Developers are unable to reason about a concern while looking only at its description, including its core goals and actions, and its structural and behavioral implications in terms of other MAS concerns. Hence its analysis inevitably forces developers to consider all the design artifacts in an ad hoc manner. For example, the designers treating the learning, security and mobility concerns in Figures 4, 5 and 6 needs to consult the goals associated with all other design concerns across the different views.

- **Reduced Evolvability and Reuse Opportunities:** Tangling and scattering are two most important anti-evolution and anti-reuse factors in any multi-agent based recommender system design. The goals associated with learning, mobility and security concerns are not logically documented in a single modular unit so that they can be easily reused in other design contexts. If the recommender system developers need to evolve the system and introduce changes related to the security, mobility and learning properties, then evolution process will become extremely difficult as those concerns are intermingled in the system design.

4.3 Solution of Crosscutting Concerns in Design of Multi-Agent Recommender Systems

Agent-oriented abstractions do not provide adequate support for the modularization of crosscutting concerns in the multi-agent recommender systems. The design of these concerns tends to affect or crosscut many classes and methods that implement other agent concerns. So Adding, removing or modifying these concerns to/from a system is an invasive task, difficult to reverse change. Hence the solution of this problem must achieve following goals.

- **Code Replication:** The design solution should minimize code replication across different classes and methods of the multi-agent recommender system.

- **Separation of Concerns:** The design solution should separate the crosscutting issues (security, learning, mobility) of multi-agent recommender system from its agents' basic structure.

- **Transparency:** The basic agent's structures of multi-agent recommender system should be unaware from the implementation of the crosscutting design issues of the recommender system. For example, external agent classes should not be changed for implementing any security or learning strategy.

- **Readability and Maintainability:** The solution should be general enough to support the modularization of the crosscutting design issues of multi agent recommender system in a way that is independent to the rest of the system. Moreover agent classes should not be mixed with invocations of methods related to these core issues of the recommender system in order to improve the system readability and maintainability.

- **Ease of Evolution:** The design solution of the crosscutting concerns of the recommender system should be easy to evolve, as future changes must be easily incorporated within the system without affecting the other part of the system.

- **Reduced Number of Components and Minimized Coupling:** Explosion in the number of agent components should be avoided as well as in the number of relationships between them.

4.4 Enhancement of Recommender System with Aspect-Oriented Approach

Creation of separate aspect for each crosscutting design issue of the multi-agent recommender systems removes all inherent problems of the recommender systems discussed in section 4.2 because AOP includes programming methods

and tools that support the modularization of concerns at the level of the source code and gives the more flexibility to implement these crosscutting concerns by integrating the aspects with the base code. These aspects (Learning Aspect, Mobility Aspect, and Security Aspect) are integrated with various agents' goals of multi-agent recommender system at well defined join points with point cuts in order to handle these crosscutting concerns effectively. These aspects completely eliminate the problem of tangling and scattering in multi-agent recommender systems easily because these just work as a plug-in with the system. So any future changes within the policies of the recommender system, can be easily handled by modification and compilation of these aspects without changing the existing code of the recommender system.

The enhanced goal view diagram of multi agent recommender system presents the system goals, i.e. the agent's goals with the learning aspect, security aspect and mobility aspect in Figure 7. The learning aspect, security aspect and mobility aspect in this diagram are represented as diamonds. Some circles are attached with these aspects. Each circle captures a crosscutting interface that an aspect crosscuts the agent goals. Crosscutting interfaces specify when and how the specific aspect (security aspect, learning aspect, mobility aspect) affects other agent's goal. The purpose of the crosscutting interfaces is to modularize parts of the learning, security and mobility concerns of the recommender system, which usually crosscut other concerns in traditional kinds of other decomposition, such as agent-orientation.

5 EXPERIMENTAL STUDY

The implementation details of AORS along with extensive description of learning aspect, mobility aspect and security aspect are shown in section 5.1. Section 5.2 illustrates the experimental results.

Figure 7. Enhanced goal view diagram of multi-agent recommender system

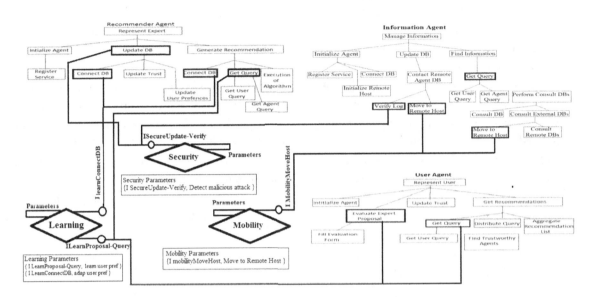

5.1 Implementation Details

AORS is designed and developed using JSP (Java Server Pages), Oracle 10g, JADE (Java Agent Development Environment) and AspectJ on Eclipse interface for tourism domain. We collected the information of various tourist zones, tourist states, tourist cities, hill stations, tourist places and available hotels at these places in India from www.touristplacesinindia.com website. This collected dataset contains the details of 4 tourist zones, 11 tourist states, 27 tourist cities, 7 hill stations, 159 tourist places and 437 available hotels at these places. We calculated the longitude and latitude values for each collected tourist places by performing reverse geo-coding using google map. The demographic information of the mobile user i.e. his physical location was extracted using the Geolocation API of HTML 5.

Initially we implemented AORS prototype using JSP and JADE on Tomcat 5.0 web server without aspects. Thereafter we have implemented mobility aspect, security aspect and learning aspect using AspectJ on Eclipse interface and integrated these aspects with the existing system. The description of these aspects is as follows:

5.1.1 Description of Learning Aspect

Learning aspect separates the learning protocol from agent classes, such as agent types, plans, and roles. By using Learning aspect, we define when and how the agent learns. It specifies how to extract information from diverse agent components which are necessary for user preference learning. The Learning aspect connects the agent classes with the corresponding learning components, making it transparent to the agent's basic functionality the particularities of the learning algorithms in use. This aspect is able to crosscut join points in the agent classes in order to change their normal execution and invoke the learning components. The join points include the change of a knowledge element, execution of actions on plans, roles, and agent types, or still some threw exception.

The Learning aspect is used for learning user preferences within AORS. Learning aspect is declared as abstract since it needs to be redefined in different context, i.e. different agent types and roles. Note that the initialization method is called by an after advice, which is in turn associated with an abstract point cut. Pointcuts are used to define which join points on the object execution

65

the aspect is interested to observe. These pointcuts must expose as parameters the information (object instances) necessary to be used in the aspect context. Advices associated with these pointcuts invoke methods on aspects and classes, and if it is necessary they pass the information gathered in the pointcuts as arguments. The learningInstantiation point cut describes when learning aspect should be initialized; it is abstract because it depends on the agent type or role class associated with the learning aspect. Learning aspect also specifies the methods: (i) learnUserPreferences() – which is responsible for invoking the learning components; and (ii) updateUserPreferences() – which updates the user preferences and his trust value on other user, after the execution of the learning algorithm. The partial code of the learning aspect is presented in Figure 8.

5.1.2 Description of Mobility Aspect

Mobility aspect is the integration of type-based and policy based mobility strategies that weave with several agents of AORS. Mobility aspect defines how and when the agents will move to other environments. The mobility aspect invokes the methods responsible for implementing the mobility-specific actions, such as IdentifyUserLocation(), move() etc. No mobility code remains in the agent classes that implement the basic functionality and collaborative activities. The Mobility aspect is declared as abstract since it needs to be redefined in different contexts, i.e. different agent types and roles. The partial code of the mobility aspect is presented in Figure 9 and descriptions of few abstract pointcuts and methods of mobility aspect are as follows:

- **moving pointcut ()**: Used to define join-points in the agent execution, where it could be moved to another environment
- **identifyUserLocation method()**: Used to define the procedure to find the user location
- **checkMobilityNeed method ()**: Identifies the mobility need of the agent.
- **init method ()**: Used to initialize the agent mobility capabilities in a specific platform

Figure 8. Snapshot of learning aspect

```
public abstract aspect Learning {
...
protected Hashtable Role.learningComponents = new Hashtable();
protected void abstract init(Role role);
protected abstract pointcut learningInstantiation(Role role);
after(Role role): learningInstantiation(role) {
System.out.println("<**** ****Learning *********> initialization:" +
((Role)role).getName());
init(role);
}
public Hashtable abstract learnUserPreferences(Hashtable
Role.learningComponents, int userTrust);
public void updatePreferences( Hashtable newPreferences, int updateTrust)
{ ...}
...
}
```

Figure 9. Snapshot of mobility aspect

```
public abstract aspect Mobility {
Agent || AbstractPlan || Goal || ... implements Serializable;
private String MobileAgent.location;
protected abstract pointcut agentInstantiation(Agent agent);
after(Agent agent) : agentInstantiation(agent) {
init(agent);     }
public abstract void init(Agent agent);
public abstract void move(Agent agent);
protected abstract pointcut moving(Plan plan);
after(Plan plan) returning (Object result): moving(plan) {
Agent agent = plan.getAgent();
boolean moveAgent = checkMobilityNeed(agent, result);
Hastable location = IdentifyUserLocation (agent, result);
if (moveAgent && (!agent.isAgentOut())) {
move(agent);     }     }
public abstract void initializeAgentInNewEnvironment(Object mobileAgent);
protected abstract boolean checkMobilityNeed(Agent agent, Object result);
...
}
```

- **move() method:** Used to define the actions to be executed to move an agent to another environment

5.1.3 Description of Security Aspect

We created the security aspect and embedded this security aspect with various agents' goals of AORS at well defined join points with point cuts to defend against security attacks. Security aspect invokes the methods responsible for implementing the security actions, such as authentication () – Which is responsible for checking the user authentication, maliciousUserAttackDetection () – Which is responsible for detection of bogus user profile in AORS. The partial code of the security aspect is presented in Figure 10.

5.2 Experimental Results

All the crosscutting concerns of multi-agent recommender system are evaluated using separation of concern (SoC) metrics (Garcia, 2004) such as CDC (Concern diffusions over components), CDO (Concern diffusions over operations), CDLOC (Concern diffusions over LOC) and coupling metric such as CBC (Coupling between components) with and without using aspect-oriented approach. The separation of concerns metrics measure the degree to which a single concern in the system maps to the design components (classes and aspects), operations (methods and advices) and line of code.

CDC is a design metric that counts the number of classes and aspects whose main purpose is to contribute to the implementation of a concern and the number of other classes and aspects that access

Figure 10. Snapshot of security aspect

```
Public aspect security {
protected void abstract init(Role role);
protected abstract pointcut SecureConnectVerify(Role role);
arround(Role role): authentictaion(role) {
if(authentication()!= admin) {
System.out.println(" non permission ");        }
else {
Object x = proceed();
System.out.println("the method is well executed");
return x;
}
init(role);
}
public void maliciousUserAttackDetection(Hashtable UserProfile)
{ ... }|
```

them. CDO counts the number of methods and advices whose main purpose is to contribute to the implementation of a concern and the number of other methods and advices that access them. CDLOC counts the number of transition points for each concern through the lines of code. Transition points are points in the code where there is "concern switch" and CBC counts the number of other classes and aspects to which a class or an aspect is coupled.

The CDC metric detected that recommender system required more components for implementing crosscutting concerns in recommender systems using conventional agent-oriented approach than the AOP approach. CDO metric required more operations (methods/advices) in the conventional agent-oriented solution than in the AOP solution. The CDLOC metric also pointed out that the AOP solution was more effective in terms of modularizing the crosscutting concerns across the lines of code. Table 1 presents the comparative results of all SoC and coupling measures for implementing crosscutting concerns in the multi agent recommender system with and without using aspect-oriented approach.

Table 1. Shows the results of SoC measures

Concerns	Separation of Concerns			Coupling
	CDC	CDO	CDLOC	CBC
Learn preferences without aspect	5	11	5	3
Learn preferences with aspect	3	7	2	1
Security without aspect	5	10	4	4
Security without aspect	2	6	2	1
Mobility without aspect	4	9	5	3
Mobility with aspect	2	5	2	1

6 CONCLUSION AND FUTURE WORK

The main objective of this chapter is to present Aspect-Oriented Recommender Systems that handle crosscutting concerns by creating various aspects such as learning aspect, security aspect, mobility aspect to remove the tangling and scattering problems of multi-agent based recommender systems. These aspects are integrated with various agents' goals of multi-agent recommender system at well defined join points with point cuts in order to handle these crosscutting concerns effectively. This approach reduces the cognitive complexity and provides better modular way to design a multi-agent recommender system, which in turn improves the system reusability, maintainability also. The main emphasis in the presented work is the identification of various crosscutting design issues of recommender systems, their side effects and their solutions by using the constructs of AOP.

As a future work, we will be working towards a recommender system to handle other crosscutting concerns such as visualization and interaction etc. of recommender systems

REFERENCES

Adomavicius, G., Sankaranarayanan, R., Sen, S., & Tuzhilin, A. (2005). Incorporating contextual information in recommender systems using a multidimensional approach. *ACM Transactions on Information Systems*, *23*(1), 103–145. doi:10.1145/1055709.1055714

Adomavicius, G., & Tuzhilin, A. (2005). Toward the next generation of recommender systems: A survey of the state-of the-art and possible extensions. *IEEE Transactions on Knowledge and Data Engineering*, *17*(6), 734–749. doi:10.1109/TKDE.2005.99

Bedi, P., & Agarwal, S. (2011a). Aspect-oriented mobility-aware recommender system. In *Proceedings of International Conference on World Congress on Information and Communication Technologies,* December 11-14, Mumbai, India, (pp. 191-196). IEEE Xplore.

Bedi, P., & Agarwal, S. (2011b). Preference learning in aspect oriented recommender system. In *Proceedings of International Conference on Computational Intelligence and Communication Systems,* October 7-7, Gwalior, India, (pp. 611-615). IEEE Xplore.

Bedi, P., & Agarwal, S. (2011c). Managing security in aspect-oriented recommender system. In *Proceedings of International Conference on Communication Systems and Network Technologies,* June 03- 05, Jammu, India, (pp. 709-713). IEEE Computer Society.

Bedi, P., Sinha, A., Agarwal, S., Awasthi, A., Prasad, G., & Saini, D. (2010). Influence of terrain on modern tactical combat: Trust-based recommender system. *Defence Science Journal*, *60*(4), 405–411.

Burigat, S., Chittaro, L., & Marco, L. (2005). Lecture Notes in Computer Science: *Vol. 3585. Bringing dynamic queries to mobile devices: A visual preference-based search tool for tourist decision support* (pp. 213–226). Springer. doi:10.1007/11555261_20

Burke, R. (2002). Hybrid recommender systems: Survey and experiments. *User Modeling and User-Adaptation Interaction*, *12*, 331–370. doi:10.1023/A:1021240730564

Burke, R., Mobasher, B., Williams, C., & Bhaumik, R. (2006). *Detecting profile injection attacks in collaborative recommender systems*. IEEE Join Conference on E-Commerce Technology and Enterprise Computing, E-Commerce and E-Services.

Burke, R., Mobasher, B., Zabicki, R., & Bhaumik, R. (2005). *Identifying attack models for secure recommendation in beyond personalization.* A Workshop on the Next Generation of Recommender systems, San Diego, CA.

Chirita, P., Nejdl, W., & Zamfir, C. (2005) Preventing shilling attacks in online recommender systems. In 7th Annual ACM International Workshop on Web Information and Data Management, New York, (pp. 67-74).

Garcia, A., Kulesza, U., & Lucena, C. (2005). Aspectizing multi-agent systems: From architecture to implementation. In *Software Engineering for Multi-Agent Systems III* (*Vol. 3390*, pp. 121–143). Lecture Notes in Computer Science Berlin, Germany: Springer-Verlag. doi:10.1007/978-3-540-31846-0_8

Garcia, A., Sant'Anna, C., Chavez, C., Silva, V., Lucena, C., & Von, S. A. (2004). Separation of concerns in multi-agent systems: An empirical study. In *Software Engineering for Multi-Agent Systems II, LNCS* (*Vol. 2940*, pp. 49–72). Berlin, Germany: Springer-Verlag. doi:10.1007/978-3-540-24625-1_4

Good, N., Schafer, B., Konstan, J., Borchers, A., Sarwar, B., Herlocker, J., & Riedl, J. (1999). Combining collaborative filtering with personal agents for better recommendations. In *Conference of the American Association of Artificial Intelligence*, (pp. 186-191).

Hussein, G. (2010). Enhanced k-means-based mobile recommender system. *International Journal of Information Studies*, 2(2).

Kass, R., & Finin, T. (1988). Modeling the user in natural language systems. *Computer Linguistic Journal*, *14*(3), 5–22.

Kiczales, G., Lamping, J., Mendhekar, A., Maeda, C., Lopes, C., Loingtier, J., & Irwin, J. (1997). *Aspect-oriented programming* (pp. 220–242). ECOOP.

Kim, B., & Li, Q. (2004). Probabilistic model estimation for collaborative filtering based on items attributes. *IEEE/WIC/ACM International Conference on Web Intelligence*, Beijing, China, (pp. 185–191).

Lam, S., & Riedl, J. (2004). Shilling recommender systems for fun and profit. In *13th International WWW Conference*, New York, (pp. 345-350).

Mehmood, T., Ashraf, N., Rasheed, K., & Rehman, S. (2005). Framework for modeling performance in multi agent systems (MAS) using aspect oriented programming (AOP). In the *Sixth Australasian Workshop on Software and System Architectures*, Brisbane Australia, (pp. 40-45).

Montaner, M., López, B., & Rosa, J. (2003). A taxonomy of recommender agents on the internet. *Artificial Intelligence Review*, *19*(4), 285–330. doi:10.1023/A:1022850703159

O'Mahony, M., Hurley, N., Kushmerick, N., & Silvestre, G. (2004). Collaborative recommendation: A robustness analysis. *ACM Transactions on Internet Technology*, *4*(4), 344–350.

Rojanavasu, P., Srinil, P., & Pinngern, O. (2005). New recommendation system using reinforcement learning. *Special Issue of the International Journal of the Computer, the Internet and Management, 13*.

Schafer, J. B., Konstan, J., & Riedl, J. (1999). Recommender systems in e-commerce. *Proceedings of 1st ACM Conference on Electronic Commerce*, Denver, USA, (pp. 43-51).

Tarr, P., Ossher, H., Harrison, W., & Sutton, S. (1999). N degrees of separation: Multi dimensional separation of concerns. In *21st International Conference on Software Engineering*, (pp. 107-119).

Tumas, G., & Ricci, F. (2009). Personalized mobile city transport advisory system. In Fuchs, M., Ricci, F., & Cantoni, L. (Eds.), *Information and communication technologies in tourism* (pp. 173–184).

Vashisth, P., Agarwal, S., Wadhwa, B., & Bedi, P. (2011). Capturing user preferences through interactive visualization to improve recommendations. In *Proceedings of International Conference on World Conference on Information Technology,* November 23-27, Antalya, Turkey, Procedia Journal of Technology, Elsevier (Accepted).

Zhang, J., Jones, N., & Pu, P. (2008). A visual interface for critiquing-based recommender systems. *EACM C, 08,* 230–239.

ADDITIONAL READING

Andreas, W. N. (2007). *Motivating and supporting user interaction with recommender systems. ECDL, LNCS 4675* (pp. 428–439). Heidelberg, Germany: Springer-Verlag.

Aspect, J. (n.d.). [*The AspectJ programming guide.* Retrieved from eclipse.org/aspectj]. *Team.*

AspectWerkz Website. (n.d.). *Simple, dynamic, lightweight and powerful AOP for Java.* Retrieved from http://aspectwerkz.codehaus.org/

Bedi, P., & Kaur, H. (2006). Trust based personalized recommender system. *Journal of Computer Science, 5*(1), 19–26.

Bedi, P., Kaur, H., Gupta, B., Talreja, J., & Sood, M. (2009). A website recommender system based on analysis of user's access log. *Journal of Intelligent Systems: Special Issue on Recent Advances in Artificial Intelligence, 18*(4), 333–352.

Bedi, P., Kaur, H., & Marwaha, S. (2007). *Trust based recommender system for the Semantic Web.* In 20th International Joint Conference on Artificial Intelligence (IJCAI), Hyderabad, India.

Bedi, P., & Sharma, R. (2012). Trust based recommender system using ant colony for trust computation. *Expert Systems with Applications, 39*(1), 1183–1190. doi:10.1016/j.eswa.2011.07.124

Bedi, P., Sharma, R., & Kaur, H. (2009). Recommender system based on collaborative behavior of ants. *Journal of Artificial Intelligence, 2*(2), 40–55. doi:10.3923/jai.2009.40.55

Bedi, P., & Vashisth, P. (2011). Interest based recommendations with argumentation. *Journal of Artificial Intelligence, 4*(2), 119–142. doi:10.3923/jai.2011.119.142

Bedi, P., & Vashisth, P. (2011). Benefits of utilizing causal purposes in interest-based recommendation. *International Conference on Computational Intelligence and Communication Systems,* October 7, Gwalior, India, (pp. 448-453). IEEE Xplore.

Chavez, C., & Lucena, C. (2003). A theory of aspects for aspect-oriented development. In *Proceedings of 17th Brazilian Symposium on Software Engineering,* (pp. 130-145).

Cheong, C., & Winikoff, M. (2005). Designing goal-oriented agent interactions. In *Proceedings of the 6th International Workshop on Agent-Oriented Software Engineering,* Hermes.

Choren, R., & Lucena, C. (2005). Modeling multi-agent systems with ANote. *Journal of Software and Systems Modeling, 4*(3), 199–208. doi:10.1007/s10270-004-0065-y

Garcia, A. (2002). Engineering multi-agent systems with aspects and patterns. *Journal of the Brazilian Computer Society, 1*(8), 57–72. doi:10.1590/S0104-65002002000100006

Garcia, A., Cortés, M., & Lucena, C. (2001). A Web environment for the development and maintenance of e-commerce portals based on a groupware approach. In *Proceedings of the Information Resources Management Association International Conference* (IRMA'01), Toronto, May, (pp. 722-724).

Garcia, A., Lucena, C., & Cowan, D. (2004). Agents in object-oriented software engineering. *Software, Practice & Experience, 34*(3), 489–521. doi:10.1002/spe.578

Hanenberg, S., Unland, R., & Schmidmeier, A. (2003). AspectJ idioms for aspect-oriented software construction. In *Proceedings of the EuroPlop'03*, Irsee, Germany, June, (pp. 235-241).

Hannemann, J., & Kiczales, G. (2002). Design pattern implementation in Java and AspectJ. In *Proceedings of the ACM Conference on Object-Oriented Programming, Systems, Languages, and Applications,* November, (pp. 161-173).

Kendall, E. (1999). A framework for agent systems implementing application frameworks. In Fayad, M. (Eds.), *Object-oriented frameworks at work.* New York, NY: John Wiley & Sons.

Masuhara, H., & Kiczales, G. (2003). Modeling crosscutting in aspect-oriented mechanisms. In *Proceedings of ECOOP2003*, Darmstadt, Germany, *LNCS 2743*, (pp. 2-28).

Mehmood, T., Ashraf, N., Rasheed, K., & Rehman, S. (2005). *Framework for modeling performance in multi agent systems (MAS) using aspect oriented programming (AOP)* (pp. 40–45). Brisbane, Australia: AWSA.

Montaner, M., López, B., & Rosa, J. (2003). A taxonomy of recommender agents on the internet. *Artificial Intelligence Review*, *19*(4), 285–330. doi:10.1023/A:1022850703159

Odell, J., Parunak, H., & Fleischer, M. (2003). The roles in designing effective agent organizations. [Springer.]. *Software Engineering for Large-Scale Multi-Agent Systems, LNCS, 2603*, 27–38. doi:10.1007/3-540-35828-5_2

Pace, A., Campo, M., & Soria, A. (2004). Architecting the design of multi-agent organizations with proto-frameworks. In Lucena, C. (Eds.), *Software engineering for large-scale multi-agent systems, LNCS 2940, February 2004* (pp. 75–92). Springer.

Rojanavasu, P., Srinil, P., & Pinngern, O. (2005). New recommendation system using reinforcement learning. *Special Issue of the International Journal of the Computer, the Internet and Management, 13*.

Ubayashi, N., & Tamai, T. (2005). Separation of concerns in mobile agent applications. In *Proceedings of the 3rd International Conference Reflection 2001, LNCS 2192*, Kyoto, Japan, (pp. 89-109). Springer.

Zambonelli, F., Jennings, N., & Wooldridge, M. (2003). Developing multi agent systems: The Gaia methodology. *ACM Transactions on Software Engineering and Methodology, 12*(3), 417–470.

Section 2
Systems Analysis, Software Design, and Design Patterns

Chapter 5
Design of Semi–Structured Database System:
Conceptual Model to Logical Representation

Anirban Sarkar
National Institute of Technology, Durgapur, India

ABSTRACT

The chapter focuses on a graph – semantic based conceptual data model for semi-structured data, called Graph Object Oriented Semi-Structured Data Model (GOOSSDM), to conceptualize the different facets of such system in object oriented paradigm. The model defines a set of graph based formal constructs, varieties of relationship types with participation constraints. It is accompanied with a rich set of graphical notations and those are used to specify the conceptual level design of semi-structured database system. The approach facilitates modeling of irregular, heterogeneous, hierarchical, and non-hierarchical semi-structured data at the conceptual level. The GOOSSDM is also able to represent the mixed content in semi-structured data. Moreover, the approach is capable to model XML document at conceptual level with the facility of document-centric design, ordering and disjunction characteristic. The chapter also includes a rule based transformation mechanism for GOOSSDM schema into the equivalent XML Schema Definition (XSD). Moreover, the chapter also provides comparative study of several similar kinds of proposals for semi-structured data models based on the properties of semi-structured data and future research scope in this area.

DOI: 10.4018/978-1-4666-2958-5.ch005

INTRODUCTION

The increasingly large amount of data processing on the web based applications has led a crucial role of semi-structured database system. In recent days, semi-structured data has become prevalent with the growing demand of such internet based software systems. Semi-structured data though is organized in semantic entity but does not strictly conform to the formal structures of strict types. Rather it possesses irregular and partial organization (Abiteboul, 1999). Further semi-structured data evolve rapidly. Thus, unlike structured database system, the schema for such data is large, dynamic, is not strict to type and also is not considered the participation of instances very strictly.

The eXtensible Markup Language (XML) is increasingly finding acceptance as a standard for storing and exchanging structured and semi-structured information over internet (Conrad, 2000). The Document Type Definition (DTD) or XML Schema Definition (XSD) language can be used to define the schema which describes the syntax and structure of XML documents (Liu, 2006). However, the XML schemas provide the logical representation of the semi-structured data and it is hard to realize the semantic characteristics of such data. Thus it is important to devise a conceptual representation of semi-structured data for efficient design of the information system based on such data. For detail reference on XML technology refer W3C Standard (2008) and W3C Standard (2012) of additional reading section.

A conceptual model of semi-structured data deals with high level representation of the candidate application domain in order to capture the user ideas using rich set of semantic constructs and interrelationship thereof. Besides some similar characteristics of structured (classical) database system, several crucial characteristics are added complexity for the design of semi-structured database system. For effective design of such system, the intended conceptual model must be capable to adopt the rapidly data evolving characteristics, representation of irregular and heterogeneous structure, hierarchical relations along with the non – hierarchical relationship types, cardinality, n – array relation, ordering, representation of mixed content etc. (Necasky, 2006). Beside these, it is also important to realize the participation constraints of the instances in association with some semi-structured entity type. Even more, the participations of instances in semi-structured data model are not strict. Thus Object Oriented (OO) paradigm is most suitable to represent the organization of semi-structured data. Further, the conceptual design of semi-structured database system should be rich enough to efficiently represent such system. Such conceptual model will separate the intention of designer from the implementation and also will provide a better insight about the effective design of semi-structured data based system. The conceptual design of such system further can be implemented in XML based logical model.

With the aforementioned objectives, the chapter has been organized in six sections. In section 2 previous researches related to the semi-structured data modeling have been summarized with major emphasize on the models based on OO paradigm. In section 3, the GOOSSDM (Sarkar, 2011 June, November) has been introduced along with the prototype CASE tools and rule based transformation mechanism of conceptual model schema to its equivalent logical model schema based on XSD technology. In section 4, major characteristics of semi-structured data model have been summarized. This section also includes a comparative study of all OO semi-structured data models. In section 5, the future research directions of semi-structured database have been summarized. Finally, the chapter has been concluded in section 6.

RELATED RESEARCH

In early years, Object Exchange Model has been proposed to model semi-structured data (McHuge, 1997), where data are represented using directed labeled graph. The schema information is maintained in the labels of the graph and the data instances are represented using nodes. However, the separation of the structural semantic and content of the schema is not possible in this approach. In recent past, several researches have been made on conceptual modeling of semi-structured data as well as XML. Many of these approaches (Badia, 2002; Mani, 2004; Psaila, 2000; Sengupta, 2003; Necasky, 2007; Lósio, 2003) have been extended the concepts of Entity Relationship (ER) model to accommodate the facet of semi-structured data at conceptual level. The major drawbacks of these proposals are in representation of hierarchical structure of semi-structured data. Moreover, only two ER based proposals (Necasky, 2007; Lósio, 2003) support the representation of mixed content in conceptual schema. In Necasky (2007), a two levels approach has been taken to represent the hierarchical relations. In first level the conceptual schema is based on extended concept of ER model and in second level, hierarchical organizations of parts of the overall conceptual schema are designed. In general, ER model are flat in nature (Choudhury, 2006) and thus unable to facilitate the reuse capability and representation of hierarchical relationship. On the other hand, ORA-SS (Wu, 2001) proposed to realize the semi-structured data at conceptual level starting from its hierarchical structure. But the approach does not support directly the representation of no-hierarchical relationships and mixed content in conceptual level semi-structured data model. For detail reference on ER model and semi-structured data refer Thalheim (2000) and Buneman (1997) respectively of additional reading section.

Object Oriented Approach Based Model

Very few attempts have been made to model the semi-structured data using Object Oriented (OO) paradigm. ORA-SS (Wu, 2001) support the object oriented characteristics partially. Also, the approach does not support directly the representation of no-hierarchical relationships and mixed content in conceptual level semi-structured data model. The approaches proposed in (Liu, 2006; Combi, 2006; Conrad, 2000) are based on UML. These approaches support object oriented paradigm comprehensively and bridge the gap between OO software design and semi-structured data schemata.

In (Conrad, 2000), essential parts of static UML notations have been used to model XML data schemata. It also provides a suitable mapping from UML into XML DTDs. To exploit all DTD constructs, authors of the proposed approach have extended few UML notations to provide more flexible modeling approach. However, the proposed model is not supported with any prototype CASE tool. Moreover, representation of irregular semi-structured data is not clear in the modeling concept.

In (Liu, 2006) a conceptual model called XUML has been proposed for XML data. The model is based on UML2 specifications. It provides clearer description for XML schemas by hiding implementation details and focusing on semantically relevant concepts. The most distinctive characteristic of XUML is that it supports the generic (asymmetric) aggregation relationship representation. The XUML meta-model is an extension to UML2 meta-model and so it supports structured class, parts, connectors and ports etc. However, this model also is not supported with any prototype CASE tools. Moreover, it does not provide any proper guidelines to convert the conceptual level model schemata into the equivalent logical level schemata based on XML technology.

In (Combi, 2006), a methodology has been proposed for the design of XML documents called, UXS. The notations of the model are based on UML static structure stereotypes. It also supports different modalities based approaches to translate conceptual UXS schemata into XML Schema documents at the logical level. UXS is a graphical language that can support all the functionalities for defining XML Schema documents. It is supported with a prototype CASE tool called UXS-Design.

All these proposals have extended the UML stereotype definitions and notations in general. However, the UML and extensions to UML represent software elements using a set of language elements with fixed implementation semantics (e.g. methods, classes). Henceforth, the proposed approaches using extension of UML, in general, are logically inclined towards implementation of semi-structured database system. In other word, semi-structured data model with UML extension cannot be considered as semantically rich conceptual level model. Moreover, majority of these proposals have been influenced by the underlying logical structures. But the conceptual model should be independent of certain logical level language like DTD or XSD (Necasky, 2006).

In (Sarkar, 2011 July; Novemver), graph semantic based conceptual model for semi-structured data called, Graph Object Oriented Semi-Structured Data Model (GOOSSDM) has been proposed. The model is comprehensively based on object oriented paradigm. Among others, the proposed model supports the representation of hierarchical structure along with non-hierarchical relationships, mixed content, ordering, participation constraints etc. The GOOSSDM reveals a set of concepts to the conceptual level design phase of semi-structured database system, which are understandable to the users, independent of implementation issues and provide a set of graphical constructs to facilitate the designers of such system. The schema in GOOSSDM is organized in layered approach to provide different level of

abstraction to the users and designers. In this approach a rule based transformation mechanism also has been proposed to represent the equivalent XML Schema Definitions (XSD) from GOOSSDM schemata. Moreover, the concepts of GOOSSDM have been implemented using Generic Modeling Environment (GME) (Lédeczi, 2001) which is a meta-configurable modeling environment. The GME implementation can be used as prototype CASE tools for modeling semi-structured databases using GOOSSDM. The GOOSSDM has been discussed further in section 3. For detail reference on UML refer OMG Standard (2011) of additional reading section.

GOOSSDM: THE CONCEPTUAL MODEL FOR SEMI-STRUCTURED DATABASE

The GOOSSDM extends the object oriented paradigm to model semi-structured data. It allows the entire semi-structured database to be viewed as a Graph (V, E) in layered organization. At the lowest layer, each vertex represents an occurrence of an attribute or a data item, e.g. name, day, city etc. A set of vertices semantically related is grouped together to construct an Elementary Semantic Group (ESG). So an ESG is a set of all possible instances for a particular attribute or data item. On next, several related ESGs are grouped together to form a Contextual Semantic Group (CSG) – the constructs of related data items or attributes to represent one semi-structured entity or object. A CSG is also capable to encapsulate loosely related ESGs or ESGs with non-strict participations. The edges within CSG are to represent the containment relation between different ESG in the said CSG. The most inner layer of CSG is the construct of highest level of abstraction in semi-structured schema formation. This layered structure may be further organized by combination of one or more CSGs as well as ESGs to represent next upper level layers and to achieve further lower level abstraction in the semi-structure data schema hierarchy. From the topmost layer the entire database appears to be a graph with CSGs as vertices and edges between CSGs as the association amongst them. The CSGs of topmost layer will act as roots of semi-structured data model schemata.

Modeling Constructs in GOOSSDM

Since from the topmost layer, a set of vertices V is decided on the basis of level of data abstraction, whereas, the set of edges E is decided on basis of the association between different semantic groups. The basic components for the model are as follows,

A set of t distinct *attributes* $A = \{a_1, a_2, ..., a_t\}$ where, each a_i is an attribute or a data item semantically distinct.

1. **Elementary Semantic Group (ESG):** An elementary semantic group is an encapsulation of all possible instances or occurrences of an attribute, that can be expressed as graph ESG (V, E), where the set of edges E is a null set $\emptyset$ and the set of vertices V represent the set of all possible instances of an attribute $x_i \in A$. ESG is a construct to realize the elementary property, parameter, kind etc. of some related concern. Henceforth there will be set of t ESGs and can be represented as $E_G = \{ESG_1, ESG_2, ..., ESG_t\}$. The graphical notation for the any ESG is *Circle*.

2. **Contextual Semantic Group (CSG):** A lowest layer contextual semantic group is an encapsulation of set of ESGs or references of one or more related ESGs to represent the context of one entity of semi-structured data. Let, the set of n CSGs can be represented as $C_G = \{CSG_1, CSG_2, ..., CSG_n\}$. Then any lowest layer $CSG_i \subseteq C_G$ can be represented as a graph (V_{Ci}, E_{Ci}) where vertices $V_{Ci} \subseteq E_G$ and the set of edges E_{Ci} represents the association amongst the vertices. For any CSG, it is also possible to designate one or more encapsulated ESGs as *determinant vertex* which may determine an unordered or ordered set of instances of constituent ESGs or CSGs. The graphical notation for any CSG is *square* and determinant vertex is *Solid Circle*.

Composition of multiple CSGs can be realized in two ways. *Firstly*, the simple *Association* (Discussed in subsection 3.2) may be drawn between two or more associated CSGs either of same layer or of adjacent layers to represent the non-hierarchical and hierarchical data structure respectively. The associated CSG will be connected using *Association Connector*. Those CSGs may share a common set of ESGs or referred ESGs.

Secondly, lower layer CSGs may maintain an *Inheritance* or *Containment* relationship (Discussed in subsection 3.2) with the adjacent upper layer CSG to represent the different level of abstraction. Thus, the upper layer CSG can be formed by inheritance or composition of one or more lower layer CSGs along with encapsulation of zero or more related ESGs or reference of ESGs. Any upper layer $CSG_i \subseteq C_G$ can be represented as a graph (V_{Ci}, E_{Ci}) where vertices $V_{Ci} \subseteq C_G \cup E_G \cup$ *Reference* (E_G) and the set of edges E_{Ci} represent the association amongst the vertices.

3. **Annotation:** Annotation is a specialized form of CSG and can be expressed as $G(V, E)$, where $|V| = 1$ and $E = \emptyset$. Annotation can contain only text content as tagged value. Annotation can be containment in or associated with any other CSG. Further the cardinality constraint for Annotation construct is always *1:1* and ordering option can be *1* or *0*, where *1* means content will be in orderly form with other constituent ESG and *0* means text content can be mixed with other constituent ESGs. The annotation construct will realize the document-centric semi-structured data possibly with mixed content. This concept is extremely important

Table 1. Summary of GOOSSDM constructs and their graphical notations

GOOSSDM Constructs	Description	Graphical Notation
ESG	Elementary Semantic Group	○
Determinant ESG	Determinant vertex of any CSG which will determine the other member vertices in the CSG	●
CSG	Contextual Semantic Group	▭
Annotation	Specialized form of CSG. Contain only Text Content.	▭
Association Connector	Connect multiple associated CSGs	◆

for mapping semi-structured data model in XML. Graphically Annotation can be expressed using *Square with Folded Corner*.

The summary of GOOSSDM constructs and their graphical notations have been given in Table 1.

Relationship Types in GOOSSDM

The proposed GOOSSDM provides a graph structure to represent semi-structured data. The edges of the graph represent relationships between or within the constructs of the model. In the proposed model, *four* types of edges have been used to represent different relationships. The types of edges and their corresponding meanings are as follows,

1. **Containment:** Containments are defined between encapsulated ESGs including determinant ESG and parent CSG, or between two constituent CSGs and parent CSG, or between CSG and referential constructs. The Containment relationship is constrained by the parameters tuple $<p, \theta>$, where p determines the participation of instances in containment and θ determines the ordering option of constituent ESGs or CSGs. With any CSG, this represents a bijective mapping between determinant ESG and other ESGs or composed CSG with participation

constraint. Graphically association can be expressed using *Solid Directed Edge* from the constituent constructs to its parent labeled by constraint specifications. The possible values for p is as follows,

a. **1:1:** Represents ESG with mandatory one instantiation or total participation in the relationship. This is default value of p.

b. **0:1:** Represents ESG with optional one instantiation in the relationship.

c. **1:M:** Represents ESG with mandatory multiple instantiation in the relationship.

d. **0:M:** Represents ESG with optional multiple instantiation in the relationship.

e. **0:X:** Represents ESGs with optional exclusive instantiation in the relationship. If a CSG contain single such ESG then it will act like 0:1 value option. Otherwise one such ESG will optionally instantiate among all ESGs with p value 0:X.

f. **1:X:** Represents ESG with mandatory exclusive instantiation in the relationship. If a CSG contain single such ESG then it will act like 1:1 value option. Otherwise it is mandatory that one such ESG will instantiate among all ESGs with p value 1:X.

The possible values for θ are as follows,

a. **1:** Represents that for any CSG, the constituent ESGs and CSGs are ordered and order must be maintained from left to right in the list of ESGs with θ value 1.

b. **0:** This is default value of θ and represents that for any CSG, the constituent ESGs and CSGs are not ordered.

2. **Association:** Associations are defined between related CSGs of same layer of adjacent layers. The Association relationship is constrained by the parameters tuple $<P, \theta>$, where P determines the cardinality of Association and θ determines the ordering option of associated CSGs. Graphically association can be expressed using *Solid Undirected Edge*. Any CSG wish to participate in association will be connected with association relationship. On next, multiple associated CSGs will be connected through *Association Connector*. For semi-structured it is sometime important to have specific context of some association. Such context can be represented using *Associated CSG* defined on *Association Connector*. Association Connector facilitates the n – array relationship. Graphically association can be expressed using *Solid Undirected Edge*, Association connector can be expressed using *Solid Diamond* and Associated CSG can be connected with Association Connector using *Dotted Undirected Edges* with Participation constraint specifications. The values for P can be *1:1* or *0:1* or *1:N* or *0:N* or *0:X* or *1:X* with corresponding meaning and possible values for θ can be *1* or *0* with corresponding meaning.

3. **Link:** Links are used to represent the inheritance relationships between two CSGs. Graphically link can be expressed using *Solid Directed Edge with Bold Head* from the generalized CSG to the specialized one.

4. **Reference:** In semi-structured data model, it is important to represent the symmetric relationship between ESGs or CSGs. Reference can be used to model such concepts. Reference relations are defined either between ESG and referred ESG or between CSG and referred CSG. Graphically reference can be expressed using *Dotted Directed Edge*.

The summary of GOOSSDM relationship types and their graphical notations have been given in Table 2.

Table 2. Summary of GOOSSDM relations types and their graphical notations

GOOSSDM Relationships	Description	Graphical Notation
Containment	Defined between Parent CSG and constituent ESGs and CSGs	$<p, \theta>$ →
Association	Defined between CSGs of same layer or adjacent layers.	$<P, \theta>$ —
CSG Association	Defined between association and associated CSG	$<P, \theta>$ -·-·-·
Link	Defined between two adjacent layer parent CSG and inherited CSG	→
Reference	Defined either between ESG and referred ESG or between CSG and referred CSG.	-·-·-·›

Transformation of GOOSSDM into XSD

In general, the proposed GOOSSDM can be useful to realize the semi-structured data schema at conceptual level. The logical structure of such schema can be represented using the artifacts of XSD. Moreover, XSD is currently the de-facto standard for describing XML documents. An XSD schema itself can be considered as an XML document. Elements are the main building block of any XML document. They contain the data and determine the elementary structures within the document. Otherwise, XSD also may contain sub-element, attributes, complex types, and simple types. XSD schema elements exhibit hierarchical structure with single root element.

A systematic rule based transformation of GOOSSDM schema to XSD is essential to express the semi-structured data at logical level more effectively. For the purpose, a set of rules have been proposed to generate the equivalent XSD from the semantic constructs and relationship types of a given GOOSSDM schema. Based on the concepts of GOOSSDM constructs and relationship types the transformation rules are as follows,

Rule 1: An ESG will be expressed as an *element* in XSD. For example, ESG_{City} can be defined on attribute *City* to realize Customer city.

Rule 2: A CSG will be expressed as a *complexType* in XSD. For example, $CSG_{Customer}$ can be defined to realize the detail of Customer.

Rule 3: Any Annotation construct will be expressed as a *complexType* in XSD with suitable *mixed* value. On containment to other CSG, if θ value is 0 then it will be treated as mixed content in the resulted XML document. Otherwise if θ value is 1 then it will be treated as annotation text in resultant XML document in orderly form.

Rule 4: A Reference of ESG and CSG will be expressed as a *complexType* in XSD. For example, a reference of ESG_{City} can be de-

fined on attribute *City* to realize a referential attribute on Customer city. *Rule 5:* CSGs of topmost layer will be treated as root in XSD declaration.

Rule 6: Any lowest layer CSG with containment of some ESGs will be expressed as a *complexType* with *elements* declaration in XSD. Further the participation constraint (*p value* in GOOSSDM concept) can be expressed using *minOccurs* and *maxOccurs* attribute in XSD. The ordering constraint (θ *value* in GOOSSDM concept) can be expressed using compositor type of XSD. If θ value is 1 then compositor type will be *sequence* otherwise *all*. For ordered set ESGs, the order will be maintained from *left to right*. If any subset of ESGs contain the *p value X:1* then those ESGs will be composite using *choice* compositor type in XSD.

Rule 7: Any upper layer CSG with containment of ESGs, reference of ESGs and adjacent lower layer CSGs will be expressed as a *complexType* in XSD.

Rule 8: Any upper layer CSG with *Link* relationship with adjacent lower layer CSGs will be expressed as a *complexType* with inheritance in XSD. Upper layer CSG will be the child of lower layer CSG. An example of XSD representation of upper layer CSG with inheritance with adjacent lower layer CSG has been shown in Figure 1.

Rule 9: Any upper layer CSG with *Association* relationship with adjacent lower layer CSGs will be expressed as a *complexType* with nesting in XSD. Upper layer CSG will be treated as root element.

Rule 10: *Association* relationship between any two CSGs in the same layer will be expressed as a *complexType* with nesting in XSD. Rightmost CSG will be treated as the root element and on next nesting should be done in *right to left* order of the CSG in the same layer.

Rule 11: N–array *Association* relationship within a set of CSGs spread over several layer will

Figure 1. Representation of relationships

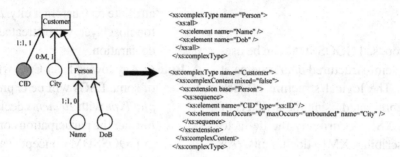

be expressed as a *complexType* with nesting in XSD. Topmost layer CSG will be treated as the root element in XSD. Then, in the adjacent lower layer the rightmost CSG should be treated as nested element within the root element. Further the nesting should be done in right to left order of the CSG in the same layer and on next moving on the adjacent lower layers.

Rule 12: With several *Association* relationships (composition of n – array and simple types) within a set of CSGs spread over several layer will be expressed as a *complexType* with nesting in XSD. Topmost layer CSG will be treated as the root element in XSD.

Then, if available, the directly associated CSGs in each adjacent lower layer will be nested till it reaches to the lowermost layer of available associated CSG. On next, the CSGs of adjacent lower layer of the root element will be nested from *right to left* order in the same layer along with the nesting of directly associated CSGs (if available) in each corresponding adjacent layers. An example has been shown in Figure 2 for XSD representation of GOOSSDM schemata where associated CSGs are spread over three layers and contain both n – array and simple associations.

Figure 2. Representation of associated CSGs spread over several layers (ESG layer is hidden)

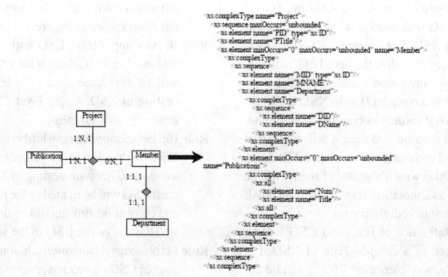

Case Study

Let consider an example (Necasky, 2007) of *Patient and Doctor* where a *Patient* can visit to a *Doctor* either at *Hospital Department* or at *Clinic*. Any Patient can visit several times to different doctors. Figure 3 shows an irregularly structured XML representation of visit records of two patients. *Patient 1* visited twice to two different *Doctors*, one at *Hospital Department* and another at *Clinic. Patient 2* visited once to one *Doctor* who is common to *Patient 1* but at different *Clinic*. All though in the document, the Date of Visit, Doctor and option of Hospital Department and Clinic are in order. The XML document of Figure 3 represents the semi-structured data. The suitable GOOSSDM schema for such data and its equivalent XSD have been shown in Figure 4.(a). The equivalent XSD of GOOSSDM schema of Figure 4.(b) can be generated using the rules described in Section 3.3.

Implementation of GOOSSDM Using GME

The Generic Modeling Environment (GME) provides meta-modeling capabilities and where a domain model can be configured and adapted from meta-level specifications (representing the Conceptual modeling) that describe the domain concept. It is common for a model in the GME to contain several numbers of different modeling elements with hierarchies that can be in many levels deep. The GME supports the concept of a viewpoint as a first-class modeling construct, which describes a partitioning that selects a subset of conceptual modeling components as being visible.

Moreover, GME support the programmatic access of the metadata of GME models. Most usual techniques for such programmatic access is to write GME interpreter for some meta-model. The interpreter will be able to interpret any domain model based on that predefined meta-model. GME interpreters are not stand-alone programs, they are components (usually Dynamic Link Libraries) that are loaded and executed by GME upon a user's request. Most GME components are built for the Builder Object Network (BON), an inbuilt framework in GME and provide a network of C++ objects. Each of these represents an object in the GME model database. C++ methods provide convenient read/write access to the objects' properties, attributes, and relations described in GME meta-model.

In the context of GOOSSDM, the lower layers can be conceptualized using levels in GME. The semi-structured data definitions for

Figure 3. Irregular structure in visit records XML

```
<Patient>
<name>Patient 1</name>
<Visit>
        <Date>10-JAN-2009</Date>
        <Doctor>
                <RegID>1234</RegID>
                <DName>Dr. P. Roy</DName>
        </Doctor>
        <Dept><DID>1</DID><DeptName>General</DeptName>
            <Hospital><Name>Hospital A</Name> </Hospital>
        </Dept>

        <Date>15-MAR-2010</Date>
        <Doctor>
                <RegID>4321</RegID>
                <DName>Dr. T. De</DName>
        </Doctor>
        <Clinic><Name>Clinic B</Name></Clinic>
</Visit>
```

```
<name>Patient 2</name>
<Visit>
        <Date>12-SEPT-2009</Date>
        <Doctor>
                <RegID>4321</RegID>
                <DName>Dr. T. De</DName>
        </Doctor>
        <Clinic><Name>Clinic D</Name></Clinic>
</Visit>
</Patient>
```

Figure 4. (a) Corresponding GOOSSDM schemata; and (b) Equivalent XSD of Figure 3

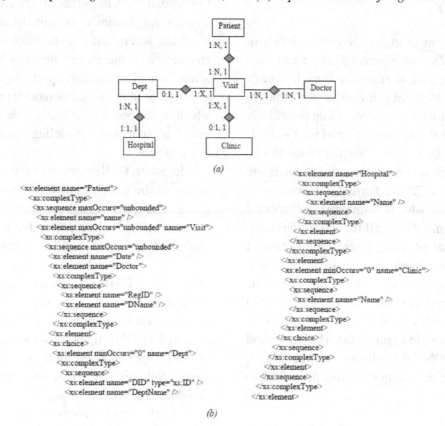

(a)

(b)

any given GME model can be configured using meta-level specifications of GOOSSDM. The interpreter will generate the equivalent XML Schema Definitions for any given GME model configured using meta-level specifications of GOOSSDM to represent the semi-structured data at logical level.

The meta-level specifications of GOOSSDM using GME have been shown in Figure 5. The GOOSSDM schema specification of *Patient and Doctor* Example (Figure 3 and Figure 4) using GOOSSDM meta-level specifications has been shown in Figure 6. The BON based interpreter for GOOSSDM can run from the GME interface to interpret any GOOSSDM schema and to generate the equivalent XSD code. For detail reading on GME refer (Ledeczi, 2001; Institute for Software Integrated System, 2008) of additional reading section.

FEATURES OF SEMI-STRUCTRED DATA MODEL

As stated earlier, For efficient design of semi-structured database system, the intended conceptual model must support the representation of rapidly data evolving characteristics, irregular and heterogeneous structure, hierarchical relations along with the non – hierarchical relationship types, cardinality, n – array relation, ordering, representation of mixed content etc. In Necasky (2006), several properties of semi-structured data models have been listed and also several non-object-oriented semi-structured data models have compared in that literature based on those properties. In this section an extended set of features for semi-structured data models are being listed, specifically which are crucial for object-oriented semi-structured data models. The list of

Figure 5. Meta-level specifications of GOOSSDM model using GME

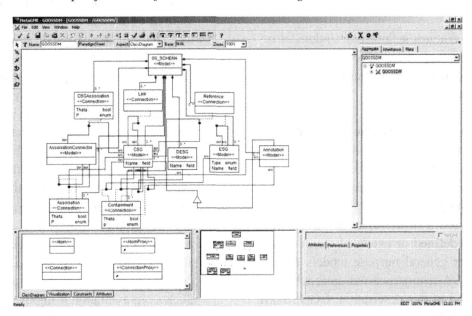

Figure 6. GOOSSDM schema of patient and doctor example using GME

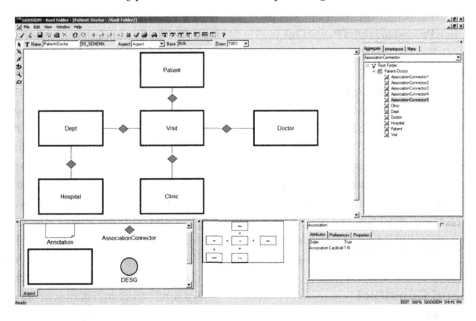

features also has been discussed in the context of the GOOSSDM model. The major advantages of the GOOSSDM are that it defines each level of structural detail on the constructs which are independent of the implementation issues and moreover, the graph structure maintains the referential integrity inherently. For better clarifications, the features are divided into different groups and are as follows.

Meta-Model Level Features

These set of features include descriptions of related concepts those are used for the purpose for devising the conceptual modeling constructs. The set of features are as follows,

1. **Language Used to Define the Model:** This shows the language mainly used by semi-structured data model to express its meta-schema. GOOSSDM used graph semantic based language.
2. **Extended Framework:** Some models have redefined or extended the concepts of other general purpose models for the design of semi-structured data, which is reflected in this description. GOOSSDM extended the concepts of Graph Data Model (GDM) (Choudhury, 2006) and Graph Object Oriented Multidimensional Data Model (GOOMD) (Sarkar, 2009), which supports structural abstraction of OnLine Transaction Processing (OLTP) and OnLine Analytical Processing (OLAP) databases respectively.
3. **Mathematical Formalism:** This feature indicates the formalism used to describe the conceptual model. GOOSSDM is however formal in that sense.
4. **Graphical Notations:** This feature indicates regarding the graphical notations provided by the conceptual model to represent the semi-structured database system domain concepts. GOOSSDM provides rich set of graphical notations to model such system.

Semantic and Construct Level Features

These set of features are used to describe the expressiveness of a conceptual model towards realizations of the target domain. The set of features are as follows,

5. **Explicit Separation of Structure and Content:** This feature enhances the capability for reuse of the elements of any conceptual model. The GOOSSDM provides a unique design framework to specify the design for the semi-structured database system using semantic definitions of different levels (from elementary to composite) of data structure through graph. In the model, the nature of contents that corresponded with the instances and the functional constraint on the instances has been separated from the system's structural descriptions.
6. **Abstraction:** Abstraction mechanism is an essential property in OO models to reduce the complexity of the system design. Such a representation is highly flexible for the user to understand the basic structure of semi-structure database system and to formulate the alternative design options. In GOOSSDM, the concepts of layers deploy the abstraction in semi-structured data schema. The upper layer views will hide the detail structural complexity from the users.
7. **Reuse Potential:** This is another important property in OO models. This can be achieved either using whole-part relationship or inheritance mechanism. The GOOSSDM is supported with inheritance mechanism using the *Link* relationship. Henceforth, there is no binding in the model to reuse some CSG constructs of any layer. Moreover, lowest layer ESG or lower layer can be shared and reused with different CSGs of the upper layers using *Containment* relationship.
8. **Disjunction Characteristic:** The instances of semi-structured data schema are likely to be less homogeneous than structured data. Disjunction relationships facilitate the possibility of non-homogeneous instances. The proposed GOOSSDM supports disjunction relationship using the participation constraint attribute *p* or *P* (by setting *p or P* value either *0:X* or *1:X*). The Containment

relationships between constituent ESGs or CSGs with the parent CSG can be disjunctive or Association relationships between two or more CSGs can be disjunctive.

9. **Hierarchical and Non-Hierarchical Structure:** The GOOSSDM explicitly supports both hierarchical and non-hierarchical representation in semi-structure data modeling at conceptual level. Associated CSGs of different or same layers form the hierarchical or non-hierarchical structure in semi-structured data model. At the logical level modeling of semi-structured data using XSD supports only hierarchical structure. For the purpose, the set of rules have been proposed to transform more generous conceptual level schema to hierarchical logical schema.

10. **Ordering:** Ordering is one important concept in modeling of semi-structured data. One or more attributes or relationships in semi-structured data schema can be ordered. GOOSSDM supports ordering in two ways using the relationship ordering constraint attributeθ. Firstly, the ordering may be enforced between parent CSG and any set of constituent ESGs and CSGs by specifying the θ value on containment relationship. Secondly, the ordering can be enforced on the any set of Association relationships within CSG.

11. **Irregular and Heterogeneous Structure:** By characteristic the semi-structured data is irregular and heterogeneous. The GOOSSDM supports disjunction characteristic, ordering and representation of both hierarchical and non-hierarchical structure in the same schema. With all these facets, the model can efficiently model the irregular and heterogeneous semi-structured data.

12. **Participation Constraint:** Instances participations in the semi-structured data schema are not followed strictly. Participations of instances can be optional or mandatory or even exclusive for such schema. All these

participation constraint can be modeled in proposed by specifying the value for participation constraint attribute p or P. That can affect the participation of constituent ESGs and CSGs in the parent CSG or may affect the participation of CSGs in some association relationship either of simply type or n-array type.

13. **N-Array Relationship:** The feature is important where there exist irregular and disjoint characters in the instance data. GOOSSDM is supported with this feature.

14. **Document-Centric and Mixed Content:** In real world, document texts are mixed with semi-structured data. The feature is more important and frequent in XML documents. Thus it is an essence that the conceptual model for semi-structured data must support modeling of such feature. In GOOSSDM, the *Annotation* construct facilitates to model document centric design of semi-structured data at conceptual level. Moreover, the modeling of the *Annotation* construct in schema allows the instances of CSG and ESG to be mixed with the text content. The presence of this construct along with the other defined constructs and relationships, the GOOSSDM is also capable to model XML document at conceptual level.

Logical Model Level Features

These features are used to describe the corresponding logical level representation of some conceptual model for semi-structured data. The features are as follows,

15. **Logical Model Used:** As specified earlier, that XML techniques are the de-facto standard for the logical representation of semi-structured data. Majority of the proposed semi-structured data models in the literatures varies on representation of logical models, which are either based on DTD

or XSD. GOOSSDM used XSD concepts for representation of the logical model for semi-structured data.

16. **Transformation Mechanism:** This feature is important as a guideline towards correctly transformations of conceptual level semi-structured data schema into its equivalent logical level schema. Also it is useful to devise a tool to generate the logical schema automatically from the related conceptual level schema in such system. GOOSSDM used rule based transformation mechanism for this purpose.

17. **Prototype CASE Tools:** This feature is important as it provides the proof of the concepts of some conceptual model. Also a prototype CASE tool is the basis for automatic transformation of the conceptual schema into its equivalent logical schema. GOOSSDM is supported with prototype CASE tool with automatic transformation features.

18. **Alternative Design Pattern in Logical Schema:** This feature is useful as it can facilitate more flexibility for the designer of semi-structured database system. GOOSSDM prototype CASE tool is partially support this feature. The alternative logical level design pattern can be achieved by changing the ordering rules of the nesting mechanism (specified in Rule 9, 10, 11 and 12 in section 3.3).

Comparison of OO Models for Semi-Structured Data

The set of features described in subsections 4.1, 4.2 and 4.3 are used to compare the conceptual level semi-structured data models those are based on object-oriented paradigm. The models described in [Liu (2006)], Combi (2006), Wu (2001), Conrad (2000), Sarkar (Nov. 2011)] are used for the purpose. Interested readers can also

follow the [Necasky (2006)] for the comparison study related to the non-object-oriented models for semi-structured data. The comparison has been summarized in Table 3.

Majority of the models do not support representation of disjunction characteristics, ordering and n-array relationships of the semi-structured data. Very few conceptual models are supported with the prototype CASE tools as the proof of concepts. Also majority of the modeling concepts are not formal. Moreover, it is interesting to note that majority of the conceptual models do not support document-centric design of semi-structured data. The conceptual models for semi-structured data or XML must allow to model document-centric data. Thus, there should be corresponding modeling constructs offered by the conceptual model to realize the representative objects and relationships of the intended domain mixed with text content when represented in XML based document content.

FUTURE RESEARCH DIRECTIONS

Various potential research agendas still exist for the field of semi-structured database system design. Several research proposals are there in literatures for the conceptual design of such system. Many of those approaches are also included with the mechanisms for transformation of conceptual level semi-structured data schema to its equivalent logical schema based on XML techniques. However, none of those proposals are still accepted as standard. Most of those proposals are varied in the representation of logical design model for semi-structured database system, which has been explored using either DTD or XSD. So, more researches are required towards the conceptual level modeling of semi-structured database domain with the aim of realizing the facets of such system more comprehensively. Besides this, several other research directions are as follows,

Table 3. Comparison of OO based conceptual model for semi-structured data

Model Name / Reference	Meta-Model Level				Semantics and Constructs Level										Logical Model Level			
	(a)	(b)	(c)	(d)	(e)	(f)	(g)	(h)	(i)	(j)	(k)	(l)	(m)	(n)	(o)	(p)	(q)	(r)
[Conrad (2000)]	UML	UML	--	Y	Y	Y	Y	--	P	--	P	--	--	--	DTD	--	--	--
ORA-SS [Wu (2001)]	ORA	OR	P	Y	Y	Y	P	Y	P	Y	Y	Y	P	--	DTD	Y	--	--
XUML [Liu (2006)]	UML	UML	--	Y	Y	Y	Y	--	P	--	P	Y	--	--	XSD	--	--	--
UXS [Combi (2006)]	Graph	UML	--	Y	Y	Y	Y	--	P	--	P	Y	--	--	XSD	Y	Y	Y
GOOSSDM [Sarkar (Nov. 2011)]	Graph	GDM	Y	Y	Y	Y	Y	Y	Y	Y	Y	Y	Y	Y	XSD	Y	Y	P

Y: supported in the model, Hyphen: not supported or not explained how to support it, P: partially supported, UML: unified modeling language, GDM: Graph Data Model, XSD: XML Schema Definition, DTD: Data Type Definitions, OR: Object Relational Model, ORA: Object-Relation-Attribute

1. **Query Language Design for Semi-Structured Data:** Management of semi-structured data requires typical database features such as a language for forming adhoc queries and updates. Query Language design for such system is one of the challenging research issues. Compare to the proposals of conceptual modeling, very few proposals are there for the query language design for semi-structured data. XQuery language proposed in (Boag, 2010), is applicable across majorly on XML data sources and accepted as standard. However, it does not have any formal background of query language design. Some other proposal like, LOREL (Abiteboul, 1997) is a query language based on LORE model (McHuge, 1997). LOREL is an extension of object query language and can be implemented top of the object oriented database system. GLASS (Ni, 2003) is a graphical query which has been derived over ORA-SS model (Wu, 2001). However, both of these proposals lack from the validation with the standard like XQuery. On the other hand, WebDB (Li, 2002) is a query language for web based system and is based on object relational concepts. WebDB is capable to query the semi-structured data at intra-document and inter-document

level. TQL (Cardelli, 2004) is another query language for semi-structured data based on ambient logic and is expressive like XQuery language. Both WebDB and TQL are rigorously formal and not based on any specific semi-structured data models. More research trials are required towards the design of query language for semi-structured database system based on conceptual level semi-structured data model and which will be formal, expressive, complete, user friendly and at the same time will be conform to the XQuery standard.

2. **Validation of Semi-Structured Data Model:** Among all the proposed approaches for conceptual data models of semi-structured data only ORA-SS model has been validated using tools like Alloy analyzer (Wang, 2006). The authors of the model also has expressed an important fact about semi-structured database design and it states that "A primary concern in designing a semi-structured data model for a particular application is to reveal any possible inconsistencies at both the schema and instance levels" (Wang, 2006). Thus for conceptual model it is essential to prove properties like correctness and completeness while transforming it to equivalent logical model. On

model level transformation, conceptual modeling concepts should capable to preserve all possible facets of the target domain. Large research initiative is required towards the mechanism for model transformation validation for semi-structured database domain.

3. **CASE Tools for Semi-Structured Database Design:** Very few models are supported with the CASE tools for design of semi-structured database [see Table 2]. Moreover, those proposals also are at prototype levels. Further tool level researches are required towards the proposal of full-fledged tools with the support of designing semi-structured database, automatic transformation of conceptual schema into equivalent logical schema, mechanism of validation and semi-structured query builder.

4. **Semi-Structured Data Warehouse Design:** Complex, online and multidimensional analysis of data is done by fetching just-in-time information from subjective, integrated, consolidated, non–volatile, historical collection of data. Data Warehouse (DW) and On Line Analytical Processing (OLAP) in conjunction with multidimensional database are typically used for such analysis. With the growing availability of XML data in web based applications, the integration of XML data and technology with data warehouse has become a challenging area of research (Perez, 2008). The existence of semi-structured nature of data raises new difficulties for the design of XML based data warehouse (Rizzi, 2006). Thus design of XML based DW requires far more complex engineering task than traditional data warehouse design due to the existence of semi-structured nature of data like irregular and heterogeneous structure, hierarchical relations along with the non – hierarchical relationship types, cardinality, n – array relationships, ordering, representation of mixed content etc. Though several research methods are available in

literatures for conceptual modeling of XML based semi-structured databases, but none of these models are extended to support the multidimensional data in XML based data warehouse system. Hence potential research agendas exist regarding the semi-structured data warehouse design possibly by extending the available conceptual model for semi-structured data model.

Due to the high availability of web data and ever-increasing need for more accurate analysis, enterprises are interested towards more powerful infrastructure towards maintaining the analytical databases. Data availability and durability are typically two properties to maintain such large scale analytical databases. Several literatures have speculated that analytical data management systems are well-suited to run in a Cloud Environment (Abadi, 2009). Many enterprises have proposed their cloud infrastructure to support the maintenance of massively distributed web based historical data (structured, semi-structured and unstructured), such as those from Amazon (DeCandia, 2007), Google (Chang, 2008; Baker, 2011), Microsoft (Bernstein, 2011), and Yahoo (Cooper, 2008). Research efforts are important towards producing sustainable semi-structured data warehouse design over the cloud environment by incorporating the cloud properties in such database design.

For additional references on Data Warehouse system design refer Abelló (2006), Binh (2001), Datta (1999), Franconi (1999), Franconi (2004), Golfarelli (1998), Hüsemann (2000), Lechtenbörger (2003), Malinowski (2006), Prat (2006), Sarkar (2009), Schneider (2008), Tryfona (1999), and Tsois (2001) from the additional reading section.

For additional reference on Cloud data management refer Chin (2005) and Ramakrishnan (2012) from additional reading section. Interested reader can also refer Buyya (2009), Dillon (2010) and Goyal (2010) from the same section for general study on cloud computing environment.

5. **Quality Evaluations of Semi-structured Database Design:** Efficient semi-structured database design depends on the quality of the conceptual model. According to ISO/IEC 9126-1 (ISO/IEC, 2001), the quality characteristic called *Usability* includes the factors, such as operability, understandability, learnability, attractiveness, and compliance. These concepts are abstracts and cannot be measured directly, but the evaluation of the factors of usability at early design phase is important in order to produce an improved semi-structured database system. In view of this, there is a necessity of a set of objective quality measurements at the conceptual level design phase of such system to assess the factors of model usability. The operability factor of the underlying conceptual data model is another issue that also influences the quality of early design of such system. Thus research effort is required to devise suitable framework for quality evaluation of semi-structured database design.

CONCLUSION

In this chapter, a graph-semantic based model has been introduced for the conceptual level design of semi-structured data, called GOOSSDM. This is a comprehensive object oriented conceptual model and the entire semi-structure database can be viewed as a Graph (V, E) in layered organization. The graph based semantics in GOOSSDM model extracts the positive features of both Object and Relational data models and also it maintains the referential integrity inherently. Moreover, a rules based mechanism also has been described for systematic transformation of GOOSSDM schema to its equivalent XSD structure. The expressive powers of the set of transformation rules have been illustrated with suitable example and case study. Further the layered organization of the model facilitates to view the semi-structured data

schema from different level of abstraction. The approach also can be automated through the GME based meta-model configuration of GOOSSDM. The meta-level specification of GOOSSDM along with interpreter can be used as prototype CASE tool for the model by the semi-structured database designer. The tools facilitates the automatic generation of XML Schema Definitions from the conceptual level graphical model, using the rule based transformation mechanism.

The GOOSSDM is enriched with set of constructs, variety of relationship types and rich set of participation constraints semantics. It provides better understandability to the users and high flexibility to the designers for creation and / or modification of semi-structured schema as well as XML document at conceptual level independent from any implementation issues.

The chapter also has highlighted the essential features for semi-structured data models, specifically which are based on object oriented paradigm. A detailed comparison study also has been performed among the available object oriented conceptual model for such system and GOOSSDM. Further, the chapter also has included several future research directions with high potential for semi-structure database domain.

REFERENCES

Abadi, D. J. (2009). Data management in the cloud: Limitations and opportunities. *A Quarterly Bulletin of the Computer Society of the IEEE Technical Committee on Data Engineering, 32*(1), 3–12.

Abiteboul, S., Buneman, P., & Suciu, D. (1999). *Data on the web: From relations to semistructured data and XML*. Morgan Kaufman.

Abiteboul, S., Quass, D., Mchugh, J., Widom, J., & Wiener, J. (1997). The Lorel query language for semistructured data. *International Journal on Digital Libraries, 1*, 68–88.

Badia, A. (2002). Conceptual modeling for semistructured data. *3rd International Conference on Web Information Systems Engineering*, (pp. 170–177).

Baker, J., et al. (2011). Megastore: Providing scalable, highly available storage for interactive services. *Conference on Innovative Database Research* (CIDR 11), ACM (pp. 223-234).

Bernstein, P. A. (2011). Adapting Microsoft SQL server for cloud computing. *IEEE 27th International Conference on Data Engineering* (ICDE 11) (pp. 1255-1263).

Boag, S., Chamberlin, D., Fernández, M. F., Florescu, D., Robie, J., & Siméon, J. (2010). *XQuery 1.0: An XML query language.* Object Management Group. Retrieved from http://www.w3.org/TR/xquery/

Cardelli, L., & Ghelli, G. (2004). TQL: A query language for semistructured data based on the ambient logic. *Journal of Mathematical Structures in Computer Science, 14*(3), 285–327. doi:10.1017/S0960129504004141

Chang, F. (2008). Bigtable: A distributed storage system for structured data. *ACM Transactions on Computers, 26*(2). doi:doi:10.1145/1365815.1365816

Choudhury, S., Chaki, N., & Bhattacharya, S. (2006). GDM: A new graph based data model using functional abstraction. *Journal of Computer Science and Technology, 21*(3), 430–438. doi:10.1007/s11390-006-0430-0

Combi, C., & Oliboni, B. (2006). Conceptual modeling of XML data. *ACM Symposium on Applied Computing*, (pp. 467 – 473).

Conrad, R., Scheffner, D., & Freytag, J. C. (2000). XML conceptual modeling using UML. *19th International Conference on Conceptual Modeling*, (pp. 558-574).

Cooper, B. F., et al. (2008). PNUTS: Yahoo!'s hosted data serving platform. *Proceedings of the VLDB Endowment* (VLDB 08), ACM (pp. 1277-1288).

DeCandia, G., et al. (2007). Dynamo: Amazon's highly available key-value store. *21st ACM SIGOPS Symposium of Operating Systems Principles* (SOSP 07), ACM (pp. 205-220).

ISO. IEC 9126-1. (2001). *Software engineering - Product quality - Part 1: Quality model.* International Standard Organization.

Lédeczi, Á., Bakay, A., Maroti, M., Volgyesi, P., Nordstrom, G., Sprinkle, J., & Karsai, G. (2001). Composing domain-specific design environments. *IEEE Computer, 34*(11), 44–51. doi:10.1109/2.963443

Li, W., Shim, J., & Candan, K. S. (2002). WebDB: A system for querying semi-structured data on the web. *Journal of Visual Languages and Computing, 13*, 3–33. doi:10.1006/jvlc.2001.0225

Liu, H., Lu, Y., & Yang, Q. (2006). XML conceptual modeling with XUML. *28th International Conference on Software Engineering*, (pp. 973–976).

Lósio, B. F., Salgado, A. C., & GalvĐo, L. R. (2003). Conceptual modeling of XML schemas. *5th ACM International Workshop on Web Information and Data Management*, (pp. 102–105).

Mani, M. (2004). EReX: A conceptual model for XML. *2nd International XML Database Symposium*, (pp. 128-142).

McHugh, J., Abiteboul, S., Goldman, R., Quass, D., & Widom, J. (1997). Lore: A database management system for semistructured data. *SIGMOD Record, 26*(3), 54–66. doi:10.1145/262762.262770

Necasky, M. (2006). *Conceptual modeling for XML: A survey.* Tech. Report No. 2006-3, Dep. of Software Engineering, Faculty of Mathematics and Physics, Charles University, Prague.

Necasky, M. (2007). XSEM: A conceptual model for XML. *4ᵗʰ ACM International Asia-Pacific Conference on Conceptual Modeling*, Vol. 67, (pp. 37–48).

Ni, W., & Ling, T. W. (2003). GLASS: A graphical query language for semi-structured data. *8ᵗʰ International Conference on Database Systems for Advanced Applications*, (pp. 363–370).

Perez, J. M., Berlanga, R., Aramburu, M. J., & Pedersen, T. B. (2008). Integrating data warehouses with web data: A survey. *IEEE Transactions on Knowledge and Data Engineering, 20*(7), 940–955. doi:10.1109/TKDE.2007.190746

Psaila, G. (2000). ERX: A conceptual model for XML documents. *ACM Symposium on Applied Computing*, (pp. 898-903).

Rizzi, S., Abelló, A., Lechtenbörger, J., & Trujillo, J. (2006). Research in data warehouse modeling and design: Dead or alive? *9ᵗʰ ACM International Workshop on Data Warehousing and OLAP (DOLAP'06)*, (pp. 3–10).

Sarkar, A. (2011, November). Conceptual level design of semi-structured database system: Graph-semantic based approach. *International Journal of Advanced Computer Science and Applications, 2*(10), 112–121.

Sarkar, A., Choudhury, S., Chaki, N., & Bhattacharya, S. (2009). Conceptual level design of object oriented data warehouse: Graph semantic based model. *International Journal of Computer Science, 8*(4), 60–70.

Sarkar, A., & Roy, S. S. (2011, July). Graph semantic based conceptual model of semi-structured data: An object oriented approach. *11ᵗʰ International Conference on Software Engineering Research and Practice (SERP 11, WORLDCOMP 2011)*, Vol. 1, (pp. 24–30).

Sengupta, A., Mohan, S., & Doshi, R. (2003). XER - Extensible entity relationship modeling. *XML 2003 Conference*, (pp. 140-154).

Wang, L., Dobbie, G., Sun, J., & Groves, L. (2006). *Validating ORA-SS data models using alloy.* Australian Software Engineering Conference, 2006.

Wu, X., Ling, T. W., Lee, M. L., & Dobbie, G. (2001). Designing semistructured databases using ORA-SS model. *2ⁿᵈ International Conference on Web Information Systems Engineering*, Vol. 1, (pp. 171–180).

ADDITIONAL READING

Abelló, A., Samos, J., & Saltor, F. (2006). YAM2: A multidimensional conceptual model extending UML. *Information Systems, 31*(6), 541–567. doi:10.1016/j.is.2004.12.002

Binh, N. T., & Tjoa, A. M. (2001). *Conceptual multidimensional data model based on object-oriented metacube.* ACM Symposium on Applied Computing.

Buneman, P. (1997). *Semistructured data.* 16th ACM SIGACT-SIGMOD-SIGART Symposium on Principles of Database Systems.

Buyya, R., Yeo, C. S., Venugopal, S., Broberg, J., & Brandic, I. (2009). Cloud computing and emerging IT platforms: Vision, hype, and reality for delivering computing as the 5th utility. *Future Generation Computer Systems, 25*(6), 599–616. doi:10.1016/j.future.2008.12.001

Chin, O. B. (2009). Cloud data management systems: Opportunities and challenges. *5ᵗʰ International Conference on Semantics, Knowledge and Grid*, (p. 2).

Choudhury, S., Chaki, N., & Bhattacharya, S. (2006). GDM: A new graph based data model using functional abstraction. *Journal of Computer Science and Technology, 21*(3), 430–438. doi:10.1007/s11390-006-0430-0

Datta, A., & Thomas, H. (1999). The cube data model: A conceptual model and algebra for on-line analytical processing in data warehouses. *Decision Support Systems*, *27*, 289–301. doi:10.1016/S0167-9236(99)00052-4

Dillon, T., Chen, W., & Chang, E. (2010). Cloud computing: Issues and challenges. *24th IEEE International Conference on Advanced Information Networking and Applications (AINA)*, (pp. 27-33).

Franconi, E., & Kamblet, A. (2004). *A data warehouse conceptual data model*. 16th International Conference on Scientific and Statistical Database Management.

Franconi, E., & Sattler, U. (1999). A data warehouse conceptual data model for multidimensional aggregation: A preliminary report. *Italian Association for Artificial Intelligence Meeting*, Vol. 1, (pp. 9-21.

Golfarelli, M., Maio, D., & Rizzi, S. (1998). The dimensional fact model: A conceptual model for data warehouses. *International Journal of Cooperative Information Systems*, *7*, 215–247. doi:10.1142/S0218843098000118

Goyal, P. (2010). Enterprise usability of cloud computing environments: Issues and challenges. *19th IEEE International Workshop on Enabling Technologies: Infrastructures for Collaborative Enterprises (WETICE)* (pp. 54-59).

Hüsemann, B., Lechtenbörger, J., & Vossen, G. (2000). *Conceptual data warehouse design*. 2nd International Workshop on Design and Management of Data Warehouses.

Institute for Software Integrated System. (2008). *Generic modeling environment*. School of Engineering, Vanderbilt University. Retrieved from http://www.isis.vanderbilt.edu/Projects/gme/

Lechtenbörger, J., & Vossen, G. (2003). Multidimensional normal forms for data warehouse design. *Information Systems*, *28*, 415–434. doi:10.1016/S0306-4379(02)00024-8

Ledeczi, A., Maroti, M., Bakay, A., Karsai, G., Garrett, J., & Thomason, C. … Volgyesi, P. (2001). *The generic modeling environment*. Workshop on Intelligent Signal Processing. Retrieved from http://www.cs.virginia.edu/~rp2h/home/research/ReadingList/gmepaper.pdf

Malinowski, E., & Zimányi, E. (2006). Hierarchies in a multidimensional model: From conceptual modeling to logical representation. *Data & Knowledge Engineering*, *59*(2), 348–377. doi:10.1016/j.datak.2005.08.003

Prat, N., Akoka, J., & Comyn-Wattiau, I. (2006). A UML-based data warehouse design method. *Decision Support Systems*, *42*(3), 1449–1473. doi:10.1016/j.dss.2005.12.001

Ramakrishnan, R. (2012). CAP and cloud data management. *IEEE Computer*, *45*(2), 43–49. doi:10.1109/MC.2011.388

Sarkar, A., Choudhury, S., Chaki, N., & Bhattacharya, S. (2009). Conceptual level design of object oriented data warehouse: Graph semantic based model. *International Journal of Computer Science*, *8*(4), 60–70.

Schneider, M. (2008). A general model for the design of data warehouses. *International Journal of Production Economics*, *112*(1), 309–325. doi:10.1016/j.ijpe.2006.11.027

Standard, O. M. G. (2011). *Unified modeling language 2.4.1*. Object Management Group. Retrieved from http://www.omg.org /spec/UML/2.4.1/

Thalheim, B. (2000). *Entity-relationship modeling: Foundations of database technology*. Berlin, Germany: Springer Verlag.

Tryfona, N., Busborg, F., & Christiansen, J. G. B. (1999). starER: A conceptual model for data warehouse design. *2nd ACM International Workshop on Data Warehousing and OLAP.*

Tsois, A., Karayannidis, N., & Sellis, T. K. (2001). MAC: Conceptual data modeling for OLAP. In Lakshmanan, L. V. S. (Ed.), *Design and management of data warehouses.*

W3C Standard. (2008). *Extensible markup language* (XML) 1.0 (Fifth Edition). W3C. Retrieved from http://www.w3.org/TR/2008/REC-xml-20081126/

W3C Standard. (2012). *XML schema definition language* (XSD) 1.1. W3C. Retrieved from http://www.w3.org/TR/2012/REC-xmlschema11-1-20120405/

Chapter 6
A Comparative Study of Bayesian and Fuzzy Inference Approach to Assess Quality of the Software Using Activity-Based Quality Model

Kawal Jeet
D A V College, India

Nitin Bhatia
D A V College, India

Renu Dhir
Dr. B R Ambedkar National Institute of Technology, India

ABSTRACT

Maintainability is one of the important characteristics of quality of software. It is the measure of efforts needed to modify the software. Large number of subjective techniques has been developed in industry to deal with assessment or prediction of this characteristic. But these techniques generally fail due to their inability to break down maintainability to a level of actual evaluation. They also lack homogeneity in the models thus developed and so fail to take into account the cost factor associated with maintainability. Activity based quality model is found to decompose maintainability to an actual analyzable level. It manages maintainability in terms of software maintenance efforts but it lacks quantitative evaluation of this characteristic. Bayesian approach to deal with this model added quantitative feature but also added crispness to the system developed. In this chapter, the authors propose the use of fuzzy approach to correct the existing Bayesian approach to deal with activity based quality model. A comprehensive comparative study is presented to show the effectiveness of proposed technique.

DOI: 10.4018/978-1-4666-2958-5.ch006

INTRODUCTION

Overview and Motivation

According to ISO 9126 model, quality is the totality of features and characteristics of a software product that bear on its ability to satisfy stated or implied needs (Losavio et al., 2003 and Jung et al., 2004). Assessing or predicting the quality of software is a very challenging task in practice as well as research. To deal with software quality a list of attributes is required to be defined that are appropriate for software. So quality is composed of following six attributes:

1. **Functionality:** It indicates the capability of the software product to provide intended functions.
2. **Reliability:** It indicates the capability of the software product to maintain its level of performance under stated conditions for a stated period of time.
3. **Efficiency:** The ability of the software product to provide appropriate performance under stated conditions, relative to the amount of resources used.
4. **Usability:** The capability of the software product to be understood, learned and used by the user.
5. **Portability:** The capability of the software product to be transferred from one environment to another. The environment may include organizational, hardware or software environment.

6. **Maintainability:** The capability of the software product to be modified. Modifications may include corrections, improvements, or adaptations of the software to changes in the environment and in the requirements and functional specifications.

Comparison between Various Quality Models

Various quality characteristics present in different models Boehm, MacCall, FURPS, ISO9126, Dromey are shown in Table 1.

From Table 1 it can be seen that maintainability is an important characteristic that is being paid attention by almost all the models popular in research and practice (Moses, 2009). Most of the software life cycle cost is consumed by continuous adaptation, extension and bug fixing of existing software and hence the maintainability of software (Pigoski, 1996).

With the maturation of software development practices, software maintainability has become one of the most important concerns of the software industry. The total cost of maintaining a widely used program is typically 40 per cent or more of the cost of developing it (Brooks, 1995).

So it is obvious that any software dependent organization wants to reduce spending for software maintenance activities. This term is most frequently associated with more flexible software and significantly reduced long-term costs. This means the desire for high maintainability is really a desire for low maintenance efforts. Current

Table 1. Quality characteristics described by various models

Quality Characteristic	Boehm et al. (1978)	McCall & Walters (1977)	FURPS (Grady, 1992)	ISO 9126 (Jung et al., 1992)	Dromey (1996)
Functionality			X	X	X
Reliability	X	X	X	X	X
Usability	X			X	
Efficiency	X	X	X	X	X
Portability	X	X		X	X
Maintainability	X	X	X	X	X

approaches to assess and improve maintainability fail to explicitly take into account the cost factor that largely determines software maintenance efforts: the activities performed on the system or more precisely, the associated personnel costs. Although maintainability is a key quality attribute of large software systems, existing approaches to model maintainability have not created a common understanding of the factors influencing maintainability and their interrelations. Hence, no comprehensive basis for assessing and improving the maintainability of large software systems has been established so far. Typically, existing models exhibit at least one of the following problems (Deissenboeck et al., 2007).

1. They do not decompose the attributes and criteria to a level that is suitable for an actual assessment. It constrains the use of these models as the basis for analyses.
2. These models tend to omit the rationale behind the required properties of the system.
3. Existing models often use heterogeneous decomposition dimensions, e. g. the required criteria mix properties of the system with properties of the activities carried out on the system.

The point is that a good model can help maintainers guide their efforts and provide them with much needed feedback. In the present work, we use fuzzy approach to assess and predict maintainability which is proved to be better than other approaches in the field.

RELATED WORK

Guidelines

A commonly applied practice to deal with quality is to provide guidelines that state what developers should do and what they should not do in order to improve the quality of software. Such guidelines are usually composed by the software developing companies. For example, the Java coding conventions provided by Sun Microsystems (Code Conventions for the Java Programming Language, 1999 & Controller Style Guidelines for Production Intent using Matlab, Simulink and Stateflow, 2001).

Reasons for the Failure

They typically do not achieve the desired effect as developers often read them once and then may forget it. Sometimes they provide very generic explanations (Duggan & Reichgelt, 2006). For example, the statement like "respecting the guideline ensures readable models" gives quite generic information and makes its practical application difficult.

It means they fail to motivate the required practices.

Metric-Based Approaches

Berns (1984) and Coleman et al. (1994) proposed metrics-based methods to measure attributes of software systems which are believed to affect maintenance. Well-known metrics like lines of code, Halstead (1977) volume, or Mc-Cabe's Cyclomatic Complexity (McCabe, 1976) etc. are found to be benefiting in such methods.

Reasons for their Failure

First, they do not explain the way system properties influence the maintenance activities and hence the maintenance efforts. It makes their usage immaterial.

Second, they are centred only on properties which can be measured by analyzing syntactic feature i.e. the source code and hence might be ignoring the more important semantic aspects (like meaningful documentation).

Quality Modelling

One of the most promising approaches to deal with quality is quality models which aim at describing complex quality criteria by breaking them down into more manageable sub-criteria. Such models breaks quality in such a manner that abstract quality attributes like maintainability or reliability are kept at the top and more concrete ones like analyzability or changeability are at lower levels. The leaf factors are found to be detailed enough to be assessed directly with software metrics. This method is frequently called the decomposition or Factor- Criteria- Metric (FCM) approach and was first used by McCall et al. (1977) and Boehm et al. (1978).

Reasons for its failure proposed by Kitchenham & Pfleeger (1996) and Kitchenham et al. (1997):

1. Lack of a clearly defined decomposition criterion.
2. Fixed number of model levels is challenging. For example, FCM's 3 level structure is inadequate.

3. Quality models do usually not model the maintenance activities explicitly. So they do not explain how system properties influence the maintenance effort.

Activity–Based Quality Model

Deissenboeck et al. (2007) proposed the use of activity-based quality models (ABQM) in order to address the shortcomings of existing quality models. Activity Based Quality Model is a two-dimensional quality model in which maintainability is decomposed structurally. This breaks down the complex and multifaceted concept of quality into more concrete definitions. This matrix shows the relationship between facts and activities (Figure 1). The two dimensions are:

1. Facts about the system, process and environment in column form.
2. Their impact on activities performed on and with the system in row form.

Figure 1. Maintainability relationships

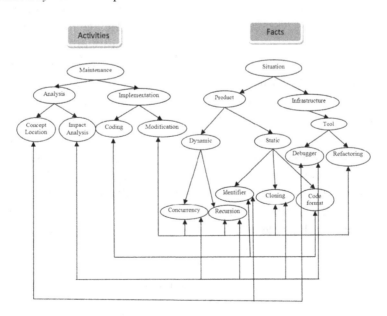

Box 1.

Entities:	These are the objects that can be observed in the real world. For example, product or available infrastructure etc.
Attributes:	These are the properties possessed by an entity like concurrency, code format etc. Some of the terms mentioned in this matrix are detailed below: 1. *Concept location* identifies parts of software that implement a specific concept originated from the problem or the requested change. Concept location is a very common software engineering activity that supports maintenance tasks such as incremental change (Marcus et al., 2004). 2. *Impact Analysis* is the process of identifying software products that is affected by proposed changes. As an example, identify hardware components that must be added, deleted or altered or identify the source code files that must be created, modified or deleted etc. (Cimitile & Fasolino, 1999). 3. *Concurrency* avoids duplication and improves maintainability and hence quality. 4. *Cloning* degrades quality and increases efforts required to design structure of software. It also reduces readability and changeability. 5. *Code Format* should be constantly followed for increasing maintainability. 6. *Refactoring* means restructure code in a disciplined manner to improve reusability.

The facts are found to be very coarse for practical evaluation. So authors further decompose facts into entities and attributes as shown in Box 1.

Shortcomings

Most facts and the relationships between facts and activities have an associated uncertainty and they cannot determine the exact relationship. So, the values measured can be uncertain (e.g. values from expert opinion). As a result a statistical method is needed to model the dependencies of diverse factors from the quality model.

Although ABQM decomposes maintainability to a manageable level but is still unable to deal with it quantitatively.

A Bayesian Approach to Assess and Predict Software Quality Using ABQM

To deal with maintainability quantitatively Wagner (2009) used Bayesian network (BN). This model predicts the maintenance of the software in term of average change efforts, average module size, average cyclometric complexity and comment ratio. This Bayesian network contains three types of nodes:

- Activity nodes representing activities.
- Fact nodes representing facts.
- Indicator nodes representing metrics for activities or facts.

The bayesian network hence developed on the basis of ABQM is shown in Figure 2.

Bayesian network is developed by using ABQM to assess or predict quality (Deissenboeck et al., 2009). Some of the relationships (between facts and activities) depicted in this BN are:

- Module Extent→Code Reading
  - The size of a module has an impact on readability of the code of the module. Fundamentally, larger the module, the longer it takes to read it.
- Regularity of Implementation→ Testing
  - An implementation is regular if it does not use unnecessarily nested branches. If software is not regular in implementation then the structure of the software will be complex which makes testing more difficult.
- Appropriateness of comments→ Modification
  - Comments need to appropriately describe the code it is associated with.

The various impacts are included in the BN (shown in Figure 2) as the arrows from the facts to the activities.

Figure 2. Bayesian network developed from activity based quality model

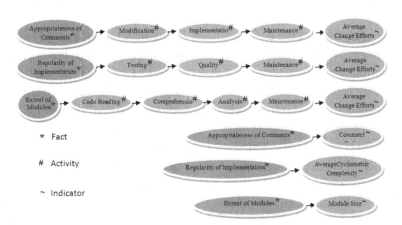

This network is developed on the basis of following four steps:

- The relevant activities are identified and appropriate assessment goal for example maintenance are defined (as shown in Figure 2).
- Other factors and sub activities that are related to the identified activities are identified recursively.
- Additional nodes called indicator nodes are identified for each fact and goal node. They act as measurement for each fact that is modelled. Edges are directed from the activity and fact nodes to the indicators. It means indicators are dependent on the facts and activities.
- Quantization is done by filling NPT (node probability tables) for each node. The most common values in use are low, medium, and high. This evaluation is easier as not precise numbers have to be determined but it actually added high uncertainty in the data. So in other words although Bayesian network is found to be much better than previous methods of evaluating maintainability but results are not very accurate due to crisp nature of input activities like extent of modules, regularity of implementation, appropriateness of comments etc.

To elaborate this, let us take domain of inputs to be 0-10. In case of BN, due to crisp nature of Bayesian approach anything values 0-3.33333 are considered low, between 3.33333-6.66666 are taken as medium and values between 6.66666-10 are high. So, in case ether input is 1, 2 or 3 the network works the same which leads to inaccuracy.

In this chapter, we overcome this shortcoming of BN by using fuzzy inference approach which takes fuzzy values as inputs.

A FUZZY APPROACH TO DEAL WITH ABQM

In order to increase accuracy of BN based approach to ABQM (Wagner, 2009), we propose to use fuzzy approach. This fuzzy inference system (FIS) is developed on the basis of dataset given by PROMISE Software Engineering Repository data set (NASA IV&V Facility). The basic topology, on the basis of which FIS is developed (Deissenboeck, 2007), is shown in Figure 2. This BN indicates that 'Average Change Effort', 'Average Module Size', 'Average Cyclometric complexity', 'Comment ratio' are the indicators of 'Maintainability' of a software project. A datasets, based on which, this assess and prediction system is developed is given in Table 2.

Basics of Fuzzy Logic

The term "fuzzy logic" emerged in the development of the theory of fuzzy sets by Zadeh (1965). It is a mean to model the ambiguity associated with vagueness. In fuzzy logic, propositions can be represented with degrees of truthfulness and falsehood. The theme of fuzzy systems is that membership values in fuzzy sets are indicated by a value on the range [0.0, 1.0], with 0.0 representing absolute Falseness and 1.0 representing absolute Truth. The tip of fuzzy logic is to map an input space to an output space, and the primary mechanism for doing this is a list of if-then statements called rules. All rules are evaluated in parallel. So fuzzy inference is a technique that interprets the values in the input and, based on set of rules, assigns values to the output.

Implementation Details

To implement the proposed system, Fuzzy logic toolbox of MATLAB has been used (*Fuzzy Logic Toolbox for MATLAB and Simulink*). Due to programmer friendly environment, availability of features required for development and analysis, we are boosted to use MATLAB for this work.

Since the inputs of the system under study could be fuzzy and the output i.e. the probability is constant (as shown in Table 4). So, Sugeno system of fuzzy inference is most appropriate for this system. A Sugeno inference system is a non linear mapping of an input data vector into a scalar output.

Various inference systems that are to be developed are given in Table 3.

Table 2. Information regarding the attributes of BN

Attribute Name	Details	Value
Average change efforts	*Indicator* of impact of activities on quality of the software. More the value of this attribute less maintainable is the software and hence lowers the quality. (effort required to make change in a software development project measured in person hours)	Numeric
Comment Ratio	*Indicator* of impact of fact 'Appropriateness of comments' on quality of the software. Commented loc/total loc The proportion of the comments in relation to the other code	
Average Cyclometric Complexity	*Indicator* of impact of fact 'Regularity of implementation' on quality of the software. Number for the decision points in the implementation (In other words, number of linearly independent paths through a program's source code)	
Average Module Size	*Indicator* of impact of fact 'Extent of modules' on quality of the software. LOC	
Extent of modules, Regularity of implementation, Appropriateness of comment	*Fact* describes a plain decomposition of the situation.	Low, Medium, High
Maintenance, Implementation, Analysis, Quality Assurance, comprehension, Modification Code Reading, Testing	*Activities* performed on or within the system	
Probability	*Probability* of occurrence of some combination of attributes	Numeric (in the range 0.0-1.0)

Table 3. Information about inference systems

Antecedents	Consequent (Probability of)
Maintenance	Average Change Effort to be in range 3.9-9.125, 9.125-14.35,14.35-19.575, 19.575-24.8,24.8- 30.025, 30.025-35.25, 35.25-40.475, 40.475-45.7,45.7-50.925, 50.925-56.15,56.15-61.375, 61.375-66.6 Person hours
Extent of Modules	Average Module Size to be in range '0.0-10.0 ','10.0-20.0','20.0-30.0', '30.0-40.0','40.0-50.0','50.0-60.0', '60.0-70.0','70.0-80.0','80.0-90.0', '90.0-Infinity'
Regularity of Implementation	Average Cyclometric complexity to be in range '0.0-1.0 ','1.0-2.0','2.0-3.0','3.0-4.0', '4.0-5.0','5.0-6.0','6.0-7.0','7.0-8.0', '8.0-9.0','9.0-10.0','10.0-Infinity'
Appropriateness of Comments	Comment Ratio to be in range '0.0-0.05 ','0.05-0.1','0.1-0.15','0.15-0.2','0.2-1.0' commented loc/total loc
Analysis, Quality Assurance, Implementation	Maintenance_low Maintenance_medium Maintenance_high
Comprehension	Analysis_low Analysis_medium Analysis_high
Testing	Quality Assurance_low Quality Assurance_medium Quality Assurance_high
Modification	Implementation_low Implementation_medium Implementation_high
Code Reading	Comprehension_low Comprehension_medium Comprehension_high
Extent of Modules	Code Reading_low Code Reading_medium Code Reading_high
Regularity of Implementation	Testing_low Testing_medium Testing_high
Appropriateness of Comments	Modification_low Modification_medium Modification_high
Type of fuzzy inference system used	Sugeno

These inference systems are motivated by BN of Figure 2.

Some of the inference systems shown in Table 2 are discussed below.

Details of Inference Systems from 'Appropriateness of Comments' to 'Comment Ratio'

The data set based on which the inference system

Table 4. Dataset about conditional probability of 'comment ratio' and 'appropriateness of comments'

Appropriateness of Comments	Comment Ratio	Probability
Low	0.0-0.05	0.21861392
Medium	0.0-0.05	0.12514098
High	0.0-0.05	0.06303138
Low	0.05-0.1	0.20460929
Medium	0.05-0.1	0.13152975
High	0.05-0.1	0.069645956
Low	0.1-0.15	0.17629181
Medium	0.1-0.15	0.13152975
High	0.1-0.15	0.07505856
Low	0.15-0.2	0.13982919
Medium	**0.15-0.2**	**0.12514098**
High	0.15-0.2	0.078898676
Low	0.2-1.0	0.2606558
Medium	0.2-1.0	0.48665854
High	0.2-1.0	0.71336544

between 'Appropriateness of Comments' and 'Comment Ratio' is developed in shown in Table 4.

Three fuzzy rules are developed in this inference system.

1. If (Appropriteness_of_comments is low) then (0.0-0.05 is z1)(0.05-0.1 is z1)(0.1-0.15 is z1)(0.15-0.2 is z1)(0.2-1.0 is z1) (1)
2. If (Appropriteness_of_comments is medium) then (0.0-0.05 is z2)(0.05-0.1 is z2)(0.1-0.15 is z2)(0.15-0.2 is z2)(0.2-1.0 is z2) (1)
3. If (Appropriteness_of_comments is high) then (0.0-0.05 is z3)(0.05-0.1 is z3)(0.1-0.15 is z3)(0.15-0.2 is z3)(0.2-1.0 is z3) (1)

where detail of output variables are given in Table 5.

Table 5. Information about output variables associated with FIS between 'appropriateness of comments' and 'comment ratio'

Output Variables	z1	z2	z3
0.0-0.05	0.21861392	0.12514098	0.06303138
0.05-0.1	0.20460929	0.13152975	0.069645956
0.1-0.15	0.17629181	0.13152975	0.07505856
0.15-0.2	0.13982919	0.12514098	0.078898676
0.2-1.0	0.2606558	0.48665854	0.71336544

Working of Sugeno Inference System

A typical rule in a Sugeno fuzzy model we developed has the form

```
If Input 1=x, then Output is z (con-
stant)
```

The output level zi of each rule is weighted by the firing strength wi of the rule. For example, for this rule, the firing strength is

```
wi = F1(x)
```

The final output of the system is the weighted average of all rule outputs, computed as

$$\text{Final Output} = \sum_{i=1}^{N} w_i * z_i \Big/ \sum_{i=1}^{N} w_i \qquad (1)$$

where N is the total number of rules.

In all the FIS discussed above, antecedents are fuzzy and consequents are constants (as indicated by sugeno inference). Each antecedent is further having three possible fuzzy sets- Low, medium and high. Gauss membership function is the membership function (a curve that defines how each point in the input space is mapped to a membership value) which is found to be most suitable for the dataset under study. Any Gauss membership function depends on two parameters σ and

Table 6. Parameter values for 'appropriateness of comments'

Fuzzy set	C	σ
Low	0	1.699
Medium	5	1.699
High	10	1.699

c. This function finds the degree of membership by putting parameters σ, c in Equation 2 (Fuzzy Logic Toolbox for MATLAB and Simulink).

$$f(x; \sigma, c) = e^{-(x-c)^2/2\sigma^2} \qquad (2)$$

where x is the value whose degree of membership (in the fuzzy set under study) is to be calculated.

For example, in case of 'Appropriateness of Comments', value of parameters x and σ are given in Table 6.

By putting value of x, c and σ in Equation 2 we can get degree of membership of value x in the fuzzy set under consideration. Similarly we can get degree of membership for other attribute inputs.

Steps to Show Working of a Sugeno Inference Rule

In order to know internal working of our FIS, let us take FIS between 'Appropriateness of comments' and 'Modification'. The rules developed on the basis of dataset of Table 3 and 4 are:

Rule 1: If (appropriteness_comments is low) then (modification_low is z1)(modification_medium is z1)(modification_high is z1) (1)

Rule 2: If (appropriteness_comments is medium) then (modification_low is z2) (modification_medium is z2)(modification_high is z2) (1)

Rule 3: If (appropriteness_comments is high) then (modification_low is z3) (modification_medium is z3) (modification_high is z3) (1)

Sugeno works as follows:

Step 1: Fuzzify Inputs

The first step is to take the inputs and determine the degree to which they belong to each of the appropriate fuzzy sets via membership functions. In Fuzzy Logic Toolbox software, the input is always a crisp numerical value limited to the universe of discourse of the input variable (in this case the interval between 0 and 10). Let us concentrate on 'Appropriateness of comments' for the FIS currently under study. Fuzzification of input 'Appropriateness of comments'=1 is shown in Figure 3 and explained in Table 7.

Figure 3. (a) Fuzzify input to resolve rule 1 (b) Fuzzify input to resolve rule 2 (c) Fuzzify input to resolve rule 3

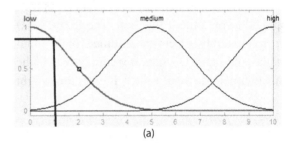

(a)

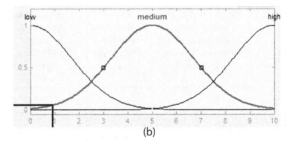

(b)

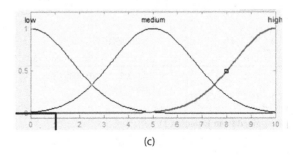

(c)

Table 7. Fuzzify inputs for FIS between 'appropriateness of comments' and 'modifications'

Rule	x (input for 'Appropriateness of Comments')	c (from Table 6)	σ (from Table 6)	Fuzzy set under consideration (For each rule)	Degree of membership $w = f(x;\sigma,c) = e^{\frac{-(x-c)^2}{2\sigma^2}}$ (From Equation 2)
1	1	0	1.699	Low	$e^{-(1-0)^2/2*1.699^2} = 0.84$
2	1	5	1.699	Medium	$e^{-(1-5)^2/2*1.699^2} = 0.0625$
3	1	10	1.699	High	$e^{-(1-10)^2/2*1.699^2} = 8.0695 \times 10^{-07}$

Step 2: Apply Fuzzy Operator

After the inputs are fuzzified, we get the degree to which each part of the antecedent is satisfied for each rule. If the antecedent of a given rule has more than one part, the fuzzy operator is applied to obtain a number that represents the result of the antecedent for that rule. This number is then applied to the output function. The fuzzy AND operator simply selects the minimum of the input values and fuzzy OR operator simply selects the maximum of the input values. It gives the weight

of the rule. For the current case there is only one antecedent. So, this step is ignored.

Step 3: Implication

From Table 5, we get value of z i.e. output level z for modification to be low, medium or high. To calculate the final outcome of FIS between 'Appropriateness of Comments' and 'Modifications' on the basis of all the three rule mentioned above see Table 8.

Table 8. Working of Sugeno inference

Rule i	Weight w (Degree of membership of 'Appropriateness of Comments' obtained from Table 7)	Z1 for modification to be low (from Table 4)	Contribution of the rule to the output 'modification_low' w*z1	Z2 for modification to be medium (from Table 4)	Contribution of the rule to the output 'modification_medium' w*z2	Z3 for modification to be high (from Table 4)	Contribution of the rule to the output 'modification_high' w*z3
1	0.84	0	0	0	0	1	0.84
2	0.0645	0	0	1	0.0645	0	0
3	8.0695×10^{-07}	1	8.0695×10^{-07}	0	0	0	0
$\sum_{i=1}^{3} wi * zi$		8.0695×10^{-07}		0.0645		0.84	
$\sum_{i=1}^{3} wi * zi / \sum_{i=1}^{3} wi$ **(Obtained from Equation 1)**		$8.0695 \times 10^{-07}/0.9045$ **=8.9211X10-07**		0.0645/0.9045 **=0.071310**		0.84/0.9045 **=0.928689**	

Figure 4. Interface to enter value of facts

The information thus generated is used as input to next inference system (as shown in Figure 2) i.e. Modification -> Implementation.

Similarly, other inference systems are processed to give the average efforts required to make changes and hence, find the maintainability of the software, which is quality factor, as discussed above.

Interface Design

In order to enter information about input activities the interface is shown below

You can enter the values for the facts 'Extent of Modules', 'Regularity of Implementation' and 'Appropriateness of Comments' in the range 0-10 (See Figure 4).

Plot

In order to compare or show the difference between fuzzy and Bayesian approach input are given for all the three facts for the three set of inputs. All the figures show the output of both fuzzy and Bayesian inference for all the three sets of inputs. The system displays the probability of occurrence of average efforts required to make changes in the software to be in a specified range as calculated by fuzzy inference system by a 'o' and that of calculated by Bayesian network by a '*'.

On clicking button 'Average Change Efforts' the output in the form of probability of average efforts required to make changes in the software to

Figure 5. Probability of average change efforts to be in range 24.8- 30.025, 30.025-35.25, 35.25-40.475, 40.475-45.7 person hours for the three given input sets

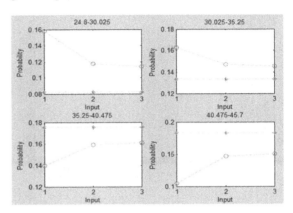

be in different range for all the three input sets is displayed. As an example we can get probability of average change efforts to be in range 24.8- 30.025, 30.025-35.25, 35.25-40.475, 40.475-45.7 person hours for the three given input sets (as shown in Figure 5).

On clicking button 'Comment Ratio' the output is in the form of probability of comment ratio to be in different range for all the three input sets is displayed. As an example we can get probability of comment ratio to be in range 0.05-1.0 for the three given input sets (as shown in Figure 6).

On clicking button 'Average Module Size' the output is in the form of probability of average size of the software module to be in different range for all the three input sets is displayed. As an example we can get probability of average module size to be in range 40.0-50.0, 50.0-60.0, 60.0-70.0,70.0-80.0 loc for the three given input sets (as shown in Figure 7).

On clicking button 'Average Cyclometric Complexity' the output is in the form of probability of average complexity of the software to be in different range for all the three input sets is displayed. As an example we can get probability of average change efforts to be in range 4.0-5.0, 5.0-6.0, 6.0-7.0,7.0-8.0 for the three given input sets (as shown in Figure 8).

Figure 6. Probability of comment ratio to be in range 0.05-0.1 for the three given input sets

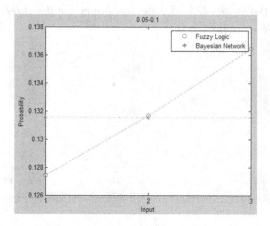

COMPARISON BETWEEN BAYESIAN AND FUZZY APPROACH TO QUANTIFY ABQM

Let us compare the outputs of the three input sets shown in Figure 5 for probability of 'Appropriateness of comments' of the software to be in range 0.15-0.2 (as shown in Table 9 and Table 10). Similar calculations could be done for other possible ranges i.e. '0.0-0.05 ','0.05-0.1','0.1-0.15' and '0.2-1.0' for these three given input sets.

Figure 7. Probability of average module size to be in range 40.0-50.0, 50.0-60.0, 60.0-70.0,70.0-80.0 loc for the three given input sets

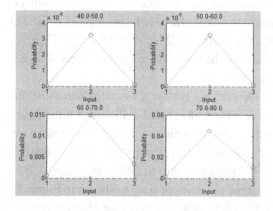

Table 9. Probability calculated for 'appropriateness of comments' to be in range 0.15-0.2 loc with Bayesian approach

Input	Input 1	Crisp Input 1	Input 2	Crisp Input 2	Input 3	Crisp Input 3
Appropriateness of comments	6	Medium	5	Medium	4	Medium
Output by Bayesian Approach	0.125		0.125		0.125	

Figure 8. Probability of average module size to be in range 4.0-5.0, 5.0-6.0, 6.0-7.0,7.0-8.0 for the three given input sets

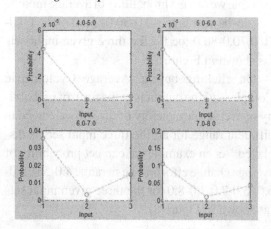

Table 10. Probability calculated for 'appropriateness of comments' to be in range 0.15-0.2 loc with fuzzy approach

Input	Input 1	Fuzzify input 1	Input 2	Fuzzify Input 2	Input 3	Fuzzify Input 3	Fuzzy set under consideration
Appropriateness of comments	6	0.84	5	1	4	0.84	Medium
Output by Fuzzy Approach	0.122		0.1247		0.1261		

Introduction to Bayesian Network

Bayesian Networks are simple visual representation of a decision problem. They offer an intuitive way to identify and display the essential elements, including decisions, uncertainties, and objectives, and how they influence each other. They provide a clear, graphical picture of a problem and helps in showing important relationships. The modeling is based on probabilistic theory. They use circle/oval called nodes and arrows called arcs (*GeNIe & SMILE*). Nodes represent system variables while arcs represent influences between variables.

If inputs are entered as shown in Table 9 then output is same in all the three cases. This is because in case of BN whether the input for 'Appropriateness of comments' is 6,5,4 it is crispfied to same set medium. From Table 5 it can be seen that for 'Appropriateness of Comments' to be medium the value for 'Comment ratio' in the range 0.15-0.2 loc is 0.125. This is how bayesian network makes inference.

In order to make inference using fuzzy approach, let us fuzzify inputs by using rules

If (appropriateness_comments is medium) then (modification_low is z2) (modification_medium is z2)(modification_high is z2)   (1)

where output variables are detailed in Table 4.

From Table 10, it can be depicted that for input 1, 'Appropriateness of comments' is 6 and its membership in fuzzy set is 0.84 for rule 1 (as discussed above). Similarly fuzzy membership for 'Appropriateness of comments' for the same rule for input 2 is 0.1 and for input 3 is 0.84 which are obviously different for each input set whereas from Table 9 we can see that for all of them single value 'Medium' is taken due to crisp nature of this approach. This is because, in case of bayesian approach (Table 9), inputs are made crisp by taking inputs in the range 0-3.3333 as low, between 3.3333-6.6666 as medium and between 6.6666-10 as high whereas in case of fuzzy approach inputs are fuzzified on the basis of rule under consideration.

So, in case of fuzzy approach overall calculations take inputs differently and behave more accurately for each input set (in the same range) which acts as an advantage of fuzzy over Bayesian approach.

CONCLUSION

Developing maintainable and hence quality software has always been responsible for the success of the software development project. Many models and techniques are developed in research and used in practice. But these are found to be inappropriate for practical use. In this chapter we developed a fuzzy based inference system which takes the fuzzy inputs whereas the already developed bayesian approach takes the inputs in a strict crisp form. So, we overcome the shortcomings of existing approach by developing a fuzzy based approach to assess or predict maintainability of software on the basis of Activity Based Quality Model.

FUTURE RESEARCH DIRECTIONS

This work revolves around prediction of maintainability of software at an early stage of development. In future the work can be carried out to predict other factors like cost of the software or the overall effort required using the proposed fuzzy technique. However, appropriate modifications are necessary for effective results.

REFERENCES

Berns, G. M. (1984). Assessing software maintainability. *ACM Communications*, *27*(1), 14–23. doi:10.1145/69605.357965

Boehm, B. W., Brown, J. R., Kaspar, H., Lipow, M., McLeod, G., & Merritt, M. (1978). *Characteristics of software quality*. Amsterdam, The Netherlands: North Holland.

Brooks, F. P. (1995). *The mythical man-month: Essays on software engineering* (2nd ed.). Pearson Education.

Cimitile, A., & Fasolino, A. R. (1999). *A software model for impact analysis: A validation experiment*. In Sixth Working Conference on Reverse Engineering.

Coleman, D. M., Ash, D., Lowther, B., & Oman, P. W. (1994). Using metrics to evaluate software system maintainability. *IEEE Computer*, *27*(8), 44–49. doi:10.1109/2.303623

Deissenboeck, F., Juergens, E., Lochmann, K., & Wagner, S. (2009). *Software quality models: Purposes, usage scenarios and requirements*. In 7th International Workshop on Software Quality (WoSQ '09), IEEE Computer Society.

Deissenboeck, F., Wagner, S., Pizka, M., Teuchert, S., & Girard, J.-F. (2007). An activity-based quality model for maintainability. In *International Conference on Software Maintenance, ICSM 2007* (pp. 184-193).

Dromey, R. G. (1996). Concerning the Chimera. *IEEE Software*, *13*(1), 33–43. doi:10.1109/52.476284

Duggan, E. W., & Reichgelt, H. (Eds.). (2006). *Measuring information systems delivery quality*. Idea Group. doi:10.4018/978-1-59140-857-4

Embedded, C. M. M. I. (2001). *Controller style guidelines for production intent using Matlab, Simulink and Stateflow*. Retrieved from http://www.embeddedcmmi.at/fileadmin/docs/reports/MAAB_v1p00.pdf

Garvin, D. A. (1984). What does product quality really mean? *Sloan Management Review*, *26*, 25–45.

GeNIe & SMILE. (n.d.). Retrieved from http://genie.sis.pitt.edu

Grady, R. B. (1992). *Practical software metrics for project management and process improvement*. New Jersey, USA: Prentice Hall.

Halstead, M. (1977). *Elements of software science*. New York, NY: Elsevier Science.

Jung, H.-W., Kim, S.-G., & Chung, C.-S. (2004). Measuring software product quality: a survey of ISO/IEC 9126. *IEEE Software*, *21*(5), 88–92. doi:10.1109/MS.2004.1331309

Kitchenham, B., Linkman, S. G., Pasquini, A., & Nanni, V. (1997). The SQUID approach to defining a quality model. *Software Quality Control*, *6*(3), 211–233.

Kitchenham, B., & Pfleeger, S. L. (1996). Software quality: The elusive target. *IEEE Software*, *13*(1), 12–21. doi:10.1109/52.476281

Losavio, F., Chirinos, L., Lévy, N., & Ramdane-Cherif, A. (2003). Quality Characteristics for software architecture. *Journal of Object Technology*, *2*, 133–150. doi:10.5381/jot.2003.2.2.a2

Marciniak, J. J. (2002). *Encyclopaedia of software engineering* (*Vol. 2*). Chichester, UK: Wiley. doi:10.1002/0471028959

Marcus, A., Sergeyev, A., Rajlich, A., & Maletic, J. I. (2004). *An information retrieval approach to concept location in source code*. In 11th Working Conference on Reverse Engineering. Washington, DC: IEEE Computer Society.

MathWorks. (n.d.). *Fuzzy logic toolbox for MATLAB and Simulink*. Retrieved from http://www.mathworks.com/products/fuzzylogic

McCabe, T. (1976). A complexity measures. *IEEE Transactions on Software Engineering*, *SE-2*, 308–320. doi:10.1109/TSE.1976.233837

McCall, J. A., Richards, P. K., & Walters, G. F. (1977). *Factors in software quality*. Springfield, VA: National Technical Information Service.

Moses, J. (2009). Should we try to measure software quality attributes directly? *Software Quality Journal*, *17*, 203–213. doi:10.1007/s11219-008-9071-6

NASA IV&V Facility. (n.d.). *Metrics data program*. Retrieved from http://promisedata.org/repository/data/cm1/cm1_bn.arff

Oracle. (1999). *Code conventions for the Java programming language*. Retrieved from http://www.oracle.com/technetwork/java/codeconv-138413.html

Pigoski, T. M. (1996). *Practical software maintenance: Best practices for managing your software investment*. New York, NY: Wiley Computer Publishing.

Wagner, S. (2009). *A Bayesian network approach to assess and predict software quality using activity-based quality models*. In International Conference on Predictor Models in Software Engineering (PROMISE '09). New York, NY: ACM.

Zadeh, L. A. (1965). Fuzzy sets. *Information and Control*, *8*, 338–353. doi:10.1016/S0019-9958(65)90241-X

Chapter 7
Data Mining Techniques for Software Quality Prediction

Bharavi Mishra
Indian Institute of Technology (BHU), India

K. K. Shukla
Indian Institute of Technology (BHU), India

ABSTRACT

In the present time, software plays a vital role in business, governance, and society in general, so a continuous improvement of software productivity and quality such as reliability, robustness, etc. is an important goal of software engineering. During software development, a large amount of data is produced, such as software attribute repositories and program execution trace, which may help in future development and project management activities. Effective software development needs quantification, measurement, and modelling of previous software artefacts. The development of large and complex software systems is a formidable challenge which requires some additional activities to support software development and project management processes. In this scenario, data mining can provide a helpful hand in the software development process. This chapter discusses the application of data mining in software engineering and includes static and dynamic defect detection, clone detection, maintenance, etc. It provides a way to understand the software artifacts and processes to assist in software engineering tasks.

INTRODUCTION

Software engineering is a complex process which has become a prominent human activity at present. Considerable amount of knowledge about the problem domain and the programming domain are needed during the software-development life cycle. Including this, different techniques are also required to combine this knowledge to provide reliable and robust software solutions. Software engineering is the application of a systematic, disciplined, quantifiable approach to the development, operation, and maintenance of software; (IEEE, 1987) that is, the application of engineering to software. Software engineering is often thought of as a series of separate, discrete

DOI: 10.4018/978-1-4666-2958-5.ch007

activities (such as design, coding, testing) that lead to a finished product. However, quality software is not composed of discrete processes; instead, it is composed of continuous processes that guide the development activity. Most of these activities are continuous; that is, the activities are performed throughout the entire software-development effort. Some of these activities, such as analysis, design, implementation, and testing are discrete. Selection of the correct life cycle is therefore, extremely important to the success of the overall software project. To support software development process, there is a need of different techniques to ensure a cost-effective and reliable software development with risk minimization.

Data Mining (sometimes called data or knowledge discovery or Knowledge Mining) is the process of analyzing data from different perspectives and summarizing it into useful information that can be used for strategic planning. Data mining techniques allow users to analyze data from many different dimensions or angles, categorize it, and summarize the relationships identified. Technically, data mining is the process of finding correlations or patterns among dozens of fields in large databases. Data Mining is a series of iterative activities that lead to identification of some interesting patterns in data set. Step by step data mining process in shown in Figure 1. Data mining techniques are now being used by the practitioners to solve several software related problem to ease the task of software development (Basili,

1996; Jing, 2007; Binkley, 1998; Mishra, 2011, December; Mishra, Sep 2011; Menzies, 2007; Zimmermann, 2007).

NEED OF DATA MINING IN SOFTWARE ENGINEERING

In the pursuit of good software, engineers have collected huge amount of data in various forms, which can be analyzed to produce better quality software (as it helps in having better comprehension of the software-development process). In software development huge amount of data is produced which can be categorized as:

- Data from software repositories
- Data from program executions

Software engineering data have a wealth of information about a software project and processes which includes:

- **Programming:** Versions of programs
- **Testing:** Execution traces
- **Deployment:** Error/bug reports
- **Reuse:** Open source packages

We can explore valuable information regarding software projects and processes to provide higher-quality software within a reasonable time and budget by using well established data mining

Figure 1. Step by step data mining process

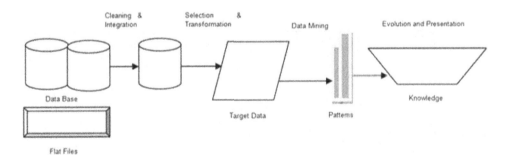

approaches. These software engineering data can be used to:

- Gain empirically-based understanding of software development.
- Predict, plan, and understand various aspects of a project.
- Support future development and project management activities.

The development of large and complex software systems is a formidable challenge which required some additional activities to support software development and project management processes. To develop quality software, software engineers need answers of following questions:

- How should one use this legacy system?
- Where are the bugs?
- How to implement a typical functionality?
- Issues in reusing software frameworks
  - Which components should one use?
  - What is the right way to use?
- Discover cross-cutting concerns that can be potentially turned into one place (an aspect in aspect-oriented programs).

An effective software development needs quantification, measurement, and modelling of the previous software artifacts. The application of data mining in software engineering, depicted in Figure

2, includes static and dynamic defect detection, testing, vulnerability analysis, clone detection, maintenance etc. Moreover, data mining can also be used in classification of the functional and non functional requirements. In summery it helps in:

- Understanding software artifacts and processes.
- Assist software engineering tasks.

The relationship of data mining techniques with software quality prediction has been reported in (Stefan Lessmann,2008), using a large-scale empirical comparison of 22 defect prediction models over 10 public domain software development data sets from the NASA MDP repository. This research work concludes that the statistical comparison of individual models on the basis of predictive accuracy does not differ significantly according to a Nemenyi post hoc test ($\alpha=0.05$). This suggests that the importance of the classification model may have been overestimated in the previous research, hence illustrating the relevance of statistical hypothesis testing. The basic linear models such as Logistic Regression, Linear Programming, and Linear Discriminant Analysis, give similar results to more sophisticated classifiers, it is evident that most data sets are fairly well linearly separable. In other words, simple classifiers suffice to model the relationship between static code attributes and

Figure 2. How data mining helps in software engineering

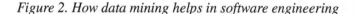

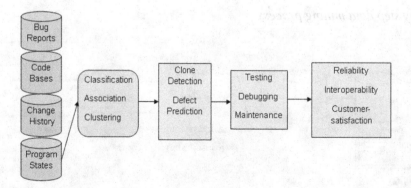

software defect. Consequently, the assessment and selection of a classification model should not be based on predictive accuracy alone but should be comprised of several additional criteria like computational efficiency, ease of use, and especially comprehensibility. Comprehensible models reveal the nature of detected relationships and help improve our overall understanding of software failures and their sources, which, in turn, may enable the development of novel predictors of fault-proneness. In fact, efforts to design new software metrics and other explanatory variables appear to be a particularly promising area for future research and have the potential to achieve general accuracy improvements across all types of classifiers.

In this chapter, we will present a wide description of two software related problems, software clones and software defects with their influence on software-development and their respective solutions using data mining techniques.

DEFECT PREDICTION: WHAT, WHY, AND WHEN

As our dependency on software is increasing, software quality is becoming gradually more and more important in the present era. Software is used almost everywhere and in every tread of life. Software defects diminish software quality because they cause failures (Tian,2005). A software failure is the departure of the system from its required behavior; error is the incongruity between the required and actual functionality; whereas hypothesized cause of an error is a fault (Laprie,1996), which is also known as a defect (or as a bug) among software professionals (Eman,2005). Incorrect and buggy behavior in deployed software costs up to $70 billion in the US on software maintenance (Report,2002;Sutherland,1995). On the other hand, the software-development companies

cannot risk their business by deploying poor-quality software because it results in customer dissatisfaction. Previous studies have shown that, of the overall development process 50% effort is consumed by testing (Pressman,2001). Maintenance cost of software increases with time. However, learning from experience, it should be possible to predict bugs in new software products. Consequently, a timely identification of these modules facilitates an efficient allocation of testing resources and may enable architectural improvements by suggesting a more rigorous design for high-risk segments of the systems. To achieve this, we must first know which components/modules/packages are more failure-prone than others. With this knowledge, we can search for properties of the components/modules/packages or its development process that are commonly correlated with bugs.

To ameliorate the testing process, we can use the defect prediction models. These models can be used in defect prediction, risk analysis, effort estimation, software testability and maintainability, and reliability analysis during early phases of software development. It can also be used in business risk minimization by predicting the quality of the software in the early stages of the software-development life cycle (SDLC). This would not only help in increasing client's satisfaction but also trim down the cost of correction of defects. It has been reported (Khoshgoftaar,1996) that the cost of defect correction is significantly high after software testing. An additional advantage of early defect prediction is better resource planning and test planning (Khoshgoftaar,1990; Khoshgoftaar,2000). Therefore, the key of developing reliable quality software within time and budget is to identify defect prone modules at an early stage of SDLC by using defect prediction models. The importance of defect prediction is evident, considering the large volume of research conducted in this regard (Basili, 1996; Jing, 2007; Binkley,1998; Mishra, 2011, December;

Mishra, Sep 2011; Menzies, 2007; Zimmermann, 2007). A basic reason behind study of defect prediction is:

- A panel at *IEEE Metrics 2002(Shull, 2002)* concluded that manual software reviews can find ≈60% of defects.
- Raffo found that the defect detection capability of industrial review methods can vary from *probability of detection (pd) = TR(35, 50, 65)%5* for full Fagan inspections(Fagan,1976) to *pd = TR(13, 21, 30)%* for less-structured inspections.

Data mining is a popular approach for defect prediction and involves categorizing modules, represented by a set of software metrics or code attributes, into a fault prone (FP) or non-fault-prone (NFP) class by a learning algorithm derived from data of previous development projects.

Defect Prediction Model and Process

In the present scenario, the main goal of data mining is to avoid the irrelevant data rather than accessing the huge amount of data. As software defect prediction is an application of the data mining process, a typical defect prediction modeling follows the traditional data mining approaches. Model creation process focuses on extracting

the hidden but useful patterns from the defect data repositories to help the developer in future development. Defect prediction process uses the techniques from statistics, artificial intelligence and machine learning disciplines to convert the data into a human recognizable form, called defect patterns. These patterns work as decision rules for the developers by providing the relevant information regarding fault proneness of software components (modules, classes, files, methods, etc.). These models may also help the software companies to enhance their process maturity level and trim down the cost of development by giving more attention to the bug prone modules. Defect pattern discovery as a process is depicted in Figure 3 and consists of following elements:

Defect Data Set

Defect predictors are learned from the historical data sets, which are the collections of static code features, object oriented features, complexity metrics or may be a collection of all these attributes. The class label of these data sets is "defective" whose value is either true or false. Each data set contains the feature's values for one project and stored with a name in public data repositories like PROMISE DATA REPOSTORIES, NASA METRIC DATA PROGRAM, and BUG PRE-DICTION DATASET. There are several defect

Figure 3. Step by step defect prediction process

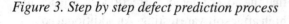

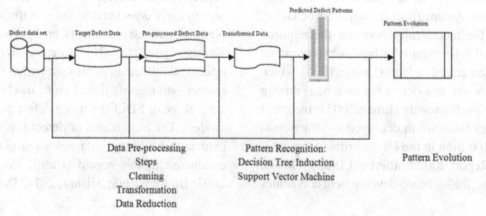

Table 1. Some defect data sets

Data set	Modules	Features	Defective	Description	Source
CM1	498	21	9.83%	Space craft instrument	Promise data Repository
KC3	458	39	9.38%	Storage management for ground data.	Promise Data Repository
MW1	403	37	7.69%	A zero gravity experiment related to combustion	Promise Data Repository
PC1	1109	21	6.94%	Flight software from an earth orbiting satellite.	Promise Data Repository
PC3	1563	37	10.23%	Flight software for earth orbiting satellite	Promise Data Repository
PC4	1458	37	12.2%	Flight software for earth orbiting satellite.	Promise Data Repository
PC5	17186	38	3.0%	A safety enhancement of a cockpit upgrades system.	Promise Data Repository
Eclipse 2.0	377	199	51%	Java IDE	Bug Prediction Dataset
Eclipse2.1	434	199	45%	Java IDE	Bug Prediction Dataset

data sets available to build a defect prediction model; some of them are listed in Table 1 and the attribute list is given in Table 2. There are three types of sources available for preparation of the defect data set.

Historical Data

It is the collection of version control and source control data in the form of CVS and subversion information. Bug tracking systems like BUG-ZILLA, GNATA and JIRA are used to mine the software engineering data using CVS and version information of a software system. Historical data

Table 2. Attribute list

Data Set	Component	Attributes	Description
Eclipse	File	ACD	Number of anonymous type declarations
		NOI	Number of interfaces
		NOT	Number of classes
		TLLOC	Total line of code
	Class	NOF	Number of fields
		NOM	Number of methods
		NSF	Number of static fields
		NSM	Number of static methods
	Method	FOUT	Number of method calls
		MLOC	Method line of code
		PAR	Number of parameters
		VG	Cyclomatic complexity
KC1		CBO	Coupling between objects
		DEPTH	Depth of inheritance
		LCOM	Lack of cohesion
		NOC	Number of children
		DOC	Dependence on an descendent
		FAN_IN	Count of calls of higher modules
		RFC	Response for a class
		WMC	Weight method per class
		loc_total	Total Line of code
		loc_blank	The number of blank lines in a module.
CM1		loc_code and loc_comments	The number of lines which contain both code and comment in a module.
KC3			
MW1		loc_executable	The number of lines of executable code.
		McCabe	
PC1		v(g)	The cyclomatic complexity of a module $v(G) = e - n + 2$
		iv(G) design complexity	The design complexity of a module.
PC3		ev(G) essential complexity	The essential complexity of a module.
PC4			
PC5		Halstead H	
		N1 num operators	The number of operators contained in a module.
		N2 num operands	The number of operands contained in a module.
		µ1 num unique operators	The number of unique operators.
		µ2 num unique operands	The number of unique operands.
		N length	
		V volume	The Halsted length metric of a module.
		L level	The Halsted volume metric of a module.
		D difficulty	The Halsted level metric of a module.
		I contentE effort	The Halsted difficulty metric of a module.
		B error_est	The Halsted effort metric of a module $E = V/L$
		T program_count	The Halsted error estimate metric of a module. T program_count The Halsted programming time metric of a module $T = E/18$.
		Miscellaneous	
		branch count	Branch count metrics
		call pairs	Number of calls to other functions in a module.
		condition count	Number of conditionals in a given module.
		decision count	Number of decision points in a given module.
		decision density	Condition_count/Decision_count.
		design density	Design density is calculated as: iv(G)/v(G).
		global data complexity	The ratio of cyclomatic complexity of a module's structure to its parameter count.

sets are very useful in defect prediction because it contains a wealth of information regarding previous software developments. According to David C. McCullough (McCullough, 1993):

History is a guide to navigate in perilous times. History is who we are and why we are the way we are.

Software Execution Information

It is composed of static (software specification information) and dynamic (run time behavior) information regarding a software system. UML diagrams such as Object diagram, sequence diagram, transition diagrams are the basic source of execution information. Besides these pre and post condition of Object's state, Method-Entry and Method-Exit are the other source of execution trace information.

Source Code Data

Source code repositories like Sourceforge.net, Google code are the basic sources of source code data. Some traditional metric extractor tools such as UC++ etc. are used to mine the value of traditional software product metrics like a line of code, cyclomatic complexity, essential complexity, etc. Feature and attribute have same meaning and are used interchangeably throughout the chapter.

Defect Data Understanding

The main task of this phase is to examine the gross properties of data and all the key attributes in the data set which can be addressed by using different statistical and visualizing test. Key analysis term includes:

- Data format analysis.
- Identify the quantity of data.
- Understanding of attributes, their meaning and values.

- Statistical analysis of each attribute.
- Check whether the attribute is appropriate for mining task.
- Detailed analysis of relevant attributes.
- Analysis of sub population characteristics of relevant attributes.

Main objectives of data understanding phase is to find the internal structure to test whether or not data contains useful and interesting information towards the mining goal. A wide range of statistical and hypothetical techniques are available for data analysis. These techniques include:

- Data distribution analysis.
- Statistical techniques for measuring central tendency (mean, median, mode, standard deviation, variance).
- Data dispersion analysis (quartile chart).
- Attributes correlation analysis.
- Attribute correlation analysis with target attribute.
- ANOVA test.
- Student T-test.
- Null hypothesis test.

Data Preprocessing

Data preprocessing is the process of data preparation for a mining task. More often data preprocessing is avoided but real data mining tasks like defect prediction, vulnerability analysis, effort estimation requires an upper hand of data preprocessing steps. In real-world scenario, data might be incomplete, ambiguous, inconsistent and noisy, which may make the result of the data mining tasks more erroneous. Data preprocessing techniques can improve the quality of data, which may further improve the accuracy and efficiency of the mining tasks. Data preprocessing steps are broadly divided into data cleaning, data transformation, data reduction. In the following sections we describe each of the terms.

Data Cleaning

Data cleaning is the process of detecting and correcting the vulnerabilities from the data sets. Data cleaning is one of the fundamental tasks of data preprocessing to ensure its correctness. For example, line of code value must not be zero for any software component. Fundamental works of data cleaning are handling missing values, data smoothing and outlier detection, etc. We can handle the missing values in the following ways:

1. Avoiding the tuples with missing values. This is usually done when the class levels of the data tuples are missing. Defect prediction is basically a supervised learning (a task of classification) due to which it is necessary to avoid the tuples with missing values to mitigate its adverse effect on the prediction results.
2. **Manual Filling:** It is a time-consuming approach for a large data set.
3. Use attribute mean value for all missing values.
4. Use attribute mean value of same class sample.
5. Use most frequently used attribute value.

1. **Data Smoothing:** This approach is used for noise reduction. The term noise denotes the variance of values in the measured variables. We can use the following techniques to mitigate the effect of noise.
2. **Binning:** In this approach attribute values are sorted in ascending order and divided into equi-width bins (buckets) then either mean value or median value or bin boundaries are used for data smoothing.
3. **Regression:** It is an approach for data smoothing. In this approach, we try to find a function which is completely suitable for data. There are two types of regression linear and multiple. In linear, a line is selected,

which considers two attributes so that one attribute can be used to find the value of another attribute. Multiple regressions are an extension of linear regression in which multidimensional surface is used for attribute value prediction.

4. **Outlier Removal:** In data set outliers are the data points which are inconsistent with the majority of data points. In statistical point of view, outliers are the measurements which pose a distance from the rest of data points. Outliers can occur in any distribution, but it is an indication of measurement error and make data heavy- tailed. Some mining approaches, which assume normal distribution of data, required outlier removal. We can use clustering, curve-fitting, hypothesis- testing for outlier detection.

Data Transformation

Data transformation is the process of making data more interpretable and easy to visualize. Data transformation is the function that maps the entire set of attribute values into a new set of values so that each attribute will get equal preference in mining task. In real-world application mining process deals with raw data which is not in a convenient form to deal with. Data transformation allows the miners to cope with this problem. Data transformation involves the followings:

1. **Normalization:** Attribute normalization is the process of scaling its values so that they fall within a small specified range, such as 0.0 to 1.0. It is a useful process for classification algorithms involving neural networks, or distance measurements such as nearest-neighbour classification and clustering. In neural network based classification, normalization of attribute value will speed up the training process. In initial data collecting phase, if variables are measured in different scale or standard devia-

tions of measured variables varies than one variable may dominate the others. So data normalization should be applied separately on each variable to give equal preference to all variables. Data normalization can be done in following ways:

a.   **MIN-MAX Normalization:** It performs a linear transformation on the original data values. Min-max normalization preserves the initial relationships of the original data values in the newly generated ones.

b.   **Z-Score Normalization:** In Z-core normalization, an attribute value is normalized using mean and standard deviation of attribute values.

c.   **Normalization by Decimal Scaling:** In this normalization, a value is normalized by moving the decimal point. The number of decimal points, moved depends on the number of absolute values associated with the attributes.

2.   **Approaching Normal Distribution:** Sometimes normal data distribution is essential in several data mining applications such as defect prediction. To test the normality data skewness chart, kurtosis Test, data frequency histogram and probability Chart can be used. Some basic transformation techniques are used for normal transformation of data such as:

a.   **Square Root Transformation:** It can be used in the case where the data distribution differs moderately from normal distribution.

b.   **Log Transformation:** In case where the data distribution differs substantially from normal distribution then log transformation can be used.

c.   **Inverse Transformation:** In case where the data distribution severely differs from normal distribution inverse transformation is applicable.

Data Reduction

Data mining is a complex process which becomes nearly impractical when it is applied on a huge amount of data. Different data reduction algorithms and techniques can be useful for acquiring a reduced image of the data set that is much smaller in volume and strongly maintains the initial characteristics such as data integrity, correlation, normal distribution, etc. of the original data. In other words, mining on the reduced data set should be more practical and produce efficient (or almost the same) analytical results. Data reduction includes different feature sub-set selection techniques and data sampling methods. In subsequent section, we will discuss briefly some of these problems and their solutions.

1.   **Feature Subset Selection:** In an abstract way, a feature represents a low-level measurement extracted from the data. For a software product, line of code, number of operands and operator, represents the attributes or features. Due to the high-throughput technologies, large data sets with an unprecedented number of features are now routinely produced, which is used in different data mining techniques. It makes the feature sub-set selection an important task in a wide range of scientific disciplines. Accordingly, building a defect prediction model with a high number of attributes becomes a very complex task. It becomes more tedious and requires more consideration when attributes are correlated. It is not an easy task even for a simple classifier to handle a large amount of data set. The main goal of attribute selection is to find a set of attributes, which have fewer numbers of attributes in comparison to original data set, and the new set posses all the data integrity of the original data set. Mathematically, feature subset selection can be stated as follows: given the p-dimensional set of attributes $A=(A_1, A_2, A_3, ..., A_p)$, find

a lower dimensional set $S=(S_1, S_2 \ldots \ldots S_n)$ with n<p that captures the characteristics of original data set. The components of S are sometimes called the hidden components. Different sub-set selection techniques that can be used in attribute selection for defect data set are:

a. **Principal Component Analysis:** Principal Component Analysis (PCA) (Pearson, 1901), linear dimension reduction technique, is a technique that is used to reduce the dimensionality (cardinality of the attribute set) of a data set from p to n, where n < p. At the same time newly extracted data set should have as much variation of the original data as possible. In PCA, a transformation of the data to a new set of coordinates or variable that are a linear combination of the original variables is taking place. In PCA, newly extracted variables are known as principal components. In addition, principal components of the new space are uncorrelated. The basic idea is that we can gain information and understanding of the data by looking at the features in the new space. It is the best dimensionality reduction technique, in the mean-square error sense. It is a second-order covariance based technique. It is also known as singular value decomposition (SVD) in different scientific disciplines. PCA tries to reduce the dimensionality of the data by finding a few orthogonal linear combinations (the PCs) of the original variables with the largest variance. The first principal component (PC) s1 of reduced data set is the linear combination with the largest variance. The second PC is the linear combination of the second largest variance and orthogonal to the first PC and so on. In real-world applications only first few PCs are required to explain most of the variance, so that rest can be discarded without or with minimal information loss. Different techniques like cumulative percentage of variance explained, screw plot, the broken stick and size of variance are used to decide how much number of PCs should be kept for data mining process.

b. **Information Gain:** In Information Gain method, each attribute of the original data set are ranked according to their information gain score in ascending order. This measurement is based on the Claude Shannon work on information theory. The information gain of an attribute A w.r.t class C is the minimization of uncertainty about the value of C when value of A is already known. For any class set C $(c_1 \ldots c_k)$ and attribute set A $(A_1 \ldots A_n)$ one calculates the information gain using following equations(Kamber,2006):

$$Infogain\left(A\right) = H\left(C\right) - H\left(C \mid A\right) \tag{1}$$

$$H\left(C\right) = -\sum_{i=1}^{n} P\left(C = C_i\right) log_2\left(P\left(C = C_i\right)\right) \tag{2}$$

$$H\left(C,A\right) = -\sum_{i=1}^{n} P\left(A = a_i\right) H\left(C \mid A = a_i\right) \tag{3}$$

c. **Correlation – Coefficient:** Some supervised learning algorithm such as Naive Bayes(NB) classification assumed class conditional independence in data set, which motivates to use uncorrelated attributes in a data mining process which is also true in the defect prediction process. In correlation- coefficient based attribute selection, the covariance between attributes is divided by the standard deviation of each variable using the following Equation 4. The set of attributes with minimum correlation- coefficients are used for data mining process and rest can be ignored.

$$\rho_{x,y} = \frac{\text{cov}(x,y)}{\sigma_x \sigma_y} \qquad (4)$$

2. **Stepwise Forward Selection:** This process starts with a null set. At each step one attribute, which has the maximum likelihood of being the best (according to some user criterion) from the others is added to the null set. This process is continued until some user defined criterion such as maximum accuracy is achieved.

3. **Stepwise Backward Elimination:** It follows the reverse approach of Stepwise forward selection. This process starts with a full set of attributes and in each subsequent step, the worst attribute from the set is discarded.

The above two approaches are time consuming when the cardinality of defect data set is too high. To solve this problem one can use a combination of the above two approaches.

4. **Data Sampling:** Sampling works in different direction to achieve a compact set of data. Instead of working on a number of attributes, it works on the number of tuples. In sampling, original data set is represented by reduced set of random data tuples. An advantage of sampling method is that its complexity depends on sample size instead of original data set size. Sampling can be done in the following ways:

a. **Random Sampling:** In random sampling, s samples (tuples) of data are drawn from the data set of n tuples in a random manner where s<n. The selection probability of each tuple is 1/n. In other words each tuple is equally likely to be sampled. Random sampling has two versions.

i. Sampling with replacement, in which sampled tuple will be replaced in the original data set to resample it again.

ii. Sampling without replacement, in which sampled tuple will not be replaced in original data.

b. **Cluster Sampling:** In cluster sampling, a data set D is divided into M mutually disjoints clusters, from this set; s clusters are obtained in a random manner. For example, tuples in a database are usually retrieved as a page at a time, so each page can be considered as a cluster.

c. **Stratified Sampling:** This method is more appropriate for defect prediction applications. In stratified sampling, data tuples are divided into mutually disjoint collection known as strata. The sampling is done by obtaining data tuples from each strata. In defect prediction application, strata represent the class variable. The basic advantage of Stratified sampling is that the class distribution of original data set is also followed in sampled data set.

5. **Class Imbalance Problem:** The class imbalance problem is a hot topic of machine learning and recognized by several scientific applications. In such a problem, most of the instances of the data are labeled as of one class (called majority class), while very few examples are labeled as of the other class (called minority class), usually considered to be a more important class in prediction.

Defect prediction is, basically, a binary classification problem in which most of the instances are labeled as non-buggy class whereas the goal of prediction is to detect buggy instances. In this scenario, a prediction result of standard machine learning algorithms such as naïve bayes, support vector machine, decision tree induction, etc. tend to be overwhelmed by the majority class and ignore the minority class since traditional classifiers looking for high accuracy over a full range of instances. To overcome the difficulty of learning associated with class imbalance data different sampling techniques are available:

a.   **Under Sampling:** In under sampling, balance class distribution is achieved by eliminating some majority class instances. The main disadvantage of this method is information loss because it leads to discard some potentially valuable instances that may be a cause of decreased accuracy. Several heuristic based under-sampling methods such as nearest neighbor can be used to reduce the information loss during under sampling.

b.   **Over Sampling:** Over Sampling is non-heuristic random replication of minority class instances to achieve balance class distribution. There are two shortcomings associated with over sampling method. 1 – Over Fitting and 2- Delay of learning process. Heuristics based over sampling methods such as SMOTE can be used to resolve these problems. SMOTE is synthetic minority over-sampling technique(Nitesh, 2002) in which over sampling is done by creating "synthetic" minority class instances rather than replicating them. SMOTE works on "feature space" rather than "data Space." The over-sampled of minority class is done by

introducing synthetic examples along with the line segment joining any or all K minority class nearest neighbors for each minority class example. The value of K depends on the ratio of the class distribution.

c.   **Cost Sensitive Learning:** Cost sensitive learning (CSL) is another way of dealing with class imbalance data set. In cost sensitive learning a cost matrix is prepared where the average cost of misclassification is stored where c_{ij} denotes the cost of misclassification of an item belongs to class i to class j. In cost matrix diagonal elements are set to zero, meaning that correct classification has no cost. The main idea behind CSL is to minimize the misclassification cost which can be achieved by choosing the class with minimum cost.

Pattern Mining

Pattern mining is a data mining method that basically works towards finding the interesting patterns in data. In defect prediction context, pattern denotes the rules which relate the data with class variable and are basically used for classification. There are several machine learning algorithms are available, some of them are described in subsequent sections.

1.   **Decision Tree Induction:** Decision tree learner such as C4.5 (Quinlan,1993) is a rooted tree-like structure where each internal node represents a test on a feature value, and a leaf node represents the class variables. The output of the decision tree induction is a single branch of satisfied test which ends on a leaf node. In decision tree induction, a splitting criterion is used to split a data set on attribute values in order to separate the possible predictions. It uses the information

theory concepts like information gain, gini index and gain ratio to assess candidate splitting ability (information gain). The best feature to split is one that has maximum information gain. Each attribute splitting trims down the set of instances (the actual data). This process is continued until either all instances belong to the same class or no other attributes remain available for splitting. For example, with three input variable a, b, and c, a might be chosen to split which splits the input space into two parts. Each of this set can be further divided into two sets at some threshold on b or c. This process is continued many times.

2. **Bayesian Classifier:** Bayesian classifiers are the statistical classifiers based on bayes posterior probability theorem and perform the classification by predicting the class membership probability of a given data instance. Naive Bayes (NB) (George and Langley, 1995), and Bayesian Belief Network (BBN) (Russel,1995) are two examples of Bayesian classifiers. NB classifier uses the statistical combination of attribute space to predict the class for a given instance. The word naïve is associated with the NB because it assumes the class condition independence; meaning all the features are statistically independent in the data set. Second classifier, BBN is a probabilistic graphical model consisting of a set of random variables (feature) and their respective conditional dependencies. It creates the compact probabilistic network which captures the current and past probabilistic relationship between variables. BBN model work well where the available information are vague, incomplete, conflicting and uncertain. In BBN, current state of a variable A is described by conditional probability table, which contains the conditional distribution $P(A|$ Parent $(A))$, where Parents(A) represents the parents of variable A.

3. **Genetic Programming:** Genetic Programming (GP) (Mishra, 2011,Jan-June; Koza, 1992) ; a branch of genetic algorithm, is a search algorithm based on the mechanics of biological evolution. This algorithm is proposed by John R. Koza. It starts with high-level of statement of what to do and automatically creates a computer program to solve the problem. It is a domain-independent method that breeds a computer program using Darwinian evolution principles (survival of the fittest) for a problem instance. The process of discovering new computer programs is based on natural occurring operations of genetic algorithm like reproduction, mutation, crossover and gene deletion. GP needs five preparatory steps to solve a problem which are specified by the user. These steps are terminal set selection, function set selection, fitness measure selection, and certain parameter selection for controlling the run and termination criteria.

4. **Nearest Neighbor Method:** It is a very straightforward method: For classification of an instance x, we test k closest training data point of x and assign the instance to the class that has a majority of points among these k points. The term close refers to a distance of points corresponding to p dimensional input space. We can use distance measures such as Euclidean distance, Manhattan distance or Mahalanobis distance to test the closest property.

5. **Support Vector Machine:** Support vector machines (SVM)(Chaves, 2005) are based on the concept of decision planes which defines the decision boundaries. SVM constructs an N- dimensional hyper-plane which defines decision boundaries between dissimilar objects. This decision plane may be a line for linear SVM or a hyper plane for non linear SVM. The fundamental of SVM modeling is to train SVM to get optimistic hyperplane which maximize the distance

between the instances of different classes. Mathematically, SVM can be defined as:

$$u = \sum_i \alpha_i \, y_k k\left(x_i, x\right) - b \, . \qquad (5)$$

Here u is the output of SVM, K stands for kernel function, $y_i \in \left(-1, +1\right)$ represent the class (buggy or nonbuggy) α_i is lagrangian multiplier and b is the bias constant. An input pattern classified according to the value of u.

$$X = \begin{cases} +1 \ \ if \ \ u > 0 \\ -1 \ \ if \, u < 0 \end{cases}$$

6. **Classification Based On Association:** Associative classification mines the rules of the form Ant => Con, where antecedent (Ant) is the collection of items (features) and consequent (Con) denotes the class level. Rules that satisfy the minimum support threshold are known as frequent rules, where minimum support denotes the percentage of instances which have antecedent and belongs to the class Con. Confidence is another criteria for rule selection which is measuring the accuracy level of that rule. Confidence measures the number of samples that contain the Ant part and have the class label Con. Association based classification is performed in two steps. In the first step, frequent and accurate association rules, also known as pattern rules, are extracted using association rule mining algorithms such as Apriori (Agrawal,1994). Second step is organizing and optimizing step in which extracted rules are organized according to their respective support and confidence than any optimization algorithm such as Ant Colony Optimization or Genetic Algorithm can be applied to extract more compact set of rules for classification.

7. **Hybrid Approach:** A hybrid combination of different learning algorithms such as SVM, Fuzzy logic provides a fruitful way for defect prediction which combines the advantages of different classifiers to enhance the predictive ability of the resulted one. One such approach in Support Vector Machine Based Fuzzy Classification optimize with Genetic algorithm (Mishra, 2011, December). This model is generated through three phases. Initially, the first set of fuzzy IF-THEN rules is obtained through SVM training. Attribute values of each support vectors combined with AND (connective) treated as antecedent part and class value work as consequent part of the rule; which is used for classification. In this model, SVM is basically used to extract the more complicated data points which are used for generating a decision hyperplane in SVM based classification. Second set of rules is generated by combining the first set based on strength of firing signals of support vectors using Gaussian kernel. The main advantage of this method is that, it guarantees that the number of final fuzzy IF THEN rules is not more than the number of support vectors in the trained SVM. Genetic algorithm is applied for rule set optimization which simultaneously enhances or maintains the performance of the model and minimizes the number of rules used for classification.

Result Measurements

The performance of defect prediction model is typically evaluated using a confusion matrix as illustrated in Figure 4. The columns of the confusion matrix represent the predicted class where rows denote the actual class labels. There are four types of results possible in confusion matrix, TN is the number of negative examples correctly classified, FP is the number of negative examples incorrectly

Figure 4. Confusion matrix

	Predictive Negatives	Predictive Positive
Actual Negatives	TN	FP
Actual Positives	FN	TP

classified, FN is the of positive examples incorrectly classified and TP is number of positive examples correctly classified.

1. **Accuracy:** It is the probability of correctly predicted positive and negative items and total number of items under consideration. In defective prediction phenomenon where the class distribution is highly Imbalance, alone Accuracy is not a suitable criteria for result assessment. Along with accuracy some more assessment criteria are needed for true assessment of prediction results.

$$\text{Accuracy} = \frac{TP + TN}{TP + FN + FP + TN} \quad (6)$$

2. **Sensitivity:** It is a proportion of actual positive, which are predictive positive .It is also known as Recall and Probability of Detection (PD).

$$\text{Sensitivity} = \frac{TP}{TP + FN}. \quad (7)$$

3. **Specificity:** It is the ratio of actual negative, which are predicted negative and can be calculated by using the confusion matrix. It works as a recall for the opposite class.

$$\text{Specificity} = \frac{TN}{TN + FP} \quad (8)$$

4. **Precision:** Precision is the measurement that works on predicted values. It is the proportion of predicted positive, which are actual positive.

$$\text{Precision} = \frac{TP}{TP + FP}. \quad (9)$$

5. **Probability of False Alarm:** It denotes the ratio between the number of non buggy files incorrectly classified and total number of non buggy files.

6. **Balance Classification Rate:** BCR is the average value of Sensitivity (proportion of actual positives which are predicted positives) and Specificity (proportion of actual negatives which are predicted negatives).

Advances in Defect Prediction

A typical defect prediction research involves the analysis of bug database that contains fault information along with software quality attributes to build a defect prediction model, which relates the fault proneness of a module with software measurements. Several studies have been carried out for defect prediction models. In this section we will discuss some of them.

Menzis (Menzies, 2007)applied three machine learning algorithms on eight MDP data sets and concluded that NB with log data filtering outperformed other classifiers.They achieved 71% probability of detection and 25% false alarm rate. Zimmermann (Zimmermann, 2007) predict defects by using data mining techniques, and their study shows that complexity of code increases the defect proneness. Pan, Kim, Whitehead (Pan, 2006) worked on bug classification and instead of using static code attributes, they used program slicing metric of modules. Bose and Srinivasan (Bose, 2005) used sequence of system calls and SVM to characterize the program execution. Koru and Liu (Koru,2005) conducted a research to find out the impact of module size in bug prediction and concluded that small components (software modules) give poor defect prediction results in comparison to large components. In (Mishra, 2011) genetic programming is used for defect prediction and concludes that genetic programming work well without any data preprocessing steps. A hybrid combination of different learning algorithms(SVM, Fuzzy logic, Genetic algotithm) (Mishra, 2011, December) is applied for bug prediction an achieved 78.6% PD on eclipse bug data set. In (Mishra, Sep 2011) a study is conducted to test the impact of attribute selection on defect prediction and conclude that a combination of l attribute selection and machine learning will improve the efficiency of prediction process.

In order to predict defect proneness information as early as possible, some studies have been conducted using requirements metrics (Jing, 2007) which shows the importance of early defect prediction. Basili (Basili, 1996) investigates the role of OO metrics in defect prediction. A survey conducted by E. Subramanyam (Subramanyam, 2003) showed that object oriented metrics are more significantly related to the fault proneness. Binkly (Binkley,1998) developed a coupling dependency metrics for predicting run time failures. Nagappan's (Nagappan,2006) study showed that the relation between the interdependency and intra dependency of components can predict the post-release defects. Xing (Xing, 2005) used support vector machines (SVM) for quality prediction using design and static code metrics and achieved up to 90% correct classification rate. Later, a comparative study of design and code metrics suggests that the combination of design metrics and static code metrics can help to develop a better defect prediction model(Jing,2008). However, it requires waiting until the development phase is completed, which is too late for prediction process. In (Yang, 2007) attempts have been made to find some useful rules in early phase of SDLC for defect proneness and reliability prediction. Yang (Yang, 2007) study suggests the use of fuzzy self-adaptation learning control network (FALCON) for quality prediction.

SOFTWARE CLONES

In terms of software engineering, redundancy is the replication of important and critical software components, modules, functions, data or more precisely a code fragment to increase the reliability of the system. In literature, software system is represented as a logical composition of data and code which executes on data to produce interesting and valuable results from the user's point of view. In terms of data, redundancy has a clear notation which leads to several level of data normalization. However, for the code base (software programs) a clear notation of redundancy has not been developed. In literature redundant code are also known as code clones, which implies that one code fragment is derived from another one. A clone may be considered as the synonym of duplicate. According to the dictionary of Merriam – "A clone is one that appears to be a copy of original one."

According to the Ira Baxter's point of view

Clones are segments of code that are similar according to some definition of similarity (Ira Baxter, 2002)

Kamiya define the clones as a portion of source code which are "identical" or "similar" to each other (Kamiya,2002).

These definitions are based on notation of similarity. It can be based on either syntax or semantics or both. In essence, two code fragments can be considered as a clone if they follow the same pattern either in form of logic (semantic) or text (syntactic).

Semantic similarity is related with the observational behavior of the system. For two code fragments A and B, A is a semantic clone of another code fragment B if B subsumed the functionality of A. In other words, two code fragments are semantically similar with each other if both code fragments have similar functionality with same pre and post conditions where pre and post conditions

Figure 5. An example of code clones

```
1 int sum = 0 ;
2
3 void addition (Iterator   iter1 ) {
4   for ( item = first ( iter1 ) ; has more (iter1) ; item = next (iter1)
) {
5             sum = sum + value ( item ) ;
6           }
7       }
8     int summation (Iterator   iter2 ) {
9     int sum = 0 ;
10 for ( item = first (iter2 ) ; has more (iter2 ) ; item = next (iter2 )
) {
11             sum = sum + value ( item ) ;
12           }
13     }
```

are the input and output patterns. An example of code clones in shown in Figure 5.

According to the earlier discussion, software clones are the result of copy-paste activities. Sometimes such types of activities are very useful in software development. It reduces the programming effort and time as developers are reused an existing fragment of the source code rather than rewriting similar code from scratch. Sometimes, clones are slightly modified to adapt the new environment and purpose. This practice is common, especially in device drivers of the operating systems where the algorithms are similar(Zhenmin,2006). However, it is also believed that software clones make the software system hard to maintain and increases the maintenance cost. It may adversely affect the software systems quality, especially their maintainability and comprehensibility (Giesecke,2006; Giesecke2003). Code cloning is not only related with escalation of maintenance costs but also adversely affects the software reliability as inconsistent code changes in duplicate code can lead to unexpected software failure. Several previous studies(Baker,1995; Kontogiannis,1996; have shown that about 5% to 20% of the software systems contain duplicated code, which is due to the use of the same code in different parts, with or without modification. Due to the adverse effect on maintenance, it is required to detect the clones.

In software development industries, clones are considered as severe software related problem. It is also considered as one of the bad smells of a software system. The presence of clones may not always affect the actual functionality, but without the proper detection further development may become more expensive as well as problematic. It is also believed that software clones have a negative impact on evolution (Laguae,1997). So during the software development it is quite beneficial to detect and remove software clones and try to prevent their introduction by constantly monitoring the source code.

Reasons for Code Cloning

Code cloning does not have to be auto generated phenomenon. Cloning occurs due to the environmental needs, programmer's abilities and programming language limitations. Besides these, code duplication by accident is also a cause of software cloning. The basic reason of cloning can be categorized in the following categories:

- Software development approaches.
- To ease the maintenance process.
- Conquer the programming language limitations.
- Cloning by accident.

Software development strategies may cause software clones. Reusing of the code logic, software architecture and software design strategies are the root cause of software cloning. Copy - paste is the simplest form of software cloning. To minimize the development time sometimes developers use the code cloning as an integral part of implementation strategy. Kasper (Kapser, 2006) discovered the cloning patterns named Forking and Templating in a large software system where these strategies were consequently, used at the implementation level.

Forking process bootstraps the development of similar functionality. Fundamental reason behind forking is "code evolution always takes a separate path, independent of the original one and so there may not be any side effect of the code changes on different cloned parts." On the other hand, Templating is the method of copying the behavior or functionality of the existing working code without considering their appropriate abstraction mechanics. It is found very often in reusable libraries, which follow a fixed protocol for execution.

Customization is another type of development approach, which is applied when the existing copied code does not satisfy the environmental needs. In this case existing code is tailored to cope with this problem.

Design patterns are another cause of code cloning. Design patterns basically provide the logic of interaction between program components. So whenever a developer uses a design pattern in development he/she unwillingly and unknowingly will produce software clones.

Besides these, cloning sometimes provides some maintenance benefits, which incur the use of cloning strategy. While implementing a new code or logic to upgrade an existing functionality of a working system there always is a risk involved like erroneous working and high cost of testing. To mitigate these types of risk involved in development, developers are used to working with existing modules, which are well tested and correctly working.

Clone Classifications

Software clone categorization is based on the type of copy –paste strategies. Widely, software clones can be classified into the following categories:

1. **TYPE I CLONES:** Type I clones are the exact copied parts of the program without any modification. In the copied part, alignment of white spaces and comments are ignored while code comparison.
2. **TYPE II CLONES:** Type II clones are the identical copy of the source code except the identifier's and function's names.
3. **TYPE III CLONES:** It is a further modified part of the source code where some extra modification such as changes in statements order, addition and deletion of statements are applied.

There is another type of software clones, which is based on the functionalities of two code fragments. If the functionalities of two code fragments are same, we call them semantic clones and can be referred as type IV clones.

4. **TYPE IV CLONES:** If two or more code fragments perform the same functionality but follow different implementation strategies.

The above classification of clones is very simple and rough. Balazinska (Balazinska.2000) introduced a more advanced and rigorous classification strategy for function clones. This classification strategy provides a helpful hand in clone removal strategy selection. For instance, Template Method (a behavioral design pattern) may be used to point out the differences in the types used in code fragments(Balazinska.2000). Furthermore, Balazinska et al. also indicates that different types of risks are associated with each class level in clone removal strategy.

A more elaborated classification strategy is proposed by Kasper (Kapser, 2003), which is based on the attributes such as location and

Figure 6. Clone taxonomy of Kasper and Godfrey

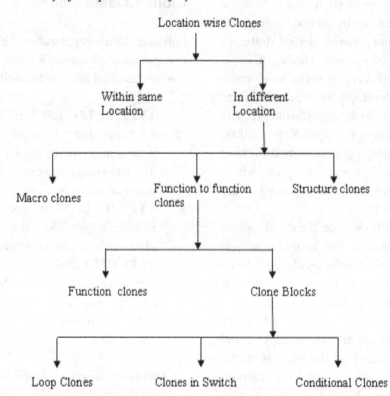

functionalities and illustrated in Figure 6. In their strategy, first level indicates the clone distance which is, where the clones are situated (within the same file or in different files). An argument can be made (although there is no empirical study on this hypothesis) that clones scattered in different files are more problematic than those scattered within the same file as it is more likely to ignore the former ones when it comes to consistent code changes. The second-level decision worked to distinguish the syntactic units which are copied. The degree of similarity is indicated by the third level of decision, and the fourth level is used to sort out the irrelevant or spurious clones.

Kontogiannis (Kontogiannis,1996) classified the clones into four basic types, which are based on types of duplication operations:

1. Exact clones where there is one to one correspondence on each nonbank character of fragment f1 to fragment *f2*.
2. Exact clones with systematically substituted identifiers and data types.
3. Clones with modified statements and expressions.
4. Clones where the code is modified (statements and expressions have been either deleted or inserted.

These types are quite similar (but not the same as) to the types we have discussed earlier.

Clone Detection

Duplicated code is a phenomenon that occurs frequently in large systems. So basic problem associated with code clones are:

- If one repairs a bug in a system with duplicated code, all possible duplications of that bug must be checked.
- Code duplication increases the size of the code, extending to compile time and expanding the size of the executable.
- Code duplication often indicates design problems like missing inheritance or missing procedural abstraction. In turn, such a lack of abstraction hampers the addition of functionality.

While there is an ongoing debate on whether remove clones or avoid them, it is required to know where the clones are in the system. Manual clone detection is infeasible and becomes a very tricky task when applied on large systems; hence, an automated clone detection strategy is required. An abstract clone detection approach is shown in Figure 7. In the following sections; we will describe some of the clone detection techniques:

Figure 7. Step by step clone detection process

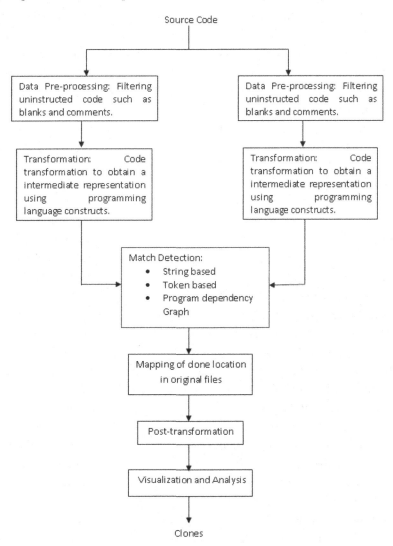

1. **String Based:** String matching techniques are based on basic string transformation and comparison algorithms, due to which it becomes a language independent ones. There are several different strings based approaches, which are based on different string comparison algorithms. Line by line signature comparison is one technique to identify matching substrings. Line matching comes in two variants and uses general string manipulation techniques (Ducasse,1999).

    a. **Simple Line Matching:** In simple line matching technique minor string transformations such as string manipulations (removal of empty lines and white spaces) are applied. In this technique only a slight knowledge of language constructs is required. In comparison phase, all lines are compared with each other using a string-matching algorithm which results in a large search space. We can use hashing to reduce the search space. In this case first of all, all the lines are hashed into n buckets than the bucket wise line by line comparison is performed to detect the similarities between the lines.

    b. **Parameterized Line Matching:** It is another variant of line matching, which detects both identical as well as similar code fragments. Fundamental behind this technique is that identifier–names and literals (we can call them changing parameters) are likely to be changed during the cloning of a code fragment. Therefore, fragments with different identifier's names are allowed. To detect these types of clones some extension of transformation such as substitution (replacing all identifiers and literals with one, common identifier symbol like"$") are required. With this substitution, comparison becomes independent of the parameters, and we

    can detect both identical as well as similar code fragments.

    c. **Substring Matching:** It is one approach to implement string matching in large bodies of source. This approach is summarized as follows:

        i. **Text-to-Text Source Transformation:** Remove all white space characters such as blank, tab, carriage return, line feed except the line separator, replace the sequence of white space with a single blank, remove comments, identifier replacing with common character such as $.

        ii. **Generation of Candidate Substrings:** The second phase is substring generation for matching. Identifying the average length of string (number of character or number of lines) is an important parameter to control the sub string generation.

        iii. **Identification of Raw Substring Matches:** This is a straightforward sorting of a file containing the content of the substring and an indication of its origin.

        iv. **Information-Preserving Simplification of Match Database:** The raw substrings used for matching purposes have more or less the same length and overlap. Raw matches will represent matches larger than the substring. To simplify the database of matches and facilitate later processing, it is important to replace the raw substring and match information by a new minimal set of non-overlapping substrings and matches that preserves the information obtained in matching phase.

v. **Data Reduction:** Another way of looking at a set of matches on non-overlapping substrings is an association between substring content sequence of characters and a set of places such that set of places collectively constitutes the total source. Since each place is an offset in a file, this information can be naturally reduced to an association between substring content and a set of files in which it occurs. For each subset of files one can then total the lengths of substring contents that occur in exactly that set of files.

vi. **Presentation of Files Clusters and Multi-File Matches:** If one considers a graph whose nodes are files and where arcs have been added whenever a match involves a set of files containing the given pair, then one can define the clusters of files corresponding to the connected components of this graph. Finally, a report is produced that groups the associations by cluster.

Phases II and III are information collecting phases, IV is an information-preserving transformation, V is an aggregation and simplification phase, and VI present's results in a useful form. Phase I provides greater sensitivity for particular types of input.

2. **Token Based:** In token based approach (Baker,1995), some more sophisticated transformations are used by constructing a token stream from the source code using the lexical analyzer. These tokens are used for comparison to detect the clones in the source code. These token sequences are compared efficiently through a suffix tree. In the first step, a lexical analyzer pass over the source text to transform the identifiers and literals in parameter symbols, while the typographical structure of each line is encoded in a non-parameter symbol known as p-string. After the lexical analysis, a data structure called a parameterize suffix tree (p-suffix tree) is built for the p-string. A p-suffix tree is a generalization of the suffix tree data structure which contains the prev()-encoding of every suffix of a P-string. Two strings are parameterized matched if one can be transformed into the other by applying a one-to-one mapping by renaming the parameter symbols. At last maximal path in the p-suffix tree is searched that are longer than a predefined character length to identify the clones.

3. **Metric Comparison:** In this approach, a feature list of source code is measured and source code is compared based on their respective metric values. Merlo et al. gather different metrics for code fragments for this purpose. An allowable distance (for instance, Euclidean distance) for these metric vectors can be used as a hint for similar code.

4. **Abstract Syntax Trees (AST) Based Approach:** In AST based approach a syntax tree is generated using lexical analyzer (such as Lex) and syntax tree generator (Yacc). After that, three levels of comparison are performed for clone detection. In the first level, sub-tree clones are detected by comparing every sub-tree to every other sub-tree for equality. In the second level, a sequence detection algorithm is used to detect variable-size sequences of sub-tree clones, and is used essentially to detect statement and declaration sequence clones. In the third level of detection, a more complex, near-miss clone are detected by attempting to generalize combinations of other clones.

5. **Program Dependency Graph Based Approach:** String based techniques; token-based techniques and syntax-based

techniques depend upon the sequence of the statements in the program and perform well in many real-life scenarios. However, If programmers modify the order of the statements in the copied code (for instance, to camouflage plagiarism) or templating of code is performed, where the basic logic of the program is reused and then certain pieces are adjusted to fulfil the environmental need, the copied code will not be found. In these changes, data dependency and control dependency of the program remain unchanged. A program dependency graph is a representation of a program that represents only the control and data dependency among the statements. Clones may be identified as isomorphic sub-graphs in a program dependency graph (Koschk, 2007).

EXPERIMENTAL STUDY

In this section we provide two experimental studies to understand the process of defect prediction and clone detection.

1. **Defect Prediction:** For this purpose we used a hybrid approach (Mishra, 2011) in which support vector machine is combined with fuzzy logic and genetic algorithm to detect the fault proneness of eclipse modules of version 2.0. In this approach prediction model is generated through three phases. Initially, the first set of fuzzy IF-THEN rules is obtained through SVM training. Attribute values of each support vectors combined with AND (connective) treated as antecedent part and class value work as consequent part of the rule; which is used for classification. The second set of rules is generated by combining the first set based on strength of firing signals of

support vectors using Gaussian kernel. The main advantage of this method is that, it guarantees that the number of final fuzzy IF THEN rules is not more than the number of support vectors in the trained SVM. Genetic algorithm is applied for rule set optimization which simultaneously enhances or maintains the performance of the model and minimizing the number of rules used for classification. In other words, the optimization is performed while considering both the minimization of the number of the extracted fuzzy rules and the maximization of the performance of the fuzzy classification system, i.e., the number of correctly classified training patterns with the less fuzzy rules. Basically the model works as zero order "Sugeno" type fuzzy inference system

a. Data sampling is done using stratified sampling. Partition the selected data set in training and testing set maintaining the same ratio of both classes in each set.

b. Normalize the test and train dataset such that they have zero mean and unit variance.

c. Perform SVM classification on training data set using the box constraint value as per number of rules desired and 'rbf' kernel function.

d. Write the if than else rule for each support vector like Rule Rq: If X1 is Vq1 and ... and Xm is Vqm then class of X = Class of V.

e. Calculate the membership degree of each feature of a data point using Gaussian Membership function,

f. Calculate the firing strength for each rule using multiplication T-norm operation.

g. Assess the performance of rule set using accuracy, precision and recall.

h.   Apply Genetic algorithm for rule set optimization by using fitness evolution function.

When this model is applied on defect data set of eclipse 2.0 version, we got 78.6% recall and 34% false alarm rate. Which indicate that, of the overall defective module we can detect nearly 78% defective modules, which is reasonably good on this data set.

2.   **Clone Detection:** KClone(Yue, 2009) is a Clone Detection algorithm that incorporates a novel combination of lexical and local dependence analysis to achieve precision, while retaining speed. It combines the software statements to find clones. Basically it performs the clone detection in three phases:

   a.   Transform the code into an internal representation.
   b.   Detect parts that denote clone pairs.
   c.   Aggregate clone pairs into clone classes.

In step 1 it filters out uninteresting statements and then extracts necessary "light-weight" information from the remaining statements(comments blank lines, C/C++ preprocessor directives (#include) and in Java the directives "import" and "package"). The Step 2 is divided into two phases: In phase 1 it identifies BCPs (basic clone pairs) created by simple copy-and-paste operations. It uses the suffix tree comparison algorithm. If two statements have the same suffix tree then they form a BCP. Phase 2 extends the results of Phase 1 to detect larger Type-1 and 2 clones as well as Type-3 clones. Phase 2 uses the control and data links to efficiently bypass potentially interjected or modified code. In this phase each BCP and repeatedly extends the fragments that make up the BCP using one of six extension functions until no functions can be applied to BCPs.

```
Extend-backwards
        Extend-forwards,
        Extend-control-back,
        Extend-control-forward,
        Extend-databack,
        Extend-data-forward
```

Extension terminates in one of three situations: the (structure of the) linked-to statements are not equal, the linked-to statements are more than a specified distance away from the current clone, or when the 'window of text' under consideration reaches the start or end of its file. Two small piece of source code detected as code clones by KClone in WelTab c program are shown below in Box 1.

When KClone is applied to this example, it first identifies as a BCP from lines 1 to 5 of both code fragments. This BCP is expanded to cover Lines 1 to 9 by the function extend-forward which stops because the two Lines numbered 10 in the two fragments are not equal. Next, the function extend-control forward identifies, through the control-link, that Line 11 of Fragment A matches Line 12 of Fragment B. After extending the clone pair to include these two statements, extend-forward adds

Box 1.

1. if (buffer[0] != '1'	1. if (buffer[0] != '1'
2. && buffer[0] != ' '	2. && buffer[0] != ' '
3. && buffer[0] != '0'	3. && buffer[0] != '0'
4. && buffer[0] != '+') f	4. && buffer[0] != '+') f
5. if (nread != 1) printf("nn");	5. if (nread != 1) printf("nn");
6. printf("%s",buffer);	6. printf("%s",buffer);
7. nwrite++;	7. nwrite++;
8. };	8. };
9. if (buffer[0] == '1')	9. if (buffer[0] == '1')f
10. printf("nf ");	10. if (nread != 1) printf("nf
11. if (buffer[0] == ' ') f	");
12. if (nread != 1)	11. };
printf("nn");	12. if (buffer[0] == ' ') f
Code segment A	Code segment B

Line 12 of A and Line 13 of B. At this point, the expansion stops. Note that in this example, even if the control-links are ignored, the extension would still have uncovered that Lines 11-12 of A match Lines 12-13 of B through the data-link for variable buffer. After dependence analysis the third and final step aggregates clone pairs into clone classes. This can be done in several ways. KClone uses transitive paring to group clones together: if code Fragments A and B form a clone pair and code Fragments B and C also form a clone pair, then A, B, and C are placed in the same clone class.

CONCLUSION

In this chapter we discussed the important problems of bug prediction in software using various data mining methods. Various stages in the data mining process were presented and their use in learning a bug predictor based on historical software repositories like NASA MDP, PROMISE DATA REPOSITORIES, BUG PREDICTION DATASET etc was described. To enhance the bug classifier design various pre processing techniques like data cleaning, smoothing, outlier removal, normalization, and feature set selection are necessary. Along with these, a few classifier designs were discussed. In the end code clones, their types and detection methods were presented. It is hoped that the information contained in this chapter will be useful to both practicing engineers and researchers in their quest for a rational and effective software testing strategy.

FUTURE DIRECTIONS

Regardless of the availability of a number of algorithms and tools, there is still no solid definition of code clones. The reason behind this is that, each clone inherently carries some values about engineering tradeoffs- weather these clones are potentially worthwhile to factor out and remove.

A better definition would allow meaningful comparisons of detection approaches to find clone classes as well as individual clones. A code clone could also be considered as a type of readymade recipe for solving some problem. Documentation of these common recipes might be extended to encompass any task that repetitively required by the developers. Linking the clones with the recipe would also remove much of their harm. One simple way of much more reliably detecting copy and paste code clones would simply be to log copy and paste. Each clone could receive some XML comment or annotation that contains a unique identifier for the clone class or a listing of links to other instances of the clone.

In defect prediction scenario several algorithms and techniques are available and worked well in defect prediction. However, despite these techniques, there is a need of programmer friendly tool which will act as a guide during software development. In defect prediction research, there is a need of improved detection methodology which helps the programmer to avoid the faults or defects during the design phase and coding phase to provide better quality software. A combined approach of different machine learning algorithms and data mining techniques is required to further improve the defect prediction accuracy. Automatic extraction of more valuable set of metrics and data samples is required for the success of cross project predictions. Finally, there is a need of researching new software metrics that are more useful in defect prediction.

FURTHER READINGS

A brief general introduction of data mining is given in Fayyad, Piateetsky, Shaprio and Smyth(1996), Glymour (1997). A detailed study of software clones is given in Roy and Cardy (2007). Strategy of clone detection using Abstract Syntax tree is proposed by Baxter (1998). Kamiya (2002) proposed a tool for clone detection using multi-linguistic tokens. Baist (2009) used market basket analysis to detect higher level clones in source code.

A study of module size impact on defect proneness is given in Koru and Hangfang (2005). Harutiko and Kenji (2008) provide a valuable study of inter and intra project defect prediction. A study of defect prediction using code change complexity is given in Hassan (2007). Statistical learning phenomenon is given in Hastie (2002).

ACKNOWLEDGMENT

The first author gratefully acknowledges the financial assistance from BHU in the form of Senior Research Fellowship.

REFERENCES

Baker, B. S. (1995). On finding duplication and near-duplication in large software systems. In L. Wills, P. Newcomb, & E. Chikofsky (Eds.), *Second Working Conference on Reverse Engineering*. Los Alamitos, CA: IEEE Computer Society Press.

Balazinska, M., Merlo, E., Dagenais, M., Lague, B., & Kontogiannis, K. (2000). Advanced clone-analysis to support object-oriented system refactoring. In *Working Conference on Reverse Engineering*, (pp. 98–107). IEEE Computer Society Press.

Basili, V. R., Briand, L. C., & Melo, W. L. (1996). A validation of object-oriented design metrics as quality indicators. *IEEE Transactions on Software Engineering, 22*, 751–761. doi:10.1109/32.544352

Binkley, A. B., & Schach, S. R. (1998). Validation of the coupling dependency metric as a predictor of run-time failures and maintenance measures. In *International Conference on Software Engineering*, (pp. 452-455).

Bose, R. P. J. C., & Srinivasan, S. H. (2005). Data mining approaches to software fault diagnoses. *Proceedings in the 15th International Workshop on Research Issues in Data Engineering*. IEEE.

Chaves, A. C. F., Vellasco, M. M. B. R., & Tanscheit, R. (2005). *Fuzzy rule extraction from support vector machines*. In Fifth International Conference on Hybrid Intelligent Systems.

Chwala, N., Kevin, W., Hall, L., & Kegelmeyer, W. (2002). SMOTE: Synthetic minority over-sampling technique. *Journal of Artificial Intelligence Research, 16*, 321–357.

Ducasse, S., Rieger, M., & Demeyer, S. (1999). A language independent approach for detecting duplicated code. In *International Conference on Software Maintenance*, (pp. 109–118).

Emam, K. E. (2005). *The ROI from software quality*. Auerbach Publications, Taylor and Francis Group, LLC.

Fagan, M. (1976). Design and code inspections to reduce errors in program development. *IBM Systems Journal, 15*(3). doi:10.1147/sj.153.0182

Giesecke, S. (2003). *Clonebased Reengineering fÄur Java auf der EclipsePlattform*. Master's thesis, Carl von Ossietzky UniversitÄat Oldenburg, Germany.

Giesecke, S. (2006). Generic modelling of code clones. In *Proceedings of Duplication, Redundancy, and Similarity in Software*, Dagstuhl, Germany. ISSN 16824405

Han, J., & Kamber, M. (2006). Data mining: Concepts and techniques, 2nd ed. Elsevier publication.

IEEE. (1987). *Software engineering standards*. IEEE Press.

Jia, Y., Harman, M., & Krinke, J. (2009). *KClone: A proposed approach to fast precise code clone detection*. Workshop on Detection.

Jiang, Y., Cukic, B., & Menzies, T. (2007). Fault prediction using early lifecycle data. In *Proceedings of ISSRE 2007*, TBF.

Jiang, Y., Cukic, B., Menzies, T., & Bartlow, N. (2008). Comparing design and code metrics for software quality prediction. In *PROMISE 2008*. New York, NY: ACM. doi:10.1145/1370788.1370793

Kamiya, T., Kusumoto, S., & Inoue, K. (2002, July). CCFinder: A multilinguistic token-based code clone detection system for large scale source code. *Transactions on Software Engineering*, *28*(7), 654–670. doi:10.1109/TSE.2002.1019480

Kapser, C., & Godfrey, M. (2003). *A taxonomy of clones in source code: The reengineers most wanted list*. In Working Conference on Reverse Engineering. IEEE Computer Society Press.

Kapser, C., & Godfrey, M. W. (2006). *Clones considered harmful*. In Working Conference on Reverse Engineering.

Khosgoftaar, T. M., & Munson, J. C. (1990). Predicting software development errors using software complexity metrics. *IEEE Journal on Selected Areas in Communications*, *8*(2).

Khoshgoftaar, T. M., Allen, E. B., Kalaichelvan, K. S., & Goel, N. (1996). Early quality prediction: A case study in telecommunications. *IEEE Software*, *13*(1). doi:10.1109/52.476287

Kontogiannis, K., Mori, R. D., Merlo, E., Galler, M., & Bernstein, M. (1996). Pattern matching for clone and concept detection. *Automated Software Engineering*, *3*(1/2), 79–108.

Koru, A. G., & Liu, H. (2005). An investigation of the effect of module size on defect prediction using static measures. *Proceedings of the Workshop Predictor Models in Software Engineering*.

Koza, J., & Poli, R. (2002). *A genetic programming tutorial*. Retrieved from http://www.genetic-programming.com/johnkoza.html

Laguae, B., Proulx, D., Mayrand, J., Ettore, M., & Hudepohl, J. (1997). Assessing the benefits of incorporating function clone detection in a development process. In *Proceedings of the 13th International Conference on Software Maintenance (ICSM'97)*, (pp. 314-321). Bari, Italy.

Laprie, J., & Kanoon, K. (1996). Software reliability and system reliability. In Lyu, M. R. (Ed.), *Handbook of software reliability engineering* (*Vol. 1*, pp. 27–69). IEEE CS Press-McGraw Hill.

Li, Z., Lu, S., Myagmar, S., & Zhou, Y. (2006). CP-miner: Finding copy-paste and related bugs in large-scale software code. *IEEE Transactions on Software Engineering*, *32*(3), 176–192. doi:10.1109/TSE.2006.28

Menzies, T., Dekhtyar, A., Distefano, J., & Greenwald, J. (2007). Problems with precision: A response to comments on data mining static code attributes to learn defect predictors. *IEEE Transactions on Software Engineering*, *33*(9), 637–640. doi:10.1109/TSE.2007.70721

Mishra, B., & Shukla, K. K. (2011, December). Support vector machine based fuzzy classification model for software fault prediction. *Proceeding in IICAI 2011*.

Mishra, B., & Shukla, K. K. (2011). Genetic programming based prediction of defects using static code attributes. *International Journal of Data Analysis and Information Systems*, *3*(1).

Mishra, B., & Shukla, K. K. (Sep 2011). Impact of attribute selection on defect proneness prediction in OO software. In *Proceedings of International Conference on Computer & Communication Technology* (ICCCT).

Nagappan, N., & Ball, T. (2006). *Explaining failures using software dependences and churn metrics*. Redmond, WA: Microsoft Research.

Nat'l, I. of Standards and Technology. (May 2002). *The economic impacts of inadequate infrastructure for software testing.* Technical Report 02-3.

Pan, K., Kim, S., & Whitehead, E. (2006). Bug classification using program slicing metrics. *Proceedings of the Sixth IEEE International Workshop on Source Code Analysis and Manipulation.*

Pearson, K. (1901). On lines and planes of closest fit to systems of points in space. *Philosophical Magazine, 2*(6), 559–572.

Russell, S., Binder, J., Koller, D., & Kanazawa, K. (1995). Local learning in probabilistic networks with hidden variables. In *Proceedings of the 1995 Joint International Artificial Intelligence (IJCAI'95),* (pp. 1146–1152). Montreal, Canada.

Shull, F. ad b., V. B., Boehm, B., Brown, A., Costa, P., M. Lindvall, Port, D., Rus, I., Tesoriero, R., and Zelkowitz, M. (2002). What we have learned about fighting defects. *Proceedings of 8th International Software Metrics Symposium,* Ottawa, Canada, (pp. 249–258). Retrieved from http://fc-md.umd.edu/fcmd/Papers/shull defects.ps

Subramanyam, R., & Krishnan, M. S. (2003). Empirical analysis of ck metrics for object-oriented design complexity: Implications for software defects. *IEEE Transactions on Software Engineering, 29,* 297–310. doi:10.1109/TSE.2003.1191795

Sutherland, J. (1995). Business objects in corporate information systems. *ACM Computing Surveys, 27*(2), 274–276. doi:10.1145/210376.210394

Tian, J. (2005). *Software quality engineering: Testing, quality assurance, and quantifiable improvement.* New York, NY: John Wiley & Sons. doi:10.1002/0471722324

Xing, F., Guo, P., & Lyu, M. R. (2005). A novel method for early software quality prediction based on support vector machine. In *Proceedings of the 16th IEEE International Symposium on Software Reliability Engineering.*

Yang, B., Yao, L., & Huang, H. Z. (2007). Early software quality prediction based on a fuzzy neural network model. In *Proceedings of Third International Conference on Natural Computation.*

Yuan, X., Khoshgoftaar, T. M., Allen, E. B., & Ganesan, K. (2000). An application of fuzzy clustering to software quality prediction. In *Proceedings of The 3rd IEEE Symposium on Application-Specific Systems and Software Engineering Technology.*

Zimmermann, T., Premraj, R., & Zeller, A. (2007). Predicting defects for Eclipse. *PROMISE '07: Proceedings of the Third International Workshop on Predictor Models in Software Engineering.*

Chapter 8
Quality Assurance of Website Structure

G. Sreedhar

Rashtriya Sanskrit Vidyapeetha (Deemed University), India

ABSTRACT

Today, the web is not only an information resource, but also it is becoming an automated tool in various applications. Due to the increasing popularity of WWW, one can be very cautious in designing the website. Poor and careless web design leads to hardship to public utility and does not serve the purpose. If the website is not designed properly, the user may face many difficulties in using the website. In last few years a set of website metrics were defined and specified based on the data collection point of view. Among hundred and fifty automated web metrics catalogued up to now, metrics for link and page faults, metrics for navigation, metrics for information, metrics for media, metrics for size and performance, and metrics for accessibility are important categories for evaluation of quality of web site. The website structure and navigation depicts the structure of the website. The navigation of website is dependent on structure of the web site. The present chapter is an attempt to develop a comprehensive quality assurance mechanism towards quality web design process. In this chapter, various measures and metrics for the quality of website structure are investigated as a part of quality assurance process.

INTRODUCTION

The web (Enrique Herrera-Viedama, 2006) is playing a central role in diverse application domains such as business, education, industry and entertainment. As a consequence, there are increasing concerns about the ways in which web applications are developed and the degree of quality delivered. Thus, there are compelling reasons for a systematic and disciplined use of engineering methods and tools for developing and evaluating web sites and applications. A website is a collection of web pages containing text, images, audio and video etc., Thus web is a vast collection of completely uncontrolled documents. Despite of many recommendations,

DOI: 10.4018/978-1-4666-2958-5.ch008

ideas and guidelines, designing a quality website is still a burning problem. The quality assurance techniques for web applications generally focus on the prevention of web failure or the reduction of chances for such failures. Due to the unceasing growth of web sites and applications, developers and evaluators have interesting challenges not only from the development but also from the quality assurance point of view.

SURVEY OF LITERATURE

Website Navigation (Darken & Siebert, 1993) is the process of determining a path to be traveled through a chosen environment. (Nielsen, 1996) claimed that the navigation design of a website answers three fundamental questions when browsing the site. They are:

1.   Where am I?
2.   Where have I been? and
3.   Where can I go?

By 1997, much of the existing navigation research literature deals with virtual reality (Brajnik, 2003). In fact, the navigation is such an important feature that (Krug, 2006) a "navigation is not just a part of the website; It is the website". Web navigation is a challenge because of the need to manage billions of information objects (Nielsen, 1998a; 1998b; 1999) which makes the measuring of navigability extremely difficult. Three major phases were proposed to tackle the navigation and search problems. In the first phase, information about hyperlinks has been used for assisting user navigation and search. The link structures of the Web and Web sites are visualized. Hyperlinks are used to cluster Web pages. Hyperlinks are used to get authoritative rankings of Web pages. In the second phase, information about Web page contents has been used for assisting user navigation and search. Web page contents are also used to cluster Web pages. Web page contents, anchor

texts, and extended anchor texts have been used to get relevance-based rankings of Web pages. In third phase, information about Website content priority has been used for assisting user navigation. Web site usage data, which contain records of how users have visited a Web site, have been used to identify collective user behavior in using the Web site. The breadth and depth web design issues were widely studied. Results from several studies have suggested that a web page with many links, the mean to reduce the depth is the optimal condition for user performance. (Zaphris & Mtei) found that in a site of 64 links, the design with 8 links per page and two levels resulted in fastest response time and lowest navigation efforts (Zhang, Huo Zhang, Zhu, & Greenwood, 2001). For web design, a widely quoted heuristic rule of navigation design is the "three click rule", which states that the user should be able to get from home page to any other page on the site within three clicks of the mouse.

OPTIMIZATION OF WEBSITE STRUCTURE FOR QUALITY ASSURANCE

The procedure of the quality assessment of website structure involves four modules:

1.   Creating a sitemap
2.   Computing path length metric
3.   Evaluating structural complexity of website and
4.   Finding broken link error index.

Creating a Sitemap

Every website must have sitemap to know the organization of web pages in the website structure. The sitemap shows all web pages in a hierarchical tree with home page as root of the tree. A web tool PowerMapper is used to construct a sitemap for the website. It selects

URL address of website and generates the tree structure for all web pages of website. In this process only markup files (html, asp, php, xml, etc.,) are considered and remaining components like graphic files script files, etc., are not included because these files do not have any significance in website structure. The sitemap of a website may be organized into various levels depending on its design. Some websites have one or two levels and some may have more levels. This idea was further investigated in (Zhang, Huo, Zhang, Zhu, & Greenwood, 2001). A metric for website structure complexity was defined as the sum of number of simple paths from the home page to each page.

Evaluating Path Length Metric

A path length is used to find average number of clicks per page. The path length of the tree is the sum of the depths of all nodes in the tree. It can be computed as a weighted sum, where weightage at each level with its number of nodes its level using Equation 1. The average number of clicks is computed using Equation 2. The width of a tree is the size of its largest level and the height of a tree is the length of its longest root path.

$$path\ length = \sum_{i=1}^{n} l_i m_i$$
$$where\quad l_i = level\ number\ i$$
$$m_i = number\ of\ nodes\ at\ level\ i$$

(1)

$$Avg\ no.\ of\ clicks = path\ length/n$$
$$where\quad n = number\ of\ nodes\ in\ the\ tree$$

(2)

To illustrate the above for a design with three levels path length (Figure 1) is computed as detailed below.

Figure 1. Tree structure of a website

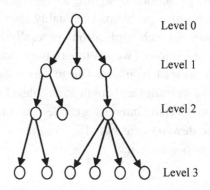

Path length = 0*1 + 1*3 + 2*3 + 3*6 = 27

AvgClicks = 27/13 = 2.07

Structural Complexity

Structural Complexity emerges from the relationships among the web pages of the website. The most basic and important relationship is that a web page is linked to another through hyperlinks. The hyperlinks between web pages of a website form the navigational paths through which users browse the website to find the required information. The more complex that the web pages are inter-linked, the more likely that a user becomes lost in the information ocean and hence, the more difficult to navigate. The structural complexity metrics are therefore based on the study of website links. The structurally simplest website consists of a single web page with no links. For more complex systems, structural complexity depends on the structure of the graph model of the website. It was decided to keep the navigation of the sites fairly simple. The home page of web site would link to all the main topics on the web site. The details of content and its relevant shall be accommodated in the pages at sub levels. An abstract model (Jin, Zhu, & Hall, 1997) of hypertext application systems is a directed graph, which is applicable to websites. In this model, a website can be modeled as a pair <G, S>, where G=(V,E) is a directed graph representing the website, V is the set of nodes representing web pages, E is the set of edges representing links between web pages and S is the start node of the graph, i.e. the home page of the website. The directed graph must also satisfy the condition that all nodes v in V are reachable, i.e., there is at least one path from the home page to node v. The Number of Independent Paths (NOIP) (Weykuer, 1988) is considered as a measure of hypertext navigation complexity. The larger the NOIP, the more complex the website structure is, the easier for a user to get lost in the network and the poor navigability. The structural complexity of website is determined with Mc. Cab's Cyclomatic Complexity Metric (Mc Cabe, 1976), which identifies NOIP in the website. This metric is used to know navigation path for a desired web page. The Cyclomatic Complexity metric is derived in graph theory as follows. A tree graph is constructed with home page as root. The tree consists of various sub trees and leaf nodes. An example tree is shown in Figure 2.

A tree graph is constructed for a website by considering various hyperlinks in the website. Each sub tree of the graph represents a web page which has further hyperlinks to the next web pages and leaf node represent a web page which do not have any further links to the web pages. In tree graph, at each level all web pages that do not have further links are represented with one leaf node at that level and a sub tree at each level consists of links to the web pages to the next level. The structural complexity is computed using Cyclomatic Complexity and it can be calculated as defined in Equation 3. According to (Mc Cabe, 1976) value of Cyclomatic Complexity Metric (CCMetric) should be less than or equal to 10.

Figure 2. Tree graph for a website

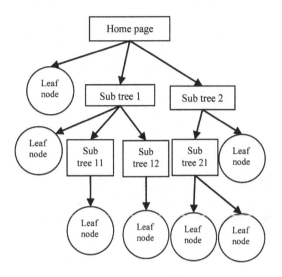

$$Cyclomatic\ Complexity\ Metric\,(CCMetric) = (e - n + d + 1)\big/n$$

(3)

where e is the number of web page links, n is the number of nodes in the graph and d is the number of leaf nodes in the graph.

Broken Link Calculation

In a website structure, navigation problem raised due to broken links. The broken link may involve at various levels of web site structure. Broken links are identified by broken link checker module. In a sitemap of website, broken links are counted at various levels and broken error index is calculated based on percentage of broken links involved in sitemap. The percentage of broken links (Sedro, 2001) is calculated using Equation 4.

$$PBL = \left(NBL/n \right) * 100$$

where $PBL = Percentage\ of\ Broken\ Links$

$NBL = Total\ number\ of\ Broken\ Links$
$\qquad in\ the\ website$

$n = number\ of\ web\ pages$

$$(4)$$

DEVELOPMENT OF METRIC FOR EVALUATING QUALITY OF WEBSITE STRUCTURE

The quality of website structure for each university is evaluated in 10-point scale. The 10-point scale value for a website is based on organization of web pages in sitemap structure, cyclomatic complexity of website, average number of clicks and broken link error index. The 10-point scale value for sitemap structure (SMP) is evaluated using SMPMetric defined in Equation 5.

$$
SMP_{Metric} =
\begin{cases}
10 & if\ webpage\ is\ home\ page \\
 & \quad \&\ wps = n\ \&\ wps \leq 20 \\
10 & if\ wps \geq 10\ \&\ wps \leq 20 \\
9 & if\ wps = 9\ or\ 21 \\
8 & if\ wps = 8\ or\ 22 \\
7 & if\ wps = 7\ or\ 23 \\
6 & if\ wps = 6\ or\ 24 \\
5 & if\ wps = 5\ or\ 25 \\
4 & if\ wps = 4\ or\ 26 \\
3 & if\ wps = 3\ or\ 27 \\
2 & if\ wps = 2\ or\ 28 \\
1 & if\ wps = 1\ or\ 29 \\
0 & otherwise \\
10 & if\ webpage\ is\ home\ page \\
 & \quad \&\ wps = n\ \&\ wps \leq 20
\end{cases}
$$

where $SMP_{Metric} = Site\ Map\ Structure\ Metric$

$wps = number\ of\ web\ page\ links\ in$

$\qquad a\ sub\ tree\ of\ sitemap$

$$(5)$$

The 10-point scale value for structural complexity (Mc Cabe, 1976) of website is calculated using Equation 6 and 7.

$$
CC_{Metric} =
\begin{cases}
10 & if\ CC \leq 1 \\
9 & if\ CC \leq 2 \\
8 & if\ CC \leq 3 \\
7 & if\ CC \leq 4 \\
6 & if\ CC \leq 5 \\
5 & if\ CC \leq 6 \\
4 & if\ CC \leq 7 \\
3 & if\ CC \leq 8 \\
2 & if\ CC \leq 9 \\
1 & if\ CC \leq 10 \\
0 & otherwise
\end{cases}
$$

where $CC = Cylomatic\ Complexity$

$CC_{Metric} = Cyclomatic\ Complexity\ Metric$

$$(6)$$

10-Point Scale value for website structure is derived using Equations 5 and 6.

$$10_{WS} = (SMP_{Metric} + CC_{Metric}) / 2$$

where $10_{WS} = 10$ - *Point Scale Value f*

or web site structure

$$(7)$$

The Web Page Click (WPClick) value is determined using Equation 8 and 10-point scale value is refined using the additional information of number of clicks as defined in Equation 9.

$$
WP_{Click} =
\begin{cases}
0.75 & if\ AvgClicks \leq 3 \\
5 & if\ AvgClicks \leq 4 \\
0.25 & if\ AvgClicks \leq 5
\end{cases}
$$

$$(8)$$

where $WP_{Click} = Web\ Page\ Click$

The adjusted 10_{WS} value can be defined as

Figure 3. Sitemap of Aligarh Muslim University website

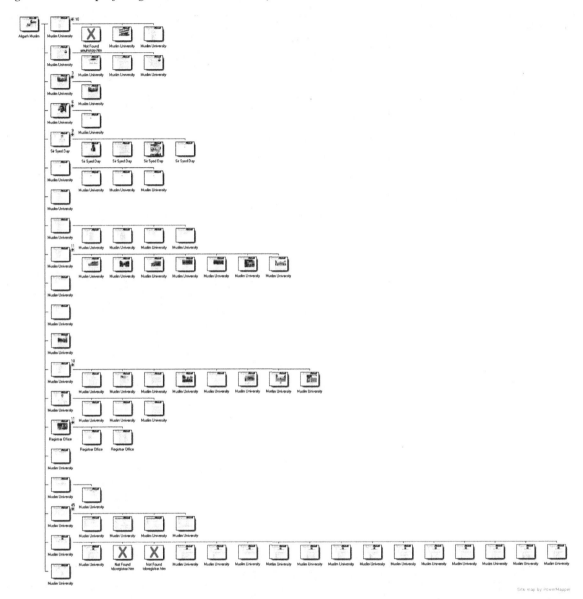

$$10_{WS} = 10_{WS} + WP_{click} \qquad (9)$$

Also the Equation 9 can be improved using BLE. The 10WS can be redefined as improved metric as defined in view of Equation 10 and it is defined in Equation 11.

$$BLE = \begin{array}{ll} 1 & if \ PBL \geq 10 \\ 0.75 & if \ PBL \geq 5 \\ 0.5 & if \ PBL \geq 2 \\ 0.25 & if \ PBL > 0 \end{array}$$

$$where \quad BLE = Broken \ Link \ Error \ Index$$

$$PBL = Percentage \ of \ Broken \ Links$$

$$(10)$$

Table 1. 10-point scale value calculation for Aligarh Muslim University website structure

AvgNoClicks	Path Length = 367 AvgNoClicks = 367/156 = 2.352564			
SMP$_{Metric}$	Level No	Sub tree in web site structure	No. of web pages in sub tree	10-Point Scale Value
	1	1	20	10
	2	1	3	3
		2	3	3
		3	1	1
		4	1	1
		5	4	4
		6	3	3
		7	4	4
		8	7	7
		9	8	8
		10	3	3
		11	2	2
		12	1	1
		13	4	4
		14	16	10
	3	1	7	7
		2	1	1
		3	5	5
		4	4	4
		5	1	1
		6	1	1
		7	1	1
		8	1	1
		9	1	1
		10	2	2
		11	9	9
		12	11	10
		13	7	7
		14	13	10
		15	9	9
	4	1	1	1
		2	1	1
	10-point scale value = 4.21875			
CC$_{Metric}$	Cyclomatic Complexity Metric (CC$_{Metric}$) = (e-n+d+1)/n = (156-20+28+1)/20 = 2.083333 10-point scale Value = 8			
BLE	% of broken links			Broken link error index
	5.769231			0.75
10-point scale value for Aligarh Muslim University website = 5.4				

$$10_{WS} = 10_{WS} - BLE \qquad (11)$$

As an example sitemap of Aligarh Muslim University website is shown in Figure 3. The corresponding web structure complexity value is calculated and it depicted in Table 1.

CONCLUSION

This chapter mainly involves various measures and metrics for the quality of website structure. In order to measure the quality of website structure two main aspects of website namely website navigation and organization of web pages in the web site need to be considered. In this chapter an attempt is made to involve all quality elements that need to be evaluated in giving assurance to the quality web design.

REFERENCES

Brajnik, G. (2003). Comparing accessibility evaluation tools: results for a case study. *Proceedings of Symposium on Human-Computer Interaction HCITALY' 2003*.

Darken, R. P., & Siebert, J. L. (1993). A tool set for navigation in virtual environments. *UIST Proceedings*, (p. 157).

Herrera-Viedama, E., Pasi, G., Lopez-Herrera, A. G., & Porcel, C. (2006). Evaluating the information quality of web sites: A methodology based on fuzzy computing with words. *Journal of the American Society for Information Science and Technology*, *57*(4), 538–549. doi:10.1002/asi.20308

Jin, L., Zhu, H., & Hall, P. (1997). Adequate testing of hypertext. *Information and Software Technology*, *39*, 225–234. doi:10.1016/S0950-5849(96)01141-X

Krug, S. (2006). *Don't make me think! A common sense approach to web usability* (2nd ed.). Indianapolis, IN: New Riders Publishing.

Mc Cabe, T. J. (1976). A complexity measure. *IEEE Transactions on Software Engineering, SE*, *2*(4), 308–320. doi:10.1109/TSE.1976.233837

Nielsen, J. (1996). *The alert box*. Retrieved from http://www.useit.com/alertbox

Nielsen, J. (1998). *Content usability. NPL: Usability forum-Making webs work*. Middlesex, UK: NPL.

Nielsen, J. (1998). *Using link titles to help users predict where they are going*. Retrieved from www.useit.com/altertbox/990530.html

Nielsen, J. (1999). *Designing web usability: The practice of simplicity*. Indianapolis, IN: New Riders Publishing.

Powermapper. (n.d.). *Home page*. Retrieved from www.powermapper.com

Sedro, N. (2001). *Experience design 1*. Indianapolis, IN: New Riders Publishing.

Weykuer, E. J. (1988). Evaluating software complexity measures. *IEEE Transactions on Software Engineering*, *14*(9), 1357–1365. doi:10.1109/32.6178

Zaphris, P., & Mtei, L. (1997). *Depth vs. breadth in the arrangement of Web links*. Retrieved from http://www.otal.umd.edu/SHORE97

Zhang, Y., Huo Zhang, L., Zhu, H., & Greenwood, S. (2001). Structure and page complexity metrics for web applications. *Proceedings of 4th Workshop on Web Engineering at 1oth WWW Conference*, Hong Kong, (pp. 72-81).

KEY TERMS AND DEFINITIONS

10-Point Scale Structural Complexity: The 10-point scale value for a website is based on organization of web pages in sitemap structure, cyclomatic complexity of website, average number of clicks and broken link error index.

Broken Link: A broken link is one which does not point to a valid web page. Broken links can also be referred to as dead links.

Cyclomatic Complexity Metric: The structural complexity of website is determined with Mc. Cab's Cyclomatic Complexity Metric which identifies Number of Independent Paths in the website.

Path Length: A path length is used to find average number of clicks per page. The path length of the tree is the sum of the depths of all nodes in the tree. It can be computed as a weighted sum, where weightage at each level with its number of nodes its level.

Sitemap: Sitemap shows all web pages in a hierarchical tree with home page as root of the tree.

Website Navigation: Website Navigation is the process of determining a path to be traveled through a chosen environment.

Website: A website is a collection of web pages containing text, images, audio and video etc., Thus web is a vast collection of completely uncontrolled documents.

Chapter 9
Resolving Conflict in Code Refactoring

Lakhwinder Kaur
Apeejay Institute of Management Technical Campus, India

Kuljit Kaur
Guru Nanak Dev University, India

Ashu Gupta
Apeejay Institute of Management Technical Campus, India

ABSTRACT

Refactoring is a process that attempts to enhance software code quality by using small transforming functions and modifying the structure of the program through slightly different algorithm. It is important to analyze the design pattern of the software code as well as the impact and possibility of the application of some conflicting refactorings on it. The objective of this chapter is to present an approach for analyzing software design patterns in order to avoid the conflict in application of available refactoring techniques. This chapter discusses the mechanism to study software code or design patterns to automate the process of applying available refactorings while addressing the problem of conflict in their application.

INTRODUCTION

The term 'Refactoring', which was first introduced by William Opdyke and Ralph Johnson, and then popularized by M. Fowler, is meant to improve internal code structure without altering external functionality of a software system. It attempts to enhance code quality by using small transforming functions and modifying the structure of the program through slightly different algorithm. After pattern analysis in programs, software code quality can be enhanced by minor modifications in the program design and that is the stage where Software Refactoring comes into play. It is observed that developers can either streamline the size of a software product after development and simplify its design, or speed up its download and execution speed with the help of Refactorings. This

DOI: 10.4018/978-1-4666-2958-5.ch009

fundamental activity also aims to help organizations in maintaining and updating their software more easily. It is an iterative process and it must result in significant improvement over original version of the software.

In fact, Refactoring facilitates reverse engineering process also, which is a process of analyzing and extracting patterns in source code programs in order to understand their system functionality and representation. As the software needs to be continuously monitored and updated in order to meet the rapid changes in requirements of the industry, there is a crucial need to exploit reverse engineering during different stages of the software development. Program design analysis is required in reverse engineering in order to ensure consistency of the software components.

In brief, when applied in a disciplined way, the summed up impact of refactoring must be significant for improving the efficiency and quality of code. But the problem is that automated, assisted or even manual application of refactorings suggested so far, may result in either negative or lesser impact on the quality of software than it was targeted. The reason is- some pairs of refactoring techniques are opposite to each other and they may nullify each other's impact when performed in a particular order. Hence, it is important to analyze the design pattern of the software code as well as the impact and possibility of the application of some conflicting refactorings on it. This chapter attempts to analyze code design patterns, which may lead to conflict in the application of refactorings and suggests a mechanism to avoid it.

BACKGROUND

Though the work of Opdyke (1992), and Johnson(1997), has been the pillar behind introducing refactoring techniques, the work by M.Fowler(1999) suggested various refactorings. Since then, a number of researchers are engaged in finding effective ways of applying refactorings

in software codes. Refactoring techniques are applied at various levels starting from design level to various control structures in a program. R. Najjar, S. Counsell, G. Loizou, and K.Mannock(2003) proved that by replacing constructors with factory methods and making minor modifications to the interface provided by the class, the lines of code can be reduced and classes can provide better abstraction. They have shown the positive effect of refactoring on softwares by improving its quality and efficiency. Mens and Tourwe(2004), performed a comprehensive survey of the research in refactoring upto that time. They classified research according to Five criteria and presented that a tool or formal model for refactoring should be sufficiently abstract to be applicable to different programming languages, but it should also provide the necessary interface to add language-specific behaviour.

Tokuda and Batory(1995) proposed automated search for refactoring trends. They implemented 12 object oriented database refactorings described by Banerjee and Kim(1987). They were able to automate thousands of lines of changes with a general-purpose set of refactorings. They implemented the refactorings in C++ and expressed the difficulty in managing C++ preprocessor Information. Beck(2000) suggested that there is correlation between characteristics of the rapid software development and the need for frequent refactorings. In case of rapid software development, programmers do not bother about code simplicity, understandability and maintainability. M. Boger et al(2002) introduced refactoring browser integrated in a UML modeling tool. They discussed how Refactorings can be extended to static architecture as well as to dynamic behaviour.

Moving state and behavior between classes can help reduce coupling and increase cohesion(Pressman,2001). The cumulative effect of several simple refactoring steps and the available tool support for their automated application has made the refactoring process a widely accepted technique for improving software design. However, identifying the places where refactoring should be applied is neither trivial nor supported by tools. Nikolaos Tsantalis and Alexander Chatzigeorgiou (2009) have proposed a methodology for locating Feature Envy bad smells and evaluating the effect of the Move Method refactorings to resolve bad smells. Daniel and his colleagues (2007) proposed a technique for automatically testing refactoring tools. They found some compilation errors introduced by Eclipse and Netbeans. The work of Balazinska et al. (2000) proposed approach to detect clones in source code. This clone analysis is required to detect the points in the source code where transformations are required. Simon et al. (2001) also worked on detecting bad smells with the help of software metrics. Kataoka et al. (2001) developed an automatic tool for detecting bad smells. This tool was named Daikon, which was able to detect invariables. Mens et al.(2007) tried to represent software refactorings as graph transformations in order to formalize the refactoring process. Tichelaar et al. (2000) has investigated Development of a Meta model for undertaking refactorings based on system change data. Their approach fits well with an agile style. It analyzes the current system version according to a list of usability principles, then reports usability problems i.e. bad smells, and then suggests improvements i.e. refactorings. They were able to automate software refactoring with existing graph transformation tools, such as PROGRES, Fujaba and AGG.

AVAILABLE REFACTORING TECHNIQUES

An exhaustive list of refactoring techniques have been proposed (Fowler, 1992) and rules to apply these refactorings are stated (Pettorossi et al, 1996). A few of most commonly used refactorings (Fowler,2007) which are used in object oriented languages like java and C++, are explained in brief below and a few are listed in Table 1.

1. **Encapsulate Field:** This refactoring allows to quickly create an accessor property from an existing field. Usages of a field are automatically replaced with usages of a corresponding property. An apparent advantage of this refactoring is that you can disallow direct access to a field through the use of properties. This refactoring suffers from the drawback that if new modules are added to the software according to previous usage of fields, the enhancement will not be compatible to the automatic changes. But this problem can be addressed by automating the process of preprocessing new modules before compilation and making them compatible with automated refactorings applied previously.

Table 1. List of commonly used refactorings (Fowler,2007)

1. Add or remove parameter
2. Change Bidirectional Association among Components to Unidirectional
3. *Change Reference(Pointer) to Value*
4. Change Unidirectional Association to Bidirectional
5. Change Value to some Reference
6. Collapse Class Hierarchy
7. Consolidate Conditional Expression
8. Convert Dynamic to Static Constructor
9. Convert Static to Dynamic Construction
10. Encapsulate Field
11. Replace Error Code with Exception
12. Replace Exception with Test
13. Replace Inheritance with Delegation
14. Replace Iteration with Recursion
15. Replace Method with Method Object
16. Replace Parameter with Method
17. Replace Recursion with Iteration
18. Replace Subclass with Fields
19. Replace Type Code with Subclasses
20. Split Loop

2. **Extract Class:** This refactoring creates a new class or struct(C++) and converts parameters of the selected method/s into encapsulated fields of the newly created class. This is implemented by making a constructor that recieves parameters, then using fields to store values and properties to retrieve values. Then all usages of parameters are translated into usages of properties of the created type. If a Class is describing too much functionality and using too many variables, then extract class refactoring can be applied. Also if you have a fixed class that does quite different and distinct things that are in no way related to each other, then separate the mutually exclusive code into varying classes, i.e. apply extract class. This refactoring definitely results in increased reusability, maintainability and adaptability of the code as small independent classes represent a well defined set of unique objects that perform a well defined task.

3. **Extract Interface or Method:** Extract Interface refactoring is used to create an interface from a class and make that class implement the newly created interface. In case of an automated tool, programmer can be provided facility to choose the members to extract to the new interface and to specify a name for the interface also. Extract Method refactoring is used when a long method needs to be broken up to enhance readability and maintainability. A section of code performing a single logical function is replaced with a call to a new method. This new method is given suitable parameters, return type and exceptions. Extracting the method also increases usability of the method as it can be used in other places, which was not possible when it was a part of a larger method. Therefore, if you are dealing with long method, then application of extract method refactoring improves code reusability.

4. **Inline Method/Inline Class:** Whenever possible, this refactoring can be used to transfer a method's body into the body of another method which is calling it. In this process the transferred method is removed altogether. This is reverse of the functionality provided by 'Extract Method'. The benefit achieved may be in terms of saving compilation time and can be used when Method is not called many times from different execution points. Similarly, if a class is relying too much on another class and doing itself almost nothing, then other class must be merged in this class, which is called Inline Class. A class can be merged in other class either by including its functionality and attributes in the other class or by making it an inner class as in Java language.

5. **Introduce Variable or Parameter:** This refactoring is used to replace an arbitrary expression inside the member code. A new local variable is declared and initialized with that selected arbitrary expression. This expression is then replaced with the name of the variable. In case of using an interactive tool for applying the refactoring, an option is provided to programmer to replace single or all occurrences of that expression by this newly created variable. In same manner constant expressions can be replaced with a constant. This refactoring maintains logic and semantics of the code while increasing its efficiency.

6. **Move Class, Method:** A Class is in the wrong package, it should therefore be moved to another package, where it fits better. All import statements or fully qualified names referring to this class also need to be updated. The compiled file will also have to be moved and updated to reflect this change. Similarly, if a method of some class is using most of the attributes of another class, then it should be made member of that other class and its container and all other callers to this method

must be modified accordingly. Similarly, if a change in one class repeatedly requires little changes in a bunch of other classes, apply move method and move field to get all the highly dependent pieces of code into one class.

7. **Pull Up Members:** This refactoring helps to move variables and methods to a superclass or to an interface. If some subclasses have the same field, then that field can be moved to the superclass. Similarly if subclasses have similar methods, then those methods can be moved to the superclass. The duplicate code will be removed this way and the interface become clear. If many subclasses in a hierarchy or peer subclasses have constructors with identical functionality, then we can create a superclass constructor and call this from the subclass methods. On the other hand when many unrelated classes use similar user interface or use same constant values, then shared methods and constant declarations can be made part of an existing Interface. This will result in enforcing standards for naming conventions used in a software project.

8. **Push Members Down:** This refactoring provides the reverse functionality of Pull Members up. It is useful when most of the subclasses do not use some functionality defined in the superclass. In that case it is better to shift the respective methods or members of the superclass to the related subclasses. This refactoring makes the interface clear and superclass more abstract.

9. **Rename:** If a method, variable, class or other item has a name that is misleading or confusing, then it must be replaced with a new meaningful name. The problem with this refactoring is that it requires all references, and sometimes even file locations to be updated. The process of renaming a method may include renaming the method in subclasses as well as clients. On the other

hand, renaming a package will also involve moving files and directories and updating the source control system. The problem with this refactoring is that little automated support can be provided for renaming. But the process can be facilitated by providing an option to replace single or all occurences of the old name with the modified name.

10. **Replace Conditional with Polymorphism:** If Methods in a class check some value using if or switch statement in order to decide some action to perform under different conditions. The code quickly becomes confusing if same 'if' or 'switch' statements are repeated throughout the class, e.g. in methods that calculate the area or perimeter of the shape instead of using multiple conditions for different shape, we can use polymorphism through which the shape specific behavior can be offloaded to subclasses, simplifying the code. This will have added benefit of allowing other subclasses, e.g. rectangle or star, to be introduced without extensive code changes. The general rule is - If too many branches of code exist, then use inheritance and polymorphism instead of 'switch.... case' or 'if...else if' type of statements.

11. **Replace Delegation with Inheritance:** Sometimes a class is delegating its work to other class or using the entire interface provided by another class. In that case it is beneficial to make the delegating class a subclass of the delegate and directly use interface provided by it. In this manner all base class functionality can be utilized in efficient manner without any need to create extra objects.

12. **Replace Assignment with Initialization:** Instead of declaring and initializing the variables in separate statements, it can be done with a single statement. It improves understandability as well efficiency of the code. This refactoring is very basic but is significant to improve execution time. This

refactoring state that instead of using the code like:

```
void abc() {
    var i;
    i = 5; }
```

Use following code:

```
void abc() {
    var i = 5;
}
```

With each of the above refactoring, a more or less obvious formalism has also been stated. However, it is trivial to every experienced software developer that there are more complicated code problems, for which simple solutions can not so easily be presented. Table 1 provides a list of 20 more refactorings. The refactoring process associated with these techniques is somewhat obvious, that is why only list is provided.

CONFLICTS AMONG REFACTORINGS

Manual refactoring may introduce many inconsistencies in different software components. Automated tools provide convenience for rapid software development and if applied in appropriate manner, refactoring definitely improves the code. But various pairs of refactoring techniques may get applied in such a way that one refactoring simply disables another refactoring or reverses the impact of other refactoring. Liu et al(2008) concluded that the conflicts among refactorings usually make it impossible to improve the code by use of refactorings. They found that application of a refactoring may change or delete elements necessary for other refactorings, and thus disables these refactorings. As a result, the application schedule of the available refactorings determines

which refactorings will be applied, and thus determines the total effect achieved by the refactoring activity. They have also proposed a conflict-aware scheduling approach.

Some of the conflicting pairs of refactorings, which are directly reverse of each other are listed below, but there are many other conflicting pairs of refactorings possible.

CONFLICT ANALYSIS OF CODE DESIGN PATTERNS IN SOFTWARES

In order to apply the refactoring techniques, software codes need to be analyzed to find certain patterns where different refactorings can be applied according to some predefined rules. A software developer will be able to apply refactorings successfully, only if he/she knows how the software should look like in the end. In other words, before trying to refactor some code, one needs to familiarize oneself with the common object oriented design patterns and refactoring. The software also needs to be analyzed to find conflicting refactoring pairs. This section introduces processes involved in code analysis techniques. These techniques can be used to identify mutual exclusions and asymmetric conflicts as identified in Table 2, and to detect sequential dependencies between refactorings. These techniques can be applied taking into consideration only the abstract refactoring specifications, without taking into account the actual code and concrete context in which they will be applied. Once an actual code is provided, the abstract analysis can be applied directly to this concrete refactoring context. The benefit of this approach is that the abstract analysis (Perez et al,2010), which is the most time-consuming operation, needs to be performed only once when the refactoring specifications are provided. These analysis techniques are discussed later.

Table 2. Direct reciprocal refactorings

Sr No	Refactoring	Counter Refactoring
1.	Change Bidirectional Association among Components to Unidirectional	Change Unidirectional Association to Bidirectional
2.	Add Parameter	Remove Parameter
3.	Change Reference(Pointer) to Value	Change Value to some Reference
4.	Convert Dynamic to Static Constructor	Convert Static to Dynamic Construction
5.	Pull Up Field	Push Down Field
6.	Pull Up Method	Push Down Method
7.	Replace Delegation with Inheritance	Replace Inheritance with Delegation
8.	Replace Error Code with Exception	Replace Exception with Test
9.	Replace Iteration with Recursion	Replace Recursion with Iteration
10.	Replace Method with Method Object	Replace Parameter with Method
11.	Replace Subclass with Fields	Replace Type Code with Subclasses

Critical Pair Analysis

Critical pair analysis was first introduced for term rewriting, and later generalized to graph re writing(Mens,Taentzer,Runge;2007). The idea of critical pair analysis is quite simple, which can be applied in different contexts. When applied in context of refactoring, given a predefined set of generic refactoring specifications (such as Push Down Method, Extract Subclass, Move Method, Create Superclass etc.), all pairs of such speci-fications are analyzed for potential conflicts. A critical pair is detected when it is possible to find a minimal critical context in the code, to which both refactorings in the pair can be applied in a conflicting way.

The critical pair analysis algorithm can be implemented using AGG tool(AGG,2011). AGG is the only available graph transformation tool that supports critical pair analysis. It is a rule based visual language that uses an algebraic approach for graph transformations. It aims at depicting the specification and prototype of applications with complex graph-structured data and models com-plex data structures as graphs. AGG may be used as a general purpose graph transformation engine in high-level codes employing graph transformation methods. When it is applied to the given refactoring specifications, then we get the actual number of critical situations that can be computed between a given pair of refactorings((Mens et al,2007). This number can be higher than one if the two considered refactorings conflict in different ways. By clicking on a number in the conflict table, all corresponding detailed conflicting situations will be displayed to the user after computing all potential conflicts. In the context of a given code for refactorings only a small fraction of these conflicts will actually occur. Therefore, the criti-cal pair analysis may be useful only at some kind of preprocessing stage which needs to be carried out only once. In case of an actual code, the set of computed critical pairs need to be filtered to find out which of the potential conflicts are actual conflicts that match with the given set. Most of the mutual exclusive and asymmetric conflicts, i.e. the refactorings that can not be applied together, become known after critical pair Analysis phase.

Dependency Analysis

In a second phase, one can consider the application of Dependency Analysis (Liu et al, 2010). In this phase actual conflicting situations are available and sequential dependencies among refactorings can be analyzed when they actually occur for a given code context. The code context can be depicted through syntax graph of software code or its design model. If refactoring applications are depicted through graph transformations, AGG can perform this applicability analysis automatically, and it reports the set of refactoring rules that are applicable for each context graph. After this analysis, the user can even go through all possible matches of each applicable rule in the given context graph. This process includes following steps:

1. **Applicability Analysis:** First of all, it is determined which refactorings are applicable in a given context. For example, in a given context refactoring Move a method to superclass may not be immediately applicable if method bodies of methods with same functionality in two peer classes are not having identical names or there may be two independent, unrelated classes may be providing similar functionality but do not have common superclass. There may be different reasons for refactorings not being applicable. Either they are sequentially dependant on other ones that have to be applied first, or they mutually exclude each other. Some refactorings may not be applicable at all for the given program design. For example, in the following code 'Move Method' refactoring can not be applied immediately as class containing method displayData() is not a derived classes:

In the above code method displayData() is performing different functions. Here we can check the applicability of 'Extract Method','Extract Superclass' and 'Move Method'. Extract method and Extract Superclass is immediately applicable, whereas Move method is not applicable in the current context. But after applying 'extract superclass', it becomes applicable.

2. **Parallel Conflict Analysis:** As discussed above, critical pairs of refactoring specifications describe only potential conflicts depending upon the refactoring specification provided. After applicability Analysis, we can further analyze which of these expected conflicts actually occur in the given code context. After applicability analysis, it can be checked which of the critical pair conflicts match and occur in the given context(Tom Mens et al,2005). For example, results of the critical pair analysis may show how refactorings 'Extract Superclass' and 'Move Method' may give rise to some conflicts. One of these expected conflicts may actually occur in the given program's code. Parallel dependency analysis is also supported by graph transformation Tools. For example, following code is received after applying 'Extract Method' refactoring to the sample code given in Figure 1.

As applicability analysis had provided the information that Move method was not applicable in the code given in Figure 1 but after applying Extract Method, it may be applicable to the code of Figure 2, especially if some other class is using this method. But at this stage Move method and Extract superclass can not be applied together as there is conflict in their application, which may become clear using Parallel analysis.

3. **Sequential Dependency Analysis:** Based on the applicability analysis of refactorings we can also analyze which refactorings are sequentially dependent of each other. For example, refactoring 'Move Method' is not immediately applicable in the context given in Figure 3, because there is no superclass. But after applying refactorings 'Extract Superclass' in this context, 'Move Method' may become applicable. On the other hand, after applying 'Replace Delegation with Inheritance', 'Move Method' may not be applicable. In a given program context, the applicability check can be performed manu-

Figure 1. Sample code for refactoring

```
Class FileDemo
{
DataInputStream dis;
        DataOutputStream dos;
        String name[]; int rno[];float per[];
        StringTokenizer stz;
Filedemo()
{
dis=new DataInputStream(System.in);
        dos=new DataOutputStream(new FileOutputStream("output.dat"));
        name=new String[10];
rno=new int[10];
per=new float[10];
    }

void displayData( ) throws IOException
{
System.out.println("Name          Rollno  Marks%age");
for(int i=1;i<=3;i++)
{
stz=new StringTokenizer(dis.readLine());
name[i]=stz.nextToken();
rno[i]=Integer.parseInt(stz.nextToken());
per[i]=Float.valueOf(stz.nextToken()).floatValue();
System.out.flush();
}
for(int i=1;i<=3;i++)
{
dos.writeChar(name[i]);dos.writeInt(rno[i]);dos.writeDouble(per[i]);
System.out.println("Name: "+name[i]+" Roll No: "+rno[i]+" Percentage : "+per[i]);
}
}
----- ---

---- --
}
```

Figure 2. Sample code of Figure 1 after applying refactoring 'extract method'

```
Class DemoInput
{
        DataInputStream dis;
    DataOutputStream dos;
    String name[]; int rno[];float per[];
    StringTokenizer stz;
DemoInput()
{ dis=new DataInputStream(System.in);
        dos=new DataOutputStream(new FileOutputStream("output.dat"));
        name=new String[10];
rno=new int[10];
per=new float[10];
        }
void readData()throws IOException                      //extracted Method
{ System.out.println("Name          Rollno  Marks%age");
    for(int i=1;i<=3;i++)
    {
    stz=new StringTokenizer(dis.readLine());
    name[i]=stz.nextToken();
    rno[i]=Integer.parseInt(stz.nextToken());
    per[i]=Float.valueOf(stz.nextToken()).floatValue();
    System.out.flush();
    }
}
void displayData( ) {

    for(int i=1;i<=3;i++)
    {
    dos.writeChar(name[i]);dos.writeInt(rno[i]);dos.writeDouble(per[i]);
    System.out.println("Name: "+name[i]+" Roll No: "+rno[i]+" Percentage : "+per[i]);
        }
    }
    ----- ---

    ---- --
        }
```

Figure 3. Two independent classes having similar functionality

Manager		Teacher	
Name		Name	
Address		Address	
Locality		Locality	
PhoneNumber		PhoneNumber	
Department		College	
		Classes	
Calsalary()		Calsalary()	
Employees()		Lectures()	

ally to find out whether new refactorings are becoming applicable, or existing refactorings are becoming non applicable as a consequences of application of some other refactorings.

AUTOMATED SUPPORT FOR REFACTORING

Refactoring can be done either manually or with the support of automated tools. Researchers have proposed several automated tools that work as preprocessor for automating the process of converting existing programs to simpler and efficient form using code refactoring (Daniel et al, 2007). Though performance of an automatic tool is excellent as compared to manual refactoring, it lacks knowledge of programmer's domain. So, it has limited applicability and still most of the code is refactored manually. The reason behind this is incapability of automated tools to consider conflicts in refactoring techniques. The programmer is expert in particular problem domain and understands the concepts and existing program characteristics that must be preserved after refactoring.

Available Refactoring tools can be classified in two categories. The first category of them provides interactive application by a programmer while operating in an IDE i.e. a refactoring browser like Visual Studio. The second category of automated tools provides facility to substitute entirely for the interactive support, and can additionally carry out code modifications, which simply may not be possible by manual or even interactive refactoring.

Interactive refactoring tool is very convenient to use. For example, an interactive tool may provide facility for an off-line application of single or multiple sets of refactorings using batch tools. This approach combines the strengths of both- the programmer (domain knowledge, seeing the big picture) and the computerized tool (fast search, remembering history, and computation). This type of tool is provided domain knowledge by the programmer and has ability to perform operations like search and compute very fast. It can also behave like an expert system and remember the past history. In this approach, the programmer simply selects code and submits the required code transformation. The tool performs the complex task of checking the transformation safety by traversing through many modules and checking various conditions (e.g. conflict in application of refactorings) and then performing the code transformation. When it is not possible to apply that transformation, it provides the specific feedback to the programmer as in the case of visual interface of an IDE such as Eclipse or VisualStudio. This way programmer is able to perform the refactoring as desired. In fact, interactive tools reduce the burden of analyzing and modifying code, are fast enough to be used interactively, and correctly apply transformations that may get otherwise overlooked by the developers.

Fully automated tool support for applying refactorings is not desirable in many situations. Some refactorings can only be semi-automated and some refactoring rules like Rename Variable are difficult to implement in automated tools. The decision of which variable should be renamed, and what the new name should be, can not be fully supported by tools. For such kind of refactoring rules, interactive tools are desirable by programmers.

ReSharper (Resharper,2011) a renowned productivity tool used to make Microsoft Visual Studio a much better IDE, provides automated support for code inspection, refactoring, fast navigation, and coding assistance. For example, it provides Move method refactoring. It analyzes all members in the current class and makes a list of members that you can pull up. Before completing the refactoring, ReSharper also checks for possible conflicts, for example, whether the members that you are trying to move to a superclass will be accessible in the destination type or not.

Madhulika Arora et al (2011) examined three pairs of subsequent major Eclipse(eclipse, 2011) releases and discovered that refactoring involves a variety of restructuring types, ranging from simple element renaming and moves to substantial reorganization of the containment and inheritance hierarchies. Many of the refactorings are behavior preserving, but may still affect behavior of the client applications.

Some of the other available refactoring tools are: Microsoft Visual Studio (visual studio, 2011), Xcode (Xcode, 2011), and Squeak (squeak,2011).

FUTURE RESEARCH DIRECTIONS

Research on robust automated tools support for detecting code segments where refactoring rule is to be applied, is still on its initial stage. Although some automated refactoring or code transformation tools make it possible to apply refactoring rules in a predefined order, there is no guidance available on how to arrange the application order (schedule) of these rules. Generally each rule can be applied at many places in the given software code design, and there can be many rules that can be applied to a given code. So research in this direction is also required. In some situations it is important to decide where to apply the rule and where not to apply. It may

be more effective to apply the rules alternately in some cases. Also deciding the schedule of a chosen set of transformations has great impact on code quality. All of these issues need to be addressed in future research.

Madhulika Arora et al (2011) suggested that an automated tool should be able to treat a refactoring as composite command possibly consisting of a set of other refactorings and each such refactoring command should remember all its effects to the framework and should be able to replay them and also propagate them in the context of the given application. Future research can be carried on in this direction.

CONCLUSION

This chapter presented a comprehensive study about refactoring techniques, problem of conflicts arising in their application and their solution strategy comprising various processes involved in analyzing the code design, and a study of automated tool support for refactoring. We can conclude that different application orders of conflicting refactorings lead to different quality improvement. It can be concluded that in order to improve the software quality as much as possible, the application order of the available refactorings is critical, and random scheduling is not a good solution. Usually, the application order of the semi-automated refactorings is determined by software engineers. But this process is time consuming, and may not be reliable. This mechanism is fully dependent upon domain knowledge and expertise of the human involved. In case of inexperienced person interacting with the system, the process may simply lead to poor results. It can be further concluded that a robust scheduling approach is required to schedule the large amount of refactorings so as to improve software quality to meet the requirements.

REFERENCES

Arora, M., Sarangdevot, S. S., Rathore, V. S., Deegwal, J., & Arora, S. (2011). Refactoring, way for software maintenance. *International Journal of Computer Science Issues, 8*(2). ISSN: 1694-0814

Balazinska, M., Merlo, E., Dagenais, M., Lag¨ue, B., & Kontogiannis, K. (2000). Advanced clone-analysis to support objectoriented system refactoring. In *Proceedings of Working Conference Reverse Engineering*, (pp. 98-107). IEEE Computer Society.

Banerjee, J., & Kim, W. (1987). Semantics and implementation of schema evolution in object-oriented databases. In *Proceedings of the ACM SIGMOD Conference*, 1987.

Beck, K. (2000). *Extreme programming explained: Embrace change*. Reading, MA: Addison-Wesley.

Boger, M., Sturm, T., & Fragemann, P. (2002). Refactoring browser for UML. In *Proceedings of International Conference on eXtreme Programming and Flexible Processes in Software Engineering*, (pp. 77–81). Sardinia, Italy: Alghero.

Daniel, B., et al. (2007). Automated testing of refactoring engines. *ACM SIGSOFT Symposium on Foundations of Software Engineering*, (pp. 185–194). ACM Press.

Fowler, M. (2003). *Refactorings in alphabetical order*. Retrieved from http://www.refactoring.com/

Fowler, M., Beck, K., Brant, J., Opdyke, W., & Roberts, D. (1999). *Refactoring: Improving the design of existing code*. Addison-Wesley.

Kataoka, T., Ernst, M. D., Griswold, W. G., & Notkin, D. (2001). Automated support for program refactoring using invariants. In *Proceedings of International Conference on Software Maintenance*, (pp. 736–743). IEEE Computer Society.

Liu, H., Li, G., Ma, Z. Y., & Shao, W. Z. (2008). Conflict-aware schedule of software refactorings. *IET Software, 2*(5), 446–460. doi:10.1049/iet-sen:20070033

Mens, T., Taentzer, G., & Runge, O. (2005). Detecting structural refactoring conflicts using critical pair analysis. *Electronic Notes in Theoretical Computer Science, 127*(3), 113–128. doi:10.1016/j.entcs.2004.08.038

Mens, T., Taentzer, G., & Runge, O. (2007). Analysing refactoring dependencies using graph transformation. *Software & Systems Modeling, 6*, 269–285. doi:10.1007/s10270-006-0044-6

Mens, T., & Tourwe, T. (2004). A survey of software refactoring. *IEEE Transactions on Software Engineering, 30*, 126–139. doi:10.1109/TSE.2004.1265817

Murphy-Hill, E., & Black, A. P. (2008). Refactoring tools: Fitness for purpose. *IEEE Software, 25*, 38–44. doi:10.1109/MS.2008.123

Najjar, R., Counsell, S., Loizou, G., & Mannock, K. (2003). The role of constructors in the context of refactoring object-oriented systems. In *Proceedings of the European Conference on Software Maintenance and Reengineering*, (pp. 111–120).

Opdyke, W. F. (1992). *Refactoring: A program restructuring aid in designing object-oriented application frameworks*. Ph.D. thesis, University of Illinois at Urbana-Champaign.

Pérez, J., Crespo, Y., Hoffmann, B., & Mens, T. (2010). A case study to evaluate the suitability of graph transformation tools for program refactoring. *International Journal of Software Tools and Technology Transfer, 12*, 183–199. doi:10.1007/s10009-010-0153-y

Pettorossi, A., & Proietti, M. (1996). Rules and strategies for transforming functional and logic programs. *Computing Surveys, 28*(2).

Pressman, R. S. (2001). *Software engineering.* McGraw Hill. ISBN-0-07-365578-3

Simon, F., Steinbruckner, F., & Lewerentz, C. (2001). Metrics based refactoring. In *Proceedings of European Conference on Software Maintenance and Reengineering*, (pp. 30–38). IEEE Computer Society.

Tichelaar, S., Ducasse, S., Demeyer, S., & Nierstrasz, O. (2000). A meta-model for language-independent refactoring. In *Proceedings of Symposium on Principles of Software Evolution*, (pp. 157–169). IEEE Computer Society.

Tokuda, T., & Batory, D. S. (1995). Automated software evolution via design pattern transformations. In *Proceedings of International Symposium on Applied Corporate Computing*, 1995.

Tsantalis, N., & Chatzigeorgiou, A. (2009). Identification of move method refactoring opportunities. *IEEE Transactions on Software Engineering*, *35*(3), 347–367. doi:10.1109/TSE.2009.1

ADDITIONAL READING

Murphy, G. C., Kersten, M., & Findlater, L. (2006). How are Java software developers using the Eclipse IDE? *IEEE Software*, *23*(4), 76–83. doi:10.1109/MS.2006.105

Murphy-Hill, E., & Black, A. P. (2008). Breaking the barriers to successful refactoring: Observations and tools for extract method. *Proceedings of 30th International Conference on Software Engineering* (ICSE 08), (pp. 421–430). IEEE CS Press.

Roberts, D., Brant, J., & Johnson, R. E. (1997). A refactoring tool for Smalltalk. *Theory and Practice of Object Systems*, *3*(4), 253–263. doi:10.1002/(SICI)1096-9942(1997)3:4<253::AID-TAPO3>3.0.CO;2-T

Spanoudakis, G., & Zisman, A. (2001). Inconsistency management in software engineering: Survey and open research issues. In Chong, S. K. (Ed.), *Handbook of software engineering and knowledge engineering* (*Vol. 1*, pp. 24–29).

Steimann, F., & Thies, A. (2009). From public to private to absent: Refactoring Java programs under constrained accessibility. In the *Proceedings of the 23rd European Conference on Object-Oriented Programming (ECOOP 09), LNCS 5653*, (pp. 419–443).

Springer.Tahvildari, L., & Kontogiannis, K. (2003). A metric-based approach to enhance design quality through meta-pattern transformations. In *Proceedings of the European Conference on Software Maintenance and Reengineering*, (pp. 183–192). IEEE Computer Society.

Tip, F., Kiezun, A., & Baumer, D. (2003). Refactoring for generalization using type constraints. In *Proceedings of SIGPLAN Conference on Object-Oriented Programming, Systems, Languages, and Applications*, (pp. 13-26).

Tourw'e, T., & Mens, T. (2003). Identifying refactoring opportunities using logic meta programming, *Proceedings of International Conference on Software Maintenance and Re-engineering*, (pp. 91–100). IEEE Computer Society.

Van Eetvelde, N., & Janssens, D. (2003). A hierarchical program representation for refactoring. In the *Proceedings of UniGra'03 Workshop*, 2003.

van Emden, E., & Moonen, L. (2002). Java quality assurance by detecting code smells. *Proceedings of Working Conference on Reverse Engineering*, (pp. 97-108). IEEE Computer Society.

Section 3
Advancements in Engineering of Systems

Chapter 10

Towards Test–Driven and Architecture Model–Based Security and Resilience Engineering

Ayda Saidane
University of Luxembourg, Luxembourg

Nicolas Guelfi
University of Luxembourg, Luxembourg

ABSTRACT

The quality of software systems depends strongly on their architecture. For this reason, taking into account non-functional requirements at architecture level is crucial for the success of the software development process. Early architecture model validation facilitates the detection and correction of design errors. In this research, the authors are interested in security critical systems, which require a reliable validation process. So far, they are missing security-testing approaches providing an appropriate compromise between software quality and development cost while satisfying certification and audit procedures requirements through automated and documented validation activities. In this chapter, the authors propose a novel test-driven and architecture model-based security engineering approach for resilient systems. It consists of a test-driven security modeling framework and a test based validation approach. The assessment of the security requirement satisfaction is based on the test traces analysis. Throughout this study, the authors illustrate the approach using a client server architecture case study.

DOI: 10.4018/978-1-4666-2958-5.ch010

INTRODUCTION

The concept of resilience was introduced in ICT systems in 1970s (Black 1976) and has been more intensively used in the research community in the very last years. By analyzing this research, we can notice that the word is used with many different definitions and at different levels (Black et al. 1997, Mostert et al., 1995, Ries, 2009, Górski et al., 2006). In (Guelfi 2011), we proposed a formal framework called DREF (Dependability and Resilience Framework) for modeling and evaluating resilient and dependable systems. In particular, it quantitatively defines resilience and satisfaction against some functional or non-functional properties of interest. In our case, we focus on the evaluation of the security requirements satisfaction at both design and deployment phases. Specifically, we are designing a novel architecture-model based security testing methodology as an operational framework associated to DREF. In fact, we propose to use the interpretation of the test traces for experimentally evaluating the satisfaction of the security requirements by the system under test (SUT).

Model-driven engineering (MDE) is a software development methodology based on the usage, creation, validation and refinement of models representing that knowledge at different levels of abstractions from requirements to executable code. This methodology is gaining approval in industry especially in critical systems development with strong security and dependability requirements, because most of the MDE development process that is automated using model transformations appears to be less error-prone than classical methodologies. In our work, we are more specifically interested in security critical systems.

Software architecture design is an important step in the development process since it considerably impacts the quality of the system.

An architectural model can be refined from the requirement phase where early model validation facilitates the detection and correction of design errors. This validation can be done either by formal verification or by testing. The architecture analysis is an activity that keeps running during the whole development process. What could be expected from testing the architecture model is the elicitation of attack scenarios exploiting some architecture level threats, like covert channels, and also lower level vulnerabilities by locating their activation and manifestation points. In addition, MDE-based development processes are based on successive model transformations from the architecture model to executable code. Consequently, we can consider that validating the system architecture model would be equivalent to validating the real system if the deployed model transformations and their automation are proved correct.

In this project, we are interested in security critical systems, which require a reliable validation process. So far, we are missing security-testing approaches providing an appropriate compromise between software quality and development cost and satisfying certification and audit procedures requirements through an automated and documented validation activities. In order to define such methodologies, we should explicitly and unambiguously define the threat and security requirements models and integrate this knowledge with the system architecture model in both design and validation phases. At design time, this knowledge influences the design choices since we must address these threats and equip the system with the necessary resources to mitigate them. At validation time, it is important to select test cases, covering both input models (requirements and threats), which correspond to potential security failures caused by malicious attacks or accidental security mechanisms failures.

We have selected the Architecture Analysis and Description Language (AADL)[1] as a modeling framework for our work. AADL is a SAE standard for system architecture description and analysis widely used in industry and supported by major avionics, automotive and telecommunications providers[2].

The chapter is structured as follows: section 2 presents the problem statements and the motivations; section 3 presents the basic concepts in DREF and overview of model based security testing state of the art; section 4 defines the running example; section 5 provides details on the proposed test-driven development process for robust secure systems.

MOTIVATIONS AND PROBLEM STATEMENT

Software architecture description languages provide a detailed view on the system's components, their interfaces and their interactions. We have in such models enough information to derive test cases relevant for the security properties of interest. What could be expected from testing the architecture model is the elicitation of attack scenarios exploiting some architecture level threats, like covert channels, and also lower level vulnerabilities, such as unchecked user input, by locating their activation and manifestation points. More importantly, architecture level vulnerabilities can be identified only by exploit-

ing the architecture model for test generation, as they don't appear in the detailed design test models. However, to the best of our knowledge, there has been no prior work on security test generation from architecture model.

The quality of the generated test cases is strongly dependent on the quality of the test model. Specifically, we need to propose a modelling framework covering the functional aspect together with the malicious aspect existing in the system and its environment. In (MAFTIA 2003), a security fault model has been proposed; it consists of 3 classes of interrelated internal and external security threats:

- **Vulnerability:** Internal fault in system design, implementation or deployment;
- **Attack:** External malicious interaction fault aiming at exploiting a vulnerability and using it to violate some security properties;
- **An Intrusion:** A composite internal fault created by a successful attack. The intrusion activation creates an error, which propagates until generating system failure.

We have adopted this fault model and analyzed it from a testing perspective in order to identify what information should be included in the security test model.

Figure 1. Relationships between attacks, vulnerabilities and test observations

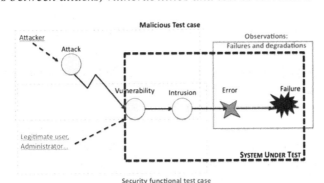

As shown in Figure 1, failures and degradations can be caused by 2 different interaction faults either executed by a legitimate user or a malicious attacker. We associate different categories to the test cases describing these scenarios:

Malicious Test Cases aim at validating the system against attack attempts. This category requires an appropriate specification of potential attackers' capabilities in terms of knowledge and interaction with the system. Consequently, an attacker model should be included in the test model.

- **Example:** A buffer-overflow attack requires a good knowledge of the system interface along with its software and hardware platform. The attacker model should include the buffer-overflow pattern that is able to execute.

Security Functional Test cases aim at validating the system against its functional security requirements. This category can be generated from the system functional specifications.

- **Example:** A legitimate user accidentally submits invalid credentials to the authentication service. However, it gets authenticated because there is a bug in the service implementation.

Therefore, testing the security of a system encompasses testing both legal and illegal means for interacting with SUT and accessing protected resources. The legal means should be derived from the system functional model while the illegal means are derived from the threat model. When analyzing the state of the arte in model based security testing, we notice that most proposals focus exclusively on one aspect.

In our work, we define an architecture model based security testing approach where threat models and security properties are explicitly specified and exploited for the security test generation and selection.

BACKGROUND

In section, we present a summary of the major trends in model based security testing and some insight on the DREF framework (Guelfi 2011).

DREF: Dependability and Resilience Framework

The Formal Framework for Dependability and Resilience (DREF) has been proposed in (Guelfi 2011). It defines the required concepts for specifying resilience requirements and evaluating their satisfaction. Hereafter, we summarize informally the basic concepts:

- **Entities:** Refer to the object of the evaluation. They are anything that is of interest to be considered. In our context, it corresponds to the system under test.
- **Properties:** Refer to the stakeholders' requirements that should be satisfied by the entities. It might be, for example, an informal requirement, a mathematical property or any entity that aims to be interpreted over entities. In our context, it corresponds to the security properties to be tested.
- **Satisfaction Function:** Is defined as a function taking as parameters properties and entities. It represents the satisfaction level of a property by an entity. Its value is a real value or undetermined $\perp$.
- **Nominal Satisfaction:** Represents the expected satisfaction against the properties of interest.
- **Tolerance Threshold:** Is used to represent the lower bound of tolerance margin with respect to a given nominal satisfaction.

- **A Tolerance:** Is defined as a tuple (property, entity) such that the corresponding satisfaction is in the tolerance margin, which refers to the zone between the nominal satisfaction and tolerance threshold.
- **A Failure:** Is defined as a tuple (property, entity) such that the corresponding satisfaction is lower than the corresponding tolerance threshold. In this case, the property fails to be satisfied by the entity.

Our objective is to quantitatively evaluate the satisfaction of the security requirements by the SUT. Testing is used as a means for evaluating experimentally the satisfaction function. Consequently, the satisfaction function must be expressed in terms of failed and successful test cases executions, which reveal failures and degradations.

Example: We present hereafter an example of satisfaction based on testing. Let **AM** be a set of architecture models, **SP** a set of security properties of interest and **sat** be a real-valued function defined on AM x SP:

$$sat: AM \times SP \rightarrow [0,1] \cup \{\perp\}$$
$$(m,sp) \rightarrow 1 - F_{m,sp} / N_{m,sp}$$

where $N_{m,sp}$ is the total number of the generated test cases from $\{m,sp\}$ and $F_{m,sp}$ is the number of test cases whose execution violates the security properties **sp**.

sat increases when the number of detected faults and vulnerabilities decrease. It reaches its maximal value (1) when all the security functional test cases pass and all the malicious test cases fail.

We might specify that sat(m,sp)>0.9 represents a nominal satisfaction while a value between 0.8-0.9 (respectively <0.8 represents a degradation (respectively a failure).

$$sat(m,sp) \begin{cases} nominal & if > 0.9 \\ degradation & if\ 0.8 \leq sat \leq 0.9 \\ failure & if < 0.8 \end{cases}$$

Resilience is defined as a change for increasing the satisfaction function, while reducing failures and tolerances. This definition implies that we are considering an evolution of an entity over a certain evolution axis, and we are characterizing each evolution state by the corresponding failures and tolerances with respect to a set of properties.

Model-Based Security Testing

Security testing is an important activity within secure software systems lifecycle. It is most popular validation technique in industry by opposition to formal verification. It is mainly used to ensure the compliance of final product with the system specification. The adoption of the model driven engineering paradigm for test generation resulted in Model-Based Security Testing (MBTS). The approach has received a lot of interest in the last years since it offers automation possibilities of test cases generation and execution tasks by model transformations

Figure 2. Classification of model-based security testing approaches

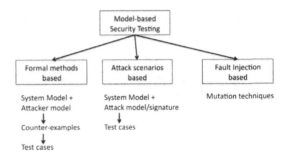

from different system models. This section provides an overview on the state of the art in model based security testing according to the classification depicted in Figure 2.

Formal Methods Based MBST Approaches

Theorem proving has been used for model-based testing (Castanet et al, 2002; Subramaniam et al, 2009; etc.) since late 90's. However, there are only few attempts in model-based security. An interesting contribution in the field is based on the UMLsec language (Jurjens 2005), which is an UML extension adding standard concepts from formal methods for security engineering to UML (i.e. security requirements: secrecy, integrity; security mechanisms: access control, encryption; or threat scenarios: adversary type, Threats). The security test cases (Jurjens 2008) are generated automatically from the SUT UMLsec specification using a theorem proofer and an attacker model generator.

Model checking has been widely used for test generation (Koo et al., 2009). In fact, the counter-examples, which are generated automatically, represent test cases violating the target properties. Recently, It has been applied to security testing. One of the recent works (Armando et al, 2010), the authors present their model checking based security testing approach for vulnerability detection and illustrate it by an analysis of a real commercial system analysis. In fact, they were able to generate an attack scenario against the authentication mechanism deployed by *google* web-based applications.

The main weakness of these approaches concerns the state explosion, which make them not suitable for validating large systems.

Attack Scenarios Based MBST Approaches

Penetration testing is a widely used method for validating secure software systems. However, it is not done systematically and it requires an in depth knowledge of security. Public databases of known vulnerabilities and attacks are used to drive penetration testing, but testers need to understand them and interpret them into executable test cases. In a MBST context, this activity is fully automated (Moutartidis et al. 2007; Xiong et al., 2009; Zulkernine et al. 2009)

These approaches should be associated to other MBST approaches that take into account the SUT architecture in order to generate SUT specific attack scenarios if applicable.

Fault Injection Based MBST Approaches

Fault injection based MBST is mostly carried out by mutation techniques. Many works, in this field, have been carried out (Marquis et al. 2005; Pretschner et al. 2008; Mouelhi et al. 2008). The purpose of these approaches is the functional testing of security mechanisms such as Policy Decision Point in access control systems.

This approach is popular for compliance testing but it is not suitable for identifying complex multi-step attacks. Moreover, the evaluation of the test generation coverage is generally disconnected from the target security properties to be satisfied.

Architecture Model Based Testing

We can find in the literature few works around test generation from architecture models. These approaches rely on the description of architecture dynamics for generating the test cases. The architecture dynamic behaviour is generally described in terms of State Machines (Richardson et al. 1996; Bucchiarone et al. 2007), Petri Nets (Schulz et al. 2007), Labelled Transition Systems (Muccini 2002; Bertolino et al. 2001) or Interaction Connectivity Graphs (Jin 2000, Debra et al. 1996). The test selection criteria are defined in terms of paths in the SM (resp. PN, LTS or ICG) modelling the properties of interest. Different reduction algorithms are proposed according to the chosen modelling framework and properties to be tested.

It is worth highlighting that to the best of our knowledge, there is no published work dedicated to security oriented test generation from architecture models.

RUNNING EXAMPLE

In this section, we present the case study, the associated security properties resulting from security requirements elicitation and the considered threats resulting from security analysis. Both security requirements and threat model are considered as input to our modelling and testing approach. Initially, they could be described in informal or formal ways. In both cases, their inclusion into the architectural model is a manual step to be performed by a security engineer.

Case Study Description

Throughout this chapter, we consider the classical client/server architecture example where we have one client and one server, namely *client1* and server1 that is considered as our system under test (SUT). The server is responsible for managing the access of a set of confidential data. These systems are interconnected through an open network (*Internet*).

In our example, *client1* and *Internet* are part of the test system (TS). *Client 1* represents a legitimate and honest client consequently the interactions with SUT describe test cases for the functional security requirements. The threat analysis results will add details about the potential malicious client profile in terms of knowlledge, capabilities and interactions with SUT. Security requirements and threat models are necessary input for testing the system security at any level of abstraction.

Security Requirements Elicitation

We will focus our study on a couple of security requirements associated to this system where server1 is responsible for managing access to some confidential information stored locally on the system.

- **Property_1:** Only authorized clients defined in the security policy, can access confidential information (sp1).
  - ○ **Example:** In a Multi-Level Security policy, security levels are associated to data and to entities accessing them. A client can access any data with same or less security level.
- **Property_2:** Confidential information must be protected during storage, transfer and processing (sp2).
  - ○ **Example:** Ensuring confidentiality property on information transfer is related to the information flow security. In fact, any information flow between authorized parties should ensure confidentiality in all its subflows in away that limit the access to parties complying with the security policy.

Threats Analysis

Threat analysis is not an additional activity required by the security testing process. On the contrary, it is a critical activity carried out in the first steps of any secure system engineering process. It aims at identifying the potential hazards menacing the system. In fact, it is needed to define their severity, activation and propagation mechanisms or impact on the system security in order to design the appropriate security mechanism to face them. The outcome of this analysis impacts heavily the architecture and implementation of the future system.

The threats analysis of our running example identified a set of security threats preventing the satisfaction of the security properties cited earlier. In this chapter, we focus on the following threats:

- **Threat_1:** The communication between client and server is done through an open network (i.e. Internet). Thus, eavesdropping attack is feasible by any malicious client connected to the network, which might intercept sensitive data such as the authentication credentials or readable protected data circulating on the network.
  - ◦ **Example:** The violation of the security property described in Property_1 can be violated when Threat_1 is exploited. Figure 5 shows an attack scenario where the malicious attacker intercept the credential of the legitimate client and use them to access the confidential data. The generation of such test case requires an explicit reasoning about the threat model.
- **Threat_2:** The confidential data stored on the server can be accessible to anyone able to circumvent the security mechanisms guarding the access to the confidential data.
  - ◦ **Example:** The data stored locally on the hard disk and accessible through the operating system might be at risk. In fact, any other corrupted process on the system having appropriate permissions can access the confidential data without going through the access control mechanisms. In this example we consider only external intruder not

insiders. Therefore, the other process has been corrupted remotely.

AADL (Analysis and Architecture Description Language)

Throughout this chapter we base our study on the Analysis and Architecture Description Language. AADL is a standardized architecture description language released in 2006 by the SAE. It is proposed for specifying a multi-aspect model suitable for analyzing both functional and non-functional requirements. In addition, it offers textual and graphic notation with precise semantics for modelling both software and hardware layers. For interoperability purposes, a UML profile representing AADL has been proposed.

The main concepts of the AADL modelling framework can be split into 3 categories related to the software system design (Software components (Feiler and al. 2006): Process, Thread, Data, Subprogram), the runtime platform (Execution Platform components: Processor, Bus, Device) and composite components (system). AADL allow the definition of component types and their implementation where the type defines the interface and their implementation an internal structure including subcomponents and their interconnections. In addition to these elements, AADL supports an annex extension mechanism to customize the description capabilities of the language by introducing a dedicated sub-language. Today, AADL has been enriched by the definition of 2 standardized annexes: a framework for supporting fault/reliability modelling and hazard analysis through the error model annex; and a framework for specifying dynamics of the system and simulation based validation through behavioural annex.

Figure 3. Graphical and textual AADL models for client server architecture

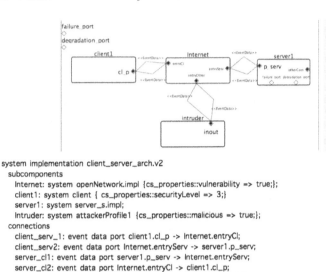

```
system implementation client_server_arch.v2
   subcomponents
      Internet: system openNetwork.impl {cs_properties::vulnerability => true;};
      client1: system client { cs_properties::securityLevel => 3;}
      server1: system server_s.impl;
      Intruder: system attackerProfile1 {cs_properties::malicious => true;};
   connections
      client_serv_1: event data port client1.cl_p -> Internet.entryCl;
      client_serv2: event data port Internet.entryServ -> server1.p_serv;
      server_cl1: event data port server1.p_serv -> Internet.entryServ;
      server_cl2: event data port Internet.entryCl -> client1.cl_p;
      attackStep1: event data port Intruder.inOut -> Internet.entryOther;
      attackStep2: event data port Internet.entryOther -> Intruder.inOut;
      annex Behavior_specification {...}
```

AN AADL MODELING FRAMEWORK FOR SECURITY TESTING

In this section, we present an overview on the AADL language and how it can be used in a test-driven security modeling approach.

Structural Modeling with AADL

At this level of abstraction, the system is seen as a set of interacting components providing globally a set of functional and non-functional properties. The AADL language allows the specification of both software and hardware parts of computing systems. The software architecture is defined as a set of interacting software components such as process, thread, subprogram, data, etc. In Figure 3, we present a sample of the AADL architecture models of the client server architecture enriched by some information from the threat model.

Figure 3 shows the global AADL architecture model for the case study. It is composed of 4 subcomponents:

- **server1:** Is a component of type *server_s*. It represents the actual access manager to the confidential data in addition to some other non-security related components that are not represented here such as some advertisement generator. The interface of this component includes an in-out event data port *serv_p* used to communicate with the other components. The notion of port here might refer to some web forms input or a smart card reader if we consider just the data input aspect.

The internal structure of the server is represented in Figure 4. This component includes: a process *server_proc* and the protected data *ConfidentialData*. In Figure 5, we define an abstract information flow (*process_req*) modelling the request processing that starts by an input on the

Figure 4. AADL architecture model for the server system

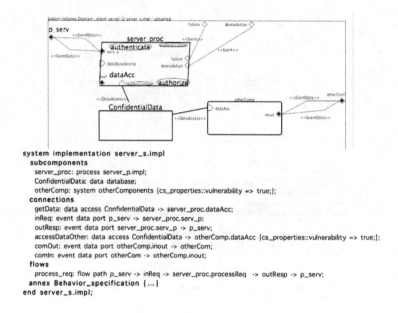

```
system implementation server_s.impl
  subcomponents
    server_proc: process server_p.impl;
    ConfidentialData: data database;
    otherComp: system otherComponents {cs_properties::vulnerability => true;};
  connections
    getData: data access ConfidentialData -> server_proc.dataAcc;
    inReq: event data port p_serv -> server_proc.serv_p;
    outResp: event data port server_proc.serv_p -> p_serv;
    accessDataOther: data access ConfidentialData -> otherComp.dataAcc {cs_properties::vulnerability => true;};
    comOut: event data port otherComp.inout -> otherCom;
    comIn: event data port otherCom -> otherComp.inout;
  flows
    process_req: flow path p_serv -> inReq -> server_proc.processReq -> outResp -> p_serv;
  annex Behavior_specification {...}
end server_s.impl;
```

Figure 5. AADL behaviour model for the client server architecture

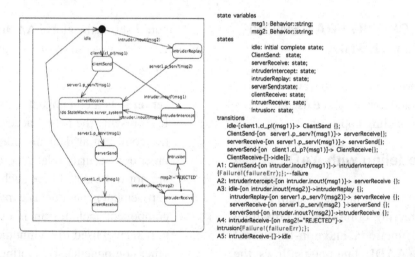

p_serv port, that is forwarded to the *server_proc* process on the *serv_p* port. Then the internal *processReq* flow of the *server_proc* is activated. Once a message is received at *serv_p* port, the message is forwarded through *p_serv* port. In addition we have 2 events ports failure and degradation for signaling any violation of the security policy.

- **intruder** is process component of type *attackerProfile1*. attackerProfile1 is expected to describe the threat model in terms of attacker capabilities to interact with the system. According to the threat model, the intruder can execute 5 actions corresponding to message interception, message replay or simple interaction with the server. The capabilities must be modeled in the in-

Figure 6. AADL behaviour model for the server process

```
state variables                      transitions
    credentials: Behavior::string;      t1:  startSession-[serv_p?(credentials)]->waitAuthentication
    response: Behavior::string;              {authentication(credentials,authenticated_r, securityLevelClient)!;};
    request: Behavior::string;
    authenticated_r: Behavior::boolean;  t2:  startSession-[]->corrupted{response:=dataAcc;
    authorized_r: Behavior::boolean;         Degradation!_port!(degradationErr);};
    securityLevelData:                       corrupted-[]->accessdata();
Behavior::integer;
    securityLevelClient:                 t3:  waitAuthentication-[on authenticated_r=true]-> Authenticated
Behavior::integer;                       {serv_p!;};
                                         t4:  waitAuthentication-[on authenticated_r=false]->reject();
states                                   t5:  reject-[]->endSession();
    startSession: initial state;
    waitAuthentication: state;           Authenticated-[serv_p?(request)]->
    Authenticated: state;                waitAuthorization{authorization(request,authorized_r)!;};
    reject: state;                       waitAuthorization-[on authorized_r=true]->Authorized();
    waitAuthorization: state;            Authorized-[on authorized_r=true]->
    Authorized: state;                   accessData{response:=dataAcc;};
    accessData: state;                   accessData-[]->endSession{serv_p(response)!;};
    endSession: complete state;          waitAuthorization-[on authorized_r=false]->reject();
    corrupted: state;
```

ternal structure of the malicious component while the strategies should be defined in the behavioral model.

- **client** is a process component of type *client1*. It represents the honest users and can execute 2 actions namely authentication request and data access request. It has one in-out data event port for communicating with the server.
- **Internet** is a system component of type *openNetwork*.

These models define the interfaces of the different components and their dependencies. More details about the internal structure of the different components are available (Saidane et 2011).

Behavioral Modeling with AADL

The AADL behaviour annex allows the specification of the software architecture dynamics. The AADL behaviour model (BM) is represented as a state-transition system consisting of: 1) states, 2) variable states, and 3) transitions.

Figure 5 presents the behaviour model of the whole client server architecture where we describe explicitly the malicious attack performed by the intruder that intercepts the client's messages and replay them. We decided to consider this simple attack where the intruder is interested in intercepting the client message in order to extract the

credentials and use them later to access the system as shown in Figure 6. Intuitively, other threats can be derived, such as intercepting the response of the server and also man-in-the middle attacks where the intruder impersonates the server from he client's view and impersonates the client from the server's view. These attacks can be modeled following the same approach by adding appropriate states and transitions to the model or any needed capability to the attacker profile.

Further, during the threat analysis we have identified the port *serv_p* as vulnerability in the system, which can be exploited to corrupt the server. The transition t2 in Figure 5 shows a possible exploitation through a buffer overflow like attack circumventing the authentication and authorization mechanisms and accessing directly the data. t2 should appear in a malicious test case testing possible protections added at the implementation level to check any user input. If the corresponding test cases fail, this shows an unsuccessful attack and, consequently, we observe a nominal behaviour.

Figure 6 presents the behavioural model for the server_p process component. It is represented as a state machine, which transitions are triggered by the reception of some events, call of server subprograms or the change of some internal state variables' values. For example, the transition (t1,

Figure 7. A test-driven security and resilience engineering process

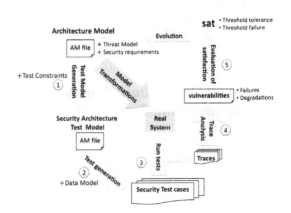

Figure 6) between *startSession* and *waitAuthentication* is triggered by the reception of data on port *serv_p*. According to the interaction protocol between the client and server, the message should include the client credentials. This corresponds to a nominal behaviour whatever is the result of the authentication that might lead to an authentication failure in the state *reject* (t4, Figure 6) or success in the state *authenticated*. Still these 2 pathes (t1.t3 and t1.t4) correspond to a nominal behaviour and should generated security functional test cases for validating the authentication mechanism.

TOWARDS A TEST-DRIVEN DEVELOPMENT PROCESS

In this section, we propose a generic test-driven development process (SETER, Figure 7) and its implementation using an AADL extension. SETER consists of a generic modeling and validation steps for developing robust secure systems. Its originality resides in defining a new test-driven security engineering approach based on the exploitation of architecture models and MDE paradigm. We can divide the process into 3 phases: the code generation, the test generation and test-based validation. In the following, we identify the objectives and required engineering artifacts for each activity.

The literature offers different solutions for code generation from architecture description languages including some proposals for AADL based code generation (Brun et al. 2008). In this study, we don't address this issue and rely on external tools.

Test Model Generation: A Test-Driven Security-Modeling Framework

The quality of the generated test cases is strongly dependent on the quality of the test model. Specifically, we need to propose a modelling

Figure 8. AADL architecture model for the server process

```
property set cs_properties is
    malicious: aadlboolean => false applies to (all);
    securityLevel: aadlinteger => 0 applies to (data, system, process);
    SecurityMechanism: aadlboolean => false applies to (subprogram,
    thread, process, device, system);
    vulnerability: aadlboolean applies to (all);
end cs_properties;
```

framework covering the security functional aspect together with the malicious aspect existing in the system and its environment. However, Most of security testing approaches proposed in the literature focus exclusively on one aspect and neglect the other (Marquis et al. 2005, Zulkernine et al. 2009, etc.). In study, we aim at validating the systems against its requirements in the presence or absence of threats. A test-driven security-modeling framework is proposed to allow this integration. An example of threat model integration has already been presented in Figure 4 where an attacker is explicitly added to the client-server system and the attacker's interactions with the other components depict its attack strategies.

In (Saidane et al. 2011), we have evaluated the expressiveness of AADL for security modeling. The lessons learned from that study could be summarized as follows:

- AADL allows specifying what components belong to the threat model and what components represent security mechanisms. This done through the definition of different AADL properties as presented in Figure 8.
- AADL does not allow an appropriate specification of the security policy that is precise enough for generating all relevant test cases. In fact, we can define the required attributes (such as credentials or location or role, etc.) as AADL properties. However, we cannot differentiate them from other non-security properties.

Figure 9. Attacker profile and behavioral model in AADL

```
package attackProfile              annex behavior_specification (**
public                             state variables
  process AttackerProfile1             msg: Behavior::string;
    features                       states
      intercept:   server    subprogram    start: initial state;
        intercepMsg;                        interceptS: state;
        replay: server subprogram replayMsg;  replayS: state;
        readData:    server    subprogram    sendServer: state;
        readConfidential;                   pingS: state;
        release:    server    subprogram    intrusion: complete state;
        releaseMsg;                         failure: complete state;
        inout: in out event data port;      endS: return state;
    properties                     transitions -- modeling attack steps
      cs_prop::attack_patterns=>       start-[on intercept!(msg->msg)]->
("eavesdropping",                interceptS{};
        "identity_theft");                  interceptS-[on replay!(msg->msg)]->
    end AttackerProfile1           replayS{};
....                                         replayS-[on    readRequest!(msg->
end attackProfile;                 msg)]->
                                       intrusion{};
```

- AADL does not allow tracing the dependencies between requirements, threats and security mechanisms. These dependencies are needed for test selection in order to ease the coverage of both legal (functional) and illegal (malicious actions) means for accessing protected resources.

Threats Modeling with AADL

In Figure 3, an intruder component has been added to the system model. It represents explicitly the threat model and it is tagged by the AADL property malicious. The malicious components model the attack patterns elicited during the threat analysis. For reuse purposes, we define a dedicated package for attack profiles where each profile consists of a set of actions modeling the capabilities of the attacker (Figure 9). Different combinations of those actions represent attack patterns that will appear at the test generation time as part of malicious test cases. We have also defined a property attack patterns, which associate to each profile the list of attacks it can perform. An example is shown in Figure 9.

AADL allows the explicit description of the attackers' profiles and their strategies, which are used to generate malicious test cases. However, we are not able to measure the coverage of the generated malicious test cases with the security requirements to be tested. An extension is needed for modeling the dependencies between requirements, threats and security enforcement mechanisms.

Security Policy Modeling with AADL

We proceeded to the extension of AADL through a security annex, where all the missing information required for the test selection can be specified. In fact, the proposed annex defines the security rule and associates it with threats in terms of malicious components and enforcement mechanism in terms of dedicated security components identified as enforcement mechanisms. All components referenced in the security annex should belong to the system architecture model.

The proposed AADL annex for security specification is called *SecureAADL*. The primary goal from extending AADL is to allow the specification of both the security policy at architecture level and the dependencies between requirement - threats - countermeasures. Among the different security policy's specification languages, XACML[3] can be considered as *de facto* standard used in both industry and academy. Moreover, we consider that a *secureAADL* annex consists of a unique security policy (Figure 10) according to the definition of a policy in XACML. As for the specification of security policies at architecture level, XACML rules' structure is well suited for this purpose. In fact, a security policy consists of a set of rules determining who are legitimate subjects to access protected resources and what actions they can execute. However, The XACML reference concepts have been refined in order to comply with AADL modeling framework.

Syntactically, the SecureAADL annex is described textually in an AADL-like style, the concrete syntax is presented in Figure 11. In the following, we redefine the XACML concept to fit the ADDL model:

Figure 10. SecureAADL annex metamodel

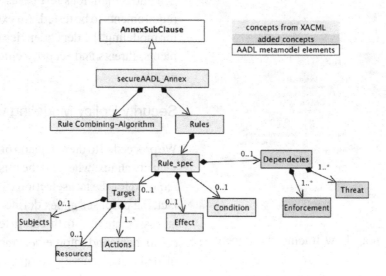

Figure 11 SecureAADL grammar

```
Security_annex ::= "security_model" "{**"
      "Combining algorithm" ["permit-overrides" | "deny-overrides"]
      Rules rule_spec+
**}
rule_spec ::= Rule {Identifier} {
      [condition_spec]
      effect_spec
      target_spec
      dependency_spec]
}
effect_spec ::= Effect [deny|allow]
condition_spec ::= Conditions
      Identifier boolean_condition {[and|or] boolean_condition }*
end conditions

target_spec ::= Target
      Subjects subject_spec* end subjects
      Resources resource_spec end resources
      Actions action_spec {; action_spec}*
end target
subject_spec ::= Identifier [attribute_identifier :
            attribute_value]*
resource_spec ::= Identifier [attribute_identifier :
            attribute_value]*
action_spec ::= action_type {, action_type}*
action_type ::= read | write | execute
dependency_spec ::= Dependencies
      enforcement_spec
      threats_spec
end dependencies
enforcement_spec ::= Enforcement  component_identifier {;
            component_idenfier}*
threats_spec ::= Threats  component_identifier {;
            component_idenfier}*
Identifier ::= Character {AlphaNum}*
Character ::= a .. z | A .. Z
AlphaNum ::= Numeric |Character | _
Numeric ::= 0 | 1 | 2 | 3 | 4 | 5 | 6 | 7 | 8 | 9
Boolean_expression : := Disjunction {or Disjunction}*
Disjunction ::= Not_Conjunction {and Not_Conjunction}*
Not_Conjunction ::= [not] Conjunction
Conjunction ::= Arith_Expression [(<|>|=|!=) Arith_Expression ] |
            Boolean_literal
Arith_Expression ::= Add_Expression {(+ | -) Add_Expression}*
Add_Expression ::= Basic_Expression {(* | /) Basic_Expression}*
Basic_Expression ::= Constant_Expression | Attribute_Identifier
Constant_Expression ::= Numeric
```

- **Attributes**: They are used to characterize subjects, resources, actions or environment. In our context, the attributes must be AADL properties derived from the system model.

- **Subjects:** A subject is an actor who makes a request to access certain protected resources. In our context, a subject could be a system, process, thread or subprogram. Therefore subject type refers to component type.

- **Resources:** A resource is a data, system component or service (AADL server subprogram). This definition remains unchanged.

- **Actions:** An action is an operation executed on a resource such as access (read/write) or execute (service call). The action should be compliant the AADL system model.

- **Rules:** A rule is a repesentation of a security requirement. It is a *tuple=(target, effect, condition, dependencies)* where *target=(subjects, resources, actions)*, effect=allow/deny, *dependencies=(threat, enforcements)*.

As shown in Figure 11, the XACML security policy has been enriched by information related to the threats and enforcement mechanisms. These information are not used for test selection and system validation. In fact, we specify for each rule what components enforce it and what components might violate it. The security-functional test cases to be derived for the rule must involve all components enforcing it. Similarly, the malicious test cases to be derived for the rule must involve all components threatening it.

Syntactically, the SecureAADL annex is described textually according to the grammar presented in Figure 12. Let's consider the following requirement:

Confidential data can be accessed only by authorized users which provide valid credentials during work hours.

This requirement can be specified in SecureAADL as shown in Figure 13. It is modeled as one secureAADL rule which target consists of the 2 kinds of subjects defined either explicitly through their credentials or with a conditions over their credentials: "credentials belong to the list of authorized users". All the attributes used to define the subjects must be defined in the AADL architecture model as AADL-properties associated to the components' types referenced as subjects.

As explained earlier, validating a secure system requires the validation of its behaviour against both trusted and hostile environment. According

Figure 12. SecureAADL example

```
Rule secReq1
  effect allow
  target
    subjects
      S1 component_type in (client, attacker)
            Credentials: in server.authorizedUsers
    end subjects
    resources
      R1   component_type in (server.confidentialData)
    end resources
    actions read, write
  end target
  dependencies
    enforcement server.authentication, server.authorization
    threats attacker
  end dependencies
End secReq1
```

Figure 13. Automated test generation

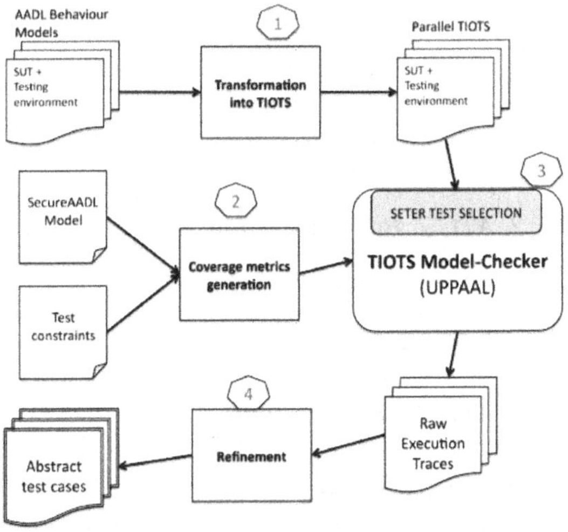

to the *secureAADL* model, we consider that a security requirement has been covered by the test selection if we find in the final test suite one or more test case involving all subjects, enforcement mechanisms, threats and actions referenced in the rule representing the requirement. Specifically we need at least 2 test cases validating a normal access to the protected resources and validating the robustness of the system against the threats. Furthermore, gathering all the components in a same test case might not be feasible in that case we need several test cases to cover the requirement. For example, the security requirement R_1 (Figure 13) is covered by the generation of 2 test cases: the first involving the client while the second involving at least the server and the attacker.

Test Cases Generation

The AADL behaviour model is defined as a state-transition system where every path is a potential abstract test cases for the SUT. We define an abstract test case (ATC) as a sequence of events complying with SUT model and used to test certain properties. ATCs represent a class of executable test cases. The state-transition system depicted in

Figure 6 combine events from the SUT (server) and the testing environment (client and intruder).

This abstract test case, presented in Box 1, corresponds to a full data access request including authentication and authorization phases. Many test cases will be derived from it. In fact, we need to test all the sub-paths such as successful and unsuccessful authentication and authorization. The non-reception of responses is considered as a failure of the test case

This abstract test case, presented in Box 2, corresponds to a malicious entry aiming at accessing the confidential data without going through the authentication and the authorization mechanisms. From the behavior model, we can extract this attack pattern corresponding to an input that executes a different code from the original and provides generally malicious services.

This test case, presented in Box 3, corresponds to a message from the client1 to server1 intercepted by the intruder and resent again in the network. The actions by the intruder are not always interactions with SUT but with its environments like in this case.

We can classify the test case in security functional or malicious test cases as explained earlier.

Box 1. ATC 1. Full Request Processing

```
client1.cl_p! (authentication_credentials). client1.cl_?(authentication_re-
sponse). client1.cl_p! (authorization_request). client1.cl_p?(authorization_
response)
```

Box 2. ATC 2. Buffer Overflow Attack

```
client1.cl_p! (malicious_input). client1.cl_p?(malicious_output)
```

Box 3. ATC 3. Eavesdropping Attack

```
client1.cl_p!(msg1). intruder.inout?(msg1). intruder.inout!(msg1)
```

Furthermore, we can refine the evaluation of the security requirements satisfaction by associating different severity levels to the test cases using the simple error model associated with the architecture Model (Saidane et al. 2012). Additionally, we need to be careful about the interpretation of the traces from security functional test cases and malicious test cases. This issue is addressed in the test-based validation section.

Automating Test Case Generation

In a test-driven development process all the models are intended to be testing artifacts. For this purpose, we integrated the environment model with the system model for studying their mutual interactions. In the example depicted in figures {4,5} (structural view) and {6,7} (behaviour model), we present the closed system composed by the SUT: server component and the environment: client1, intruder and Internet components.

The behaviour model is defined as a state-transition system that can be interpreted in terms of input/output transition systems (IOTS) (lynch et al. 1989). We consider IOTS because, from a testing perspective, we need to differentiate inputs and outputs between the SUT and the environment, and particularly, the input events and output events are the only observable events in the context of black box testing. Moreover, we can find many tools supporting the validation of such models (von Oheimb et al. 2002, Lim et al. 2005, Yang et al.2009). Some works propose to use model checkers as model analyzers supporting the automation of the test generation (Petrenko et al. 2003, Hessel et al. 2008, Zhou et al. 2009).

In AADL, the differentiation between input and output events is not explicit. However, we can distinguish them as follows:

- **AADL Input Events:** Receiving data/ events on ports (port_name?), or receiving a server subprogram call (subprogram_name ?).

- **AADL Output Events:** Sending data/ events on ports (port_name!), or sending a server subprogram call (subprogram_name !).

Figure 6 summarizes the possible interactions between the different parties. However, that model can be inferred from the parallel composition of the separate components' behavior models. Considering the detailed models of the components, allows to study about the internal mechanisms enabling and generating the observable interactions, ensures more precision in evaluating the generated test-suite in terms of some coverage criteria that might be structural, behavioral or security related. Therefore, we transform the different components' behaviour model into independent IOTS that are parallelly composed.

In addition, AADL behaviour model introduces explicitly the time notion through the predefined type *behaviour::time* and the functions timeout and delay. Therefore, Timed IOTS are more suitable in our context. From our architecture model-based security testing perspective, this representation is more interesting because it allows the specification of the SUT, trusted-parties and hostile-parties as independent autonomous systems that are interacting in the context of a closed system. This representation is closer to the real world configuration.

An Timed IOTS (Kaynar et al. 2003) is a tuple $M = (states(M), init(M), V(M), Act(M), \theta(M), transitions(M), C(M))$:

- **state(M):** A set states
- **init(M):** A set of initial states
- **V(M):** A set of variables
- **θ(M):** A set of conditions/predicates on variables V
- **Act(S):** It is the finite alphabet of actions partitioned into: *in(M)*: set of input actions; *out(M)*: set of output actions; *internal(M)*: set of internal actions. An action $a \in Act(M)$ is characterized by its signature

Table 1. Mapping the AADL behaviour model into IO transition systems

Timed IO transition system	AADL Behaviour Model[4]
Act(M)	The component interface actions in terms of port!(send event/data); port?(receive event/data); server subprogram call; in addition to internal events belonging to subcomponents
States(M)	States
Init(M)	The set of initial states
V(M)	State variables in the AADL behaviour model
θ(M)	Set of all predicates used in the guards on transitions
Transitions(M)	The transitions in the AADL behavior models are more sophisticated than the IOTS. AADL transitions allow subprogram call and executing some actions in addition to assignments.
C(M)	Set of variables of type Behaviou::time

Table 2. Interpretation test case results

	PASS	FAIL
Security functional ATC	System satisfies requirement	System does not satisfy requirement: degradation/failure
Malicious ATC	System does not satisfy requirement: degradation/failure	System satisfies requirement

$sig(a)=(p_1... p_k)$ specifying the types of parameters carried by the action a.

- **A Transition Relation Transitions(M):** A transition is a tuple $t=<S_i,G,a,A,S_j>$ where $S_i,S_j \in states(M)$; G is a predicate guard on $V \cup sig(a)$; A is a set of assignment manipulating variables V.
- **C(M):** Set of clocks

Table 1 defines a mapping between the two models. The transformation between the two models seems very intuitive since we find many similarities. Moreover, the timed IO automata model allows the definition of variables and data types.

Model-based test generation is automated using model analyzers capable of exploring the SUT and its environments models and generating execution traces based on their interactions. In our context, the execution traces of TIOTS is a sequence of inputs and outputs actions directed from the testing environment to the SUT (i.e. ATC1, ATC2 and ATC3).

The choice of a TIOTS model analyzer for our automated test generation has been based on the following requirements:

- **Scalability:** The model analyzer should be able to handle real case studies consisting of a large number of transitions and states.
- **Simulation Capabilities:** This is an important asset when building complex models. In fact, it helps the modeler in evaluating the design choices on the system's implementation and the requirements satisfaction.
- **Possible Extension on the Selection of the Test Cases:** It is mandatory to be able to customize the test cases selection in order to implement our own test selection strategy.

Figure 13 shows the full test generation process. We can divide it into 4 tasks: 1) transforming the AADL behaviour model into TIOTS according to the guidelines in Table 2. Currently, this is a manual task but it can be easily automated; 2) generating the test selection criteria according to our coverage driven approach presented in the next section; 3) using UPPAAL[5] for generating raw execution traces; and finally refinement into ATCs.

UPPAAL is a toolbox for modeling, validation and verification of real-time distributed systems modeled as networks of timed automata, extended with data types (bounded integers, arrays, etc.). As shown in (Robson 2004), UPPAAL is an interesting tool for TIO automata validation and simulation that has been used to verify real systems developed by universities and several industrial partners. Currently, there are 2 versions of the tool one research-oriented and the other commercial. UPPAAL tool environment allows the definition of complex data structures and the definition of complex internal actions in terms of C-like procedures and functions. These features will be used to develop and implement our test selection primitives as defined in the next section.

The abstract test cases generated by UPPAAL contain extra-information such as internal actions and the states and transitions activated after each step. In addition, it provides the variables values. A polishing is required in order to obtain an ATC with form presented in ATC1,2,3.

A Coverage-Driven Test Selection

Exhaustive testing is unfeasible in most real cases and consequently selection criteria are used to limit the search domain. In our study, we are targeting distributed and real time systems, which behavioral models might generate infinite traces. Thus, selection criteria such as final states and maximum test case length must be defined to avoid endless executions sequences during test generation and selection steps. Ultimately, the test suite will be evaluated using a coverage model. Coverage is a measure of the quality of a test suite that is based on some statistical measurements on the test suite and the test model.

In Coverage-driven validation process, there are 2 activities: 1) coverage metric definition and 2) test generation (Lettnin et al. 2007, Chen et al. 2008, Cichos et al. 2011). Our test selection approach comply with this framework as shown in (2, Figure 14). A test case generated through such process activate some test target and it reduces considerably the number of tests compared to random generation.

The coverage goals are defined as coverage arrays. A states-coverage-array is an array indexed by the states and specifying what states must be covered: state-coverage-array(S_i)=1 if the state

Figure 14. Coverage driven test selection algorithm

```
Coverage-driven-selection (currentState, currentTransition)

If (currentState is finalState or TemporaryTestCase.maxSize reached) then
    (a) evaluate added coverage of TemporaryTestCase
        evaluate the added coverage by comparing (TemporaryTestCaseStates_cov against
        Cstates) and (TemporaryTestCase.Transitions_cov against CTransitions) and
        (TemporaryTestCase.Requirements_cov against Crequirements )
        if there is added coverage then
            (b) accept test case
                add TemporaryTestCase to selcectedTestCases
                update Cstates, Ctransitions, Crequirements //coverage of current test suite
            (c) check is selection should end
                endSelection=true if  (Cstates covers GoalCoverage_states) and (Ctransitions
                    covers      GoalCoverage_transitions)      and      (Crequirements     covers
                    GoalCoverage_requirements) or max size reached
                if endSelection then exit end
    end
    (d) Initialize TemporaryTestCase
else
    (e) continue construction of the new test case
        if guard is IO action then add IOaction to TemporaryTestCase.IOa
        update TemporaryTestCase.States_cov by assigning true to state1, state2
        update TemporaryTestCase.Transitions_cov(currentTransition)=true
End
```

S_i should be covered and 0 if not. Similarly, we define a transitions-coverage-array as an array indexed by the transitions and specifying which transitions must be covered. Our test model consists of at least 3 components: SUT, attacker and legitimate user. A component coverage goal is refined in terms of states and transitions coverage-arrays or coverage rates if we are not targeting specific states or transitions to be covered.

The ultimate goal of this research is to evaluate the satisfaction of the security properties by the architecture model and the real system. Covering the security properties of interest implies testing all legal and illegal means to access the protected resources referenced in the requirements. According to the structure of secureAADL rules, we refine the coverage of a security requirement (i.e. a secureAADL rule) into coverage of the components appearing in the rule. We will derive two kinds of coverage criteria for each rule:

- **Security Functional Criteria:** For every security requirement SRi, we define security functional coverage goals in terms of a pair (SRi-Func-SUT transitions-coverage-array, SRi-Func-client transitions-coverage-array).
- **Threats Coverage Criteria:** For every security requirement SRi, we define threats coverage goals in terms of pair (SRi-

Threat-SUT transitions-coverage-array, SRi-Threat-attacker transitions-coverage-array). Optionally, we might add client-coverage-array in the threats coverage goals when some attack scenarios elicited during the threat analysis phase involve both attacker and client.

For the security requirements, the coverage goals satisfaction is evaluated against single test cases not against the whole test suite. A single test case covers partially the security functional criteria of a security requirement if it covers partially and simultaneously SRi-Func-SUT transitions-coverage-array and SRi-Func-client transitions-coverage-array. Similarly, a test case covers partially and simultaneously SRi-Threat-SUT transitions-coverage-array a SRi-Threat-attacker transitions-coverage-array.

In addition, we define structural coverage criteria such as components coverage, states coverage and transitions coverage. The structural coverage criteria are evaluated against the whole test suite. We use transitions and states coverage arrays to specify such coverage goals. For structural coverage, we might define the coverage goal in terms of a coverage rate(i.e. state-coverage(SUT)=90%). All coverage arrays and rates are given as input for the selection algorithm.

All these coverage goals are given as input for the test selection algorithm. This algorithm is executed at each enabled transition. It incrementally builds the test suite by adding IO actions to the test cases. We define final states and maximal length of the test cases in order to limit the test cases sizes. Internal actions and other guards on the transitions are ignored but the enabled transition and related states are marked as covered by the test case.

- A transition is reduced to *(state1,guard, state2)* the guard could be I/O action or not. In case it is an IO action, the action is added to the test case sequence of events.
- currentState is defined as tuple (SUT.state, user.state, attacker.state).
- currentTransition is defined as(componentID, TransitionID, state1,state2,guard).
- We define the following sets for expressing the coverage goals: GoalCoevrage_states/ GoalCoverage_transitions/ GoalCoverage_requirements.
- A security requirement coverage goal is defined as a record including security functional coverage criteria and malicious scenario coverage criteria. GoalCoverage_requirements is defined as an array of security

Figure 15. Example of raw traces generated by our algorithm executed on UPPAAL

```
selectedTestCases[0].n=2
selectedTestCases[0].IOa[0] = attacker.inout!
selectedTestCases[0].IOa[1] = attacker.inout?
selectedTestCases[0].param[0][0] = BOF_attack
selectedTestCases[0].param[0][1] = BOF_msg
selectedTestCases[0].param[1][0] = confidential_data

selectedTestCases[1].n = 3
selectedTestCases[1].IOa[0]'= client.clp!
selectedTestCases[1].IOa[1] = attacker.intercept!
selectedTestCases[1].IOa[2] = attacker.inout!
selectedTestCases[1].param[0][0] = Authentication_req
selectedTestCases[1].param[0][1] = invalid_credentials
selectedTestCases[1].param[1][0] = Authentication_req
selectedTestCases[1].param[1][1] = invalid_credentials
selectedTestCases[1].param[2][0] = Authentication_req
selectedTestCases[1].param[2][1] = invalid_credentials
```

This is an example of the raw traces generated by our selection algorithm on UPPAAL. In particular, these are some values from the variable selectedTestCases. The figure shows 2 test cases: one of length 2 and the other of length 3. The first 1 corresponds to a buffer offer flow attack that succeeds to access to confidential data. The second test case corresponds to an eavesdropping attack where an attacker succeeds to retrieve the credentials sent by the client. However in this case, the client is sending invalid credentials.

requirement coverage goals. Optionally, we might define coverage rates on the coverage-arrays in case we don't target 100% so that the coverage goal is satisfied once the specified rate is reached.

- Cstates, Ctransitions and Crequirements represent coverage arrays of the current test suite under construction.
- TemporaryTestCase represent the current test case under construction, it consists of the sequence of IO actions, their parameters and its coverage arrays. TemporaryTestCase = (IOa set, IOa parameters, States_cov, Transitions_cov, Requirements_cov). States and Transitions sets are used to check the coverage of security requirements.
- selectedTestCases represents the test suite under construction. Concretely it is a set of test cases.
- The algorithm is implemented with UPPAAL.

The output of the coverage-driven selection algorithm is a set of test cases satisfying all the coverage goals. The generated test suite does not contain any redundant test cases because the acceptance condition (a) states that there should be some added coverage. Figure 15 represents a sample of raw traces generated by UPPAAL and our algorithm. The tool allows non-deterministic behaviours by means of the "select" command. In fact, UPPAAL allows the specification of a definition domain for every I/O action parameter so that the engine will randomly select a different

value. at every call. Practically, it is recommended to enumerates values belonging to the different data equivalence classes identified during the analysis phase and use the command "select" over the parameter definition domain in order to make UPPAAL select a different value (i.e. different equivalence class) at every call.

This algorithm is executed at every generation step and whenever a transition is enabled. Therefore we instrument the network of timed IO automata by placing the calls at every transition in the system. In addition we keep updated the variables *currentState*, *currentTransition* and *activeComponent*.

- **Example:** Presented in Figure 16.

Once the model is instrumented we query the UPPAAL verifier with the following: ***E<> endSelection***. The model-checker will keep selecting randomly transitions and the *coverage_driven_selection* algorithm handling them until ***endSelection=true***. Therefore, we obtain a test cases set satisfying all the selection criteria.

The experiments showed a good quality of the generated test cases. In particular, we were able to generate the malicious test cases represented in ATC2 and ATC3.

Metrics and Evaluation

By construction, the test suite generated by our selection algorithm (1) satisfies all the coverage goals (structural and security) and (2) eliminates any redundant test cases. In addition, it tries to

Figure 16.

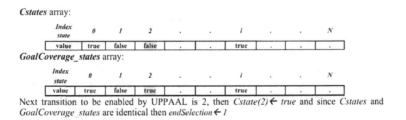

Next transition to be enabled by UPPAAL is 2, then *Cstate(2)* ← *true* and since *Cstates* and *GoalCoverage_states* are identical then *endSelection* ← *1*

minimize the test suite size through the acceptance condition requiring that any new test case must provide additional coverage in order to be added to the test suite. However, different selection strategies can be implemented by varying the acceptance condition. Therefore, the evaluation of the selection algorithm will be focused on metrics measuring the size of the generated test suite, computation time and scalability.

- **Test Suite Size:** The size of a test suite is defined by the number of the generated test cases. In the best case, we could generate the minimal test suite satisfying all the goals.
- **Computation Time:** It characterizes the cost of the test selection and generation. UPPAAL provides the computation time after each run. This metric influences the scalability capabilities of testing system.

However, in some cases we might reach the maximal length of the test suites without satisfying all the goal coverage. In this case, we need to evaluate the generated test suite in order to decide whether to accept it as-is or to increase the maximal size.

Test-Based Validation

The last step of the test-driven development process concerns the test-based validation activity.

Box 4.

	ATC1	ATC2	ATC3
Nominal	X		
Degradation		X	
Failure			X

The Objective is to evaluate the satisfaction of security properties by the SUT. For this purpose, we need to classify the test cases in nominal, degraded or faulty behaviors. The classification is based on their quantity and the severity of the identified violations. During the execution of one security test case, we might observe different violations. In such a case, the resilience policy defines to which class it belongs. We use the error model annex to describe the resilience policy.

In Figure 17, we describe the resilience policy by an AADL error model consisting of 3 error states: *nominal*, *degradation* and *failure*, and 2 error events *degradationErr* and *failureErr*. According to the error model implementation, if one test case activates a degradation violation and a failure violation, then we classify the corresponding test case into failure class. The error events generation is described in the behaviour model as highlighted in Figures 7 (*degradation_port!(degradationErr)*) and 6 (*failure_port!(failureErr)*). When the error events are raised, they trigger the corresponding transition in the error model implementation.

Figure 17. AADL Error Model for the client-server system

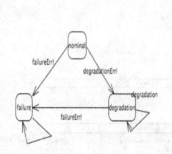

```
error model Basic
features
    nominal: initial error state;
    degradation: error state;
    failure: error state;
    failureErr, degradationErr: error event;
end Basic;

error model implementation Basic.err
transitions
    nominal-[degradationErr]-> degradation;
    nominal-[FailureErr]->Failure;
    degradation-[degradationErr]-> degradation;
    degradation-[FailureErr]->Failure;
    failure-[]->failure;
end Basic.err
```

After generating the test cases, we classify them according to the error model associated with the component.

- **Example:** During ATC2 execution an error event degradationErr is raised ➜ this test case is classified in degradation category. Similarly, we classify the rest of the ATCs as presented in Box 4.

In addition, the interpretation of the traces from security functional test cases and malicious test cases is different as showed in Table 2. A failure of a malicious test case exhibits a nominal behaviour of the system while its success demonstrates a violation of the security policy.

CONCLUSION AND FUTURE WORKS

In this chapter, we presented a test-driven and architecture model-based security engineering approach for resilient systems. The proposed process is based on a test-driven security modelling framework that integrates security functional view, in terms of security mechanisms; security requirements, in terms of security policy specification; and security threats, in terms of malicious components and interactions. The combination of these 3 elements allows the generation of both security functional test cases and malicious test cases. For evaluating the satisfaction of the system against its security requirements, we relate the test cases executions to the satisfaction function as defined in DREF. For this purpose, we use the error annex to associate a satisfaction category to each test case (nominal, degradation or failure).

REFERENCES

Armando, A., Carbone, R., Compagna, L., Li, K., & Pellegrino, G. (2010). Model-checking driven security testing of web-based applications. In *Proceedings of the 2010 Third International Conference on Software Testing, Verification, and Validation Workshops, ICSTW'10*. IEEE Computer Society Press.

Bertolino, A., Inverardi, P., & Muccini, H. (2001). *An explorative journey from architectural tests definition down to code tests execution*. Software Engineering, 23rd International Conference on Software Engineering (ICSE'01). IEEE Computer Society Press.

Brun, M., Delatour, J., & Trinquet, Y. (2008). Code generation from AADL to a real-time operating system: An experimentation feedback on the use of model transformation. In *Proceedings of the 13th IEEE International Conference on on Engineering of Complex Computer Systems* (ICECCS '08). IEEE Computer Society.

Bucchiarone, A., Muccini, H., & Pelliccione, P. (2007). *Architecting fault-tolerant component-based systems: From requirements to testing. Electronic Notes in Theoretical Computer Science*. Elsevier.

Chen, M., Mishra, P., & Kalita, D. (2008). Coverage-driven automatic test generation for UML activity diagrams. In *Proceedings of the 18th ACM Great Lakes Symposium on VLSI* (GLSVLSI '08). ACM.

Cichos, H., Oster, S., Lochau, M., & Schürr, A. (2011). Model-based coverage-driven test suite generation for software product lines. In J. Whittle, T. Clark, & T. Kühne (Eds.), *Proceedings of the 14th International Conference on Model Driven Engineering Languages and Systems* (MODELS'11). Springer-Verlag

Franca, R. B., Bodeveix, J., Filali, M., Rolland, J., Chemouil, D., & Thomas, D. (2007). The AADL behaviour annex -- Experiments and roadmap. In *Proceedings of the 12th IEEE international Conference on Engineering Complex Computer Systems* (ICECCS). IEEE Computer Society.

Górski, J., Rydzak, F., Breistrand, l., Sveen, F., Qian, Y., & Gonzalez, J. (2006). Exploring resilience towards risks in eoperations in the oil and gas industry. *Computer Safety, Reliability, and Security. LNCS.*

Guelfi, N. (2011). A formal framework for dependability and resilience from a software engineering perspective. *Central European Journal of Computer Science*, *1*(3), 294–328. doi:10.2478/s13537-011-0025-x

Hessel, A., Larsen, K. G., Mikucionis, M., Nielsen, B., Pettersson, P., & Skou, A. (2008). Testing real-time systems using UPPAAL. In Hierons, R. M., Bowen, J. P., & Harman, M. (Eds.), *Formal Methods and Testing* (*Vol. 4949*). Lecture Notes In Computer Science Berlin, Germany: Springer-Verlag. doi:10.1007/978-3-540-78917-8_3

Jin, Z. (2000). *A software architecture-based testing technique.* PhD thesis, George Mason University.

Jin, Z., & Offutt, J. (2001). Deriving tests from software architectures. In *Proceedings of the 12th International Symposium on Software Reliability Engineering* (ISSRE '01). IEEE Computer Society.

Jurjens, J. (2005). *Secure systems development with UML.* Springer-Verlag.

Jurjens, J. (2008). *Model-based security testing using UMLsec. Electronic Notes in Theoretical Computer Science.* Springer.

Kaynar, D. K., Lynch, N., Segala, R., & Vaandrager, F. (2003). Timed I/O automata: A mathematical framework for modeling and analyzing real-time systems. In *Proceedings of the 24th IEEE International Real-Time Systems Symposium* (RTSS '03). Washington, DC: IEEE Computer Society.

Koo, H.-M., & Mishra, P. (2009). Functional test generation using design and property decomposition techniques. *ACM Transactions in Embedded Computing Systems, 8*(4).

Lettnin, D., Winterholer, M., Braun, A., Gerlach, J., Ruf, J., Kropf, T., & Rosenstiel, W. (2007). Coverage driven verification applied to embedded software. In *Proceedings of the IEEE Computer Society Annual Symposium on VLSI* (ISVLSI '07). IEEE Computer Society.

Lim, H., Kaynar, D., Lynch, N., & Mitra, S. (2005). Translating timed I/O automata specifications for theorem proving in PVS. In P. Pettersson & W. Yi (Eds.), *Proceedings of the Third international conference on Formal Modeling and Analysis of Timed Systems* (FORMATS '05). Springer-Verlag

Lynch, N., & Tuttle, M. R. (1989). An introduction to input/output automata. *CWI Quarterly, 2*(3).

MAFTIA Consortium. (2003). *Conceptual model and architecture of MAFTIA (Malicious- and Accidental-Fault Tolerance for Internet Applications).* Public Deliverable, EU MAFTIA Project. Retrieved from http://spiderman-2.laas.fr/TSF/cabernet/maftia/deliverables/D21.pdf

Marquis, S., Dean, T. R., & Knight, S. (2005). SCL: A language for security testing of network applications. In *Proceedings of the 2005 Conference of the Centre for Advanced Studies on Collaborative Research* (CASCON '05).

Mouelhi, T., Fleurey, F., Baudry, B., & Traon, Y. (2008). A model-based framework for security policy specification, deployment and testing. In *Proceedings of the 11th International Conference on Model Driven Engineering Languages and Systems* (MoDELS '08).

Mouratidis, H., & Giorgini, P. (2007). Security attack testing (SAT)-Testing the security of information systems at design time. *Information Systems Journal, 32*(8).

Muccini, H. (2002). *Software architecture for testing, coordination and views model checking.* PhD Thesis, University La Sapienza, Rome.

Petrenko, A., Yevtushenko, N., & Huo, J. L. (2003). Testing transition systems with input and output testers. In D. Hogrefe & A. Wiles (Eds.), *Proceedings of the 15th IFIP International Conference on Testing of Communicating Systems* (TestCom'03), (pp. 129-145). Berlin, Germany: Springer-Verlag.

Pretschner, A., Mouelhi, T., & Le Traon, Y. (2008). Model-based tests for access control policies. In *Proceedings of the 2008 International Conference on Software Testing, Verification, and Validation* (ICST '08). IEEE Computer Society Press

Richardson, D. J., & Wolf, A. L. (1996). Software testing at the architectural level. In *Joint Proceedings of the Second International Software Architecture Workshop (ISAW-2) and International Workshop on Multiple Perspectives in Software Development (Viewpoints '96) on SIGSOFT '96 Workshops (ISAW '96)*

Ries, B. (2009). *SESAME - A model-driven process for the test selection of small-size safety-related embedded software.* PhD thesis, Laboratory for Advanced Software Systems, University of Luxembourg.

Robson, C. M. (2004). *TIOA and UPPAAL.* MIT Master thesis. Retrieved from http://dspace.mit.edu/bitstream/handle/1721.1/17979/57188153.pdf?sequence=1

Saidane, A., & Guelfi, N. (2011). Towards improving security testability of AADL architecture models. In *Proceedings of the International Conference on Network and System Security.* IEEE. Milano, 2011.

Saidane, A., & Guelfi, N. (2012). Seter: Towards architecture model based security engineering. *International Journal of Secure Software Engineering, 3*(3), 23–49. doi:10.4018/jsse.2012070102

Schulz, S., Honkola, J., & Huima, A. (2007). Towards model-based testing with architecture models. In *Proceedings of the 14th Annual IEEE International Conference and Workshops on the Engineering of Computer-Based Systems* (ECBS '07).

Subramaniam, M., Xiao, L., Guo, B., & Pap, A. (2009). An approach for test selection for EFSMs using a theorem prover. In *Proceedings of the 21st IFIP WG 6.1 International Conference on Testing of Software and Communication Systems and 9th International FATES Workshop* (TESTCOM '09/FATES '09).

von Oheimb, D., & Lotz, V. (2002). Formal security analysis with interacting state machines. In *Proceedings of the 7th European Symposium on Research in Computer Security* (ESORICS '02). Springer-Verlag

Wang, F., Wang, S., & Ji, Y. (2009). An automatic generation method of executable test case using model-driven architecture. In *Proceedings of the 2009 Fourth International Conference on Innovative Computing, Information and Control* (ICICIC '09). IEEE Computer Society

Xiong, P., Stepien, B., & Peyton, L. (2009). *Model-based penetration test framework for web applications using TTCN-3. E-Technologies: Innovation in an Open World, Lecture Notes in Business Information Processing* (Vol. 21). Springer.

Yang, Y., Jiao, J., Wang, H., & Xia, C. (2009). A task-deployment model for the simulation of computer network attack and defense exercises. In *Proceedings of the 2009 First IEEE International Conference on Information Science and Engineering* (ICISE '09). IEEE Computer Society.

Zhou, C., & Kumar, R. (2009). Modeling simu-link diagrams using input/output extended finite automata. In *Proceedings of the 2009 33rd Annual IEEE International Computer Software and Applications Conference* (COMPSAC '09), Vol. 2. IEEE

Zulkernine, M. F. R., & Uddin, M. G. (2009). Towards model-based automatic testing of attack scenarios. In *Proceedings of the 28th International Conference on Computer Safety, Reliability, and Security* (SAFECOMP '09)

ENDNOTES

1. http://www.sae.org/standards/
2. www.aadl.info
3. http://www.oasis-open.org/committees/tc_home.php?wg_abbrev=xacml
4. http://www.aadl.info/aadl/documents/Behaviour_Annex1.6.pdf
5. http://uppaal.org/

Chapter 11
Software Engineering, Process Improvement, and Experience Management:
Is the Nexus Productive? Clues from the Indian Giants

Neeraj Sharma
Punjabi University, India

Kawaljeet Singh
Punjabi University, India

D.P. Goyal
Management Development Institute, India

ABSTRACT

Software engineers have always been experimenting with various models in an endeavor to improve upon software processes. Recently, a new area of software process improvement through experience management has got attention of the software engineering community. Software developers are experimenting with experience management to improve software process. This chapter explores the role of experience management in mitigating the effects of software crisis and investigates the current state of EM in Indian software engineering environment. The chapter discusses the need and integration of knowledge and experience management practices in software engineering environments. The chapter begins with the discussion of the ills of software engineering, classically referred to as "software crisis," like late delivery of the systems, ill-functionality, and cost overruns, and justifies how managing the knowledge and experience of software engineers and practitioners can ward off these evils. The chapter then discusses the models and methodologies for knowledge and experience management in software engineering. Finally, the chapter sheds light on the major works carried out in this area and suggests possible future research avenues in this domain.

DOI: 10.4018/978-1-4666-2958-5.ch011

INTRODUCTION

Software has become '*woven into the threads of our daily lives*' (Glass, 1996). It has become an inherent constituent of survival for almost all organisations as well as for individuals in today's world of competition. May it be telecommunications, transportation, medical services or the defence of a nation, software is a critical component. With Internet and mobile technologies becoming omnipresent, and growing use of embedded software in consumer products, individuals are increasingly becoming dependent on software. For this ever increasing dependence over software, problems in developing software can have ravaging effects not only at individual and organisational levels but also at national and international levels. As a result, the improvement of software development processes has become the pressing area of concern for software engineering (SE) professionals and researchers.

Software engineering is a highly intricate, multi-stage process, usually involving teams of multi-domain experts and professionals working through different phases and activities, sometimes even beyond the boundaries of geographical space and time. Complexity in the field is further aggravated by continuous technology revisions and replacements. With the successful completion of every new project, new proportions in the SE knowledge are added. Even failures in the project execution lead to the generation of new experience that was not already known. Thus knowledge in SE is constantly growing, leading to another kind of problem – keeping track of what this knowledge is, where it is, or who owns it. Managing this knowledge in a systemic way and treating those who possess knowledge as valuable assets in an organisation, is the most potent solution to leverage the knowledge of individuals within the organisation.

Software engineering organisations qualify to be the perfect candidates for experience management initiative because of the knowledge-intensive nature of SE tasks (Birk et al., 1999; Rus and Lindvall, 2002). Understanding and balancing user requirements, applying the most appropriate development methodology, choosing suitable tools, and storing project related experience are some of the examples which justify the knowledge-intensive nature of the software engineering discipline. Software development, like any other design work, is not rigid mechanical manufacturing process. Rather, it has a strong creative component involving human and social interaction that cannot be totally pre-planned (Conradi and Fuggetta, 2002). That is why we *develop* software and not *produce* it. Every person involved in software development has to make a variety of decisions, each of them with several possible options, in contrast to a production process which is mostly structured and programmable. Choice of what software to develop, selection of the team-members to carry out the project, selection of technique of programming, finalization of design from among many available alternatives, selection of kinds of tests and test cases for testing the final product, ways of providing user-manuals or help are some of the examples of the cross-roads which every software engineer faces. What helps software engineers make the 'right choice' when in situation of doubt? Well, most of the time it is their personal experience, gut feeling and intuitions that guide the software engineers. But for bigger projects, involving large group of people, knowledge sharing among individuals in the team is indispensable. And this is where experience management comes into picture.

The major objective of the chapter is to study the use of experience management (EM) systems in software engineering environments. It is especially interesting to study this in a setting with people who are very skilled in using computers, like people developing software. The chapter also investigates the current EM practices followed by Indian software engineering organisations. For the purpose of this study, an exhaustive literature search has been carried out. For the empirical evidence of EM in Indian SE environment, five major SE companies in India were selected randomly. Primary data was collected through interviews and secondary data was collected from internal documentation and official websites of the companies.

LITERATURE REVIEW

A lot of research has been reported about KM in software engineering e.g. (Rus and Lindvall, 2002; Ward and Aurum, 2004). An infrastructure to deal with KM in software engineering environments is presented in Natali and Falbo (2002). There are studies which investigate the need for software experience bases (SEB) in software projects, e.g. Basili et al., (1992). Talking of experience management, much research exists on many aspects of EM including approaches to EM (e.g. Basili et al., 1992; Schneider, 2000), how to collect experience (e.g. Althoff et al., 2000; Land et al., 2001), how to structure experience (e.g. Houdek et al., 1998; Lindvall et al., 2001), tools for EM (e.g. Henninger and Schlabach, 2001; Mendonca et al., 2001) and applications of EM in practice (e.g. Diaz and Sligo, 1997; Brossler, 1999; Sharma et al., 2009a). Table 1 gives a summary of the EM literature.

The application of EM in the field of software engineering to improve the software process has become popular with the term SPI. However the literature on the use of EM for SPI is limited though pivotal e.g. Martinez et al., 2005. An overview of seven initiatives for improved quality in software engineering is provided in Glass, 1999: structured techniques, fourth generation programming languages, computer aided software engineering, formal methods, clean-room methodologies, process models and object-oriented technology. Common for most of these initiatives, or technologies as Glass calls them is that they show promising results, but there is a lack of research, and more studies are needed to properly determine how they work in practice and what the actual benefits are. An attempt at establishing an overview of the SPI field is described in Hansen et al. (2004) and Sharma et al. (2009b). Han-

Table 1. Summary of experience management literature

S.No.	EM Aspect	References
1.	Experience Factory approach	Basili et al., 1992
2.	Light-weight approach	Schneider, 2000
3.	How to collect experience	Althoff et al., 2000; Land et al., 2001
4.	How to structure experience	Houdek et al., 1998; Lindvall et al., 2001
5.	Tools for managing experience	Henninger and Schlabach, 2001; Mendonca et al., 2001
6.	Application of EM in practice	Diaz and Sligo, 1997; Brossler, 1999; Sharma et al., 2009a

sen et al. (2004) reviewed 322 contributions to the SPI literature in order to establish an overview of research in the field and categorized them according to a simple framework: whether the papers were prescriptive (suggesting solutions without validation), descriptive (describing an implementation of a method or technology in practice), or reflective (reflecting findings from practice with academic theory). They conclude that the field is heavily biased towards prescriptive contributions, and that the field is dominated by the CMM approach. The finding that field is biased toward prescriptive contributions is mirrored by Glass et al. (2004), who presents an overview of the literature in the whole software engineering field. Aaen et al. (2001) describes a survey of the state-of-the-art knowledge on SPI, and position SPI in the landscape of strategies aimed at maturing software organizations. They identify three fundamental concerns in SPI, the principles used to Manage the intervention, the Approach taken to guide the intervention, and the Perspectives used to focus the intervention on the target (MAP for short). According to Conradi and Fuggetta (2002), SPI efforts are characterized by two dichotomies: discipline vs. creative work and procurer risk vs. user satisfaction. Table 2 gives a summary of the SPI Literature.

Another important aspect of SPI covered in the literature review is the models for process improvement. The SPI models can be used to divide the field into two approaches. The first approach tries to improve the process through standardization; examples here are the Capability Maturity Model (CMM) (Humphrey, 1989; Paulk et al., 1995); the ISO 9000 standard (Braa and Ogrim, 1994; Hoyle, 2001); and the Software Process Improvement and Capability dEtermination, or SPICE (SPICE, 2009). Another approach, known in software engineering as the Quality Improvement Program (QIP) is a more bottom up approach involving the developers in defining their own processes (Deming, 2000). Table 3 summarizes the literature on the SPI models.

The literature on SPI implementation points towards the use of SEB as the core of the Experience Factory (EF) concept (Basili et al., 1994), an organizational unit that supports reuse of experience and collective learning by developing, updating and providing, on request, past experiences to be used by project organizations. Knowledge (in the form of processes, products, and technologies) is enriched by explicitly documented experience (e.g., lessons that were learned during the practical application of the knowledge). These experience packages are stored in a SEB, which is an organizational memory for relevant knowledge and experience. EF has to be supplemented on a technical system implementation level to realize the SEB, which give organizations

Table 2. Summary of SPI literature

S. No.	SPI Aspect	References
1.	EM in SPI	Martinez et al., 2005
2.	SPI technologies	Glass, 1999
3.	Classification by MAP framework	Aaen et al. (2001)
4.	Dichotomies in SPI	Conradi and Fuggetta, 2002
5.	Overview of research in SPI	Glass et al., 2004; Hansen et al., 2004; Sharma et al., 2009b

Table 3. Summary of literature on SPI models

S. No.	SPI Model	Process Improvement Strategy	References
1.	Capability Maturity Model (CMM)	Standardization	Humphrey, 1989; Paulk et al., 1995
2.	ISO 9000	Standardization	Braa and Ogrim (1994), Hoyle (2001)
3.	Software Process Improvement and Capability dEtermination (SPICE)	Standardization	SPICE, 2009
4.	Quality Improvement Program (QIP)	Bottom up approach	Deming (2000)

the opportunity to appreciate the challenges and complexities inherent in software development. Aurum et al. (2003) posit that software development can be improved by recognizing related knowledge content and structure, as well as appropriate knowledge and engaging in planning activities.

SOFTWARE PROCESS IMPROVEMENT AND EXPERIENCE MANAGEMENT

Knowledge and experience are closely associated and the latter can be conceived as a special form or instance of the former. Experience is defined as previous knowledge or skill one obtained in everyday life (Sun and Finnie, 2004). Commonly experience is understood as a type of knowledge that you have gained from practice. In this sense, experience can be regarded as a specialization of knowledge consisting of the problems encountered and successfully tackled in the past. The salient distinguishing characteristic of experience is that it resides in humans and moving it from one person to another is almost impossible as one has to experience it to call it an experience.

The area of EM is increasingly gaining importance. EM can be defined as a special kind of KM concerned with discovering, capturing, storing & modeling and re-/using knowledge of the members of an organisation, who acquired this knowledge through learning from experience (Althoff et al., 2001; Bergmann, 2002). Therefore, methodologies, tools and techniques for KM can be directly reused for EM. However management of experience warrants different methods as experience has some special features different from knowledge. A unique differentiating feature of EM is the additional stage where experience is transformed into knowledge (Bergmann, 2002). Since the evolution of the human race, all invaluable experience is transformed into knowledge and this knowledge is shared among humans in varied forms. Creation of knowledge is an indispensable stage in the KM process (exemplified by data mining and knowledge discovery techniques); generation of experience from heaps of knowledge is still a challenging task and is not addressed in EM research (Nilsson, 1998; Bergmann, 2002; Sun and Finnie, 2004).

The major problem with the existing SPI approaches is that none of these explicitly value the knowledge and experience of software engineers in improving the software processes in an organisation and nor do they provide for any system or method to capture, manage and use this accumulated knowledge to avoid repeating the mistakes and to enable the software engineers learn from past experience. There is no denying the fact that accumulating and managing software development experiences plays a very significant role in improving the software process. Reusing experience in the form of processes, products, and other forms of knowledge is essential for improvement, that is, reuse of knowledge is the basis of improvement (Basili et al., 1994). The fundamental idea is to improve the software process on the basis of the accumulated knowledge and experiences of the software engineers working in the organisation. Insights from the field

of knowledge and experience management are therefore potentially useful in software process improvement efforts so as to facilitate the creation, modification, and sharing of software processes in an organisation. Management of knowledge and experience are key means by which systematic software development and process improvement occur (Ward and Aurum, 2004). They further assert that although remedies such as fourth generation programming languages, structured techniques and object-oriented technology, software agents, component based development, agile software practices, etc. have been promoted; a silver bullet1 has yet to be found (ibid.). EM provides for the systems and mechanisms for managing the knowledge and experience of software engineers in an organisation that becomes the basis of process improvement. SPI in practice is about managing software knowledge.

It was in 1968 NATO conference that the problems of project overruns, over budgeting and poor functionality of the software were discussed and eventually identified as software crisis or software gap to expose the gravity of the problems in the discipline. But even after over 40 years, not much seems to have changed; late delivery of the systems, ill-functionality and cost overruns are commonly reported by companies (ACM, 2007).

Following text discusses the common SE problems and explains how EM can address these issues to a great extent, thus promising a silver bullet of some sort.

Reinventing the Wheel

SE is an extremely experimental discipline (Basili and Rombach, 1991). With every software development project, new experience is gained but this experience is seldom captured and stored systematically so as to learn from it in future projects to avoid project delays and cost overruns. Often software development teams carry out similar kinds of projects without understanding that they could have achieved the results more easily by following the practices adopted in previous projects (Brossler, 1999; Basili et al., 2001). In every project, software engineers acquire new knowledge and experience and this new knowledge can be used to better the future projects but much of this knowledge and experience goes unnoticed and is hardly shared among team members in an organisation. The underlying fact is that SEs do not benefit from existing experience and instead repeat mistakes over and over again by reinventing the wheel (Basili et al., 2001).

EM in general and SEB in particular can help SE organisations capture the experience from across the projects and store it in a central repository so as to make it available to the whole organisation. An experience management system encourages knowledge growth, communication, preservation and sharing. EM in SE projects can be used to capture the knowledge and experience generated during the software development process and these captured experiences can be used to better the performance of the developers in similar kinds of projects in future. Reusing experience forbids the repetition of past failures and steers the solution of recurrent problems.

Understanding Problem is the Problem

SE is also highly interdisciplinary in approach. A software engineer is required to have knowledge not only about its own domain but must also possess sufficient knowledge about the domain for which software is being developed. Many a times writing software for a new domain demands learning a new technique or tool or a programming language or application of a new project management technique. Even when the organisation has been working on a particular domain extensively, the deep application-specific knowledge required to successfully build complex software is thinly spread over many software development engineers (Curtis et al., 1988). Although individual development engineers understand different components

of the application domain, building large and complex software requires integration of different pieces of domain knowledge. Software developers working in these complex domain environments admit that "writing code is not the problem, understanding the problem is the problem" (ibid.). EM serves two goals in this direction – (a) identifying expertise or competence already existing in the organisation and helping leverage and package this knowledge in a reusable form and (b) helping organisation in acquiring new domain(s) knowledge by identifying the knowledge gaps that exist in the organisation.

Here Today, Gone Tomorrow Technology

Emergence of new technologies makes software more powerful, but at the same time new technologies is every project manager's worst nightmare (Brossler, 1999). The fast pace of technology change makes the already complex software development business a highly demanding one, necessitating software developers to acquire knowledge of emerging technologies while at the same time adhering to organisational processes and methodologies. Though these problems are ubiquitous across industries, but the software industry is probably worse than other industries due to the fact that the pace of change is faster here. Lack of time causes a lack of experience, constantly pushing the boundaries of an organisation's development set of skills and competencies (Henninger and Schlabach, 2001). When a project team uses a new technology, the software engineers all too often resort to the 'learning by doing' approach, often leading to serious project delays (Brossler, 1999).

EM provides an opportunity to SE organisations to create a common language of understanding among software developers, so that they can interact, negotiate and share knowledge and experiences (Aurum et al., 2003). Furthermore, an EM system compliments the organisational ability to systematically manage innovative knowledge in the SE domain. Experience management nurtures a knowledge sharing culture within the company and eases sharing of knowledge about new technologies. EM also provides for the systems that help in actively searching for knowledge not only within organisation but outside as well. Knowledge sharing among communities of practice is the best example of such a system.

Knowledge Walks Home Everyday

The success of any organisation in performing its core business processes depends heavily upon the employees' relevant knowledge about these processes. But the problem is that this knowledge is within the control of its employees and not with the organisation as such. Serious knowledge gaps are created when the employees who possess this core knowledge leave the organisation. The problem becomes graver if the outgoing employee is the only expert in that field of activity. Still serious is the case when no one else in the organisation knows what knowledge he possesses (Basili et al., 2001). Also in usual working culture of SE organisations, people from different departments with different sets of skills and knowledge are taken together to form a team for a specific project. These teams dissolve after the completion of the project, taking the cross-functional experience along, without storing these experiences in organisational repository of some sort. These experiences remain with the individuals who will take it with them when they leave the organisation.

EM helps organisations in systematically capturing, storing (in a repository called experience base) and disseminating knowledge and experience at all levels of the organisation, by creating a knowledge-sharing culture. EM also facilitates employees by providing who knows what. EM helps organisations create systems and frameworks for capturing core competency that can help retain some knowledge when employees leave. This core competency would at least help

in getting insights as to what the employee who left knew and what profile his successor needs to have to fill the position. This is even more relevant in the current scenario of economic slowdown.

Trust in Virtual Teams

Another important trend being witnessed by SE organisations is the development of the systems through, what is called, the virtual teams. A virtual team consists of its members who are not co-located but separated by geographic distances and national cultures. Increase in globalization has led to this trend (Nonaka, 1994; von Krogh, 2000). Other reasons behind the popularity of virtual teams in SE are availability of experts at cheap costs in other parts of the world, enhanced telecommunication infrastructure, and competitiveness. Members of the virtual teams are required to complete interdependent tasks, requiring different sets of technical skills. Collaboration among members, having different domain expertise and cultural backgrounds, requires knowledge transfer among them so as to create a sense of mutuality. Knowledge transfer across space and time has problems in virtual teams. The root-cause of this problem, among other things, is the concept of 'localness of knowledge'. People usually get knowledge from their organisational neighbours. The knowledge market depends on trust, and individuals usually trust people they know. Face-to-face meetings are often the best way to get knowledge. Reliable information about more distant knowledge sources is not available. Also, mechanisms for getting access to distant knowledge tend to be weak or nonexistent (Davenport and Prusak, 1998).

EM can redress the problem of localness of knowledge as it acknowledges the value of knowledge transfer and communication. Collaboration among members of virtual teams is related to mutual sharing of knowledge which is facilitated if the software artifacts and their status are stored and made part of an organisational repository.

Organisational Culture

It is a well known fact that every software development organisation fosters a specific software development culture and creates (and thus promotes) policies and conventions in the light of this culture. Often this type of culture exists as folklore and is informally maintained within the brains of the experienced developers (Rus and Lindvall, 2002). This knowledge is passed on to new and/or inexperienced developers through informal meetings with the effect that not everyone gets the knowledge they need (Terveen et al., 1993). 'Water-cooler meetings' are the common sight in SE environments where software engineers share their knowledge informally but this shared knowledge never becomes available to everyone who needs it in the organisation as it is not formalized in any repository.

EM provides for both formal as well as informal ways of sharing SE knowledge and effective means of communication accessible to every member of the organisation. Lightweight knowledge management approaches attempt to capture the informal knowledge that is shared on a daily basis so that it can be disseminated on a larger scale.

THE INDIAN SCENARIO

To identify the EM practices and use of SEB in software engineering environment in Indian context, the software firms have been categories in two categories – large-sized and medium & small-sized, on the basis of their size and volume of their business. A sample of five software organizations has been taken in each category as a representative of the Indian software industry. The large-sized companies selected are Infosys, Wipro, Satyam, TCS and Patni. The major state of EM in software engineering environments in India can be summarized as follows.

Infosys Technologies, founded in 1981, has been a pioneer in the Indian software industry for implementing a comprehensive KM program. Infosys has won four Global Most Admired Knowledge Enterprise (MAKE) awards and has thus become the first Indian company to be inducted into the Global MAKE Hall of Fame. The knowledge management portal, K-Shop supports process management as the repository of over 30,000 knowledge components, best practices and experiences across all projects managed for clients across domains and technologies. This knowledge can be drawn upon for reference when appropriate. In addition to hosting a rich content in a central repository, KShop also provides access to knowledge assets across Infosys – termed satellite repositories: e.g. QSD, web sites of the company's domain competency group, links to external market intelligence sources such as Q's Lab, Gartner, Forrester etc. "People-Knowledge Map", an application, locates experts within Infosys who have volunteered to be knowledge resources for others. Since tapping knowledge of employees is vital for sustaining KM, Knowledge Currency Units (KCU) were designed to reward and encourage experts to submit papers and volunteer on People-Knowledge Map. High KCU scorers are awarded with incentives. Infosys has pioneered a five-stage Knowledge Management Maturity Model (KMM), which is a framework to enable organizations to deploy KM practices and harness the benefits.

Wipro Technologies, the first PCMM Level 5 and SEI CMM Level certified IT Services Company globally, has been awarded KMWorld's prestigious KM reality award for best practices in knowledge and experience management. The company has devised a KNet Framework to convert the explicit knowledge of documents and other reusable components into tacit knowledge and store it into a SEB. The main components of this repository are DocKNet (The repository of documents), KoNnEcT (yellow pages with an associated database of experts, queries, responses and ratings), War Rooms (a virtual workspace for time-bound and task-oriented jobs) and the repository of software reusable components and tools developed in-house. Konnect helps share the tacit knowledge within the organization, above and beyond the explicit knowledge captured in the KNet Repositories. War Rooms facilitate document sharing, exchange of information, real-time online discussions, sharing work plans and online updates, monitoring the progress of activities.

Satyam Computers Services Ltd. started the KM programme, called Knowledge Initiative (KI), to address the pain-areas of its project managers by filling the current knowledge gaps. Satyam also has the knowledge networking portal called K-Window. Some of the highly successful ideas implemented in Satyam's KI programme include Satyam Pathshala, Communities of Excellence (CoE), K-Radio and the K-Mobile. Satyam Pathshala is a tacit knowledge sharing program facilitated by employees volunteering to share their experiences with fellow colleagues and has four objectives: experiential knowledge sharing, connecting employees with experts in the field, capturing tacit knowledge in documented form for further dissemination, and enhancing the breadth of knowledge of various domains and technologies among its software engineers. CoE are virtual communities of professionals who volunteer to share their experience with fellow employees across Satyam. K-Radio is a query broadcast and response service provided under K-Window, wherein employees can post their queries online and can receive responses-all pooled at one place-from the members of the targeted CoE. K-Mobile is an application of SMS in the field of knowledge management, with the aim of facilitating knowledge request by employees who are on the move. K-Mobile enables software engineers to request for critical documents through their mobile phones.

Tata Consultancy Services (TCS) is the leading Indian software solutions provider and has been providing KM solutions to a wide spectrum of organizations. The KM philosophy of TCS is manifested through its motto of managing mind-

sets. The KM initiative of TCS is known for its 5iKM3 Knowledge Management Maturity Model.

Patni Computer Systems, India's software services giant is also one of the few organisations that make extensive use of SEB in software engineering. The company has created a knowledge centre, which allows its employees to learn about new technologies, have discussions and get technical queries answered. The knowledge portal of the company has a searchable SEB of large reusable software components.

The companies in the medium-sized and small-sized sectors do not have formal EM system in place. Most of the respondents in the sample were unaware of the use of SEB to improve their software proceses. Almost all the firms were reluctant to introduce SEB in their organisations in the near future. Lack of awareness, lack of infrastructure, ROI justification and dearth of required manpower were cited as the main reasons for the absence of EM systems in their organisations.

FUTURE RESEARCH DIRECTIONS

Various attempts have been made to improve the quality of software. Of course, quality is a very broad term, and we can think of many areas where quality can be improved, like in the final software product, the documents being created whilst developing a product, the models in use to understand user requirements and so on. In the software development context, SPI can be viewed as the foundation for continuous improvement of the software process and consequently, the resulting products. Using an SEB approach, knowledge created during software processes can be captured, stored, disseminated, and reused, so that better quality and productivity can be achieved. SEB can be used to better support several activities, such as software process definition, human resource allocation, estimation, requirement analysis, quality planning, and so on.

Finally, it is also observed that most of the work that has been reported on SPI is from large organizations. Such organizations can devote a lot of resources on organizational issues such as experience bases. Use of experience bases for software process improvement is also catching up with large sized Indian software companies. Software organizations in India have well realized the importance of leveraging the knowledge of its software engineers and are already using software platforms to capture, organize, use and disseminate experience among its software engineers. It is evident that the major software engineering organizations in India are quite aware of the benefits of SEB and are applying EM practices in software engineering to improve their processes. The technique used to manage software engineering knowledge is through some form of experience factory in almost all the organizations studied. Also all major software engineering firms in India use a knowledge management maturity model to assess their KM stage and identify the bottlenecks in the KM process. But the same is not true of small-scale and medium-scale software organizations in India, which do not use any formal EM in software process. Therefore, it is concluded that the use of SEB in software engineering is restricted to only large-sized organizations. Small- and medium-sized software organizations are not implementing EM systems, either because of ROI issues or the lack of infrastructure and/or required personnel. This could be an area of research for future in software experience bases in small and medium software engineering organizations, thereby adding to the body of empirical research both in the field of EM and software engineering.

CONCLUSION

For the continuous improvement of software process, the knowledge and experience of its employees can not be overemphasized in an organisation. Large amounts of knowledge in the form of project data, lessons learnt, software artifacts, code libraries etc. could be accumulated for a software organisation but to make this knowledge usable, it needs to be structured, organized, modeled and stored in a generalized and reusable form in an organisational repository or experience base.

However, learning and reuse of knowledge usually occur only because of individual efforts or by accident. This necessarily leads to a loss of the experience and knowledge after the completion of the project and therefore a reuse-oriented software development process in which learning and feedback are regarded as integrated components, and experiences are stored in an experience base, is potentially the best solution. Reuse of experience in SE environments requires that processes and products from software development projects are systematically collected, packaged and stored in an experience base. Managing experiences through experience bases will potentially provide SE organisations with some remedies against the software crisis and help them not only in improving their software processes but will also lead them to a learning organisation that constantly improves its work by letting employees share experience with each other, thus proving to be a silver bullet of some sort. This enlightenment seems to be following major software engineering organisations in India.

REFERENCES

Aaen, I., Arent, J., Mathiassen, L., & Ngwenyama, O. (2001). A conceptual map of software process improvement. *Scandinavian Journal of Information Systems*, *13*, 81–101.

Althoff, K., Birk, A., Hartkopf, S., Muller, W., Nick, M., Surmann, D., & Tautz, C. (2000). Systematic population, utilization, and maintenance of a repository for comprehensive reuse. In Ruhe, G., & Bomarius, F. (Eds.), *SEKE 1999, LNCS (Vol. 1756*, pp. 25–50). Heidelberg, Germany: Springer.

Althoff, K., Decker, B., Hartkopf, S., Jedlitschka, A., Nick, M., & Rech, J. (2001). Experience management: The Fraunhofer IESE experience factory. In P. Perner, (Ed.), *Industrial Conference on Data Mining*. Leipzig, Germany: Institute for Computer Vision and applied Computer Sciences.

Aurum, A., Jeffery, R., Wohlin, C., & Handzic, M. (2003). *Managing software engineering knowledge*. Berlin, Germany: Springer-Verlag.

Basili, V., Caldiera, G., Mcgarry, F., Pajerski, R., Page, G., & Waligora, S. (1992). *The software engineering laboratory - An operational software experience factory*. Paper presented at the 14th International Conference on Software Engineering.

Basili, V., Costa, P., Lindvall, M., Mendonca, M., & Seaman, C. (2001). *An experience management system for a software engineering research organisation*. Paper presented at the 26th Annual NASA Goddard Software Engineering Workshop.

Basili, V., & Rombach, H. D. (1991). Support for comprehensive reuse. *IEEE Software Engineering Journal*, *22*(4), 303–316.

Basili, V. R., Caldiera, G., & Rombach, H. D. (1994). The experience factory. In Marciniak, J. J. (Ed.), *Encyclopedia of software engineering* (*Vol. 1*, pp. 469–476). New York, NY: John Wiley & Sons.

Bergmann, R. (2002). *Experience management: Foundations, development methodology and internet-based applications. Lecture Notes in Artificial Intelligence* (*Vol. 2432*). Berlin, Germany: Springer.

Birk, A., Surmann, D., & Althoff, K.-D. (1999). Applications of knowledge acquisition in experimental software engineering. *International Conference on Knowledge Acquisition, Modeling and Management, LNCS, vol. 1621*, (pp. 67-84), Springer Verlag, Germany.

Braa, K., & Ogrim, L. (1994). Critical view of the ISO standard for quality assurance. *Information Systems Journal*, *5*, 253–269.

Brossler, P. (1999). Knowledge management at a software house: An experience report. In Ruhe, G., & Bomarius, F. (Eds.), *Learning Software Organizations: Methodology and Applications, SEKE '99* (pp. 163–170). Berlin, Germany: Springer-Verlag.

Conradi, R., & Fuggetta, A. (2002). Improving software process improvement. *IEEE Software*, *19*(4), 92–99.

Curtis, B., Krasner, H., & Iscoe, N. (1988). A field study of the software design process for large systems. *Communications of the ACM*, *31*(11), 1268–1289.

Davenport, T. H., & Prusak, L. (1998). *Working knowledge: How organizations manage what they know*. Boston, MA: Harvard Business School Press.

Deming, E. W. (2000). *Out of the crisis*. Cambridge, MA: The MIT Press.

Diaz, M., & Sligo, J. (1997). How software process improvement helped Motorola. *IEEE Software*, *14*, 75–81.

Glass, R. L. (1996). The relationship between theory and practice in software engineering. *Communications of the ACM*, *39*(11), 11–13.

Glass, R. L. (1999). The realities of software technology payoffs. *Communications of the ACM*, *42*, 74–79.

Glass, R. L., Ramesh, V., & Iris, V. (2004). An analysis of research in computing disciplines. *Communications of the ACM*, *47*(6), 89–94.

Hansen, B., Rose, J., & Tjornhoj, G. (2004). Prescription, description, reflection: The shape of the software process improvement field. *International Journal of Information Management*, *24*(6), 457–472.

Henninger, S., & Schlabach, J. (2001). A tool for managing software development knowledge. In Bomarius, F., & Komi-Sirvio, S. (Eds.), *PROFES 2001, LNCS* (*Vol. 2188*, pp. 182–195). Heidelberg, Germany: Springer.

Houdek, F., Schneider, K., & Wieser, E. (1998). *Establishing experience factories at Daimler-Benz: An experience report*. Paper presented at the 20th International Conference on Software Engineering.

Hoyle, D. (2001). *ISO 9000 quality systems handbook*. London, UK: Butterworth-Heinemann.

Humphrey, W. S. (1989). *Managing the software process*. Reading, MA, USA: Addison-Wesley.

Inside Risks. (2007). *Communications of the ACM, 50*(8). Retrieved December 22, 2011, from http://www.csl.sri.com/users/neumann/insiderisks.html

Land, L., Aurum, A., & Handzic, M. (2001). *Capturing implicit software engineering knowledge*. Paper presented at the 2001 Australian Software Engineering Conference.

Lindvall, M., Frey, M., Costa, P., & Tesoriero, R. (2001). *Lessons learned about structuring and describing experience for three experience bases*. Paper presented at the 3rd International Workshop on Advances in Learning Software Organisations.

Martinez, P., Amescua, A., Garcia, J., Cuadra, D., Llorens, J., & Fuentes, J. M. Feliu, T. S. (2005). Requirements for a knowledge management framework to be used in software intensive organizations. *IEEE International Conference on Information Reuse and Integration,* (pp. 554-559).

Mendonca, M., Seaman, C., Basili, V., & Kim, Y. (2001). *A prototype experience management system for a software consulting organization*. Paper presented at the International Conference on Software Engineering and Knowledge Engineering.

Natali, A. C. C., & Falbo, R. A. (2002). *Knowledge management in software engineering environments*. Paper presented at the 14th International Conference on Software Engineering and Knowledge Engineering, Ischia, Italy.

Nilsson, N. J. (1998). *Artificial intelligence: A new synthesis*. San Francisco, CA: Morgan Kaufmann Inc.

Nonaka, I. (1994). A dynamic theory of organizational knowledge creation. *Organization Science, 5*(1), 14–37.

Paulk, M. C., Weber, C. V., Curtis, B., & Chrissis, M. B. (1995). *The capability maturity model for software: Guidelines for improving the software process*. Reading, MA: Addison-Wesley.

Rus, I., & Lindvall, M. (2002). Knowledge management in software engineering. *IEEE Software, 19*(3), 26–38.

Schneider, K. (2000). LIDs: A light-weight approach to experience elicitation and reuse. In Bomarius, F., & Oivo, M. (Eds.), *PROFES 2000, LNCS* (*Vol. 1840*, pp. 407–424). Heidelberg, Germany: Springer.

Sharma, N., Singh, K., & Goyal, D. P. (2009a). Knowledge management in software engineering environment: Empirical evidence from Indian software engineering firms. *Atti Della Fondazione Giorgio Ronchi, 3*, 397–406.

Sharma, N., Singh, K., & Goyal, D. P. (2009b). Knowledge management in software engineering: Improving software process through managing experience. In Batra, S., & Carrillo, F. J. (Eds.), *Knowledge management and intellectual capital: Emerging perspectives* (pp. 223–235). New Delhi, India: Allied Publishers Pvt. Ltd.

SPICE. (2009). *Website*. Retrieved December 22, 2011, from http://www.sqi.gu.edu.au/Spice

Sun, Z., & Finnie, G. (2004). *Intelligent techniques in e-commerce: A case-based reasoning perspective*. Heidelberg, Germany: Springer-Verlag.

Terveen, L. G., Sefridge, P. G., & Long, M. D. (1993). *From 'folklore' to 'living design memory'*. Paper presented at the ACM Conference on Human Factors in Computing Systems.

von Krogh, G., Ichijo, K., & Nonaka, I. (2000). *Enabling knowledge creation*. New York, NY: Oxford University Press.

Ward, J., & Aurum, A. (2004). *Knowledge management in software engineering - Describing the process*. Paper presented at the Australian Software Engineering Conference, IEEE Computer Society, Los Alamitos.

ADDITIONAL READING

Althoff, K.-D., Bomarius, F., & Tautz, C. (2000). Knowledge management for building learning software organizations. *Information Systems Frontiers*, 2(3/4), 349–367.

Florac, W. A., & Carleton, A. D. (1999). *Measuring the software process – Statistical process control for software process improvement*. Addison Wesley, SEI Series on Software Engineering.

Housel, T., & Bell, A. H. (2001). *Measuring and managing knowledge*. Boston, MA: McGraw-Hill Irwin.

Jalote, P. (2002). *Software project management in practice*. Addison-Wesley.

McFeely, B. (1996). *Ideal: A user's guide for software process improvement*. Technical Report CMU/SEI-96-HB-001, Software Engineering Institute, Carnegie-Mellon University.

Wenger, E., McDermott, R., & Snyder, W. M. (2002). *Cultivating communities of practice: A guide to managing knowledge*. MA: Harvard Business School.

Wohlin, C., Runeson, P., Höst, M., Ohlsson, M., Regnell, B., & Wesslén, A. (2000). *Experimentation in software engineering – An introduction*. London, UK: Kluwer Academic Publishers.

KEY TERMS AND DEFINITIONS

Experience: Experience is understood as a type of knowledge that one has gained from practice.

Experience Management (EM): Defined as a special kind of KM concerned with discovering, capturing, storing & modeling and using/ reusing knowledge of the members of an organisation, who acquired this knowledge through learning from experience.

Knowledge: Information that changes something or somebody either by becoming grounds for action, or by making an individual or an institution capable of different and more effective action.

Knowledge Management (KM): In the context of software engineering, KM is defined as a set of activities, techniques, and tools supporting the creation and transfer of SE knowledge throughout the organisation.

Software Process Improvement (SPI): Aims at providing SE organisations with mechanisms for evaluating their existing processes, identifying possibilities for improving as well as implementing and evaluating the impact of improvements.

ENDNOTES

[1] A term rooted in folklore of the American Civil War, supposedly became popular from the practice of encouraging a patient who was to undergo field surgery to bite down hard on a lead bullet to divert the mind from pain. According to another folklore, one seeks bullets of silver to magically lay to rest the werewolves who could transform unexpectedly from the familiar into horrors. The software project is capable of becoming a monster of missed schedules, blown budgets, and flawed products, calling desperately for a silver bullet.

Chapter 12
Usability Engineering Methods and Tools

Amandeep Kaur
Apeejay Institute of Management Technical Campus, India

ABSTRACT

Usability engineering is a field that focus on the human-computer interaction and exclusively in making the GUI's with high usability. A Usability Engineer validates the usability of an interface and recommending methods to improve its purview. This chapter elaborates various techniques to improve usability of websites: software graphical user interfaces (GUIs). It includes details on assessing and making recommendations to improve usability than it does on design, though Usability Engineers may still engage in design to some extent, particularly design of wire-frames or other prototypes. They conduct usability evaluations of existing or proposed user-interfaces and their findings are fed back to the designer.

INTRODUCTION

Usability engineering is a cost-effective, user centered process that ensures a high level of effectiveness, efficiency, and safety in complex systems. (Andrew, 2000; Nielsen, 1998) This chapter discusses a usability engineering approach for the design and the evaluation of interactive systems, focusing on practical issues. A list of

methods has been presented, considering a user-centered approach. This chapter describes the evaluation methodologies following the temporal phases of evaluation, according to a user-centered approach. Today's customer is well aware of his requirements and is unwilling to compromise. Whether customer purchases a mobile phone, a microwave oven, or a washing machine – the focus has now shifted from features offered, to the ease

DOI: 10.4018/978-1-4666-2958-5.ch012

and convenience of operation, and how fast the gadget can be mastered – i.e. the focus is now on the "USER INTERFACE".

LITERATURE REVIEW

Down the time usability has been studied and discovered by great researchers and scholars. It is a multidimensional concept that opens areas for research. It has evolved over time and has got its relevance in many aspects.

"Usability Engineering" is a science which studies how to understand and systematically address the usability demand of a customer (Jacko & Andrew, 2000) Thus, usability engineering deals with design of Web sites, computer portals, computer keyboard design, car dashboard design, washing machine front panel layout, etc. Even people who are already experts in the application of usability methods are aware of potential adaptations and extensions to the methods when applied to systems that are designed to incorporate significant use of AI. According to (Lieberman & Jameson 2009), some of the ways in which systems that incorporate intelligence tend to differ from systems that do not, both in terms of their potential to help users and in terms of possible side effects. These and other properties of usability systems can affect the application of design and evaluation methods in various ways, some of which are illustrated in the case studies by(Czerwinski, Horvitz, & Wilhite, 2009) which yield records of user activities at set points throughout the day and are useful for gathering evidence about the nature and duration of users' activities Questionnaires can ask about many different types of users' needs, though the data collected is not always as reliable and informative as the more direct methods just listed.

The first, and very important, aspect (Marca, 2012) about usability modeling with today's commonplace methods is that UML, Agile Software Development and Usability Engineering have their origins rooted in software systems. When used in combination, these methods have a strong track record for developing software for many kinds of problems and domains. The tools, techniques and technology (Clark 2011) for usability experts today is creating a win-win outcome. Inzunza, Juarez-Ramirez, & Mejia (2011), in their paper discuss that Usability can be attended from early phases by incorporating task and user analysis with framework's components. This fact benefits also the development of mobile applications, obtaining more usable systems tailored to the needs of a specific user with unique characteristics.

Seffah & Metzker (2009) discussed several usability cost/benefits and demonstrated the importance of usability while highlighting the current gap between usability and software engineering methods and tools. In this introductory chapter we outline the importance of usability as a software quality attribute as well as the importance and fundamentals of its engineering and integration into the mainstream software development lifecycle.

Usability Engineering (Durrani & Qureshi, 2012) is being partially followed in organizations. In planning phase, usability activities are not estimated and it propagates the absence of usability tasks in next phases. User involvement in SDLC phases is limited to requirement gathering and testing phase. In requirement phase, main focus is on the functionality of the system. User profiling is largely missing in organizations. In design phase, usability factors are somehow explored and organizations intend to do detailed designing. Usability testing is not focused by many organizations and this leads to post-release defects. To convince management regarding benefit of usability practices it may be a better idea to perform videotaped usability tasks of some recently developed system and share the results with development and management teams. (Gardner-Bonneau D. 2010), talked about the software system's capability to sustain the changes in the technical prospects without hampering the usability effectiveness. (Jennifer C. Romano Bergstrom 2011) carried out a demonstration and explained the benefits and challenges faced by the designers while usability testing of website design.

USABILITY ENGINEERING LIFECYCLE

The Usability Model is comprised of five stages, four of which are implicitly joined in a loop. Usability engineering is not typically hypothesis-testing based experimentation, but instead is structured, iterative user-centered design and evaluation applied during all phases of the interactive system development lifecycle.

The model is graphically depicted in Figure 1.

The usability process (Leventhal & Barnes, 2001) and a system's usability depend on the interaction design. Therefore, we must deal with system usability throughout the entire development process. Usability testing alone is not enough to output a highly usable product, because usability testing uncovers but does not fix design problems. Furthermore, usability testing has been viewed as similar to other types of software quality assurance testing, so developers often apply the techniques late in the development cycle—when major usability problems are very costly, if not impossible, to fix. Therefore, it is crucial to evaluate all results during the product development process, which ultimately leads to an iterative development process. A pure waterfall approach to software development makes introducing usability techniques fairly impossible. All software applications are tools that help users accomplish

certain tasks. However, before one can build usable software tools— or, rather, designs a UI— information is needed about the people who will use the tool:

- Who are the system users?
- What will they need to accomplish?
- What will they need from the system to accomplish this?
- How should the system supply what they need?

The usability process helps user interaction designers answer these questions during the analysis phase and supports the design in the design phase (see Figure 1).There are many usability methods—all essentially based on the same usability process—so we have abstracted a generic usability process from the different approaches to usability mentioned earlier.

Usability Analysis Phase

First, we have to get to know the users (Gabbard & Brown, 1998) and their needs, expectations, interests, behaviours, and responsibilities, all of which characterize their relationship with the system. There are numerous approaches for gathering information about users, depending on each individual system under development and the effort or time constraints for this phase. The main methods are *site visits*, *focus groups*, *surveys*, and *derived data*. The primary source for user information is site visits. Developers observe the users in their working environment, using the system to be replaced or performing their tasks manually if there is no existing tool. In addition, developers interview the users to understand their motivation and the strategy behind their actions. A well-known method or doing user analysis jointly with task analysis is *contextual inquiry*. This method provides a structured way for gathering and organizing information. A focus group is an organized discussion with a selected group

Figure1. The usability process

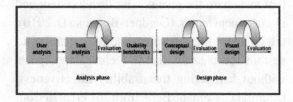

of users. The goal is to gather information about their views and experiences concerning a topic. (Benyon, 1993) It is well suited for getting several viewpoints about the same topic—for example, if there is a particular software product to discuss—and gaining insight into people's understanding of everyday system use. In a survey, the quality of the information depends on the quality of the questions. Surveys are a one-way source, because it is often difficult or even impossible to check back with the user.

There are a variety of different usability analysis tools available on the web today. They all perform tasks differently ways, but in the end, they are all carefully working on helping the user gather data that will help to improve the usability of your website or software. Some of the popular UA tools include, Quantivo, OpinionLab, ClickTale, Five Second Test, Concept Feedback, Clixpy, Ethnio.

Task Analysis Phase

Task analysis describes a set of techniques people use to get things done. The concept of a task is analogous to the concept of a use case in object-oriented software development; a task is an activity meaningful to the user (Bunt, 2005). User analysis is taken as input for task analysis, and both are sometimes performed jointly. Users can analyze tasks because one can use the located tasks to drive and test UI design throughout the product development cycle. It focus on a small set of tasks helps rationalize the development effort. So, one should prioritize the set of tasks by importance and frequency to get a small task set. This guarantee that you'll build the most important functions into the system and that the product will not suffer from "futurities." These tasks should be the starting point for developing the system. One approach to analysis is to build a task model within the Usage-Centered Design method, a model-driven approach for designing highly usable software applications, where tasks, described as essential use cases, are the basis for a well structured process and drive UI design.

Task analysis ends when we evaluate the discovered task set, which is best done collaboratively with users. When the user population is already performing a set of tasks, user can perform task analysis during user analysis to apprehend the tasks the user performs routinely and how the user perceives these tasks. After the optional first analysis, next task is to identify the tasks our system will support, based on a study of the goals the user wants to attain. Then, one can break the tasks into subtasks and into particular actions that the user will perform and take the identified tasks as the basis for building the usability specifications. It can then be instantiated into real-world examples and present them to test participants in a usability test.

The Task Analysis sequences and describes measurable behaviors (observable if possible) involved in the performance of a task. It provides a thorough analysis of each task in terms of occurrence, difficulty and importance. Jobs are a series of tasks. A *task* is an act designed to contribute a specific end result to the accomplishment of an objective. It has an particular beginning and end that is a measurable element of the duties and responsibilities of a specific job.

Even though each job has a title, the work that is likely to be done by that job can vary widely. Tasks are the means of describing a job in detail. The following are characteristics of tasks:

- A task has a specific beginning and end.
- It is performed in relatively short periods of time.
- Tasks are observable.
- Each task is autonomous of other actions.
- Tasks are not dependent on components of a procedure. A task is performed by an individual for its own sake.
- A *task statement* is a statement of a extremely specific action. It always has a verb and an object. It should not be baffled with an *objective* that has conditions and standards.

A task analysis defines a job in terms of KSA essential to bring out daily tasks. It is a planned framework that dissects a job and help to arrives at a reliable process of describing it across time and people by composing a detailed listing of all the tasks. The first product of a task analysis is a task statement for each task on the list.

Usability Benchmarks Phase

We set usability benchmarks as quantitative usability goals, which are defined before system design begins. They are based on the five basic usability attributes or their sub attributes. We need these benchmarks because, if we want to assess the value of the usability attributes for the system under development, we need to have a set of operationally defined usability benchmarks. We establish usability benchmarks by defining a set of benchmarks for each usability attribute we want to evaluate—that is, for each usability attribute we consider important for our system. We must define the benchmarks in a way that makes them calculable in a usability test or through a user satisfaction questionnaire.

Usability Design Phase

Once we have analyzed the tasks our system will support, we can make a first attempt at the UI's conceptual design, which we will evaluate and possibly improve in the next iteration.

1. **Conceptual Design:** During the conceptual design (Beyer & Holtzblatt, 1998) phase, we define the basic user–system interaction and the objects in the UI and the contexts in which interaction takes place. The findings of the user and task analysis are the basis for the conceptual design. The deliverables from this phase are typically paper prototypes, such as pencil drawings or screen mock ups, and a specification, which describes the UI's behaviour. Conceptual design is the most crucial phase in the process, because it defines the foundation for the entire system. Unfortunately, design is a very creative process, and it can't be automated with a method. There is a set of design principles and rules that we must creatively adapt for a certain design problem. The main principles of UI design cover feedback, reuse, simplicity, structure, tolerance, and visibility in UIs. Knowing usability design principles is the basis for good design. Compare this to an adult drawing class. Not everyone will be Picasso by the end of the course, but the students will be able to paint reasonable pictures if they use the principles they learned. Another way to improve design ability is to examine UIs. Analyzing the UIs of every software application you can access is very helpful and can sometimes be a source of inspiration for finding innovative, alternative solutions.

2. The conceptual design phase also ends with evaluating the results. It is a good idea to test the paper prototypes against the defined task set to check that all the prioritized tasks can be enacted. The last test in this phase is run together with users as a usability test or usability inspection of the paper prototype.

3. **Visual Design:** Having completed the conceptual design, the final step in our process is visual design, where we define the UI's appearance. This covers all details, including the layout of screens and dialog boxes, use of colors and widgets, and design of graphics and icons. There are also rules and principles for visual design, addressing use of color, text, screen layout, widget use, icon design, and so forth. It pays to have a professional screen designer, especially in this phase. Recommended readings about visual and conceptual design are *About Face* and *Software for Use*, which both include numerous design tips. *Designing Visual Interfaces* focuses on screen design and

graphics design in the context of UIs, as well as the underlying principles of visual design. The deliverables of this phase are prototypes that must be tested, an exact specification of the UI appearance, and behaviour plus the specification for new widgets that must be developed.

Prototyping

Prototypes are not exclusive to UI design, but they are valuable for performing usability testing in early development phases. (Brusilovsky & Millan, 2006) We need to build prototypes because abstract technical specifications are not a good way of communicating when we want to involve users in the design process—users understand tangible system prototypes much better. Some prototyping techniques help perform usability testing and require little implementation effort. We create prototypes to test them on the user through usability evaluation techniques. The prototyping techniques with which software developers usually are not familiar include

- **Paper Mock-Ups:** At the beginning of the design process, the designer creates paper prototypes—usually pencil drawings or printouts of screen designs—for the user. The designer ill act as the computer, showing the user the next element when a transition between graphical elements occurs.
- **"Wizard of Oz" Technique:** A human expert acts as the system and answers the user's requests, without the user's knowledge. The user interacts normally with the screen, but instead of using software, a developer sits at another computer (network-connected to the user's computer) answering the queries. The user gets the impression of working with a real software system, and this method is cheaper than implementing a real software prototype.

- **Scenarios, Storyboards, and Snapshots:** A scenario describes a fictional story of a user interacting with the system in a particular situation; snapshots are visual images that capture the interaction occurring in a scenario; and storyboards are sequences of snapshots that focus on the main actions in a possible situation. They make the design team think about the appropriateness of the design for a real context of use, and they help make the process user-centric.

USABILITY EVALUATION METHODS

Usability evaluation is a central activity in the usability process. It can determine the current version's usability level and whether the design works (Lewis & Wharton, 1997). It is the activity of performing usability tests in a laboratory with a group of users and recording the results for further analysis. We can't predict a software system's usability without testing it with real users. First, we must decide which groups of users we want to use to test the system and how many from each group we will try to recruit as test participants. Then, we must design the test tasks we'll ask the participants to perform. We usually take them from the results of the task analysis activity and apply them to hypothetical real-life situations. Some characteristics of the test require consideration, such as

- Whether the participant can ask the evaluator for help;
- Should two participants jointly perform each test task to observe the remarks they exchange in the process;
- What information participants will receive about the system prior to the test; and
- Whether to include a period of free system access after completing the predefined tasks to get the user's overall impression of

the system. Following is the description of commonly used evaluation methods.

After we prepare the test and recruit test participants, we run the tests, optionally recording them with video cameras or audio recorders, and log the users' actions in the system for further analysis. Once we have performed all the tests, we analyze the data and gather results to apply them in the next iterative cycle. Following is the description of commonly used evaluation methods.

Thinking Aloud Protocol

Formative evaluation seeks to learn which detailed aspects of the interaction are good and how to improve the interaction design. This opposes summative evaluation, which is performed at the end of the development process, after the system has been built. The results of summative evaluation do not help shape the product. Thinking aloud helps perform formative evaluation in usability tests. We ask the test participant to think aloud while using the system in a usability test, to verbalize his or her actions so we can collect the remarks. For example, a participant might say, "First, I open the file, and I click once on the file icon. Nothing happens. I don't know why this is not working like the Web. I press the Enter key, and it opens. Now I want to change the color of the label, so I search in the Tools menu, but I can't find any option for what I want to do." User remarks obtained in usability tests can provide significant insight into the best way of designing the system interaction. By detailing their mental process, test participants can uncover hidden usability problems. Formative evaluation is the usual form of evaluation in a usability process, combining qualitative data gathered from user comments with quantitative data to check against previously defined usability specifications.

Heuristic Evaluation

A usability expert can perform a heuristic evaluation of the system to make some development iterations shorter and to perform more iteration in the development process. Experts provide a different kind of feedback than final users through usability testing. Expert suggestions for modification are usually more applicable, and they are more precise about the underlying usability problems, such as a lack of consistency or poor navigation. On the other hand, usability testing must be performed with real users to identify specific usability problems. Heuristic evaluation can complement but not replace usability testing.

Collaborative Usability Inspection

A collaborative usability inspection is a systematic examination of a finished system, design or prototype from the end user's viewpoint. A team of developers, end users, application or domain experts, and usability specialists collaboratively perform the review. (Bunt A., 2005) Collaborative usability inspections (CUIs) use features and techniques from heuristic evaluation, pluralistic usability walkthroughs, and expert evaluations and are less expensive and faster than usability testing. Behind this technique is a set of strict rules to avoid the problems that typically arise if end users discuss their work together with designers or developers. CUIs uncover more—albeit different—usability defects (up to 100 defects per hour) than usability testing. Apart from efficiency, one advantage is that people with multiple perspectives and expertise examine the test object. Another advantage is that the participating developers build skills and know-how about how to make software more usable.

Interviews

In this technique, human factors engineers formulate questions about the product based on the kind of issues of interest. Then they interview representative users to ask them these questions in order to gather information desired. It is used for obtaining thorough information as well as information that can only be obtained from the interactive process between the interviewer and the user. In an evaluation interview, an interviewer reads the questions to the user, the user replies verbally, and the interviewer records those responses. The methods of interviewing include the following two types: Unstructured interviewing methods are used during the earlier stages of usability evaluation. The objective of the investigator at this stage is to gather as much information as possible concerning the user's experience. The interviewer does not have a well-defined agenda and is not concerned with any specific aspects of the system. The primary objective is to obtain information on procedures adopted by users and on their expectations of the system. Structured interviewing has a precise, determined agenda with specific questions to guide and direct the interview. Structured interviewing is more of a cross-examination than unstructured interviewing, which is closer to a conversation.

Focus Group

This is a data collecting technique where about 6 to 9 users are brought together to discuss issues relating to the system. A usability engineer plays the role of a mediator, who prepares the list of issues to be discussed beforehand and seek to gather the needed information from the discussion. It can confine spontaneous user reactions and ideas in the dynamic group process. The general procedures for conducting a focus groups study is to locate representative users who are willing to participate and select a moderator, prepare a list of issues to be discussed and goals for the type of information to gather, keep the discussion on track without inhibiting the free flow of ideas and comment. It is ensured that all participants get to contribute

to the discussion. Guard against having a single participant's opinion dominate the discussion.

Cognitive Walkthroughs

To determine the level of usability for a website, one or more usability (Beyer & Holtzblatt,1998) experts "walk" through a set of the most typical user tasks supported by the website, one-step-at-a-time. At each step in a task procedure, the evaluator(s) asks herself the following four questions about her expectations of users' behaviors:

1. Will the user try to achieve the right effect?
2. Will the user notice that the correct action is available?
3. Will the user associate the correct action with the effect to be achieved?
4. If the correct action exits, will the user see that progress is being made toward solution of the task?

The evaluator(s) attempts to come up with a "success story" for each step in the process. If user cannot come up with one, user instead creates a "failure story" and assesses why the user might not accomplish the task based on the interface design.

Contextual Task Analysis

A contextual task analysis, or contextual inquiry, is a user research method that applies ethnographic observation and one-on-one interviewing to understand the task procedures that users follow to reach their goals. The examiner silently observe the user at work in his or her natural work environment and notes any tools and people that support the user as they work on the way to task goals. For example, if a user is booking a vacation online, he may look up hotels online and then call the hotel front desk to learn more about the hotel. He may also review consumer ratings online to determine if the hotel offers amenities and services that meet his needs and preferences. In this example, the researcher would simply observe the user while he finds a hotel that is suitable. The researcher will take notes, and possibly use audio and/or video recording to capture key moments in the process. Following the observation, the researcher may conduct a one-on-one interview to understand the procedure from the user's point of view. In order to analyze a task procedure in terms of the average emotional and behavior patterns experienced by all participants in a study, the researcher may conduct exercises that let users map out the task procedure on paper and indicate their emotional reactions to specific procedural steps.

Questionnaires/Surveys

Surveys are a good way to collect quantitative data about users' opinions about an application or website. Traditionally, surveys have been mailed to consumers through the postal service, and today, the internet is a great resource for distributing and collecting survey feedback from hundreds or thousands of participants in a short period of time. Surveys are best used as tools to rate user experiences and users' needs and preferences as they relate to system features. Surveys should be used when users' task procedures are clearly defined, and when researchers are interested primarily in opinions about a task procedure. As a result, survey questions should be planned well. Additionally, surveys may include some open-ended questions; however, if time is a concern, analysis of these types of questions may lead to postponement of the project. Lastly, when creating a survey, it is best to judge how each question will be analyzed to determine its utility.

Usability Testing

Usability testing (Carroll, 2000) is the best way to understand how real users experience your website or application. Unlike interviews or focus groups that attempt to get users to accurately self-report their own behavior or preferences, a well-

designed user test measures actual performance on mission-critical tasks. To carry out a usability test, begin by identifying the end audience. It will consist of one or more user groups. For example, a single website may have content for consumers and a separate login area for site administrators. It is probable that these two user groups carry out different tasks as part of their normal website usage. Each user group should be given tasks to perform during testing that reflect their different usage patterns.

COMPARISON OF USABILITY ENGINEERING METHODS

Various usability methods are compared based on various criteria's like number of usability problems, performance, accuracy, requirement of number of evaluators, equipments.(Andreas Holzinger,2000) The above usability inspection and test methods are compared by various criteria's with the help of Table 1.

ADVANTAGES OF HIGH USABILITY

Following a product development process that includes usability engineering principles and usability tasks, deliverables and evaluation methods (Jacko & Andrew, 2000) ensures an enhanced appreciation of the user. Apart from enhanced customer satisfaction, following benefits are also observed for efforts for high usability

1. **Reduced Cost and Time to Market:** Usage of usability engineering principles ensures and user experience models are factored in the product design and validated at early stage. This ensure minimum iterations and little rework, resulting in reduced time to market. The fewer number of iterations and shorter product development cycle also provide major cost savings to the ISV.

Table 1. Comparison of evaluation methods

	Heuristic Evaluation	Cognitive Walkthrough	Action Analysis	Thinking Aloud	Field Observation	Questionnaires
Phase Applicability	All	All	Design	Design	Testing	All
Required Time	Low	Medium	High	High	Medium	Low
Users Needed	none	none	none	3+	20+	40+
Evaluators Required	3+	5+	1-2	1	1+	1
Equipment Required	Low	Low	Low	High	Medium	Low
Expertise Required	Medium	High	High	Medium	High	Low
Intrusive	No	No	No	Yes	Yes	No

2. **Reduced Support Cost:** 80% of software lifecycle costs occur during the maintenance phase. Every $1 invested in user-centered design returns between $2 and $100 (Pressman, 1992). As the product is built using user experience models, one of the key cost savings can be obtained by a significant reduction in the support, the product requires when it reach the market and there is reduction in the expected support of the product by implementing an innovative method of user interaction.

3. **Improved Brand Value:** In today's world, the impression of a company's brand is linked to the usability of its products. Various companies have created a mark for themselves by improving usability of existing products.

4. **Competitive Advantage:** For a competitive and commoditized software product market, usability provides many options to create differentiators by bringing a product with enhances user experience, patenting a user-centric design, or simply by building a product that attracts the users with its simplicity and ease of use.

5. **Improved Productivity:** The average software program has 40 design flaws that impair employees' ability to use it. The resulting cost of lost productivity can be up to 720%. Productivity within the service sector would rise 4% - 9% annually if every software program were designed for usability. Approximately one-fifth of the workers'

time is spent waiting for programs to run or for help to arrive, with double-checking printouts for accuracy and format following as a close second.

6. **Reduced Training Time:** The number of computer users in the workplace has increased today. A survey of MIS managers found that the training time for new users of a standard personal computer was 21 hours, whereas it was only 11 hours for users of a more usable computer. Hence the training time is reduced.

7. **Increased Sales and Revenues:** Combining hardware, software, networks and the people needed for computer support and training, the total spending has increased. Statistics indicate one-third of the overall real growth attributed to IT, and IT will continue to be the "engine of continued economic growth" for decades to come.

8. **Reduced Development Time and Costs:** According to a study (Bosert, 1991):
   a. 9% - 16% of software development projects are completed on time and on budget. Large companies have a 9% success rate. Medium-sized companies succeed with 16% of projects. Small companies had the greatest success rate at 28%.
   b. Overall, 31% of software development projects are cancelled before completion. Another 52% of projects eventually do get completed, but end up cost-

ing 189% of their original budget. In terms of time, they take between twice and three times as long as originally anticipated.

c. When software projects are completed, they only have 42% of the features originally intended.

d. More than 30% of software development projects are cancelled before completion, primarily because of inadequate user design input. The result is an annual loss of $80 billion to the economy.

The implementation of usability engineering techniques has demonstrated a reduction in the product development cycle by 33% - 50%.

Good usability is no more an optional requirements for software products but is a mandatory criterion for a successful product. It also helps the ISVs to fulfill its users need in a cost effective way.

USABILITY ENGINEERING INTERACTIVE TECHNOLOGIES

In this section we present an existing case study as an example to depict how usability engineering is applied to Complex Interactive Systems. This case study (Gabbard, Brown, & Livingston, 2000) was conducted at the Naval Research Laboratory's (NRL) Virtual Reality Lab where a system has been developed as a virtual environment application, called Dragon, for next-generation battlefield visualization. In Dragon, a responsive workbench provides a three-dimensional display for observing and managing battle space information shared among commanders and other battle planners. As described in, Dragon is a battlefield visualization system that displays a three-dimensional map of the battle space, as well as military entities represented with semi-realistic models. Dragon allows users to navigate and view the map and symbols, as well as to query and manipulate entities, us-

ing a modified flight stick. During early Dragon demonstrations and evaluations, it was observed that the user task of "navigation" – how users manipulate their viewpoint to move from place to place in a virtual world – profoundly affects all other user tasks. This is because, when using a map-based system, users must always first navigate to a particular area of the map. Thus, all the usability engineering methods, including domain analysis, user task analysis, expert evaluation, formative evaluation, and summative evaluation, that we applied to Dragon focused on the key user task of navigation.

Domain Analysis

Early in its development, Dragon was demonstrated as a prototype system at two different military exercises, where feedback from both civilian and military users was informally elicited. This feedback was the impetus for a more formal domain and user task analysis that included subject matter experts from naval personnel. Important Dragon-specific high-level tasks identified during domain and user task analysis included planning and shaping a battlefield, comprehending situational awareness in a changing battle space, performing engagement and execution exercises, and carrying out "what if" (contingency planning) exercises. In the user task analysis, it was also examined how personnel perform their current battlefield visualization tasks. Navigation is critical to all these high-level tasks.

Expert Evaluations

During expert evaluations, three user interface design experts assessed the evolving user interface design for Dragon. In early evaluations, the experts did not follow specific user task scenarios per se, but simply engaged in exploratory use of the user interface. The subsequent expert evaluations were guided largely by our own knowledge of interaction design for virtual environments and, more formally, by the Dragon user task analysis, as well as a framework for usability characteristics for virtual environments. Major usability design problems revealed by four major cycles of expert evaluations and subsequent redesign based on findings included poor mapping of navigation tasks to flight stick buttons, difficulty with damping of map movement in response to a user's flight stick movement, and inadequate graphical and textual feedback to the user about the current navigation task, the problems were discussed and a cycle of expert evaluations began to reveal fewer and fewer user interface design issues.

Formative Evaluations

Based on domain and user task analyses, a set of user task scenarios consisting of benchmark user tasks, carefully considered for coverage of specific issues related to navigation. A thoroughly pre-tested and debugged all scenarios before presenting them to users. During each of six formative evaluation sessions, each with an individual subject, a formal protocol designed to elicit both quantitative (task time and error counts) and qualitative errors. Time to perform the set of scenarios ranged from about 20 minutes to more than an hour. During each session, at least two and sometimes three evaluators were present. The evaluation leader ran the session and interacted with the user; the other one or two evaluators recorded timings, counted errors, and collected qualitative data. It was found that the quality and amount of data collected by multiple evaluators greatly outweighed the cost of those evaluators. After each session, it was analyzed that both the quantitative and qualitative data based the next design iteration on results.

Summative Evaluation

Expert and formative evaluation work using Dragon revealed four variables most likely to influence virtual environment navigation tasks.

Subsequently, summative evaluation manipulated and studied those four independent variables and their values, specifically:

- **Display Platform (CAVETM, Wall, Workbench, Desktop):** A standard immersive room, a single wall, a responsive workbench, and a standard desktop monitor, respectively.·
- **Stereo Sis (Stereo, Mono)**
- **Movement Control (Rate, Position):** How a subject's navigational hand gesture controls the resulting map movement.·
- **Frame of Reference (Egocentric, Exocentric):** Whether the user's actions with the flight stick appear to move the user through the world, or whether actions appear to move the virtual world around the user Thirty-two subjects performed a series of 17 carefully designed and pre-tested tasks, each requiring the subject to navigate to a certain location, manipulate the map, and/or answer a specific question based on the map.

Results

The summative evaluation yielded interesting results. A striking finding of results was that the desktop had the best overall user performance time of all display platforms. Many user tasks required finding, identifying, and/or reading text or objects labelled with text. While all displays were set to 1024 x 768 pixels, the size of the projection surface varied enough to conjecture that pixel density is more critical than field of view or display size. The observations and qualitative data support this claim. This research suggests one should further research user task performance using high resolution displays. Also interestingly, it was found no effect of platform at all in map tasks and geometric object tasks.

CONCLUSION

This chapter has presented a review of methods and techniques for design and evaluation of interactive systems under a usability engineering perspective. Even though improvement has been registered in a number of evaluation studies in the recent years, the evaluation of interactive systems needs to reach a more rigorous level in terms of subject sampling, statistical analysis, correctness in procedures, experiment settings, etc. Evaluation studies should benefit from the application of qualitative methods of research and from a rigorous and complete application of user-centered design approach in every development phase of these systems. To conclude, we advocate the importance of evaluation methods and tools in every design phase of a human centric system and at different layers of analysis. Significant testing results can lead to more appropriate and successful systems and the user's point of view can be a very inspiring source of information for adaptation strategies. From our point of view, both quantitative and qualitative methodologies of research can offer fruitful contributions and their correct application has to be carried out by the researchers working in this area in every design phase. Finally, since evaluation of such systems is still in exploratory phase, new approaches are strongly called for and these can include combining together different techniques, exploring new metrics to assess usability.

REFERENCES

Beck, J. E., Stern, M., & Woolf, B. P. (1997). Using the student model to control problem difficulty. In A. Bednarik, R. (2005). *Potentials of eye-movement tracking in adaptive systems*. In the 10th International Conference on User Modeling UM2005, Edinburgh, (pp. 1-8).

Begg, C., Cho, M., Eastwood, S., Horton, R., Moher, D., & Olkin, I. (1996). Improving the quality of reporting randomized trials (the ONSORT Statement). *Journal of the American Medical Association*, 276(8), 637–639. doi:10.1001/jama.1996.03540080059030

Bellotti, V., & MacLean, A. (n.d.). *Design space analysis* (DSA). Retrieved from http://www.mrccbu.am.ac.uk/amodeus/summaries/DSAsummary.html

Bental, D., Cawsey, A., Pearson, J., & Jones, R. (2003). Does adapted information help patients with cancer? In Brusilovsky, P., Corbett, A., & De Rosis, F. (Eds.), *User Modeling 2003 (Vol. 2702*, pp. 288–291). Lecture Notes in Computer Science Berlin, Germany: Springer. doi:10.1007/3-540-44963-9_38

Benyon, D. (1993). Adaptive systems: A solution to usability problems. *User Modeling and User-Adapted Interaction, 3*, 65–87. doi:10.1007/BF01099425

Berkovsky, S., Coombe, M., Freyne, J., Bhandari, D., & Baghaei, N. (2010). Physical activity motivating games: Virtual rewards for real activity. *Proceedings of, CHI2010*, 243–252.

Bevan, N. (1995). Measuring usability as quality of use. *Software Quality Journal, 4*, 115–130. doi:10.1007/BF00402715

Beyer, H., & Holtzblatt, K. (1998). *Contextual design: Defining customer- centered systems*. San Francisco, CA: Morgan Kaufmann Publishers, Inc.

Billsus, D., & Pazzani, M. (1998). Learning collaborative information filters. In *Proceedings of the International Conference on Machine Learning*, Madison, Wisconsin, (pp. 116-118). Morgan Kaufmann Publishers.

Bosert, J. L. (1991). *Quality functional deployment: A practitioner's approach*. New York, NY: ASQC Quality Press.

Brunstein, A., Jacqueline, W., Naumann, A., & Krems, J. F. (2002). Learning grammar with adaptive hypertexts: Reading or searching? In P. De Bra, P. Brusilovsky, & R. Conejo (Eds.), *Proceedings of the Second International Conference, AH 2002*, Málaga, Spain, May 29-31, 2002.

Brusilovsky, P., & Millan, E. (2006). *User models for adaptive hypermedia and adaptive educational systems*. Springer.

Bunt, A. (2005). User modeling to support user customization. In *Proceedings of UM 2005, LNAI 3538*, (pp. 499-501).

Burke, R. (2002). Hybrid recommender systems: Survey and experiments. *User Modeling and User-Adapted Interaction*, *12*(4), 331–370. doi:10.1023/A:1021240730564

Card, S. K., Moran, T. P., & Newell, A. (1986). *The psychology of human- computer interaction*. Hillsdale, NJ: Erlbaum.

Carroll, J. M. (2000). *Making use: Scenario-based design of human-computer interactions*. Cambridge, MA: MIT Press.

Carroll, J. M. (2007). *Making use is more than a matter of task analysis*. Hershey, PA: Idea Group Inc.

Cena, F., Gena, C., & Modeo, S. (2005). How to communicate commendations: Evaluation of an adaptive annotation technique. In the *Proceedings of the Tenth IFIP TC13 International Conference on Human-Computer Interaction* (INTERACT 2005), (pp. 1030-1033).

Clark, K. A. (2011). Human interaction and collaborative innovation human centered design. *Lecture Notes in Computer Science*, *2011*, 13–21. doi:10.1007/978-3-642-21753-1_2

Dillon, A. (2000). *Group dynamics meet cognition: Combining socio-technical concepts and usability engineering in the design of information systems*. Retrieved from http://dlist.sir.arizona.edu/1282/01/Ad2000.pdf

Gabbard, J. L., Brown, D., & Livingston, M. A. (2011). *Usability engineering for complex adaptive systems* (pp. 513–525).

Holzinger, A. (2000). Usability engineering methods for software developers. *Communications of the ACM*, *48*(1), 71–74. doi:10.1145/1039539.1039541

Holzinger, A. (2004). Application of rapid prototyping to the user interface development for a virtual medical campus. In *Proceedings of the IEEE VR'03 Conference*, (pp. 92-99). Los Angeles, CA: IEEE Computer Society Press.

Inzunza, S., Juarez-Ramirez, R., & Mejia, A. (2011). *Implementing user oriented interface: From user analysis to framework's components* (pp. 107–112). IEEE Computer Society Press. doi:10.1109/URKE.2011.6007858

Jacko, J. A. (2000). *The human-computer interaction handbook: Fundamentals, evolving technologies* (pp. 247–257). New York, NY: Springer.

Jameson, C. Paris, & C. Tasso (Eds.), *User Modeling: Proceedings of the Sixth International Conference, UM97*, Vienna, (pp. 277-288). New York, NY: Springer.

Leventhal, L. M., & Barnes, J. (2008). *Usability engineering: Process, products, and examples*. Pearson/Prentice Hall.

Lewis, C., & Wharton, C. (1997). Cognitive walkthroughs. In Helander, M. (Ed.), *Handbook of human-computer interaction* (2nd ed., pp. 717–732). Amsterdam, The Netherlands: Elsevier.

Marca, D. A. (2012). *SADT/IDEF0 for augmenting UML, agile and usability engineering methods*. (SADT/IDEF01-11).

Marcus, A. (2002). Dare we define user-interface design? In *Proceedings of the IEEE VR'04 Conference*, (pp. 19–24). Los Angeles, CA: IEEE Computer Society Press.

Nielsen, J. (1998). *Usability engineering*. Boston, MA: Academic Press.

Pressman, R. S. (1992). *Software engineering: A practitioner's approach*. New York, NY: McGraw-Hill.

Proyova, R., Peach, B., Wicht, A., & Wetter, T. (2010). Lecture Notes in Computer Science: *Vol. 6182. Use of personal values in requirements engineering-A research preview* (pp. 17–22). Berlin, Germany: Springer.

Rosson, M. B., & Carroll, J. M. (2001). *Usability engineering: Scenario-based development of human-computer interaction*. San Francisco, CA: Morgan Kaufmann Publishers Inc.

Seffah, A., & Metzger, E. (2009). *Adoption-centric usability engineering: Systematic deployment, assessment*. San Francisco, CA: Morgan Kaufmann, Inc. doi:10.1007/978-1-84800-019-3

Seffah, A., & Metzker, E. (2009). On usability and usability engineering. *Adoption Centric Usability Engineering*, 3-13. Springerlink.

Sharp, H., Robinson, H., & Segal, J. (2009). Integrating user centered design and software engineering: A role for extreme programming. *BCS-HCI Group's 7th Educators Workshop: Effective Teaching and Training in HCI, Learning and Teaching Support Network's Subject Centre for Information and Computer Science*, (pp. 98-107).

Sohaib, O., & Khan, K. (2010). Integrating usability engineering and agile software development: A literature review. *2010 International Conference on Computer Design and Applications*, Vol. 2, (pp. 32-38).

Swan, J. E., Gabbard, J. L., Hix, D., Schulman, R. S., & Kim, K. P. (2003). A comparative study of user performance in a map-based virtual environment. In *Proceedings of the IEEE VR'03 Conference*, (pp. 259-266). Los Angeles, CA: IEEE Computer Society Press.

Thomas, C., & Bevan, N. (Eds.). (1996). *Usability context analysis: A practical guide*. Teddington, UK: National Physical Laboratory.

ADDITIONAL READING

Carroll, J. M. (2002). *Usability engineering: Scenario-based development of human-computer interaction (Interactive Technologies)*. Morgan Kaufmann Publisher. ISBN-1-55860-712-9

Kushniruk, A. W., & Patel, V. L. (2008). *Cognitive and usability engineering methods for the evaluation of clinical information systems*. Hershey, PA: Idea Group Inc.

Memmel, T. (2011). *Agile usability engineering*. McGraw-Hill Professional.

Nebe, K., Zimmermann, D., & Paelke, V. (2008). *Integrating software engineering and usability engineering*. Wiley Publishers.

Rogers, Y., Sharp, H., & Preece, J. (2007). Interaction design, 3rd ed. Wiley Publishers. DOI 9780470018668

Rosson, M. B., & Carroll, J. M. (2008). *Usability engineering: Scenario-based development of human-computer interaction*. Morgan Kaufmann.

Chapter 13
Innovative Strategies for Secure Software Development

Punam Bedi
University of Delhi, India

Vandana Gandotra
University of Delhi, India

Archana Singhal
University of Delhi, India

ABSTRACT

This chapter discusses adoption of some proactive strategies in threat management for security of software systems. Security requirements play an important role for secure software systems which arise due to threats to the assets from malicious users. It is therefore imperative to develop realistic and meaningful security requirements. A hybrid technique has been presented in this chapter evolved by overlapping the strengths of misuse cases and attack trees for elicitation of flawless security requirements. This chapter also discusses an innovative technique using fuzzy logic as a proactive step to break the jinx of brittleness of present day security measures based on binary principle. In this mechanism, partially secure state evolved between safe state and failed state using fuzzy logic provides an alert signal to take appropriate additional preventive measures to save the system from entering into the failed state to the extent possible.

INTRODUCTION

The term "secure software" describes the state of software, where no unauthorized access, no manipulation, and no attacks on the software itself are successful. It is concerned with confidentiality (information disclosed only to authorized users), integrity (information modification only by users who have the right to do so, and only in authorized ways) and availability (use of the system cannot be maliciously denied to authorized users) (Brunil et al., 2009). Unfortunately, it is not possible to achieve such software security with the traditional methods which are post-development

DOI: 10.4018/978-1-4666-2958-5.ch013

activities and are not supported by appropriate methodologies to manage the high complexity of the securing process. Software researchers and practitioners have therefore come up with the view that we should focus on security from early phases of development life cycle as it is much cheaper to prevent than to repair to justify investment (Stoneburner et al., 2004; Davis et al., 2004). A number of security experts have therefore enhanced existing software development life cycle by incorporating various security techniques in all phases for developing secure software systems. Secure software engineering has thus been evolved as a new approach wherein security features are 'in-built' rather than 'on-bolt'.

We have extended this area of research and presented some proactive measures in this chapter to be adopted at the design level itself as a part of secure software engineering. This helps in reducing design-level vulnerabilities which are a major source of security risks in software and has accounted for around 50% of the security flaws (Hoglund & McGraw, 2004). Exploitation of these vulnerabilities result in security threats which are potential attacks, i.e. misuses and anomalies that violate the security goals of system's intended functions. Managing these threats suggests what, where and how security features for threat mitigation should be applied in secure software engineering. This chapter presents some of the proactive strategies in threat management like hybrid technique for elicitation of security requirements and use of fuzzy logic to help avert failed state in security of software systems to meet the challenges of changing security scenario of modern times.

Security requirements form the very basis for developing secure software systems. These requirements identify the vulnerable points in the system that an attacker can exploit to carry out threats. It is therefore necessary to determine realistic and meaningful security requirements. Any flaw in these requirements will mean faulty development of the security system making it vulnerable to threats. A new technique named as Hybrid Technique has therefore been presented in this chapter for elicitation of effective security requirements. This technique has been evolved by overlapping the strengths of misuse cases and attack trees as they provide complementary information which becomes much more comprehensive for the designers for enhancing the security of software systems. This proactive step in threat management is instrumental in enhancing in-built security to meet present day threat perceptions (Gandotra et al., 2009; Gandotra et al., 2011).

Traditional security mechanisms these days are based on binary principle making the system to be in either of the two states i. e. safe state or failed state. We have no means or mechanism to protect our system from complete failure which is a bad omen from security point of view. This can result in catastrophic consequences in terms of leakage of confidential data so vital to the users. A proactive security measure using fuzzy logic has therefore been discussed in this chapter to avert the failed state of the software system to the extent possible. This mechanism helps evolve an intermediate stage i.e. Partially Secure State (Yellow Zone) between the Safe State (Green Zone) and the Failed State (Red Zone). Here, the Yellow Zone provides an 'Alert Signal' in case the security of system starts moving towards Red Zone. This prevents the system from being compromised as the additional preventive measures become operative immediately on sensing this alert signal. This mechanism helps in designing more secure software systems thus eliminating the possibility of catastrophic failure of traditional security measures based on binary principle (Gandotra et al., 2010; Gandotra et al., 2011).

Thus, integration of the above proactive steps in threat management with traditional security development process has the potential to positively influence the level of security inherent in the developed software products.

BACKGROUND

This section discusses some important definitions relating to the subject discussed in this chapter. Works done by leading researchers in this area alongwith factors that have motivated us for evolving and enhancing innovative security solutions have also been presented as a part of secure software engineering.

Definition

- **Asset:** An abstract or concrete resource that a system must protect from misuse by an adversary.
- **Threat:** The adversary's goals or what an adversary might try to do to a system.
- **Vulnerability:** A security flaw in the system that represents a valid way for an adversary to realize a threat.
- **Risk:** A characterization of the danger of a vulnerability or condition.
- **Risk Management:** Risk management consists of risk assessment, risk reduction, and risk acceptance. There are four possible ways to manage a risk:
  ○ **Accept the Risk:** The risk is so low and so costly to mitigate that it is worth accepting.
  ○ **Transfer the Risk:** Transfer the risk to somebody else via insurance, warnings etc.
  ○ **Remove the Risk:** Remove the system component or feature associated with the risk if the feature is not worth the risk.
  ○ **Mitigate the Risk:** Reduce the risk with countermeasures.
- **Security Strength:** The effectiveness of the system at mitigating a threat.
- **Security Requirements:** Security requirements provide foundations upon which the security of a software system is built. Security requirements are driven by security threats, whereas most requirements are based on higher level goals. While most requirements are stated in terms of what *must* happen, security requirements are often specified in terms of what *must not* be allowed to happen.
- **Threat Modeling Process**: It involves understanding an adversary's goal in attacking a system based on system's assets of interest (Swiderski & Snyder, 2004). It is important to be systematic during the threat modeling process to ensure that as many as possible threats and vulnerabilities are discovered by developers not by attackers (Myagmar et al., 2005). Threat modeling process consists of characterizing the security of the system, identifying assets and access points and determining threats. Characterizing the security of the system involves complete understanding of the system. This includes gathering information about different components and their interconnections, usage scenarios and identifying assumptions and dependencies. This will help us in creating a system model that will detail out the necessary features of the system. Understanding the system completely will help us to identify vulnerable assets that need to be protected from malicious users. It will also assist us to find out the weak points that can be targeted by the attacker to enter into the system to steal precious assets (Swiderski and Snyder, 2004). Thereafter threats can be identified by going through each of these security critical entities and creating threat hypotheses that violate confidentiality, integrity, or availability of the entity.
- **Fuzzy Logic:** The concept of Fuzzy Logic (FL) was conceived by Lotfi Zadeh, a professor at the University of California at Berkley. FL is a superset of conventional logic (Boolean) that has been extended to handle the concept of partial truth. The

central notion of fuzzy system is that truth values (in fuzzy logic) or membership values (in fuzzy sets) are indicated by a value on the range [0.0, 1.0], with 0.0 representing absolute Falseness and 1.0 representing absolute Truth. FL deals with real world vagueness.

Overview of Existing Literature and Motivation

Software systems these days are increasingly facing with both internal and external penetrations. This has given rise to organized and motivated hacking. That might be the reason why Cheng and Atlee (2007) have highlighted security as the research hotspot and also pointed it as the future subject of research in this area. Many researchers have emphasized the need to build software security from the ground level. Lipner (2004), McGraw (2004) and Davis et al. (2004) have discussed how software security can be improved by focusing on its development process since the early phases. Essafi et al. (2006; 2007) have also augumented the concept of secure software systems. Yasar et al. (2008) have proposed the best practices in software development which the developer has to follow during different phases of the software development life cycle. Jan Juriens (2003) has done a lot of work regarding secure systems development with UML.

Many researchers have published their work on threat modeling and risk estimation which are considered as the basis for obtaining security requirements (Swiderski and Snyder, 2004; Myagmar et al., 2005). There are several existing works on Misuse Cases for determining security requirements (Sindre & Opdahl, 2000, 2005; Alexander, 2003). Similarly numerous works have been published on use of Attack trees associated with security requirements of the system (Lamsweerde, 2004; Schneier, 1999). Opdahl & Sindre (2009) have drawn experimental comparison of attack trees and misuse cases for security threat

identification. Diallo et al. (2006) have made the comparative evaluation of three approaches: The Common Criteria, Misuse Cases, and Attack Trees for elicitation of security requirements. They have stated that each approach has its own strengths and weaknesses, and that they can be complimentary when combined. The Common Criteria are difficult to learn and use, but are easy to analyze. Misuse Cases are easy to learn and use, but produces output that is hard to read. In contrast, Attack Trees produce clear output, but are difficult to analyze. They have proposed that by combining techniques, more information can be obtained regarding the security of a system. We have therefore been motivated to carry forward their work by evolving Hybrid Technique which merges the strengths of misuse cases and attack trees for developing realistic and meaningful security requirements making the system stronger to mitigate weaknesses effectively in large and complex systems (Gandotra et al., 2009; Gandotra et al., 2011).

In 1965 Lofti Zadeh proposed fuzzy set theory and later established fuzzy logic based on fuzzy sets. His research in this area has been extensive and is available in the various volumes to his credit (Zadeh et al., 2009). Mamdani and Assilian (1975) have extended this area of research and developed algorithm for fuzzy inference system. Sodiya et al. (2007) have presented a technique for software security risk analysis using fuzzy expert system. Olthoff (2001) has come with some observations on the security requirements engineering and obliquely pointed out some of the deficiencies in the present day security mechanisms which are based on binary principle making the system to be in either of the two states i. e. safe state or failed state. The failed state can be catastrophic and is not acceptable in this information age as it handles secret and confidential data. We have therefore been motivated to evolve a proactive defense mechanism to break this jinx of brittleness. This jinx has been broken using fuzzy logic by generating an intermediate state i.e. Partially Secure State (Yellow Zone) in between Fully Secure State (Green Zone) and Failed State (Red Zone). Here yellow zone provides an 'Alert Signal' for taking additional preventive measures to save the system from entering into the red zone (Gandotra et al., 2010; Gandotra et al., 2011). This unique security solution thus overcomes the deficiency of existing security solutions which are based on binary principle.

PROACTIVE STEPS IN THREAT MANAGEMENT FOR SOFTWARE SECURITY

In this section we have discussed some of the proactive strategies in threat management like hybrid technique for elicitation of security requirements and use of fuzzy logic to help avert failed state in security of software systems. These strategies may be adopted during design phase of software life cycle to meet new threat perceptions of this digital era.

Elicitation of Security Requirements Using Hybrid Technique

Hybrid Technique has been evolved for developing realistic and meaningful security requirements by merging the strengths of misuse cases and attack trees as they form the very basis of security of software systems (Gandotra et al., 2009). At present Common Criteria, Misuse Cases and Attack Trees are adopted for elicitation of security requirements as explained below.

- **Common Criteria:** The Common Criteria (CC) is a comprehensive, standardized method for security requirements elicitation, specification, and analysis developed by the National Institute for Standards and Technology (Common Criteria implementation Board, 1999; Vetterling, 2002). Output document produced by this tech-

nique is very clear and helpful in evaluating general security requirements of information technology systems. CC produces two kinds of documents, a Protection Profile (PP) and a Security Target (ST). The PP is a document used to identify the desired security properties of a product created by a group of users while the ST identifies what a product actually accomplishes that is security-relevant. The drawback of Common Criteria is that it is a complex activity involving many special work products: security objectives, security requirements, security policies, functional specifications, and security policy models. These work products are essential in a process that aims to create trustworthy information security products. But the work products and relationships between them can be hard to understand, even for persons with a strong technical background, but little knowledge of security engineering which add complexity and compromise to its usability (McDermott & Fox, 1999).

- **Misuse Cases:** Use cases are helpful in describing functional requirements of a system, but they are less helpful with non-functional requirements, such as security. Misuse Cases were introduced to address this shortcoming of use cases by Sindre and Opdahl (2000; 2005). A misuse case is a use case model adopted by the attackers hostile to the system. Misuse case diagrams show the mappings between use cases, misuse cases and mitigations against threats. The graphical representation of these relationships facilitates the analysis of the security requirements. This technique is simple to learn, use and complete as the solution is included in the same diagram. Although the combination of threats and their remedies in the same diagram helps to analyze the threats but it has the deficiencies where the clarity of output is concerned specially w.r.t. large systems. These diagrams provide information of all attacks but do not indicate how the attacker will achieve his objective of the attack.

- **Attack Trees:** Attack trees were defined by Schneier (1999) to model threats against computer systems. Attack trees provide a formal, methodical way of describing the security of systems, based on varying attacks. A tree structure is used to represent attacks against a system, with the goal as the root node and different ways of achieving that goal as leaf nodes (Swiderski & Snyder, 2004). An attack tree represents step by step realization of the attack and provides systematic way to symbolize attacks. This characteristic gives better understanding and provides clarity of output. Although it states clearly the mode of attack but remedy does not find place in this technique. Furthermore, attack trees capture attacks that are sequences of events and may not be appropriate for attacks that involve concurrent actions.

Diallo et al. (2006) have made the comparative evaluation of the above three approaches to specify security requirements. Each of these approaches were applied to a common problem, a wireless hotspot, and evaluated for learnability, usability, completeness, clarity of output, and analyzability. They have concluded that each approach has its own strengths and weaknesses and can be complimentary when combined. This fact has led us to evolve a hybrid technique as a framework wherein we have combined misuse cases and attack trees for elicitation of effective security requirements as explained below.

- **Hybrid Technique:** We have seen each elicitation technique mentioned above has its own advantages and disadvantages. For large and complex systems having more threats misuse case diagram is not suitable

as it will be difficult to read so many cross edges in the diagram. Also a misuse case diagram shows attacks or threats but does not give details on how these attacks can be realized. However it is achievable using attack trees. Although attack trees have some advantages over misuse case technique, they do not provide information about preconditions and mitigation policies corresponding to the threats. We have therefore proposed Hybrid Technique which overlaps the strengths of these two techniques to overcome the above said deficiencies and is shown in Figure 1(Gandotra et al., 2009; Gandotra et al., 2011).

Hybrid technique has been used here in security requirement generation cycle for deriving security requirements as indicated in Figure 2.

In this security requirement generation cycle, threat modeling process has been used to enumerate and identify threats to the system. After enumerating various threats, these are first classified using STRIDE model and thereafter prioritized on the basis of risk associated with each threat using DREAD algorithm. Threats needing mitigation are then mapped into security requirements using hybrid technique as explained below.

At first, all possible threats to the system and the assets under attack are identified using threat modeling process (Swiderski & Snyder, 2004). Various entities defined during the threat modeling

Figure 1. Evolution of hybrid technique

Figure 2. Security requirement generation cycle

Figure 3. Threat entity relationship diagram

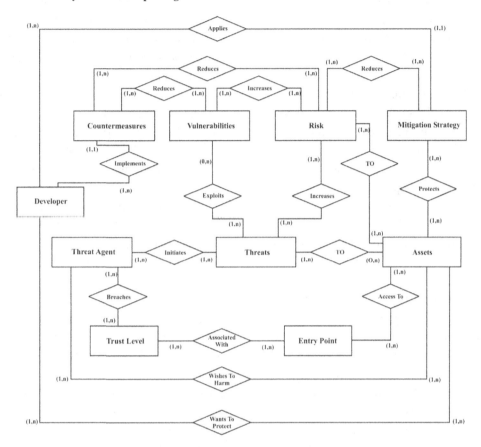

process and their relationship has been indicated in the Threat Entity Relationship (T-E-R) diagram as shown in Figure 3.

In the diagram above (min, max) notation has been used for displaying cardinality ratio. In this notation a pair of integer numbers (min, max) is associated with each participation of an entity type E in relationship type R, where $0 \leq min \leq max$ and $max \geq 1$. The numbers mean that for each entity e in E, e must participate in at least min and at most max relationship instances in R at any point of time. In this method, min=0 implies partial participation, whereas min> 0 implies total participation (Elmasri et al., 2006).

As indicated in the diagram, a threat agent is an adversary who is motivated to harm/exploit the system in an unauthorized manner to drive benefit. He is primarily responsible for threat to the assets

of the system and can traverse the privilege boundaries in an illegal way to reach the access points to realize the threat. The vulnerabilities not covered by countermeasures are very easily exploited by threat agents to meet their objective of exploiting the system maliciously and fraudulently to their advantage. The responsibility of the developer is to adopt appropriate countermeasures to reduce the identified vulnerabilities to the minimum. He will also incorporate mitigation techniques at the design level to reduce the risks due to these identified threats (Gandotra et al., 2012).

Thus threat modeling helps in identifying all the vulnerable points in the system that an attacker can exploit to carry out threats and is a base of any secure software system. It also helps the designers anticipate attack goals and determine: 'what' the system is designed to protect; from 'whom' and 'how' it can be done. Microsoft's Threat Modeling Tool supports and facilitates the designers and developers in this respect (Microsoft ACE Team). Once threats are identified, they are categorized using STRIDE model. STRIDE is a classification of the effects of realizing a threat: Spoofing, Tampering, Repudiation, Information disclosure, Denial of service and Elevation of privilege.

- **Spoofing:** Allows an adversary to pose as another user, component, or other system that has an identity in the system being modeled.
- **Tampering:** The modification of data within the system to achieve a malicious goal.
- **Repudiation:** The ability of an adversary to deny performing some malicious activity because the system does not have sufficient evidence to prove otherwise.
- **Information Disclosure:** The exposure of protected data to a user that is not otherwise allowed access to that data.
- **Denial of Service:** Occurs when an adversary can prevent legitimate users from using the normal functionality of the system.
- **Elevation of Privilege:** Occurs when an adversary uses illegitimate means to assume a trust level with different privileges than he recently has.

This high level of classification of threat makes it easier to understand what that threat allows an attacker to do. These classified threats are then prioritized on the basis of quantum of risk each threat poses. DREAD algorithm is used in the step to compute a risk value for prioritization of threats to drive guidelines for mitigation. DREAD name is an acronym derived from: Damage potential, Reproducibility, Exploitability, Affected users, and Discoverability as explained below.

- **Damage Potential:** Ranks the extent of the damage that occurs if vulnerability is exploited.

- **Reproducibility:** Ranks how often an attempt at exploiting vulnerability works.
- **Exploitability:** Assigns a number to the effort required to exploit the vulnerability. In addition, exploitability considers preconditions such as whether the user must be authenticated.
- **Affected Users:** A numeric value characterizing the ratio of installed instances of the system that would be affected if an exploit became widely available.
- **Discoverability:** Measures the likelihood that vulnerability will be found by external security researchers, hackers and the like if it went unpatched (Swiderski & Snyder, 2004).

Risk posed by each threat is calculated by taking an average of the numbers assigned (on a scale of 1-10) to these five factors ((D+R+E+A+D) /5). After calculating the overall risk factor for each threat, sort the threat list by decreasing order of risk. Threats can be addressed starting at the top of the list. Next step in this process is how to respond to threats. Threats needing mitigation are then mapped into security requirements using hybrid technique. In this technique, we first enumerate the required conditions for a successful attack to an asset. Thereafter different paths adopted by the attacker to achieve its goal are identified. Remedial measures are then worked out to ensure that the attacker does not succeed in his mission. Hybrid Process Diagram used in this technique is the manifestation of various stages starting from threat to mitigation level. This diagram is created through the following steps.

- Representation of threat and asset threatened.
- Preconditions prevailing at the time of threat.
- Mode of realization of threat by an attacker to achieve its goal.
- Application of mitigation techniques to neutralize the threat.

The graphical representation of this complete information about a threat in a single diagram helps in better analysis of security requirements and is useful to the designers and developers for incorporation of appropriate countermeasures for software security. Illustrative example for mapping of a threat into security requirements using hybrid technique has been given below for better understanding.

Illustrative Example

Let's say that a threat model for electronic mail has been defined. Here we are mapping one specific threat i.e. "Attacker is stealing information being sent by E-mail" into security requirements

with the help of hybrid technique. This threat has been chosen for mitigation because of high risk factor associated with it. Hybrid process diagram corresponding to this threat is shown in Figure 4.

Threat in the diagram above is the root node and involves stealing of e-mail by malicious user. E-mail is the asset under threat. Left side of the threat shows preconditions, i.e. reading e-mail by user that has necessitated attack. Mode of realization of threat has been shown by drawing nodes indicating ways of accomplishing the threat. Right side of the threat indicates mitigation policies i.e. encrypt message and enforce strong password to be adopted to neutralize this threat. These mitigation policies are attached to the root threat only and have not been shown individually correspond-

Figure 4. Hybrid process diagram representing threat of e-mail stealing

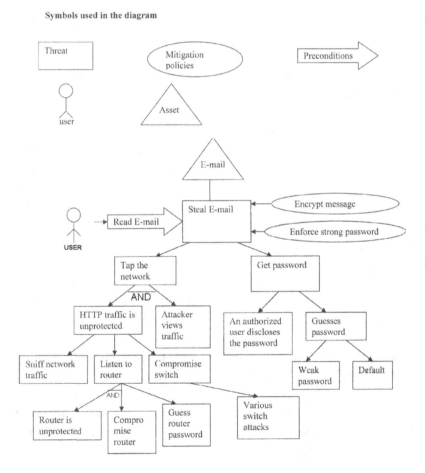

ing to the attacks as one mitigation policy can be responsible for neutralization of other threats in the process.

Security requirements generated corresponding to mapped threat from the above graphical representation using hybrid technique is: data encryption as a security feature in the system helps to protect the data from being compromised as the adversary will get encrypted text even if he succeeds in tapping the network. A strong password policy guards against the misuse of password to enter in the system by the attacker. Similarly other threats to the system can also be mapped into security requirements using this technique.

Thus addressing security concerns during early phases of development life cycle eliminates patch work making software security much more economical and less time consuming. This in turn will increase the confidence of end users due to adoption of this proactive measure in secure software engineering (Gandotra et al., 2009; Gandotra et al., 2011).

Use of Fuzzy Logic to Avert Failed State in Software Security

Traditional security mechanisms adopted at present are primarily based on binary principle making the system to be in either of the two states i. e. safe state or failed state.

1. **Safe State:** In this state, security measures are sufficient to avoid threats to keep the system in safe mode.
2. **Failed State:** In this state, security measures adopted have failed to avert the threat bringing the system in failed mode.

We have no means or mechanism at present to protect our system from complete failure which is unacceptable in this information age as it can result in catastrophic consequences in terms of leakage of confidential data. We are therefore presenting a proactive strategy in threat management using fuzzy logic to break the jinx of brittleness of present security measures which are based on binary principle. Fuzzy logic is basically a multi-valued logic that allows intermediate values to be defined between conventional evaluations like yes/no, true/false, black/white etc. Fuzzy logic is derived from fuzzy set theory to deal with reasoning that is approximate rather than precise. Lofti Zadeh (1965) has proposed fuzzy set theory and later established fuzzy logic based on fuzzy sets. Fuzzy variables may have a membership value between 0 and 1 and is not having the constraint of two truth values like true and false as is the case with binary logic or crisp logic. This feature of fuzzy logic fills an important gap in engineering design methods which are either based on purely mathematical approaches or purely logic based approaches in system design. The proactive strategy presented in this chapter uses fuzzy logic which enables us to generate more states in between safe state and failed state thus eliminating the deficiencies observed in case of binary system. An intermediate stage i.e. Partially Secure State (Yellow Zone) generated between the Safe State (Green Zone) and the Failed State (Red Zone) provides an 'Alert Signal' in case the security level of the system starts moving towards Partially Secure State (Yellow Zone). It helps save the system from moving into failed state as the additional countermeasures become operative to strengthen the since applied mitigation policies for different threats before the attacker is successful in his mission(Gandotra et al., 2010; Gandotra et al., 2011). These stages are associated with security level which in turn depends upon security goals of the software system under development as explained below.

Major goals of any secure software system are:

*   **Preservation of Confidentiality (C):** i.e. ensuring that an asset is visible only to actors authorized to see it.
*   **Preservation of Integrity (I):** i.e. to ensure that an asset is not corrupted.

- **Preservation of Availability (A):** i.e. ensuring that the asset is readily accessible to agents needing it.

The degree to which each of these factors or properties is needed varies from application to application. For example the defense industry is primarily interested in confidentiality. In contrast the banking industry is primarily interested in integrity and the telephone industry may value availability most. The exact requirements that are needed for a particular system or application are expressed in security policy for that system or application (Madan et al., 2002). This is also indicated as guidelines by Natioanl Institute of Standards and Technology as basis for achieving information technology security (Stoneburner et al., 2004).

In this mechanism, above security goals have been used as input variables while designing the fuzzy inference system which in turn generates security level as output to be monitored for any variations. In literature, commonly two different types of fuzzy inference systems are used. These are the Mamdani and the Takagi-Sugeno-Kang algorithms (Jang, 2007). We are here using Mamdani Fuzzy Inference System for the prediction of security level of the system as given below.

Application of Fuzzy Inference System for Determination of Security Level of the System

Fuzzy inference system is a popular computing framework based on the concepts of fuzzy set theory, fuzzy if-then rules and fuzzy reasoning and a defuzzification interface.

1. **Fuzzification:** This is the first step in the fuzzy inference system i.e. to fuzzify inputs. Designing the fuzzy system requires that the input parameters to the system be represented as fuzzy sets. A fuzzy set is a collection of paired members consisting of members and degrees of "support" and "confidence" for those members. A linguistic variable whose values are words, phrases or sentences are labels of fuzzy sets (Zadeh, 1973). Values for C, I and A as input parameters and their corresponding weights depend upon the application and the environment in which they work. All the input values in respect of the above parameters are defined as a fuzzy number instead of crisp numbers by using suitable fuzzy sets. Levels of three input variables i.e. Confidentiality, Integrity and Availability as fuzzy sets are given below.

a. Confidentiality = {Not Confidential, Partially Confidential, Very Confidential}
b. Integrity = {Low Integrity, Medium Integrity, High Integrity}
c. Availability = {Non Availability, Partial Availability, Full Availability}

The fuzzy sets shown above in turn are represented by a membership function. The membership function is the graphical representation of the magnitude of the participation of each input. Designing membership function is the most difficult, laborious and critical stage of building a fuzzy model. This can be best achieved by partitioning the numerical domain of the fuzzy input/output variables into specified number equally spaced membership functions. This number depends upon security concerns of the software system as per user's requirement. In this case, the domain is divided into three regions for better understanding. Thus we have used triangular membership function to represent three regions for each input variable. The representation for input parameter Confidentiality is shown in Figure 5. Similarly the other two input parameters Integrity and Availability can also be represented.

Levels of output variable i.e. Security Level as fuzzy set is

Figure 5. Triangular membership function for input parameter: Confidentiality

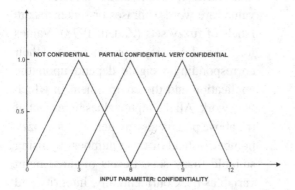

○ Security Level = {Not Secure, Partially Secure, Fully Secure}

As can be seen in Figure 6, a Partially Secure state (PS) has been created in between Fully Secure (FS) and Not Secure (NS) state. It is like providing a Yellow Zone (PS) between Green (FS) and Red (NS) zones. The intermediate zone (Yellow Zone) provides an 'alert signal' prompting additional security measures to strengthen the since applied countermeasures to avoid the system reaching the Red Zone i.e. failed state.

2. **Rule Evaluation:** Once the input and output fuzzy sets and membership functions are constructed, the fuzzy if-then rules are then framed to reflect the relationships between any possible relation of input variables C,

Figure 6. Triangular membership function for output parameter: Security level

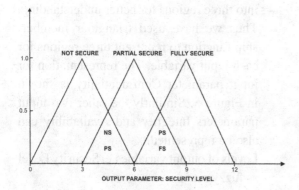

I, A and the output variable i.e. security level. The levels of input parameters defined in above step are used in the antecedent of rules and the level of the security as the consequent of rules. Usually T-norm and T-conorm operators are used in the evaluation of antecedent and consequents respectively given as follows:

T-norm operator is $T_{min}(a, b) = min(a, b)$ and

T-conorm operator is $T_{max}(a, b) = max(a, b)$.

The rules are formulated using Mamdani's inference method (Mamdani & Assilian, 1975). Rules formulated in the rule base of the fuzzy inference system are represented in the format as follows:

1. *If (Confidentiality is 'Not Confidential') AND (Integrity is 'Low Integrity') AND (Availability is 'Non Availability') THEN Security Level is 'Not Secure'.*

2. *If (Confidentiality is 'Not Confidential') AND (Integrity is 'Low Integrity') AND (Availability is 'Partial Availability') THEN Security Level is 'Not Secure'.*

3. *If (Confidentiality is 'Not Confidential') AND (Integrity is 'Low Integrity') AND (Availability is 'Full Availability') THEN Security Level is 'Partially Secure'.*

4. *If (Confidentiality is 'Not Confidential') AND (Integrity is 'Medium Integrity') AND (Availability is 'Non Availability') THEN Security Level is 'Not Secure'.*

5. *If (Confidentiality is 'Not Confidential') AND (Integrity is 'Medium Integrity') AND (Availability is 'Partial Availability') THEN Security Level is 'Partially Secure'.*

6. *If (Confidentiality is 'Not Confidential') AND (Integrity is 'Medium Integrity') AND (Availability is 'Full Availability')*

THEN Security Level is 'Partially Secure'.

7. If (Confidentiality is 'Not Confidential') AND (Integrity is 'High Integrity') AND (Availability is 'Non Availability') THEN Security Level is 'Partially Secure'.

8. If (Confidentiality is 'Not Confidential') AND (Integrity is 'High Integrity') AND (Availability is 'Partial Availability') THEN Security Level is 'Partially Secure'.

9. If (Confidentiality is 'Not Confidential') AND (Integrity is 'High Integrity') AND (Availability is 'Full Availability') THEN Security Level is 'Fully Secure'.

10. If (Confidentiality is 'Partially Confidential') AND (Integrity is 'Low Integrity') AND (Availability is 'Non Availability') THEN Security Level is 'Not Secure'.

11. If (Confidentiality is 'Partially Confidential') AND (Integrity is 'Low Integrity') AND (Availability is 'Partial Availability') THEN Security Level is 'Partially Secure'.

12. If (Confidentiality is 'Partially Confidential') AND (Integrity is 'Low Integrity') AND (Availability is 'Full Availability') THEN Security Level is 'Partially Secure'.

13. If (Confidentiality is 'Partially Confidential') AND (Integrity is 'Medium Integrity') AND (Availability is 'Non Availability') THEN Security Level is 'Partially Secure'.

14. If (Confidentiality is 'Partially Confidential') AND (Integrity is 'Medium Integrity') AND (Availability is 'Partial Availability') THEN Security Level is 'Partially Secure'.

15. If (Confidentiality is 'Partially Confidential') AND (Integrity is 'Medium Integrity') AND (Availability

is 'Full Availability') THEN Security Level is 'Fully Secure'.

16. If (Confidentiality is 'Partially Confidential') AND (Integrity is 'High Integrity') AND (Availability is 'Non Availability') THEN Security Level is 'Partially Secure'.

17. If (Confidentiality is 'Partially Confidential') AND (Integrity is 'High Integrity') AND (Availability is 'Partial Availability') THEN Security Level is 'Fully Secure'.

18. If (Confidentiality is 'Partially Confidential') AND (Integrity is 'High Integrity') AND (Availability is 'Full Availability') THEN Security Level is 'Fully Secure'.

19. If (Confidentiality is 'Very Confidential') AND (Integrity is 'Low Integrity') AND (Availability is 'Non Availability') THEN Security Level is 'Partially Secure'.

20. If (Confidentiality is 'Very Confidential') AND (Integrity is 'Low Integrity') AND (Availability is 'Partial Availability') THEN Security Level is 'Partially Secure'.

21. If (Confidentiality is 'Very Confidential') AND (Integrity is 'Low Integrity') AND (Availability is 'Full Availability') THEN Security Level is 'Fully Secure'.

22. If (Confidentiality is 'Very Confidential') AND (Integrity is 'Medium Integrity') AND (Availability is 'Non Availability') THEN Security Level is 'Partially Secure'.

23. If (Confidentiality is 'Very confidential') AND (Integrity is 'Medium Integrity') AND (Availability is 'Partial Availability') THEN Security Level is 'Partially Secure'.

24. If (Confidentiality is 'Very Confidential') AND (Integrity is

'Medium Integrity') AND (Availability is 'Full Availability') THEN Security Level is 'Fully Secure'.

25. *If (Confidentiality is 'Very Confidential') AND (Integrity is 'High Integrity') AND (Availability is 'Non Availability') THEN Security Level is 'Partially Secure'.*

26. *If (Confidentiality is 'Very Confidential') AND (Integrity is 'High Integrity') AND (Availability is 'Partial Availability') THEN Security Level is 'Fully Secure'.*

27. *If (Confidentiality is 'Very Confidential') AND (Integrity is 'High Integrity') AND (Availability is 'Full Availability') THEN Security Level is 'Fully Secure'*

3. **Defuzzification:** After if-then rules are applied, the crisp output is calculated through a process called defuzzification. Defuzzification refers to the way a crisp value is extracted from a fuzzy set as a representative value. Defuzzification is briefly defined as a transformation of a fuzzy set into a numerical value. The most widely adopted method for defuzzifying a fuzzy set A of a universe of disclosure Z is centroid of area.

Centroid of area $Z_{COA} = \int_z \mu_A(z)\, z\, dz / \int_z \mu_A(z)\, dz$

where $\mu_A(z)$ is the aggregate output MF (Jang, 2007).

Determination of security level using fuzzy inference system helps us to know whether the security measures adopted to counter the threats are adequate or not. In case the output security level is found below the threshold level defined by the user, additional security measures are taken to achieve the desired results. In turn this helps us to define the initial values for security goals as input parameters to the system to achieve threshold value of security level as output parameter required by the user.

Once we apply the countermeasures, it is presumed that system is in the safe state and is able to maintain the security goals i.e. C, I, A of the system. When the threat starts taking place the values for security goals also start coming down. This correspondingly changes the output security level. Variations in the security goals during threat are fed as input to the fuzzy inference system which in turn evolves new security level at any given point of time. Actors which can be software agents or human agents can be associated for monitoring this security level constantly. They implement their predetermined action plans as soon as they find that the security level is entering in the 'Partially Secure State (Yellow Zone)' thus saving the system from entering into the failed state i.e. red zone. These action plans may consist of induction of complex algorithms, biometric features, multifactor security mechanism or other additional features which are considered necessary to prevent the attacker from achieving its goal. This ensures that the security level is not allowed to move towards 'Not Secure State (Red Zone)'. The innovations in this proposed proactive strategy once incorporated at the design level may prove a forerunner towards flawless secure software systems to help avert the failed state to save the system from being compromised to the extent possible.

Implementation Using MATLAB

We have used MATLAB Fuzzy Tool Box which is a graphical user interface tool required to build fuzzy inference system. Primary GUI tools for building, editing and observing fuzzy inference systems in the toolbox used in this case are:

- Fuzzy Inference System Editor
- Membership Function Editor
- Rule Editor
- Rule Viewer

Figure 7. Representation of input and output parameters using FIS editor

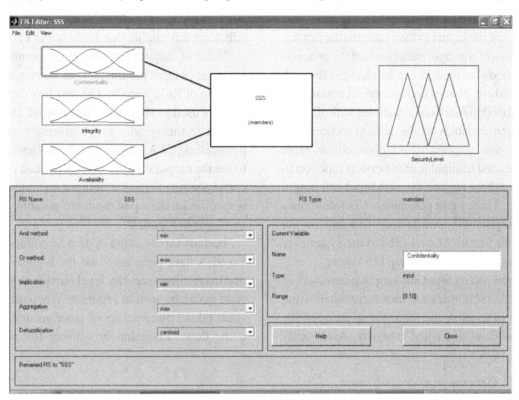

Figure 8. Formulation of rules using rule editor

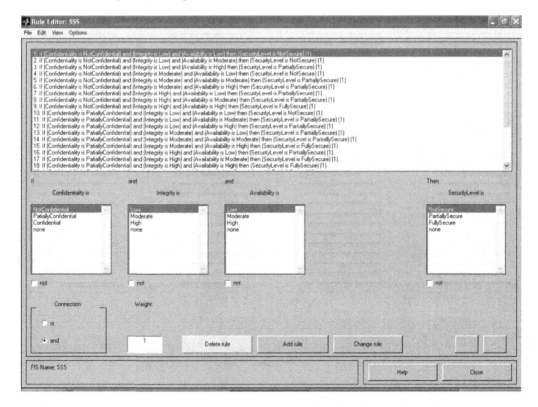

The fuzzy inference system editor shows a summary of the fuzzy inference system. It shows the mapping of the inputs to the system to the output. The names of the input variables and the processing methods for the FIS can be changed through the FIS editor. Names and numerical parameters of membership functions associated with all input and output variables can be defined and changed through the membership function editor. Here we have used triangular membership function to represent three regions for each input and output variable. Three input parameters Confidentiality (C), Integrity (I), Availability (A) and output parameter Security Level (SL) to the system are represented in Figure 7 using FIS Editor.

After defining input and output parameters of this application, rules are then formulated using rule editor to show the relationship between the levels of Confidentiality, Integrity, Availability

and also the levels of output parameter. Rule editor is used to add, delete or change a rule. Rule editor for this application is shown in Figure 8.

Value of output parameter corresponding to a given set of input parameters can be viewed with the help of Rule Viewer. The text box captioned input is used to supply the three input variables needed in the system. For a given set of input parameters [C I A] say [9 9 9], Rule Viewer helps to see the output security level generated i.e. 8.94 corresponding to this set of input variables which is specified at the top of the corresponding graphs as shown in Figure 9.

Initially inputs to the system i.e. values for C, I, and A have been taken on the higher side so that the resultant security level remains in the safe state as can be seen in Figure 9. When the threat starts taking place values of these security goals come down immediately causing the security

Figure 9. Generation of security level

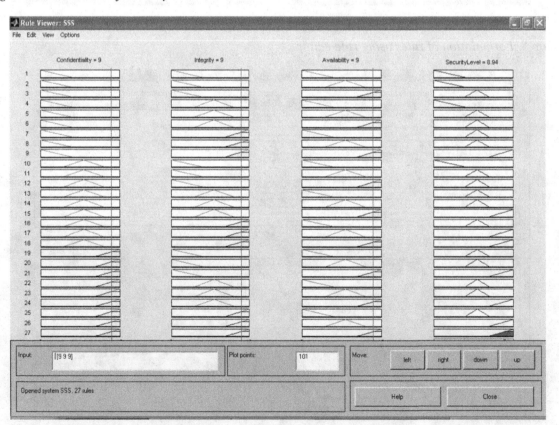

level to move from safe state to partial secure state and then towards failed state if not attended earlier. Actors which can be software agents or human agents are associated for monitoring this security level constantly and take appropriate preventive measures to save the system from entering into the failed state. Study on this subject reveals that high security level has to be maintained to reduce the probability of failed state. It has therefore to be ensured by agents that values of security goals are not allowed to fall beyond a certain value so that the defined threshold value of security level is maintained (Gandotra et al., 2010; Gandotra et al., 2011).

FUTURE RESEARCH DIRECTIONS

As a future work, we mean to develop innovative security techniques which are adaptive and dynamic in nature to respond proactively in real time to constantly evolving threats from sophisticated hackers. Once fully developed as a tool it may provide auto-remediation capability to safeguard against changing threat environment.

CONCLUSION

In this chapter, we have presented some proactive steps in threat management as a part of secure software engineering to meet the present day security requirements of software systems. Elicitation of flawless security requirements forms the very basis of secure software systems. We have therefore developed hybrid technique by combining the strengths of attack trees and misuse cases for eliciting realistic and flawless security requirements which has a definite edge over the existing ones. Present day security measures are primarily based on binary principle which make the system strong up to a point and then fail catastrophically. We have therefore tried to break this jinx of brittleness

by inducting fuzzy logic to evolve an intermediate state between the safe state and failed state. This intermediate state provides an alert signal as soon as the system starts moving towards failed state and additional security measures employed therein save the system from being compromised to the extent possible.

REFERENCES

Alexander, I. (2003). Misuse cases help to elicit non-functional requirements. *Computing & Control Engineering Journal, 14*(1), 40–45. doi:10.1049/cce:20030108

Brunil, D., Haddad, H. M., & Romero, M. (2009). Security vulnerabilities and mitigation strategies for application development. In *Sixth International Conference on Information Technology: New Generations* (pp. 235-240). Las Vegas, NV: IEEE Press.

Cheng, B. H. C., & Atlee, J. M. (2007). Research directions in requirement engineering. In *Future of Software Engineering* (pp. 285–303). Minneapolis, MN: IEEE Press. doi:10.1109/FOSE.2007.17

Common Criteria Implementation Board. (1999). *Common criteria for information technology security evaluation, Part 2: Security Functional Requirements*. CCIB.

Davis, N. (2005). *Secure software development life cycle processes: A technology scouting report*. Pittsburgh: Software Engineering Institute, Carnegie Mellon University.

Diallo, M. H., Romero-Mariona, J., Sim, S. E., Alspaugh, T. A., & Richardson, D. J. (2006). *A comparative evaluation of three approaches to specifying security requirements*. In 12th Working Conference on Requirements Engineering: Foundation for Software Quality (REFSQ'06). Luxembourg: Springer.

Elmasri, R., Navathe, S. B., Somayajulu, V. L. N. D., & Gupta, K. S. (2006). *Fundamentals of database systems. Dorling Kindersley.* India: Pvt. Ltd., Licensees of Pearson Education in South Asia.

Essafi, M., Labed, L., & Ghezala, H. B. (2006). Addressing software application security issues. In *10th WSEAS International Conference on Computers* (pp. 361-366). Athens, Greece: ACM Digital Library.

Essafi, M., Labed, L., & Ghezala, H. B. (2007). S2D-Prom: A strategy oriented process model for secure software development. In *International Conference on Software Engineering Advances* (p. 24). France: IEEE Computer Society.

Gandotra, V., Singhal, A., & Bedi, P. (2009). Identifying security requirements hybrid technique. In *4th International Conference on Software Engineering Advances* (pp. 407-412). Porto, Portugal: IEEE Computer Society and ACM Digital Library.

Gandotra, V., Singhal, A., & Bedi, P. (2010). A step towards secure software system using fuzzy logic. In *IEEE 2nd International Conference on Computer Engineering and Technology* (pp. 417-422). China: IEEE Press.

Gandotra, V., Singhal, A., & Bedi, P. (2011). Layered security architecture for threat management using multi-agent system. *ACM SIGSOFT Software Engineering Notes, 36*(5), 1–11. doi:10.1145/2020976.2020984

Gandotra, V., Singhal, A., & Bedi, P. (2012). Threat-oriented security framework: A proactive approach in threat management. In *Second International Conference on Computer, Communication, Control and Information Technology*. West Bengal, India: Elsevier.

Haley, C. B., Laney, R. C., Moffett, J. D., & Nuseibeh, B. (2004). The effect of trust assumptions on the elaboration of security requirements. In *12th IEEE International Conference on Requirements Engineering* (pp. 102-111). Kyoto, Japan: IEEE Computer Society Press.

Jang, S. R., Sun, T., & Mizutani, E. (2007). *Neuro-fuzzy and soft computing.* Pearson Education.

Juriens, J. (2003). Lecture Notes in Computer Science: *Vol. 2863. Developing safety-critical systems development with UML* (pp. 360–372).

Lamsweerde, A., Brohez, S., De Landtsheer, R., & Janssens, D. (2003). From system goals to intruder antigoals: Attack generation and resolution for security requirements engineering. *In Workshop on Requirements for High Assurance Systems (RHAS'03), Pre-Workshop on the 11th IEEE International Conference on Requirements Engineering* (pp. 49-56). Monterey, CA: IEEE Computer Society Press.

Lipner, S. (2004). The trustworthy computing security development lifecycle. In *20th Annual Computer Security Applications Conference* (pp. 2-13). Arizona: IEEE Computer Society Press.

Madan, B. B., Popsotojanova, K. G., Vaidyanathan, K., & Trivedi, K. S. (2002). Modeling and quantification of security attributes of software system. In *International Conference on Dependable Systems and Networks* (pp. 505-514). Bethesda, MD: IEEE Computer Society Press.

Mamdani, E. H., & Assilian, S. (1975). An experiment in linguistics synthesis with a fuzzy logic controller. *International Journal of Man-Machine Studies, 7*(1), 2–15. doi:10.1016/S0020-7373(75)80002-2

McDermott, J., & Fox, C. (1999). Using abuse case models for security requirements analysis. In *15th Annual Computer Security Applications Conference* (p. 55). Arizona: IEEE Computer Society.

McGraw, G. (2006). *Software security: Building security in.* Boston, MA: Addison Wesley Software Security Series.

Microsoft, A. C. E. Team. (n.d.). *Microsoft threat analysis and modeling* [EB/OL]. Retrieved January 1, 2012, from http://www.microsoft.com/en-us/download/details.aspx?id=14719

Myagmar, S., Lee, A. J., & Yurcik, W. (2005). *Threat modeling as a basis for security requirements*. In IEEE Symposium on Requirement Engineering for Information Security (SREIS). Paris, France.

Olthoff, K. G. (2001). *Observations on security requirements engineering*. In Symposium on Requirements Engineering for Information Security.

Opdahl, A. L., & Sindre, G. (2009). Experimental comparison of attack trees and misuse cases for security threat identification. *Journal of Information and Software Technology, 51*(5). doi:10.1016/j. infsof.2008.05.013

Schneier, B. (2000). *Secrets and lies: Digital security in a networked world*. John Wiley & Sons.

Sindre, G., & Opdahl, A. L. (2000). Eliciting security requirements by misuse cases. In *37th International Conference on Technology of Object-Oriented Languages and Systems* (pp. 120-131). Sydney, Australia: IEEE Computer Society.

Sindre, G., & Opdahl, A. L. (2005). Eliciting security requirements with misuse cases. *Requirements Engineering, 10*(1), 34–44. doi:10.1007/s00766-004-0194-4

Sodiya, A. S., Longe, H. O. D., & Fasan, O. M. (2007). Software security risk analysis using fuzzy expert system. *Journal of INFOCOMP: Journal of Computer Science, 7*(3), 70–77.

Stoneburner, G., Hayden, C., & Feringa, A. (2004). *Engineering principles for information technology security. Recommendations of the National Institute of Standards and Technology, Computer Security Division*. Gaithersburg, MD: Information Technology Laboratory, National Institute of Standards and Technology.

Swiderski, F., & Snyder, W. (2004). *Threat modeling*. Redmond, WA: Microsoft Press.

Vetterling, M., Wimmel, G., & Wisspeintner, A. (2002). Secure systems development based on the common criteria: The PalME Project. In *10th ACM SIGSOFT Symposium on Foundations of Software Engineering* (pp.129-138). Charleston, SC. New York, NY: Association for Computing Machinery.

Xu, D., & Nygard, K. (2006). Threat-driven modeling and verification of secure software using aspect-oriented petri nets. *IEEE Transactions on Software Engineering, 32*(4), 265–278. doi:10.1109/TSE.2006.40

Yasar, A. U. H., Preuveneers, D., Berbers, Y., & Bhatti, G. (2008). Best practices for software security: An overview. In *12th IEEE International Multitopic Conference* (pp. 169-173). Karachi, Pakistan: IEEE Press.

Zadeh, L. A. (1965). Fuzzy sets. *Information and Control, 8*(3), 338–353. doi:10.1016/S0019-9958(65)90241-X

Zadeh, L. A., Klir, J. G., & Yuan, B. B. (1996). *Fuzzy sets, fuzzy logic, and fuzzy systems: Selected papers by Lofti A. Zadeh (Vol. 6)*. London, UK: World Scientific Publishing Co Pte Ltd.

ADDITIONAL READING

Ashbaugh, D. A. (2008). *Security software development addressing and managing security risks*. Boca Raton, FL: CRC Press. doi:10.1201/9781420063813

Beznosov, K., & Chess, B. (2008). Security for the rest of us: An industry perspective on the secure-software challenge. *IEEE Software, 25*(1), 10–12. doi:10.1109/MS.2008.18

Dalila, B., Marino, R., & Haddad, M. H. (2009). Security vulnerabilities and mitigation strategies for application development. In *Sixth International Conference on Information Technology: New Generation* (pp. 235-240). IEEE Press.

Essafi, M., & Ghezala, H. B. (2005). *Secure software engineering processes*. In Third International Conference on Computing, Communications and Control Technologies, Austin, Texas, USA.

Essafi, M., Labed, L., & Ghezala, H. B. (2007). Towards a comprehensive view of secure software engineering. In *International Conference on Emerging Security Information, Systems and Technologies* (pp.181-186). Spain: IEEE Computer Society.

Firesmith, D. G. (2005). *Analyzing the security significance of system requirements*. In Symposium on Requirement Engineering for Information Security in conjunction with RE 05-13th IEEE International Requirements Engineering Conference. Paris, France.

Futcher, L., & Solms, R. V. (2008). Guidelines for secure software development. In *Annual Research Conference of the South African Institute of Computer Scientists and Information Technologists on IT Research in Developing Countries* (pp. 56-65). South Africa: ACM Press.

Gandotra, V., Singhal, A., & Bedi, P. (2009). Threat mitigation, monitoring and management plan - A new approach in risk management. In *International Conference on Advances in Recent Technologies in Communication and Computing* (pp. 719-723). India: IEEE Computer Society, ACM Press.

Graham, D. (2006). *Introduction to the CLASP process*. Secure Software Inc. Retrieved January 2012 from https://buildsecurityin.us-cert.gov/bsi/articles/best-practices/requirements/548-BSI.pdf.

Hein, D., & Saiedian, H. (2009). Secure software engineering: Learning from the past to address future challenges. *Information Security Journal: A Global Perspective*, 18, 8–25. DOI: 10.1080/19393550802623206.

Helmer, G., Wong, J., Slagell, M., Honavar, V., Miller, L., & Lutz, R. (2002). A software fault tree approach to requirement analysis of an intrusion detection system. *Requirement Engineering Journal*, 7(4), 207–220. doi:10.1007/s007660200016

Hoglund, G., & McGraw, G. (2004). *Exploiting software: How to break code*. Boston, MA: Addison-Wesley.

Howard, M., & LeBlanc, D. (2003). *Writing secure code*. Redmond, WA: Microsoft Press.

Howard, M., & Lipner, S. (2006). *The security development life cycle*. Redmond, WA: Microsoft Press.

Matulevicius, R., Mayer, N., & Heymans, P. (2008). Alignment of misuse cases with security risk management. In *Third International Conference on Availability, Reliability and Security* (pp. 1397-1404). Barcelona, Spain: IEEE Computer Society.

Mauw, S., & Oostdijk, M. (2006). Foundations of attack trees. In *8th International Conference on Security and Cryptology - ICISC 2005, LNCS, Volume 3935/2006*, Seoul, Korea, (pp.186-198). DOI: 10.1007/11734727_17.

Mouratidi, H., & Giorgini, P. (2006). *Integrating security and software engineering: Advances and future visions*. Hershey, PA: IGI Global. doi:10.4018/978-1-59904-147-6

OMG. (2004). *UML profile for modeling quality of service and fault tolerance characteristics and mechanisms*. Object Management Group (OMG), Document ptc/04-09-01.

Pressman, R. S. (2005). *Software engineering: A practitioner's approach*. New York, NY: McGraw Hill.

Rodgers, D. H. (2002). *Implementing a project security review process within the project management methodology. GIAC Security Essentials Certification (GSEC)*. SANS Institute.

Saini, V., Duan, Q., & Paruchuri, V. (2008). Threat modeling using attack trees. *Journal of Computing Sciences in Colleges, 23*(4), 124–131.

Verdon, D., & McGraw, G. (2004). Risk analysis in software design. *IEEE Security and Privacy, 2*(4), 79–84. doi:10.1109/MSP.2004.55

Viega, J., & Mcgraw, G. (2001). *Building secure software: How to avoid security problems the right way*. Boston, MA: Addison-Wesley. ISBN 0-201-72152-x

Whittle, J., Wijesekera, D., & Hartong, M. (2008). Executable misuse cases for modeling security concerns. In *30ᵗʰ International Conference on Software Engineering* (pp. 121-130). Leipzig, Germany: ACM Press.

Section 4
Case Studies and Emerging Technologies

Chapter 14
Case Study:
Secure Web Development

Daljit Kaur
Lyallpur Khalsa College, India

Parminder Kaur
Guru Nanak Dev University, India

ABSTRACT

This chapter is an effort to develop secure web applications based on known vulnerabilities. It has been seen that in the rapid race of developing web applications in minimum time and budget, security is given the least importance, and a consequence of which is that web applications are developed and hosted with a number of vulnerabilities in them. In this race, one thing is constant that attackers take advantage of weaknesses existing in technology for financial gain and theft of intellectual property. In this proposed method of secure web development, most common vulnerabilities and their occurrence in development process is discussed. Mapping vulnerabilities to the actions needed to take during development process may help developers to understand vulnerability and avoid vulnerabilities in application.

INTRODUCTION

Since the development of internet, web applications have become very popular, and, nowadays, they are used in every environment, such as medical, financial, military systems. But in the race to develop these online services, web applications have been developed and deployed with minimal attention given to security risks, resulting in surprising number of corporate sites that are vulnerable to hackers (Halkidis, 2008). With the rise in web applications for security critical environment, number of attacks against these applications has grown as well. Organizations face more security risks imposed upon them by hackers on achieving fame, glory, profit or information. Malicious

DOI: 10.4018/978-1-4666-2958-5.ch014

hackers are finding out constructively new ways to exploit web applications. According to study conducted by Imperva's Application Defense Center (ADC), web sites experience an average of 27 attacks per hour or about every two minutes (Be'ery et al, 2011). When sites come under automated attack, the target can experience up to 25,000 attacks per hour or 7 per second (Be'ery et al, 2011). The number of daily web based attacks observed was 93% higher in 2010 as compare to 2009, according to report by Symantec on attack Kits and malicious websites (SYM).

Web based attacks are rising consistently and there are number of reasons that make applications so vulnerable. The rise in attack volume in web applications is due to ready availability of attack toolkits, many of which exploit known vulnerabilities (Malek, 2004). Hacking tools and guides are available on-line, almost anyone can launch attack using these resources. Web applications have become interesting target for many for achieving fame, profit or information. Hackers continue to focus on web applications because these are easy points of entry and valuable data is exchanged in business processes run by these web applications. Developers are mandated to deliver functionality on time and on budget but not to develop secure applications. Developers are not generally educated in secure code practices. According to CERT/CC, more than 90% of vulnerabilities leak out during development. They are result of ignoring known vulnerabilities found in other systems (Nany and Gary, 2005). Keeping this fact in mind, this chapter is an attempt that will help to develop partially secure web applications avoiding vulnerabilities.

The chapter describes related work, the development life cycle, most common vulnerabilities in web applications and then explains the actions proposed to avoid vulnerabilities. In the end, mapping of vulnerability to action is done to understand and avoid the vulnerabilities and future scope is discussed.

RELATED WORK

There are existing processes, standards, life cycle models, frameworks, and methodologies that support or could support secure software development. Security Development Lifecycle (SDL), which focuses on producing secure software, is a software assurance methodology and tool that aims at assisting software developers, designers, builders, and educators in improving the security of software production. SDL prescribes activities to embed security into applications and supplies the foundation for a broad software security assurance that extends across an IT enterprise (FOR), (Hajar and Salman, 2011). The SDL introduces security and privacy throughout all phases of the development process. SDL includes five phases: Training, policy, and organizational capabilities, Requirements and design, Implementation, Verification, and Release and response. It includes mandatory security activities executed as part of a software development process.

The Requirements phase of the SDL includes consideration of security and privacy at a foundational level. The best opportunity to build trusted software is during the initial planning stages, when development teams can identify key objects and integrate security and privacy (MSD). The Design phase includes building the plan for implementation, release, and functional and design specifications, and performing risk analysis to identify threats and vulnerabilities. Functional specifications may describe security and privacy features directly exposed to users, such as requiring user authentication to access specific data or user consent before use of a high-risk privacy feature. Design specifications describe how to implement these features and how to implement all functionality as secure features (MSD). An extra security activity includes a final code review of new as well as legacy code during the Verification phase. Finally, during the release phase, a Final Security Review is conducted by the Central Microsoft Security team, a team of security experts who are also available to the product development team throughout the development life cycle, and who have a defined role in the overall process (Steve and Howard, 2005).

Microsoft Trustworthy Computing Software Development Lifecycle, the Team Software Process for Secure Software Development (TSP-Secure), Correctness by Construction, Agile Methods, etc. are process models for secure software development (Davis, 2005). Also, it is important to understand the processes that an organization is using to build secure software, because unless the process is understood, its weaknesses and strengths are difficult to determine.

DEVELOPMENT LIFE CYCLE

The development of the web application goes through different phases: Requirement, Design, Coding, Testing and Deployment. Secure web application can be developed only by securing all these phases of development life cycle. Ignoring security at any of these phases can result in insecure web application. Moreover, flaws that experts discover at the deployment level of web application are expensive and time-consuming to fix (IBM). As Table 1 shows that fixing a design error in deployment phase is 30 times more costly than fixing it in design phase.

Error in early phase persists in later phases and later in the application too (Bar-Gad and Klein, 2002). For this reason, a flaw should be discovered and removed at the earliest. Figure 1 illustrates a development life cycle based on known vulnerabilities and agile development. Also, this

Figure 1. Development lifecycle with security

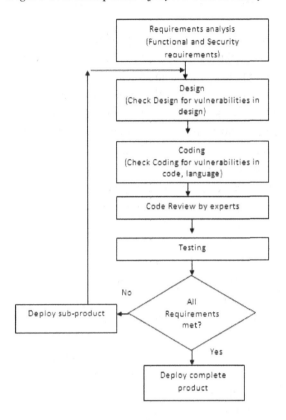

model assumes that developers, project manager and everyone associated with product development are aware of security and their common breaches.

The basic idea of this model is develop product in increments i.e., develop a small sub-product with few requirements and then in next iteration, develop another sub-product and integrate with existing one. Keep on repeating the iterations until the final complete product is not ready. Also one important thing is that security is inculcated in each phase of development life cycle.

Table 1. Cost of fixing error

Error Found in phase	Corrected in Design	Corrected in Coding	Corrected in integration Testing	Corrected in Beta Testing	Corrected in Deployment
Design	1X	5X	10X	15X	30X
Coding		1X	10X	20X	30X
Integration			1X	10X	20X

COMMON VULNERABILITIES

Vulnerability is a hole or weakness in application, which can be design flaw or implementation bug that allows an attacker to cause harm to stakeholders of an application (Chunguang et. al, 2006). Almost 80% of web application attacks are from known vulnerabilities (Raviv, 2012). This is shown in Figure 2. This section introduces 20 common vulnerabilities and also includes the general description, creation phase of development life cycle. For reference, these vulnerabilities are assigned a code.

- **WV 1- SQL Injection:** SQL injection is a very old approach but it's still popular among attackers. This technique allows an attacker to retrieve crucial information from a Web server's database. Constructing a dynamic SQL statement (constructing SQL queries by string concatenation) with user input may allow an attacker to modify original statement to illegal SQL statement. The cause of this vulnerability is weak input validation and can be avoided by allowing only alphanumeric characters,

especially avoid double quote ("), single quote ('), semicolon (;), colon (:) and dash(-). Most SQL injection vulnerabilities can be easily fixed by avoiding use of dynamically constructed SQL queries and using parameterized queries or stored procedures instead (WVR), (Uzi Ben-Artzi and Donald, 2003).

- **WV 2- Cross Site Scripting (XSS):** XSS is a kind of injection vulnerabilities, attacker injects malicious tags and/or script code that is executed by user's web browser when accessing the vulnerable website. The injected code takes the benefit of trust given by user to vulnerable site These attacks are targeted to all users of web application instead of web application itself (Impact2009). Every technology or language like ASP, PHP, CGI, Perl, Asp. NET, JSP, VB.NET and C# may face this vulnerability (Shirazi, 2009). The results of these XSS attacks range from revealing authentication credentials to feeding sensitive information to a remote user or host, propagating the attack to other members or administrators of the site, and cre-

Figure 2. Different web application attacks

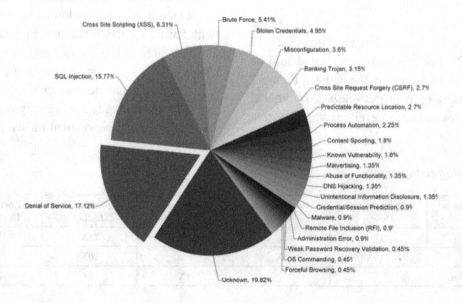

ating Man-in-the-Middle attacks such as Phishing attacks. Data validation, data cleansing, disabling scripting languages, limiting cookie access and not saving sensitive data in the cookies reduce the risk of XSS (Micha, 2009).

- **WV 3- Invoking Untrusted Mobile Code/ Malicious File Execution:** Malicious File execution flaw could allow attackers the opportunity to include hostile code and data, resulting in devastating attacks, such as total compromise of the server. Uploading and executing code from external sources causes this vulnerability. Malicious file attack can an affect PHP, XML and any framework that accepts filenames or files from users (OWA). In case of using such files, demand adequate certificates to ensure safety (Michal et al, 2009).
- **WV 4- Weak Cryptography and Insecure Cryptography Storage:** Poorly protected data may be used by attackers to steal identity, credit card information or to conduct other crimes. Web applications must properly protect sensitive data such as credit cards, Social Security numbers (SSN) and authentication credential with suitable encryption or hashing. Countermeasure to this flaw is to make proper use of cryptographic functions to protect data and credentials (OWA). At coding level, avoid hard coding of data.
- **WV 5 -Information Leakage:** Applications can unintentionally leak information about their configuration, internal workings, or violate privacy through a variety of application problems (OWA). Attackers can use this weakness to steal sensitive data, or conduct more serious attacks. Error messages should be checked for unnecessary or extra information. Data must be encrypted is another consideration (Jay and John, 2004).

- **WV 6- Broken Authentication and Session Management:** Broken access and session is due to authentication and authorization flaws. Applications built using custom authentication and session management schemes may have flaws in the areas such as logout, password management, timeouts, remember me, secret question, account update. Such flaws may allow accounts to be attacked and compromise passwords, keys, session tokens, or exploit implementation flaws to assume users' identities (OWA), (Metula, 2012). This flaw is caused when account credentials and session tokens are not protected properly.
- **WV 7- Cross Site Scripting Forgery(CSRF):** A CSRF attack creates forged HTTP requests and tricks a victim into submitting them via image tags, XSS, or other techniques. If the user is authenticated, the attacker succeeds (OWA). As browsers send credentials like session cookies automatically, attackers can create malicious web pages which generate forged requests that are indistinguishable from the legitimate ones. Forcing users to log off and checking referrer headers can help but for complete solution include authentication tokens in the body of every request (Walker, 2012).
- **WV 8- Format String:** This vulnerability occurs when the user is able to control format string used in printf style functions. This attack alters the flow of application by using string formatting library features to access other memory space (WAS). Attackers can set buffer overflow attack taking control over format string. To avoid this, user input should not be passed to formatting functions directly (Shirazi, 2009). Formatting functions should accept only static string as input.

- **WV 9-Security Mis-Configuration:** A secure web application requires a strong server configuration. A poorly configured server can potentially create multiple security vulnerabilities. A default server may have many features turned on for convenience and may have software packages that are pre-installed and should be removed. Operating a server with a default software setup and configuration may cause multiple security vulnerabilities that may be exploited by hackers. Server configuration is not typically the responsibility of the programmers, and should be addressed by server and network administrators. The host server should be assessed for security issues, which will usually reveal what packages are installed and their versions, missing patches and updates or upgrades, and provide a hit list for which packages should be removed, disabled or correctly configured (Shirazi, 2009).

- **WV 10- Failure to Restrict URL Access:** Failure to restrict URL access may enable attackers to forge URLs to access hidden pages or admin pages (OWA). Countermeasure to this vulnerability is to check URL access rights or perform access control checks when these pages are requested. In case of violation of URL access, an error page should be return to user.

- **WV 11-Invalidated Redirects and Forwards:** Invalidated redirects and forwards take place when the attacker redirects the users to malicious web pages or phishing web sites.

- **WV 12-Insufficient Transport Layer Protection:** Protecting network traffic for sensitive communication is necessary as it can be stolen by attackers. Mostly applications don't encrypt sensitive traffic and even if they do, they use weak algorithms, expired or invalid certificates, or do not use them correctly (OWA).

- **WV 13- Brute Force:** Brute force attack automates a process of trial and error to guess a person's user name, password, credit-card number or cryptographic key (WAS). In this method unknown value is determined by using automated process to try large number of possible values. To avoid this always select a password with minimum of 8 character alphanumeric and do not use common words and terms as passwords.

- **WV 14- Content Spoofing:** Content spoofing is a client side attack by illegal execution of foreign code (WAS), (WHW). In this technique attacker can inject malicious payload that is later misrepresented as legitimate content of web application.

- **WV 15- Buffer Overflow:** Buffer Overflow attack is performed by submitting more information than a variable is expecting to receive, causing the "overflow" of data to write over a section of memory where another process may subsequently access and execute it. If the section of overwritten code contains the correct executable content for the process that happens to access it, the results could range from a defunct server or process to a compromised server with associated exploitations. Some web applications components in some languages do not correctly validate user-submitted input and may crash or freeze a server. Languages like Java, C# are good options as they are less vulnerable to buffer overflow attacks (Shirazi, 2009). While coding, input variables should be given appropriate size to reduce this vulnerability.

- **WV 16- Injection Flaws (LDAP, SSI, XPath):** Injection flaw basically allows to insert specially formulated data, code, script in order to affect normal execution (CUS). Mostly injection flaw attacks occur when user sends some illegal input. LDAP (Light weight directory access Protocol) injection attack exploit web sites by constructing LDAP statements from user supplied inputs. XPath injection constructs queries from user supplied input. SSI (server Side Include) sends code to web server which is then executed locally (WAS]. To avoid injection flaws user inputs should be validated properly.

- **WV 17- Denial of Service (DoS):** A denial-of-service attack or distributed denial-of-service attack (DDoS attack) is an attempt to make a resource unavailable to its intended users. DoS attackers typically target sites or services hosted on high-profile web servers such as banks, credit card payment gateways etc. One common method of attack involves saturating the target (victim) machine with external communications requests, such that it cannot respond to legitimate traffic, or responds so slowly as to be rendered effectively unavailable. Preventing DoS and DDoS attacks requires the integration of multiple prevention techniques such as firewalls, routers, switches. Low-volume web environments may make more use of programming-level prevention, but DoS/DDoS prevention is more of a server and network level approach.

- **WV 18- Directory Indexing and Path Traversal:** Directory indexing is an automatic listing of web server function that shows all files in requested directory if normal base file is not present (WAS). Path Traversal allows to track paths used in system files (Shirazi, 2009). Best solution is to adequate input validation.

- **WV19- Improper Error Handling:** Many vulnerabilities occur when errors are not handled properly. A server that is configured to operate in Debug mode may offer considerable information about the error, which may reveal server and ap-

plication pathways, file names, code segments, server types and versions, and other information. All of these contribute to resources the attacker will use to exploit the web application and server. Once a poorly handled error is discovered, an attacker may iterate man types of errors to collect a wide range of information about the server. Some errors, especially crafted errors by an attacker, may result in denial of service or cause the server to fail in some form. Some security features of the web application may become voided by some error situations, creating yet more vulnerabilities. To counter this, errors should be handled in such a way that system preserves its secure state (Shirazi, 2009). All the expected and unexpected errors should be handled in a proper way and error message generated by application should be issued only as needed void of any extra information (Younan, 2003).

- **WV20- Insecure Direct Object References:** A direct Object reference occurs when a reference to an internal implementation object, such as file, directory, or database key is exposed. Applications do not always verify the user is authorized for the target object, resulting in an insecure direct object reference flaw (OWA). These flaws can compromise all the data that is referenced by the parameter.

ACTIONS TO AVOID VULNERABILITIES

Secure software engineering is an approach for secure software development which means that security must be implemented during the software development phases. Keeping this thing in mind, this section lists the actions needed to take during design, coding, testing, configuring and hosting of the web application to avoid most common

Box 1.

Act-1:	Only accept input values specified in white list and if user supplies any other input, reject it.
Act-2:	When it is not possible to predict exactly type or form of input use sanitization strategy i.e. use escaping or encoding characters so that it will not affect back end system.
Act-3:	Along with validating external boundaries, each component of application must validate data coming from and going to other components.
Act-4:	Make sure that if an attacker manages to cause an exception, there is no way for execution flow to reach at end of function. Exceptions should be handled properly.
Act-5:	Implementing resource locking for shared resources and complete transactions. Understand the thread safety mechanisms provided by development framework and database.
Act-6:	A structured approach must be followed for error handling. Sensitive information or technical details like background operation causing exception, stack traces, file system paths should not be disclosed in error messages. Standard HTTP error codes should be handled by application and never returned to users.
Act-7:	Sensitive data should be transmitted to remote storage in an encrypted and authenticated fashion.
Act-8:	Choose a proper development framework, programming language with respect to requirements and expected functionality as this decision can mitigate much possible vulnerability.
Act-9:	Applying least privileges and separating duties.
Act-10:	Storing sensitive data using appropriate access control and encryption technique.
Act-11:	Secure data transmission by using secure data transfer protocols especially for sensitive data.
Act-12:	Validating remote codes including data type and size of uploaded file or attachment.
Act-13:	Filter unnecessary requests or decrease requests in order to avoid DoS or low performance
Act-14:	Inactivity of users for a specific period should fore the system to log out and login in again.
Act-15:	Use library functions instead of using external/system calls. Avoid invoking operating system calls directly.
Act-16:	Simple Coding according to coding standards and well-defined programming structure.
Act-17:	Using validated SSL (Secure Socket Layer) certificates.
Act-18:	In order to ensure that design is implemented in a correct and secure way, code should be reviewed for issues like memory allocation and free up, variable initialization. Tools are also available for automated code review.
Act-19:	Do not save password directly, encrypt them using appropriate cryptographic function. For additional level of protection add randomly generated data to user inputted password.
Act-20:	Re-authenticate users before any critical transaction is authorized to ensure that if a user session is compromised an attacker would not be able to perform sensitive transaction on behalf of user unless he/she is also in possession of user's credentials.
Act-21:	Locking the account after predefined number of unsuccessful login attempts and also increasing the response time after each failed login attempt.
Act-22:	Minimize the number of authentication interfaces.
Act-23:	The application should be able to detect if a single source IP is responsible for multiple authentication failures.
Act-24:	Reissue a new token after successful authentication and protect it throughout session's lifespan.
Act-25:	Session tokens need to be unpredictable and sufficiently random. They should be independent on ser credentials. They must expire after a reasonable period.
Act-26:	Manage session to user mapping safely on server side. Transmit session tokens over secure channel only. Use cookies to store them not query string parameters.
Act-27:	Set "Secure" and "HttpOnly" flags to secure cookies and do not store sensitive information in cookies.
Act-28:	Deny access by default unless it is explicitly granted.
Act-29:	Use parameterized queries and avoid string concatenation.
Act-30:	Disable the functionality not required by application such as operating system calls, HTTP interfaces, built in compilers, etc.
Act-31:	Storing content outside the web root and using and indexed list of accessible resources instead.
Act-32:	Isolate the resource required by the application from other resources in the underlying server.
Act-33:	Store any uploaded content in a directory outside of web server's document root or best practice is to store it in database so that it can not get executed by web server.
Act-34:	Perform security focused code review. Ensure that dynamic execution functions such as eval(), include() or those inside templates do not take user-supplied data as inputs without strict validation.

continued on following page

Box 1. Continued

Act-35:	Do not use persistent cookies to store sensitive information.
Act-36:	Instead o fusing query string, favor requests that send information as HTML form parameter.
Act-37:	Before performing requested operation make sure that requests are legitimate.
Act-38:	Token regeneration should be performed prior to any significant transaction, after a certain number of requests, as a function of time.
Act-39:	Do not rely on client-side security measures. Security must be enforced by the server.
Act-40:	Disable standard HTTP methods that are not used by application.
Act-41:	The Web server should run with minimum privileges required and must apply security patches.
Act-42:	Output validation with respect to type and amount of outputted information based on security policies.
Act-43:	Using stored procedures instead of dynamic SQL.
Act-44:	Validating function's return value and calling error/exception handlers if required.
Act-45:	Avoid hard coding of data.
Act-46:	Re-implementing unsafe functions using standard library functions.
Act-47:	Generating awareness among users and guiding them to differentiate between original and phishing sites.
Act-48:	Addressing with arrays instead of direct pointers manipulation.
Act-49:	Static creation of external commands in a program and passing static string which can not be controlled by user, to format string function and checking the number of arguments sent to that function.
Act-50:	Choose a proper and hard to guess location for temporary files and applying access control mechanisms on them (encrypt if required). Try to create lent side temporary files.

Table 2. Mapping actions to vulnerability

Vulnerability	Actions Required
WV1	Act-1, Act-2, Act-9, Act-29, Act-34, Act-42, Act-43, Act-39
WV2	Act-1, Act-2, Act-9, Act-34, Act-35, Act-42
WV3	Act-8, Act-12, Act-17, Act-33
WV4	Act-10, Act-11, Act-19, Act-45
WV5	Act-6, Act-11, Act-27, Act-40, Act-41, Act-44
WV6	Act-7, Act-10, Act-20, Act-24, Act-25, Act-26, Act-27, Act-36
WV7	Act-24, Act-38
WV8	Act-1, Act-8, Act-9, Act-34, Act-46, Act-49
WV9	Act-9, Act-28, Act-30, Act-32, Act-39, Act-40, Act -41
WV10	Act-20, Act-37
WV11	Act-3, Act-17, Act-47
WV12	Act-7, Act-17
WV13	Act-21, Act-22, Act-23
WV14	Act-1, Act-3, Act-12, Act-30, Act-31, Act-32, Act-33
WV15	Act-1, Act-8, Act-18, Act-48
WV16	Act-1, Act-5, Act-16, Act-29, Act-34, Act-36, Act-39, Act-49, Act-50
WV17	Act-5, Act-13, Act-14, Act-15, Act-28, Act-30, Act-32, Act-40
WV18	Act-1, Act-31, Act-32, Act-44
WV19	Act-4, Act-6, Act-8
WV20	Act-16, Act-48

vulnerabilities. For further references, code is assigned to each action as presented in Box 1.

MAPPING ACTIONS TO VULNERABILITIES

This section shows the actions required to avoid a particular vulnerability in tabular form. This mapping is done in such a way so that it becomes easier for developers to implement it and understand the vulnerability. By incorporating various security actions early in development life cycle, developers can understand the threats faced by application and security risks to which they expose organizations through application.

From the Table 2, it is clear that a vulnerability can be closed by taking number of actions and a single activity can be essential in closing many vulnerabilities. Depending on the action repeated in top 20 web vulnerabilities, Table 3 shows the no. of occurrences and most important few actions that are essential to make web application more secure.

These are the actions that are commonly overlooked by developers and have given advantage to attackers. And most important thing is training and awareness among developers to implement these actions in development process.

Table 3. Top actions

Actions	No. of occurrences
Act1	7
Act8	4
Act9	4
Act32	4
Act34	4
Act17	3
Act30	3
Act39	3
Act40	3

CONCLUSION AND FUTURE RESEARCH DIRECTIONS

Implementation of security in early phases of development life cycle can save time and cost of removing flaws after the software has been developed. Relying on this idea of secure web development, this chapter describes most common known vulnerabilities and proposed model for software development.

The activities described in this chapter do not grantee absolute secure web applications but can help web applications to fortify against number of attacks. It is very important that web developers keep themselves up to date with new risks which their applications could face and also understand their nature to ensure that the mitigations implemented are effective.

In the future, we can expect more security solutions and more awareness of their implementation.

REFERENCES

Bar-Gad, I., & Klein, A. (2002). *Developing secure web applications*. Sanctum Inc. Retrieved from http://www.cgisecurity.com/lib/WhitePaper_DevelopingSecureWebApps.pdf

Be'ery, T. N., Shulman, A., & Rachwald, R. (2011). *Imperva's Web application attack report -2011*. Retrieved from http://www.imperva.com

Chunguang, K., Qing, M., & Hua, C. (2006). Analysis of software vulnerability. In N. Mastorakis & A. Cecchi (Eds.). Proceedings of the 5th WSEAS International Conference on Information Security and Privacy (ISP'06), (pp. 218-223). Stevens Point, WI: World Scientific and Engineering Academy and Society (WSEAS).

CUS. (2010, March). *Web app security- Managing web app security risks*. CUSIP (Web App Security Working Group). Retrieved from http://www.cusip.com/cusip

Davis, N. (2005). *Secure software development life cycle processes: A technology scouting report.* December 2005.

FOR. (2010). *Optimizing the Microsoft SDL for secure development.* Whitepaper, Fortify Solutions to Strengthen and Streamline a Microsoft Security Development Lifecycle Implementation. Retrieved from http://www.fortify.com/servlet/download/public/Optimizing_the_Microsoft_SDL_for_Secure_Development.pdf

Hajar, M. J., & Salama, A. M. (2011). Implementing case-based reasoning technique to software requirements specifications quality analysis. *International Journal of Advancements in Computing Technology*, 3(1), 23–31. doi:10.4156/ijact.vol3.issue1.3

Halkidis, S. T., Tsantalis, N., Chatzigeorgiou, A., & Stephanides, G. (2008). Architectural risk analysis of software systems based on security patterns. *IEEE Transactions on Dependable and Secure Computing, 5*(3), 129-142. DOI=10.1109/TDSC.2007.70240

IBM. (2008, January). *Understanding web application security challenges.* Web Application Security Management whitepaper by IBM.

Malek, M. (2004). Security management of Web services. *Network Operations and Management Symposium, NOMS 2004,* IEEE/IFIP, Vol. 2, (pp. 175–189).

Mead, N. R., & Mcgraw, G. (2005). A portal for software security. *IEEE Security & Privacy, 3*(4), 75–79. doi:10.1109/MSP.2005.88

Metula, E. (2012). *Web application attacks.* NET Security User Group, from 2BSecure. Retrieved May 9, 2012, from http://www.microsoft.com/download/7/7/b/77b7a327.../m1-1p.pdf

Michal, H., David, L., & John, V. (2009). *19 deadly sins of software security, programming flaws and how to fix them* (1st ed.). McGraw-Hill Osborne Media.

MSD. (2010). *The Microsoft security development lifecycle* (SDL). Microsoft, Version 5.0, 2010. Retrieved from http://msdn.microsoft.com/en-us/security/cc448177.aspx

OWA. *The open web application security project (OWASP): Top ten project theme page.* Retrieved from http://www.owasp.org/index.php/

Raz, R. (2012). *Web application security: Cyber fraud & hacktivism.* Retrieved from http://chaptersinwebsecurity.blogspot.com/

Shirazi, H. M. (2009). A new model for secure software development. *Proceedings of International Journal of Intelligent Information Technology Application, 2,* 136–143.

Steve, L., & Michael, H. (2005). The trustworthy computing security development lifecycle. Retrieved from http://msdn.microsoft.com/security/default.aspx?pull=/library/en-us/dnsecure/html/sdl.asp

SYM. (2009). *Threat activity trends- Web based attack report 2009-10.* Retrieved from http://www.symantec.com/business/threat-report/

Tevis, J.-E. J., & Hamilton, J. A. (2004). Methods for the prevention, detection and removal of software security vulnerabilities. In *Proceedings of the 42nd Annual Southeast Regional Conference* (ACM-SE 42), (pp. 197-202). New York, NY: ACM. DOI=10.1145/986537.986583 http://doi.acm.org/10.1145/986537.986583

Uzi Ben-Artzi, L., & Donald, S. (2003). *Web application security: A survey of prevention techniques against SQL* injection. Thesis Stockholm University/Royal Institute of Technology, June 2003.

Walker, J. (2012). *Web application security-- Keeping your application safe*. Retrieved May 9. 2012, from http://ajaxexperience.techtarget.com/ images/Presentations/Walker_Joe_WebAppSecurity.pdf

WAS. (n.d.). *Web app security—How to minimize prevalent risk of attacks*. Retrieved from www.qualys.com

WHW. (2010). *White Hat Website security statistic report*, 10th edition. Retrieved from www.whitehatsec.com

WVR. (2009, January). Webapps vulnerability report. *Core Impact Professional*. Retrieved from http://www.coresecurity.com/files/attachments/ core_impact_webapps_vulnerabilities_report.pdf

Younan, Y. (2003). *An overview of common programming security vulnerabilities and possible solutions*. Master's thesis, Vrije University Brussel.

ADDITIONAL READING

Cencini, A., Yu, K., & Chan, T. (2005). *Software vulnerabilities: Full, responsible and non-disclosure programming series* (1st ed.). Charles River Media.

Huang. Y.-W., Yu, F., Hang, C., Tsai, H.-H., Lee, D.-T., & Kuo, S.-Y. (2004). *Securing Web application code by static analysis and run time protection*. 13th Acm International World Wide Web Conference, 2004.

Seacord, R. (2011). *Top 10 secure coding practices*. Secure Development Series: Secure Development Lifecycles whitepaper by Apex Assurance Group. Retrieved from https://www.securecoding.cert.org/confluence/display/seccode/Top+10+Secure+Coding+Practices

The Open Web Application Security Project (OWASP). (n.d.). *Secure coding principles*. Retrieved from https://www.owasp.org/index.php/ Secure_Coding_Principles

Chapter 15
Galileo Case Study:
A Collaborative Design Environment for the European Space Agency's Concurrent Design Facility

Aggelos Liapis
European Dynamics SA, Greece

Evangelos Argyzoudis
European Dynamics SA, Greece

ABSTRACT

The Concurrent Design Facility (CDF) of the European Space Agency (ESA) allows a team of experts from several disciplines to apply concurrent engineering for the design of future space missions. It facilitates faster and effective interaction of all disciplines involved, ensuring consistent and high-quality results. It is primarily used to assess the technical and financial feasibility of future space missions and new spacecraft concepts, though for some projects, the facilities and the data exchange model are used during later phases. This chapter focuses on the field of computer supported collaborative work (CSCW) and its supporting areas whose mission is to support interaction between people, using computers as the enabling technology. Its aim is to present the design and implementation framework of a semantically driven, collaborative working environment (CWE) that allows ESA's CDF to be used by projects more extensively and effectively during project meetings, task forces, and reviews.

INTRODUCTION

The particular chapter focuses on the field of computer supported collaborative work (CSCW) and its supporting areas whose mission is to support interaction between people, using computers as the enabling technology.

Researchers and scientists from fields such as computer science, sociology, psychology, anthropology, and information science seek to understand the nature of work and the complexities of human interaction for the express purpose of building computer-based systems which support and enhance inter-personal activities.

DOI: 10.4018/978-1-4666-2958-5.ch015

CSCW looks at the way users interact and collaborate with each other, and attempts to develop guidelines for developing technology to assist in the communication process. These systems are known as Groupware. A successful groupware should fulfil the following requirements:

- Make its users aware of being participants within a collaborative effort.
- Provide cues regarding the actions and their effects taken by the other participants.
- Enable communication between the participants.
- Allow the sharing of resources
- Awareness features built into the application.
- Fully customisable and highly integrable environment.
- Cross domain collaboration support through different collaboration modes (synchronous, semi-synchronous and asynchronous).

The chapter describes the delivery of a prototype Collaborative Working Environment (CWE) that leverages the functionality of the Concurrent Design Facility (CDF) of the European Space Agency (ESA). In particular, it will address the needs for three main activities:

- Distributed design sessions
- Concurrent reviews
- Distributed Anomaly Investigation Boards (ESA, 2011)

Ultimately, it will allow the CDF to be used more extensively and effectively and extend its use in later phases of the design of space missions.

THE TARGET DOMAIN

Founded in 1975, the *European Space Agency (ESA)* is the independent space organisation of Europe, and its purpose is to promote cooperation between European States in space research and technology and their space applications.

The *Concurrent Design Facility (CDF)*, ESA's main assessment center for future space missions, is located at *ESTEC* (European Space Research and Technology Centre) in the Netherlands. It uses the concurrent engineering (CE) methodology to perform cost-effective, fast and high-quality space mission studies (Wikipedia, 2011). Equipped with state of the art network of computers, multimedia devices and software tools, the CDF allows interdisciplinary teams of experts to perform design studies. It has achieved this through the use of its *Integrated Design Model (IDM)*, which makes use of spreadsheet technology, both as data storage and as engineering tool, to achieve interdisciplinary collaboration (Integrated Design Model, 2012).

The growing interest of ESA partners, Industry and Academia in the ESA CDF core IDM, revealed the need for standardised data representation and exchange, and common design methodologies, but at the same time exposed the limitations of the IDM communications layer for use in distributed concurrent design. This has motivated the creation of the *Open Concurrent Design Server (OCDS)*, which makes use of a Service Oriented Architecture (SOA) using web services, a centralised database and many client tools such as the OCDS Study Manager (OSM) and OCDS enabled spreadsheets. An initiative of ESA, the OCDS provides the building blocks of a Concurrent, Collaborative and Distributed Engineering for the European Space Industry, using Open Standards Information Models and Reference Libraries (OCDS User Community Portal, 2012)

The OCDS is the vehicle to distribute CDF's concurrent design methodology and a set of tools to the Space industry, organisations and academia. At the same time, it distributes an open data exchange standard for early phase space system engineering and design activities.

The OCDS is built on a common *Space Engineering Information Model (SEIM)*, which is the common upper level ontology for early phase concurrent design and engineering in ESA. It describes the structure and content (ontology and semantics) of CDF Space Engineering activities carried out by ESA/ESTEC and its partners. A standard model-based data exchange will allow more effective engineering design collaboration and iterations.

The goal of this chapter is to define an environment that allows the Concurrent Design Facility (CDF) to be used by projects more extensively and effectively during project meetings, task forces and reviews in later phases.

OBJECTIVES

This chapter elaborates on the design and implementation of the Galileo prototype Collaborative Working Environment (CWE) that leverages the functionality of ESA's CDF. The three main activities that will be addressed by the envisioned CWE are:

1. **Distributed Design Sessions (DDS):** Are meetings with participants such as engineers, sub-contractors, as well as scientists, contract officers and others, depending on the subject, who may be distributed across different locations. Those meeting focus on design aspects which may not only be discussed but also implemented on the fly in the design definition. Galileo must allow for fast analyses of system project changes with regard to engineering and programmatic aspects, multidisciplinary involvement of sub-contractors, scientists etc. in decision making, and requirements specification coverage and tracing during the sessions.

2. **Concurrent Reviews (CR):** Are project meetings between the review team and the customer/supplier to solve issues raised in Review Item Discrepancies (forms where identified problems, questions and solutions arising from the examination of the documentation are recorded (ESA, 2008)) to consolidate findings and to provide recommendations for RID closure. Those meetings must be held via an on-line shared data exchange model. Using this model, concurrent sessions can be held for various panels dedicated to different sub-systems, systems or functional breakdowns. Galileo can help to reduce the amount of RIDs demanding explanation of unclearly formulated phrases or grammatical errors, enhance visibility of the review to the project team, and enhance consistence between various review components. Galileo can facilitate the classification of RIDs into contexts e.g. assign RIDs to documents, document versions, authors, system or sub-systems related to the RID, data package and version, relation to other RIDs, requirements linked to the RID including data, project milestone, answer to the RID, RID status (open/closed) and more.

3. **Distributed Anomaly Investigation Boards (DAIB):** Are called upon to investigate an anomaly that occurred during a space system development or operation phase. Anomaly is defined as "any deviation from the expected situation" (ESA, 2004). A board is called for when it is important to determine the cause and take corrective actions for a deviation in behaviour or performance of a space system. Often a multi-disciplinary team of highly qualified experts is needed on short notice to resolve the situation, usually under great time pressure as well. Galileo can provide an effective collaborative working environment where distributed teams can be created and have access to all relevant information, models and tools.

Ultimately, Galileo will allow the CDF to be used more extensively and effectively and extend its use in later phases of the design of space missions.

CURRENT STATE OF THE ART

Several technologies are available for supporting teams collaborating via a computer network. The technology that CSCW systems employ can be split into four categories:

- Communication
- Shared workspace
- Shared information
- Group activity support

Group activity support is the technology which supports multiple users collaborating on a series of tasks. Current groupware applications host the majority of the above technologies. Figure 1 describes in detail the different modes of collaboration in a time and place communication diagram.

Table 1 illustrates a summary of projects/ systems on collaborative product design and a summary of projects/systems on agent-based collaborative product design.

The software tools classification described in this section are not confined to a particular domain and cover a wide spectrum from somewhat domain independent to highly domain specific tools. Current collaborative design tools are focusing on the

Figure 1. Time and place communication diagram

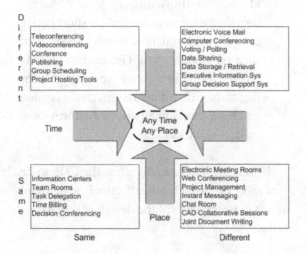

modelling stages of the design process leaving the conceptual stages of the design process totally unexplored. Figure 2 illustrates in more detail the technological gap amongst the various stages of the design process.

The dynamics of collaborative design are typically characterised by the following challenges:

- Multiple iterations and/or heavy reliance on multi-functional design reviews, both of which expensive and time-consuming.
- Poor incorporation of some important design concerns such as environmental impact.
- Reduced creativity due to the tendency to incrementally modify known successful designs rather than explore radically different and potentially superior ones.

Previous research on design dynamics has focused on routine design where the design space is well-understood, and the goal was to optimize a design via incremental changes for requirements similar to those that have been encountered many times before (Eppinger 1997; Smith and Eppinger 1997).

Current research identified that rapid technological changes have made it increasingly clear, many of the most important collaborative design problems begin in the early stages of the design process (Klein 2002; Fan, Oliveira et al. 2004; Mitchell 2004). The majority of the commercial

Figure 2. Availability of collaborative design tools

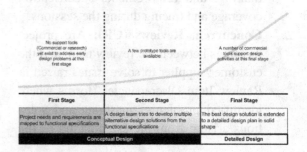

Table 1. Summary of projects/systems on collaborative and agent-based product design

Name of Project/ System	R&D Group	Key Features	Implementation Technologies
Projects/systems on collaborative product design			
CPD	Roy et al., KBEL., Syracuse Univ.	Shared product design web pages; shared geometric models in VRLML; shared databse; multi-server architecture	Web, HTML, VRML, RD-BMS, CAD Tools
DFX Shell	Huang et al., Univ. of Hong Kong	Web-based deployment of DFX tools using ActiveX	Web, HTML, ActiveX
DOME	Pahng et al., KIST, Korea	Use distributed object technology; multi-server architecture	Web, CORBA, Java, HTML
ipTeam	NexPrise Inc	Primarily a virtual entrprise integration system with a suitc of tools for supporting collaborative product development	Web, E-mails, Multimedia and much more
KA Framework	Sony System Design Corp.	A collaborative design system architecture from KA point of view; an interesting approach for tacit knowledge capture and sharing	Web, CORBA, OODB, Distributed DB, STEP
Schemebuilder	Bracewell et al., Lnacaster Univ	Scheme based knowledge representation, and sharing via the web	Web, HTML, CLIPS, Matlab, CAD tools
WebCADET	Rodgers et al., Univ. of Cambridge	Web based deployment of CADET as a decision support system for evaluating conceptual designs	Pro-Web server toolkit, Prolog
Web-based Morphological Chart	Huang et al., Univ. of Hong Kong	Web-based collaborative environment using morphological chart	Web, HTML, ActiveX
WWDL	Zdrahal et al., KMI, Open Univ.	Tadzebao metaphor for guiding designers around ongoing design dialogues; Distributed CBR using agents	Web, HTML, Java, Lisp, Lisp-Web, CBR tool, Agents
Projects/systems on agent-based collaborative product design			
A-Design	Campbell et al, CMU	Two tier representation; Multi-objective optimisation; evaluation-based iterative algorithm	Agents, Internet Lisp
Concept Database	Varma et al., UC Berkeley	Provide strategic support for version control, workflow management, and information gathering	Agents, Internet/Web, Relational Database
Co-Designer	Hague et al., CSCE, Univ. of Derby	Localised design agents with high degree of authority for decision-making based on the rich downstream product life cycle information	Agents, Internet/Web
DIDE	Shen et al., UTC	Autonomous agents approach; wrapper for legacy system integration; Web for system monitoring	Agents, Internet/Web, ELM, Lisp, MOSS
ICM	Fruchter et al., Stanford	Shared graphical modelling; iterative communication approach	Agents, Internet/Web, Auto-CAD, ProKappa
Madefast	Madefast Consortium	No formal top-down management structure and no central authority; Web for posting, access, sharing of design info & data; synchronous & asynchronous communication	Internet/Web, Agents, CSCW, HyperMail, and much more
RAPPID	Parunak et al., ERIM	Characteristic agents, marketplace approach, set-based design	Agents, Internet
PACT	Cutkosky et al., CDR, Stanford	Federation architecture using facilitators; wrapper for legacy system integration	Agents, Internet/Web, KQML, Lisp
SHARE	Toye et al., Stanford	Federation architecture, Asynchronous communication using emails; Web-based tools for information capturing and sharing	Agents, Internet/Web, KQML, NoteMail, ServiceMail, and more
SiFAs	Brown et al., WPI		Agents, Internet CLIPS

collaborative design environments focus on the modelling stages of the design process leaving the early stages totally unexplored.

DOMAIN REQUIREMENTS

The following paragraphs describe generic groupware technologies and features, which form the core non-functional and functional requirements for CSCW systems in general and for the envisioned CWE.

Non-Functional Requirements

The inherent complexity of CSCW systems, and the particularities and scope of the target domain, demand a set of requirements to be fulfilled for its development to be considered successful. Below is a (non-exhaustive) description of the main non-functional requirements to be taken into account for the design of Galileo.

Security

The domain in which the Agency operates, more often than not, involves confidential documents and information which need to be protected. The need for security at all levels needs to be taken into account, especially when providing access to sensitive data from remote and uncontrolled locations.

In particular the following aspects of security need to be considered:

- **Network Security:** The Agency is planning to use the CWE developed in this activity for distributed collaboration sessions, allowing experts from various locations (inside or outside ESA's Local or Wide Area Network) to cooperate. The current network security measures implemented at ESA (such as firewalls, networking access control lists, packet filtering etc) and the requirements in terms of security may affect the CWE's design dramatically and need to be identified early in the project and taken into consideration.

- **Transport Security:** Depending on how users connect to the CWE, data will have to travel over public networks (the Internet) or private networks. It is crucial to investigate the requirements for secure transport of confidential data when necessary. Connections from within ESA's network may be over private leased lines, VPN connections (which are already encrypted) or local area connections. However, connections from mobile users will likely be over an unprotected public network and special measures may need to be taken, such as VPN Client connections, to preserve confidentiality.

- **Access Control:** The ability to control access to resources is vital, especially in an environment where a hierarchical organisational structure is employed, with varying levels of exposure to information. Access control includes *Authentication* (confirming the identity of the user who tries to access a system), *Authorisation* (controlling the resources the user can or cannot access) and *Audit* (a record of the users actions while in the system). The way Access Control is implemented (Role-based, Discretionary, Mandatory access control etc) will heavily affect the environment's design.

Scalability and Extensibility

Scalability of a software system is its ability to handle growing amounts of work in a graceful manner or its ability to be enlarged to accommodate that growth. The scalability of a system subject to growing demand is crucial to its long-term success (Bondi 2000). In the context of a CWE the workload may increase in various ways, including the number of concurrent users or the amount and type of data processed.

Extensible is a system which supports the addition of new functionality or the modification of existing functionality without considerable changes in its core. Extensibility is a desirable trait of a software system, especially if the processes it is meant to support are likely to change over time.

Reliability and Availability

Availability refers to a system's ability to be accessible and serve its intended purpose when needed. High availability and minimised downtime is of the essence in concurrent collaboration environments, where collaborators and auxiliary resources may be available for a limited period of time.

Reliability is the ability of a system to function as required within a specified time-frame and under specified conditions. Software reliability, however, is not directly a function of time because it depends mostly on the quality of its design.

Both these concepts must be taken into consideration when designing any business-grade real-time system.

Maintainability

It is a software product's ability to allow for modifications after delivery to correct faults, to improve performance or other attributes. However meticulous the design of a software platform may be, maintenance issues may arise. From this standpoint, a web-based approach to the design of a CWE may be advantageous, because it involves centralised administration and maintenance and eliminates the need for client software maintenance. The CWE design proposed in this activity will be as modular as possible to allow for future modifications with minimal disruption.

Usability

Usability of a software product refers to its ease of use, learnability and efficiency. In the case of a collaborative work environment, where a multidisciplinary team of users have to cooper-ate, the product has to be equally usable by both technical and non-technical members, which poses special considerations regarding user-friendliness, intuitiveness and responsiveness of the system.

Usability inspections of the initial prototype is necessary so as to uncover the main design flaws and allow a clean up of the design, meanwhile adapting the method to the collaborative aspects. Usability and interaction are very much interrelated.

Several HCI rules for display design must be taken into account when implementing the proposed CWE. These include consistency of data display, efficient information assimilation by the user, use of metaphors, minimal memory load on user, compatibility of data display with data entry, flexibility for user control of data display, presentation of information graphically where appropriate, standardized abbreviations, and presentation of digital values only where knowledge of numerical value is necessary and useful.

As the proposed platform will be used for synchronous creative sessions, such as conceptual modelling and brainstorming, the proposed CWE should be usable enough to encourage creativity and not hinder it. Adhering to usability criteria, enables the improvement of usability and create pleasing, fast and accurate interaction between the technology and the user. The author takes into account the following usability characteristics during the implementation of Gallileo:

- **Efficient:** Efficiency can be described as the speed (and accuracy) with which users can complete the tasks for which they use the product. ISO 9241 defines efficiency as the total resources expended on a task. Efficiency metrics include the number of clicks or keystrokes required or the total "time on task".

- **Effective:** Effectiveness is the completeness and accuracy with which users achieve specified goals. It is determined by looking at whether the user's goals are met successfully and whether all work is correct.

- **Engaging:** An interface is engaging if it is pleasant and satisfying to use. Visual design is the most obvious element of this characteristic. The style of the visual presentation, the number, functions and type of graphic images or colours, and the use of multimedia elements are all part of a user's immediate reaction.

- **Error Tolerant:** The ultimate goal is a system, which has no errors. But, product developers are human, and computer systems far from perfect, so errors may occur. An error tolerant program is designed to prevent errors caused by the user's interaction, and to help the user in recovering from any errors that do occur.

- **Easy to Learn:** One of the biggest objections to "usability" comes from people who fear that it will be used to create products with a low barrier to entry, but which are not powerful enough for sustained use.

Accessibility

Recent advancements in the field of Information and Communications Technology have brought about radical changes in the way people conduct their business. Company resources can become available from almost any location and through a variety of means, using the Internet. The advantages of remote accessibility become evident in cases of distributed synchronous collaboration, where professionals need to share their expertise within a restricted time-frame. The Galileo environment will be web-based, to maximise accessibility from any suitable device with a connection to the Internet.

Customisability

Customizability is the activity of modifying a computer application within the context of its use (Angehrn 2001). Customisability is therefore valued from both users and developments, as it allows the system to adapt to the needs of the user. Customisability is widely assumed to be a key requirement for the design of groupware systems (Mørch, Stiemerlieng et al. 1998).

While customisability is very much motivated by a user-centred perspective on the design and use of technology, the question of how to design customizable environments that go beyond the scope of user interface remains unanswered (Fan, Gao et al. 2007);(Jordan 2001); (Leevers 1999); (Liapis 2007); (Mayhew 1997); (Metros 1997). Adding customization features to a collaborative environment requires advanced development; hence it is clear that high customizability requires advanced development efforts. User interface customization is not enough; hence support for customising the tools of groupware environments is essential (Liapis 2008). The particular issue will be taken into serious account when designing and implementing the CWE.

Functional Requirements

Unlike single-user systems, CWEs require a particular set of technologies to be effective and within the scope of CSCW. The following generic set of technologies form the core on which the envisioned CWE is designed.

Virtual Workspace

When people use computers for supporting geographically dispersed groups a virtual workspace is being created (Bardram 1998). In CSCW, the shared, virtual workspace is the communications medium. The characteristics of cooperative applications can be summed up as follows (Rodden, Mariana et al. 1992):

- The system is distributed, using a grouping of machines to support many users.
- The system needs to establish and maintain a shared context for users.

- The system should attempt to capture and support, rather than hide, the activities involved in the collaborative process.

A virtual workspace in a groupware application is a shared electronic workspace. There are different types of virtual workspace, depending on the type of work that needs to be done (Plowman, Rogers et al. 1995). Workspaces can be seen as a "free" field of interaction as they allow users to socialize around a process and also to move the tacit knowledge to explicit knowledge (Pinsonneault and Kraemer 1989; Plowman, Rogers et al. 1995).

An essential feature when developing virtual workspaces is customisability (Borghoff 2000). Users should be able to customize the environment according to their needs. The virtual workplace simulates the physical workspace of the team members as if they were located around the same table with access to all information necessary to carry out the work (Borghoff 2000). The shared workspace should provide access to the needed information, tools and communication mechanisms (Sommerville and Rodden 1994). In addition team members should have private workspaces where they can work independently (Nam 2000).

Concurrency Control

Concurrency control mechanisms are required in order to handle conflicting actions (Neale and Rosson 2004). However, concurrency control in groupware must be handled differently than traditional concurrency control methods because the user is an active part of the process (Neale & Rosson, 2004). For example, professionals will not tolerate delays introduced by duplicates or conflicts because of the tight deadlines that they have to meet. Concurrency control problem occur in groupware when it is implemented as a distributed system (Bardram 1998). Methods, such as locking, serialization, and their degree of optimism, are shown to have quite different impacts on the interface and how operations are displayed and perceived by group members (Greenberg and Marwood 1994).

Calendaring and Scheduling

Shared calendaring and scheduling applications enable coordination of activities without the burden of personally contacting each participant multiple times to verify open dates and confirm attendance (Henry 2001). Scheduling tasks are common in group working environment (Neumann 2007). Group members can find an appropriate meeting time by collecting information about available time of all participants and coordinating the different individual schedules. This process is traditionally done by phone calls, email, and voice mail. Interpersonal communication increases exponentially as the number of target people engaged in the scheduling process increases (Neale and Rosson 2004). A calendaring tool keeps all public and private schedules of individual group members. In addition provides a more convenient way to access and make changes to current data.

Recording Mechanisms

When a team collaborates using a groupware system its members must be co-ordinated in order to avoid possible conflicts. To preserve the integrity of the project throughout its complete lifecycle appropriate recording mechanisms should be integrated into the system (Grinter 1996).

Recording mechanisms provide participants with a verification mechanism with regards to the evolution of the project. Users can use the outputs as a reference for future work or to review the process. Most importantly recording mechanisms allow participants to coordinate their work without communicating with others. This is an important characteristic and can help prevent coordination breakdowns which frequently occur during collaborative design.

Recording mechanisms try to support collaboration by providing information about other participants' contributions. They consist of four major activities (Grinter 1996; Bayles 1998):

- Who made the changes?
- What changes were made to the project?
- When were the changes made?
- Why were the changes made?

As project requirements may change during the design and engineering process, the design objects should also change to address the up-to-date requirements. It is important that team members easily can identify which requirements versions belongs to which design versions.

Version control is the process of managing and maintaining multiple revisions of the same file in an archive (Forbes 1997). An archive contains information about each revision of the file, allowing participants to retrieve, modify, and return any version of a file in a safe, organised and consistent manner (Forbes 1997). The proposed environment will depend on various recording mechanisms to track the contributions of the participants during a collaborative session.

Information Sharing and Knowledge Management

Collaborative working is also a learning process and an important aspect of learning is access to information. However information sharing is not only a matter of making data available to team members (Coleman and Furey 1996). The data will be interpreted by the recipient depending on their experience and skills and on the context. It is therefore necessary that the collaborative process is supported by technologies for managing knowledge (Coleman and Furey 1996).

Knowledge management is the process by which individual learning and experience can be accessed, reflected upon, shared and utilised in order to foster enhanced individual knowledge and,

thus, organizational value (Wolf 2002). Hence, knowledge management is important for building team memory which is essential for the success of a collaborative design project (Agarwal 2004). To support long-term asynchronous collaboration it is crucial to provide an archive or repository that functions as a group memory (Adams, Toomey et al. 1999). Then professionals engaged later in the design life cycle can understand reasons for what might otherwise be obscure decisions taken by others (Chen and You 2003). The repository should record both what was done in a project and why, recording both decisions and rationale underlying those decisions (Borghoff 2000).

Technologies for Synchronous, Remote Group Activities

Groupware for real time distributed collaboration allows people to work together at the same time, even when some or all participants and their work products are in different physical locations (Greenberg and Marwood 1994). To do this effectively, groupware and its components must support 'telepresence' and 'teledata' (Greenberg and Roseman 1997).

Telepresence is defined as a way of giving distributed participants a feeling that they are in the same meeting room (Herlea and Greenberg 1998). During meetings a sense of presence is necessary to help participants mediate and coordinate their real time discussions, and to achieve a common understanding of the work process (Herlea and Greenberg 1998). Teledata is a way of having participants bring into the meeting the materials and on going work they wish to share with others (Herlea and Greenberg 1998). Bringing documents or other work artefacts in the shared workspace is essential during collaborative sessions (Herlea and Greenberg 1998).

Synchronous tools enable real-time communication and collaboration in a "same time-different place" mode. These tools allow people to connect at a single point in time, at the same time. Synchronous tools possess the advantage of being able to engage people instantly and at the same point in time. The primary drawback of synchronous tools is that, by definition, they require same-time participation different time zones and conflicting schedules can create communication challenges. In addition, they tend to be costly and may require significant bandwidth to be efficient. Table 1 describes the most characteristic synchronous collaboration tools.

Technologies for Asynchronous Group Activities

Asynchronous groupware applications support users that are generally not working together in the same place at the same time.

Asynchronous tools possess the advantage of being able to involve people from multiple time zones. In addition, asynchronous tools are helpful in capturing the history of the interactions of a group, allowing for collective knowledge to be more easily shared and distributed. The primary drawback of asynchronous technologies is that they require some discipline to use when used for ongoing communities of practice (e.g., people typically must take the initiative to "login" to participate) and they may feel "impersonal" to those who prefer higher-touch synchronous technologies. Table 2 describes the most characteristic asynchronous collaboration tools.

Distributed Collaborative Design

When a product is designed through the collective and joint efforts of many designers, the design process may be characterised as Collaborative Design, Co-operative Design, Concurrent Design and Interdisciplinary Design. A collaborative design team often works in parallel and independently with different engineering tools distributed in separate locations, even across various time zones around the world.

Table 2. Synchronous and asynchronous collaboration tools

Tool	Useful for...
Synchronous Collaboration Tools	
Audio Conferencing	Discussing and dialogue
Web Conferencing	Sharing presentations and information
Video Conferencing	In-depth discussions with higher-touch interactions
Chat	Information sharing of low complexity issues
Instant Messaging	Ad hoc quick communications
White-boarding	Co-development of ideas - brainstorming
Application Sharing	Co-development of documents
Asynchronous Collaboration Tools	
Discussion Boards	Dialogue that takes place over a period of time
Web logs (Blogs)	Sharing ideas and comments
Messaging (e-mail)	One-to-one or one-to-many communications
Streaming Audio	Communicating and/or training
Streaming Video	Communicating and/or training
Narrated Slide-shows	Communicating and/or training
"Learning objects" Web-based training	Training
Document Libraries	Managing Resources
Databases	Managing information and knowledge
Web books	Training
Surveys and polls	Capturing information and trends
Shared Calendars	Coordinating activities
Web site links	Providing resources and references

To support collaborative design, computer technology must not only augment the capabilities of the individual specialists, but must also enhance the ability of collaborators to interact with each other and with computational resources. However, engineering design has to address several complex characteristics (e.g. diverse and complex forms of information, interdisciplinary collaboration, heterogeneous software tools etc.)

and these make interaction difficult to support. Traditional approaches to sharing design information among collaborators and their tools include the development of integrated sets of tools and the establishment of data standards. These approaches are becoming insufficient to support collaborative design practices, because of the highly distributed nature of the design teams, diversity of the engineering tools and the complexity and dynamics of the design environment.

The ability of the Web for designers to combine multimedia to publish information relevant to the spectrum of the design process (e.g. moodboards, storyboards), from concept generation and prototyping to product realisation and virtual manufacturing. motivated the adoption of the Web as a design collaboration tool. A web-based collaborative design system would primarily provide:

- Access to catalogue and design information on components and sub-assemblies.
- Communication among multi-disciplinary design team members in multimedia formats.
- Authenticated access to design tools, services and documents.

CURRENT CHALLENGES IN GROUPWARE AND COLLABORATIVE DESIGN SYSTEMS

Current computational workspaces do not naturally provide the rich information landscape available in a face-to-face setting (Gutwin 1997). As a result, many of the perceptual cues that people use to maintain workspace awareness are missing in a groupware system. This problem exists for two reasons:

- The technical and physical environment of groupware (the input and output devices) that participants use to interact with the workspace often imposes severe con-

straints on how users interact with artefacts, how the workspace is perceived, and what can be seen of others.
- The ways that software developers think about groupware systems have also limited the awareness information available in the shared workspace.

The main limitation of current groupware systems is that most of them are focusing on the shared data, rather than the shared space. This approach is evident in many current groupware systems, such as Google docs, Microsoft Office Groove 2007 and ShrEdit. By ignoring this reality, software developers often create collaborative workspaces where there is a paucity of workspace awareness information and where human interaction becomes difficult and awkward.

This proposal aims to approach the area from a different perspective. Before initiating the development of the CWE we will perform a thorough investigation of the concurrent engineering process followed by ESA adopting rapid ethnographical methodologies such as "quick and dirty" observation focusing on the tools that domain experts use to be able to collaborate efficiently. Furthermore a series of rapid prototypes will be implemented and evaluated from domain experts against a series of criteria before the development of the final prototype takes place.

Problem Areas

Risk is a major factor to be considered during the management of any project. Project management must control and contain risks in order to ensure the successful outcome of the project. Risk can be defined as uncertainty of outcome.

The task of risk management is to manage the project's exposure to risk (that is, the probability of specific risks occurring and the potential impact if they occur). The aim is to manage exposure by taking action to keep exposure to an acceptable level in a cost-effective way. Risk management and control will involve:

- Access to reliable up-to-date information about risks.
- Decision-making processes supported by a framework of risks analysis and evaluation.
- Processes in place to monitor and control risks.
- The right balance of control in place to deal with those risks.

Table 3 provides an overview of the currently identified risks regarding the development of Galileo, as well as possible risk mitigation strategies.

THE GALILEO PROTOTYPE

Despite the abundance of existing commercial and open source CWE solutions, the features required to cover the particular needs of a domain specific community of end-users such as this of ESA does not exist in a single platform. Therefore a com-

Table 3. Overview of identified risks

Identified threats	Risk	Risk reduction plan
Errors in system design.	System malfunction or failure to achieve the expected results which will lead to eventual fadeout of its use and abandonment.	Provide a specific meeting plan for acquiring information about all external system interfaces.
Errors in Galileo specifications.	System malfunction or failure to achieve the expected results, which will lead to eventual fadeout of its use and abandonment.	Arrange more meetings with ESA to define as clearly as possible all technical and functional requirements for the CWE.
Loss of credibility of the system.	System malfunction or failure to achieve the expected results which will lead to eventual fadeout of its use and abandonment.	Comply with security standards in order to provide maximum security to the system. If necessary, security experts of the company will be involved.
Low system use.	Build a system that no one uses and is state of the art only on paper. This inevitably leads to system abandonment.	Re-design the system GUI based on previous experience and after the collection of specific requirements from ESA.
Significant delays in the development and deployment of Galileo components.	Late delivery of the system in production mode.	The modular nature of Galileo allows for more resources to be allocated for each component's development. Allocate more resources for the development of critical components first and speed up delivery of the system.
System crashes or delay in achieving performance requirements and loss of system credibility.	Problematic implementation of the system and loss of valuable time and resources in rectifying problems.	Specify the minimum requirements for the ESA infrastructure to host the system. Ensure that the system architecture is capable to provide services inline with the requirements. Request any changes to ESA's infrastructure if required.
System might not be able to cope with other systems or supplier technologies.	Poor performance of the system as well as incompatibility problems.	The system will be implemented following the latest standards and technologies available. In particular, functionalities that relate to system interconnections will follow official industry-wide standards.
ESA will not be able to take over the operational support of Galileo after development and integration.	Hindered system operation and eventual fadeout of usc.	Produce detailed documentation for both business and technical administration of the system, while additionally provide transfer of know-how supporting the proper operation of the system.
Uncontrolled additional requirements and change requests cause serious schedule and resource overruns.	Late delivery of CWE in production mode.	All user requirements and system specifications are clearly documented and all system stakeholders review and approve them before system implementation commences.

bination of solutions will have to be provided in terms of an integrated solution which covers the conceptual stages of design (such as gathering experts, brainstorming, sharing resources and ideas, drafting etc.), as well as the more concrete aspects (such as requirements analysis, planning, resource management etc.).

Overview of the Conceptual Framework of Galileo

Design commences with high-level descriptions of requirements and proceeds with a high level description of a solution. It involves formulation of abstract ideas with approximate concrete representations. The early or conceptual stage of the design process is dominated by the generation of ideas, which are subsequently evaluated against general requirements' criteria.

The conceptual design is crucial, particularly, when designing new and innovative products, or when generating a completely new design for an existing product. It is common knowledge that the majority of the product cost is committed by the end of the conceptual design phase. At this stage information is very fuzzy and incomplete, which makes the design process quite difficult and challenging. It also renders a problem for representing the designed product.

Most common techniques used in the conceptual design include problem solving strategies, genetic algorithms, case-based reasoning, and agent-based technology. The author adopted a recurring DAER technique (Design - Analysis - Evaluation - Redesign) for the conceptual design stage of Galileo which led to the high-level architecture design outlined below.

Galileo High Level Architecture

The general infrastructure of Galileo is organised into three levels:

- **Configuration Level:** The main metaphor of the environment is the concept of customisability. We acknowledge that designers tend to reject applications that may limit their creativity. However they embrace tools that are easy to customise according to their needs. Galileo will allow the user to customise the tools according to the needs of the mission by simply dragging and dropping them into the categorised tabs. For example users will be able to keep the tools required for the project and drop the tools that rarely use in the unused tools category. The environment will automatically save user settings in an xml file, so there is no need for the user to customise the environment again for the particular mission.

- **Reuse Level:** Generally, the ability to reuse relies in an essential way on the ability to build larger projects from smaller parts, and being able to identify commonalities among those parts. Galileo will provide users' with a series of tools to record the methodology followed towards the completion of a project, for example real time recording mechanisms and snapshots. In addition, the prototype can provide the user with online file repositories where users are able to store their projects and review them at any time. Meta information with regard to contributors, date and time as well as automatic versioning will be provided automatically by the platform.

- **Reflection Level:** The concept behind the implementation of Galileo is to provide the client with appropriate tools to help them reflect on their ideas and prototypes. The tools will be implemented and arranged in a way that a user is constantly reminded of the next step, related sources that may be of help, and reusable material from past and present projects.

Galileo was designed in a way that allows users to work collaboratively as well as individually simultaneously. The individual tools will allow the users to try solutions without feeling that they are being watched or criticised. When all the participants have indicated readiness they can begin to place components of their solutions in the collaborative space synchronously or asynchronously. All the contributions are monitored and recorded by appropriate mechanisms providing Meta information as to the date and time the contribution took place, and the name(s) of the contributor(s).

In the conceptual design of the system, features and services have been created and an initial integration plan with existing ESA infrastructure will be made. The goal is to identify any possible problems and solve them before the implementation stage.

The high-level architecture identifies the components of the system, and the relationships among them. Its purpose is to direct attention at an appropriate decomposition of the system without delving into details. Moreover, it provides a useful vehicle for communicating the architecture to non-technical audiences, such as management, marketing, and users. It consists of the Architecture Diagram illustrated in Figure 3.

Galileo Front-End

The user interface determines the way the user interacts with Galileo and will be designed according to the needs and priorities of ESA. Through the User Interface design process, the navigation options and system functions are organised. In this phase, the "look-and-feel" (visual layout) of Galileo and the navigational elements will be designed based on the specification and conceptual design. This ensures that there is an agreement on the high-level navigation, look and architecture

Figure 3. Galileo high-level architecture

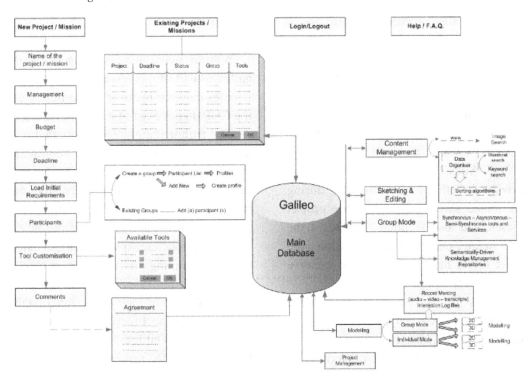

Figure 4. Galileo front end

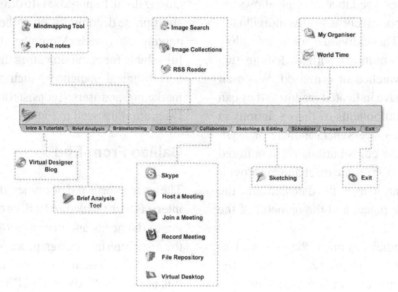

of the platform before significant development work has been done.

Galileo Features

Based on an initial requirements analysis and a relevant background study, the author has drawn two main conclusions regarding the purpose of Galileo (See Figure 4):

- As in any engineering process, there is a coexistence of sub-processes which can be creative and conceptual during the initial phases and become low-level and strictly technical towards the final stages of the project. Since the Agency aims at improving the efficiency of the CDF during distributed sessions in early space project phases, and also facilitate the use of the CDF in later phases of space missions, the target CWE must enhance both creative and technical design skills.
- Semantics play an important role in the collaboration between multidisciplinary teams of experts, because it minimises ambiguity in the use of technical terms and

reduces the time needed for clarifications. A remarkable effort has been made on the part of the Agency to standardise the semantics of the space mission process and the design parameters involved. The author intents to comply with those standards and apply the semantic models to the supported processes.

A preliminary investigation performed by the author as part of this research has shown that the features required to cover the particular needs of the CDF do not exist in a single platform.

The author therefore believes that a combination of solutions will have to be provided and foresees the need for an integrated solution, which can cover the more conceptual/creative stages of design (such as gathering experts, brainstorming, sharing resources and ideas, drafting etc.) as well as the more concrete aspects (such as requirements analysis, planning, resource management etc).

Figure 5 describes how features which can provide the abovementioned functionality are mapped onto the lifecycle of an ESA mission and the phases Galileo could cover. It also shows how the supported processes and their respective

Figure 5. Creative and technical features of Galileo

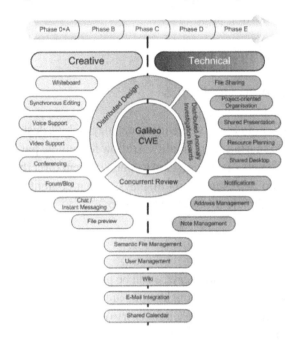

features are separated into creative and technical, and the relationships between them. The CWE-related features and services in this section have been selected as part of the initial concept of the envisioned CWE. The descriptions that follow summarize the key functionality and the relationship of each feature with CDF processes.

Creativity-Related Features

Forum/Blog

The blog module allows users to create and manage their own blogs in order to share their thoughts with other domain experts. Each user can create a personal blog which will be visible by other domain experts. This CWE module can support all the functionalities of modern blogs, such as dividing posts in categories, assigning tags to better describe their content as well as a trackback functionality which allows users to indicate posts they find interesting, thus connecting discussions with each other.

The environment can also include a forum service, which allows the exchange of views and positions among the members of a workgroup for any subject of common interest. A user may read and/or contribute to a forum discussion. The forum access can be controlled allowing moderation of forum posts and/or restricted read or write access to different types of users.

Chat/Instant Messaging

Instant Messaging (IM) allows users to exchange real time messages with domain experts. A short message history will be available, which will be retained between different pages of the CWE platform, thus allowing users to participate to an IM session while at the same time working on their other tasks on the system.

Whiteboard

The collaborative whiteboard is not as restrictive as other common means of communication like instant messaging and voice conference.

The whiteboard feature can help designers and other external domain experts to communicate visual information to a large group of experts. The particular feature can enhance the brainstorming process as it helps designers to emphasise on a model (image) or a problem area before using a more feature-enhanced tool such as a collaborative design editor.

Synchronous Editing

The CWE's synchronous editor can be developed to support groups of domain experts editing a document (collaborative writing), a model (Collaborative Computer Assisted Design-CAD) and CASE (Computer Aided Software Engineering). Consistency coupled with good performance of a synchronous editing tool can be the answer to the social challenges of supporting group activities.

Video & Voice Support

The CWE platform can be linked to a VoIP platform. It can be configured so that selected services are provided to different users, allowing the definition of user groups based on the VoIP services they are allowed to use. In addition, it allows existing client applications to use the basic and additional telephone services provided by the VoIP server.

The system may also provide enhanced services, including the possibility to call a user through their name or their extension number.

Conferencing

Through the use of a specialised server, the envisioned CWE can provide extensive video/voice conference support including control through web services.

The following services can be supported:

- **Ad Hoc Conference:** Two or more users will be able to activate a teleconference service and invite additional participants to it.
- **Conference Rooms:** A registered user may see an existing teleconference room of the system as well as create/modify/delete one if suitably authorised. The conferencing rooms are accompanied with a set of useful metadata including their name, phone number, etc.

File Preview

The file preview feature enables users to upload and preview files (documents, images etc) in the CWE. To that front, in addition to the functionalities offered by the File Management module, such as organising files into folders or specifying custom attributes for images, it will also offer image preview functionalities. In the case of DAIB or CR sessions, this may prove to be an invaluable

tool for incorporating photographs or designs as supporting information.

Technical Features

Shared Desktop

The collaborative environment may include desktop sharing functionality, to allow for remote participants of a CE session to share content directly from their individual displays, if that content is not already available on Galileo.

Notifications

The notification service can be provided through regular e-mail. Notifications are offered in conjunction with the user directory of the system and allow users to keep track of actions of interest taking place in the system. This functionality allows users to be notified on real time of important events.

Notes

The system will allow the creation of session notes, which may be semantically annotated with concepts and terms from the existing data model, or linked to processes, documents, participants and requirements, therefore giving them context.

Project-Oriented Organisation

The CWE may include an engine to support teamwork and cooperation between the members of a study. It can support the assignment and processing of tasks and assures better communication and control by the team leaders and team members.

File – Sharing

The file sharing functionality of Galileo will enable registered users to manipulate the access permissions of resources which they own, to change them from private to public or give them more specific permissions for individuals and teams.

Resource Planning

A more specialised module for the organisation of resources, such as technical equipment and meeting rooms may be included in the CWE, to ensure proper conduct of studies. Through this module, users can view available resources and their availability in terms of quantity, time and location, and arrange study sessions and meetings accordingly.

Shared Presentation

Galileo may provide special functionality to support the delivery of presentations to all collaborators, synchronously. This can be a valuable tool for any distributed collaborative design effort, since it does not restrict the location of the presenter, while at the same time it does not compromise the quality of presentation material. Accompanied by appropriate conferencing functionality, this module can also be used for remote training/ briefing sessions.

Address Management

The CWE may support a centralised contact repository, which is easier to access and maintain. It can be used to share e-mail, telephone or other contact information, which can also be used by other modules for the organisation of tasks and conferences. Access to this information can also be controlled to ensure integrity and security.

Added Value Services

Semantic File Management/ Version Control

Semantic file management allows a workgroup to maintain online document libraries. The docu-

ments may be of any format, size, and language. Galileo can provide a private work space for each geographically distributed workgroup where access is provided through simple web browsers.

All the documents will be stored in a hierarchical structure and may be annotated with terms and concepts from a semantically grounded reference library. Workgroup coordinators may provide as detailed access rights as necessary, according to the specific workgroup needs. In addition, the file management service may support multiple document versions, allowing for an organised document evolution through the CDF design iterations.

User Management

The envisioned CWE includes an extensive administration suite of tools for the management of user accounts, their access rights, and all the necessary functionality for identity information storage and manipulation.

A high-level category of users may include users in the following hierarchical structure:

- **Domain Expert:** Varying access rights as set by the Workgroup coordinator.
- **Workgroup Coordinator:** Responsible for the administration of workgroup-related resources and Domain Expert's access rights to them. May add/remove users and user profiles.
- **Team Leader:** May create/modify/delete workgroups and CDF study sessions; responsible for the maintenance of the user directory.
- **Administrator:** May create/modify/delete studies and authorise their Team Leaders, and has access to all the functionality.

The system may support different access rights models depending on access levels and provides varying levels of data protection. Access rights can be based on user profiles. Currently, the OCDS infrastructure supports user roles and separates them into "outside-study roles" and "inside-study roles" and therefore Galileo may be adopted to reflect those user categories.

Shared Calendar

The calendar service allows the management of meetings and other events and can be shared among the members of a workgroup or study. In addition, it supports meeting preparatory actions, announcements as well as meeting and event management. In a shared calendar users may organise the reservation of meeting rooms and other relevant equipment.

Wiki

The wiki module provides a set of functionalities that help domain experts to share knowledge and information. Users are able to create and edit wiki entries whose content can be easily formatted and may include pictures, hyperlinks and cross-links to other pages of the wiki. Each wiki entry will have a full history which allows keeping track of all the changes on the entry and the user who performed them.

E-Mail Integration

This service provides the study members with the functionality to send email messages to one or more users. The emails are sent via SMTP to the recipient's normal email mailbox. The recipients do not have to be members of the workgroup or exist in the System Directory.

GALILEO EVALUATION AND TESTING

Overview of the Adopted Evaluation Process

During the evaluation stages of Galileo the researchers applied usability testing for the assessment of the environment. Usability testing is a means of testing how well end users can operate human-made objects (such as a web page, a computer interface, a document, or a device) for its intended purpose (Perlman 1997; Hix, Gabbard et al. 1999). The advantage of this approach is that it focuses on particular aspects of the produced environment whereas general human computer interaction studies attempt to formulate universal principles (Millen 2000). The authors adopted this method to measure the usability as well as the functionality of the Galileo environment. Furthermore other important factors found to be of great significance include:

- **Consistency:** Consistent use of terminology, abbreviations, formatting, titles and navigation within and across outputs. Response time whenever a function is performed.
- **Efficiency:** Formatting should be designed with an understanding of the task being performed. Graphics, text and data should be aligned and sorted for efficient navigation and entry. Manual entry of data should be avoided where possible.
- **Ease of Use:** Output should be self explanatory and not require users to remember information from prior outputs in order to complete tasks.
- **Format:** The format should be consistent between information entry and display. Format should distinguish each piece of data and highlight important data.

- **Flexibility:** Information should be viewed and retrieved in a manner most convenient to the user.

The evaluators were briefly introduced to the purpose of the project and are informed about the services that the environment provides. The researchers aimed to maintain the same conditions throughout the evaluation for all respondents, since this is necessary when comparing numerical results.

Setting up a usability test involves development of scenarios based on realistic situations, where participants performed a list of tasks using the product being tested while observers take notes (Hix and Hartson 1993; Dray 1997; Perlman 1997; Pinelle, Gutwin et al. 2003). As soon as the users finish evaluating the prototype they are required to fill in a questionnaire and critically evaluate the tools provided in terms of usefulness and usability as well as the entire environment in terms of usability, supportiveness and potential.

Research supports that user friendliness is a term often used, and misused since it is too vague from a design point of view to provide adequate information. This is because it means different things to different people (Dray 1997; Mayhew 1997; Perlman 1997; Spool, Scanlon et al. 1997; Hix, Gabbard et al. 1999).

This research has evaluated the proposed environment against the following criteria:

- **Learning Curve:** Reflects on how long it takes the average user to become proficient using the proposed environment.
- **Process Measures:** Look for patterns in behavioural or verbal activity during a collaborative session and connect these to issues of effectiveness or efficiency. Process measures are often obtained by observation or through video and protocol analysis.
- **Subjective Satisfaction:** Records the participants' subjective experience with the groupware system, and investigates whether people find the system to be a

good setting for collaboration. In addition, measures of usability can also explore people's perceptions of a system's efficiency and effectiveness. These measures are usually obtained through questionnaires and interviews.

The research applied several data collection methods during the usability testing of the prototype such as "quick and dirty" observation combined with open-ended and scalar questionnaires, to extract feedback from the participants.

Overview of the Adopted Testing Process

Testing involves the critical analysis of the final results produced during the design and implementation stages. The testing phase highlights the strengths and weaknesses perceived by team members, outside parties and the CDF personnel. In an ideal situation, the content of the site needs to be "frozen" before the final testing begins. Rigorous testing ensures the highest possible level of quality and client satisfaction. Hence, the following factors play a particularly important role during the testing phase. Testing consists of the following stages:

- Platform Testing
  - **Conduct CWE Tests:** Performing test steps according to scripts, registering timings, performance diagnostics, and noting all significant events.
  - **Analyse CWE Test Results:** Revisiting test outputs systematically, checking accuracy and consistency and identifying non-conformity.
  - **Support Corrective Actions:** Diagnosing and correcting faults, retesting according to CSCW standards completing the relevant documentation under configuration management.

○ **CWE Test Report:** Evaluation of the complete test process and production of a test file which will contain information on test log and results analysis, error correction and re-test and final reporting.

- **Component Testing:** Activities during the Component Testing stage will involve:
  ○ Testing of individual CWE collaborative and knowledge management components.
  ○ Combined tests as a group of collaborative features as well as the general functionality of the CWE.

The following tasks are performed which may be conducted in an incremental, iterative approach:

- **Coding and Unit Testing:** The service team implement the changes in the existing platform and perform unit testing (automated). Other quality assurance and verification and validation processes may be required for safety-related code development.
- **Integration:** The changes are integrated with the system and integration and regression tests are refined and performed. All effects (functional, performance, usability, safety) of the change on the existing platform are assessed. A return to the coding and unit testing tasks will be necessary in order to remove any unacceptable impacts.
- **Test Readiness Review:** A test readiness review is conducted in order to determine if items, including source code, documentation, libraries, hardware, telecommunication lines, are ready for system test to begin.

The control activities during this stage include:

- Conduct structured walkthroughs of the code.

- Ensure that unit and integration testing are performed and documented.
- Ensure that test documentation (test plans, test cases, and test procedures) are either updated or created.
- Identify, document and resolve any risks exposed during software and test readiness reviews.
- Verify that the new software is placed under software configuration control.
- Verify that the training and technical documentation have been updated.
- Verify the traceability of the design of the code.

Integration of Galileo with CDF Infrastructure

Two important issues arise from the deployment of Galileo in the ESA CDF: its integration with the existing CDF ICT infrastructure, and the deployment of secure user account management integrated with ESA's single sign-on services.

At the time of writing, the ESA CDF information and communication technology infrastructure comprised of the following server platform: Microsoft Windows Server 2008 SP2 with Hyper-V virtual machines and multi-core Intel Xeon CPUs, and the following client platform: Citrix ICA clients running on either Windows XP SP3 PCs or Windows 7. Typical resources for client workstations are: Intel 2.5 GHz CPU or better with a minimum of 1 GB RAM and 100 GB of hard disc space.

The existing server infrastructure is based on virtualisation technology, which is flexible and scalable enough to accommodate additional servers if necessary, and can therefore provide a secure and reliable hosting solution for the Galileo server features. The web-based design of Galileo will allow it to run on existing clients without requiring additional resources.

The CWE is designed to provide a secure collaboration environment that can implement the following essential aspects: user authentication, certification of valid participating computers across the network, encrypted network connections and controlled secure access through the ESA firewalls. The importance and convenience of single sign-on access control has been taken into account in this design and the Galileo user account management can be integrated with ESA's single sign-on services on the Windows platform, therefore minimising password fatigue by using existing user credentials.

Testing Results

Graphical User Interface (GUI) of Galileo

Participants' thought that the environment was simple to use and reliable featuring useful tools focussed to serve the early stages of the design process. They highlighted that it was easy to understand the next steps because of the categorization of the tools mirrored on the stages of the design process. In addition it helped the search for related information and repurposes them according to the needs of the project.

According to the participants the prototype encourages project management and security keeping the users focussed on the needs of the project. They thought that being able to build your own tool palette is an essential feature in a domain specific collaborative environment. Evaluators asked for an additional tab named "Material Research". "Material Research tab" could help designers gather information using a series of data mining tools with regards to the materials used for a specific project.

Evaluators found that the linear menu was a great start since it was fully customizable and organised into categories. However they thought that a non linear, more flexible menu could be better. A characteristic example was quicksilver's constellation menu used in MacOS X as it suggests a more flexible metaphor, similar to that of

the design process. According to the participants one of the strongest points of the prototype is its ability to reorganise and manage the complexity of a collaborative design project.

Brainstorming Tools

ESA scientists and designers already use handwritten mind-maps and post-it notes when brainstorming. This can be verified from the literature as well. For example Ivashkov (Ivashkov, Souchkov et al. 2000) who builds on (Hymes and Olson 1992) supports that one of the most important techniques that designers use when developing new concepts is brainstorming. By the end of the brainstorming session there will be a list of ideas that may have the potential to be developed into concepts.

Collaborative Tools

Design projects cannot be generated by a single professional and usually involve the co-ordinated effort of many professionals (Curtis, Krasner et al. 1988; Günther, Frankenberger et al. 1996; Popovic 1996). Since design is a collaborative process many professionals become actively involved in the design of large or complicated products and their actions are co-dependant on the simultaneous decisions of the participants working on the project. Collaborative design is a highly complex process because decision makers and designers may have different perspectives, solutions and personal agendas that may wish to follow which may not be compatible. In addition participants may have different levels of problem understanding and experience in different areas.

Exploration of the literature indicated that designers already have tools that are able to host collaborative sessions during the modelling phases of the process. However participants' could be assisted by tools supporting the collaborative aspects of the design process, when in its initial stages. This research has indicated that providing tools to support collaboration in design is an important goal which has already been the subject of research in the computer supported collaborative work community (CSCW) (Maclean, Bellotti et al. 1990; Boland, Schwartz et al. 1992; Muller 1992; Gaver, Sellen et al. 1993). Most collaborative environments are focussing on aiding individual problem solving rather than co-ordinating and organising user activities (Bannon 1986; Anderson, Button et al. 1993; Cross and Christiaans 1996; Cross 1997). Mulder and Swaak (Mulder and Swaak 2003) support the view that current collaborative technology still fails to support real life collaboration. In addition Bardram (Bardram 1998) argues that this problem is a direct result of not looking at the dynamic aspects of collaborative work. For example this would involve interaction protocols, recording mechanisms and group decision mechanisms to avoid confusion. As a result new tools and integration methods for more interactive and dynamic collaboration need to be investigated for better collaboration amongst virtual design teams (Nam 2000; Klein, Sayama et al. 2001; Yingfei, Mingxi et al. 2002).

During the usability studies participants thought that the collaborative tools were extremely efficient and friendly allowing them to communicate and co-operate securely with their colleagues. However there were times where users could not identify who had the main control of the system, hence they thought that the implementation of a collaboration protocol is essential. The file-sharing feature allowed users instant access to the host's workstation.

In the usability studies participants thought that the tool's interface seemed awkward during the first use and was in great need of better graphics. However even a non IT literate user could communicate and collaborate with the rest of the team within few minutes of using the tool.

Participants already use voice over Internet protocol by means of Skype communicator technology for communicating with colleagues and clients. They usually demonstrate their work in front of the camera to get feedback from a remote client. Furthermore they are writing by hand the meeting notes and minutes. Participants acknowledged that the prototype could save them time and effort with its integrated recording mechanisms.

Online File Repository

Design is also a learning process and an important aspect of learning is access to information. However information sharing is not only a matter of making data available to team members (Coleman and Furey 1996). Data will be interpreted by the recipients' depending on their experience, skills and context. It is therefore necessary that the design process is supported by technologies for managing knowledge (Coleman and Furey 1996). To support long-term asynchronous collaboration it is crucial to provide an archive or repository that functions as a group memory (Adams, Toomey et al. 1999). Then professionals engaged later in the design life cycle can understand reasons for what might otherwise be obscure decisions taken by others (Chen and You 2003). Ideally the repository should record both what was done in a project and why, recording both decisions and rationale underlying those decisions (Borghoff 2000).

Participants commented positively on the user interface and the simplicity of the online file repository tool.

Participants characterised as 'useful' the following features of the online file repository:

- Being able to create a default folder or space where all the files produced will be stored.
- Automatic file versioning.
- Meta information.
- File and area restrictions.
- User roles and authentication.

Participants reflected on the security features of the tool focussing on the user restrictions. In addition they acknowledged the automatic versioning feature as well as the creation of logs with detailed Meta information with regards to the users activities in the environment and in the tool it self. For example logs were being created in the case of files uploaded, downloaded and were contribution were made.

However they noted that the integration of graphics was essential allowing them to substitute the lists with icons, in this way customizing their view of the data. In addition the integration of a tracking mechanism demonstrating who has viewed the files and when, was considered to be essential.

Record Meeting

When a team collaborates using a groupware environment its members should be co-ordinated to avoid possible conflicts occurring. In order to protect the integrity of the project throughout its complete lifecycle appropriate recording mechanisms should be integrated into the system (Grinter 1996). Grinter (1996) supports the view that recording mechanisms have more than one uses in a collaborative environment:

- They provide participants with a verification mechanism with regards to the evolution of the project.
- Users can use the outputs as a reference for future work or to review the current process, hence a recording mechanism improves the designer's learning curve and experience.
- Recording mechanisms allow participants to coordinate their work without communicating with the rest of the team. In this way preventing that way a coordination breakdown that may occur during a collaborative session.

Recording mechanisms support collaboration by providing information about the contribution of other participants' (Grinter 1996; Bayles 1998) for example:

- Who made the changes?
- What changes were made to the software?
- When were the changes made?
- Why were the changes made?

It is important that team members can see the project as it evolves from one version to another. This research considers the integration of tracking and recording mechanism essential features to a collaborative design environment

During the evaluation of the storyboards participants thought that the ability to track project members' activities could be an extremely useful tool assisting users who are not familiar with the project to evaluate the progress and the process.

During the usability studies the recording tool was thought as an extremely powerful tool and an essential part of the prototype. The recording mechanism of the prototype helped participants keep tack of the collaborative activity and secure their ideas as they were contributing to the project. Participants acknowledged that they were able to record voice and video saving valuable time as they did not have to keep minutes of meeting. However one of the limitations of the tool was the fact that the participants could not tell whether was active or not. Designers also added that they might need a transcript as well as an output. Furthermore the transcript could be further analysed with the brief analysis tool or the brainstorming tools of the prototype.

Sketching

Designers tend to capture their ideas by sketching them on paper. According to Lawrence (Lawrence 1964) sketching helps designers identify key points, which then can be communicated with the rest of the team.

The sketching tool of Galileo was thought to be very handy for reviewing and evaluating purposes when the team is distributed. Participants characterised the collaborative history box as the strongest point of the tool as it allowed designers to identify the different stages towards the evolution of the project. They commented that the history box was another mechanism provided to log the collaborative session similar to the record meeting tool. However it was suggested to expand the collaborative history box demonstrating the reason behind each contribution.

FUTURE DEVELOPMENTS AND CONCLUSION

Overall, the findings revealed in the analysis support the aim of the project in gaining a deeper understanding of the collaborative nature of the design process and developing a prototype collaborative design environment to support ESA designers and scientists during its early stages. Through highlighting the tools and services used to co-ordinate collaborative work, the research revealed areas where particular forms of context sensitive technology could be introduced that would increase the effectiveness and productivity of designers when in remote collaboration.

Proposed future research derives from two elements of the work undertaken. The first of these arises from the limitations of the study in the number and range of settings examined. The other is further development of the proposed prototype, undertaking further work to evaluate how the proposed prototype could be used to support designers working in different design contexts within ESA.

In addition, further research could examine the impact of the technologies developed in the prototype in an educational context. Most current educational tools are focussed on supporting individual development. A tool could be developed which focussed on exploring the collaborative side of the education process by repurposing some of the tools and services provided in the prototype and combining them with appropriate training material, with a focus on assisting ESAs trainees and instructors.

CHAPTER SUMMARY

The Concurrent Design Facility (CDF) is ESA's center for the assessment of future space missions and it is located at ESTEC (European Space Research and Technology Centre) in the Netherlands. It uses Concurrent Engineering (CE) to perform space mission studies, which increases their cost-effectiveness and quality.

Galileo will enable the extensive and effective use of the Concurrent Design Facility (CDF) during project meetings, task forces and reviews by addressing the needs of address the needs of Distributed Design Sessions, Concurrent Reviews and Distributed Anomaly Investigation Boards. With Galileo, the CDF will not be restricted to initial space mission phases but also extended to later phases.

The research behind Galileo takes into account several state-of-the-art technologies which are available for use in CSCW systems. Traditional approaches to sharing design information among collaborators and their tools, such as the development of integrated sets of tools and the establishment of data standards, are considered insufficient to support collaborative design. The often distributed location of contemporary design teams, the diversity of the tools and the dynamics of the design process itself, require more advanced means of collaboration. Galileo augments the capabilities of the individual specialists, but also facilitates the collaboration and interaction between experts in a multidisciplinary team.

Commercial off-the-shelf and open source CWE solutions exist, but the particular requirements of the design teams of ESA cannot be fulfilled by the features existing in a single platform. An integrated and flexible solution must be provided, combining features which cover the conceptual stages of design as well as the more technical aspects.

A preliminary requirements analysis and background study, revealed that the target CWE must enhance both creative and technical design skills, in order to improve the efficiency of the CDF during initial mission phases, and also in later phases. Semantics must play an important role in the reduction of effort and time required for the disambiguation of technical terms during sessions which involve multidisciplinary collaborators.

Galileo takes into account the functionality needed by the CDF and relevant technical requirements, and integrates them into a state-of-the-art CWE. The authors have presented the study which has led to the design of Galileo and the first iteration towards its development.

FURTHER READING

Although there is much research on collaborative working environments, there has been little systematic research on the linkages between collaborative behaviour, organizational effectiveness and physical space, for example:

- Full links between spatial features, collaborative behaviours and organizational outcomes. At present, most research addresses parts of the linkage. For instance, links between space and brief interactions have been studied, as have links between interaction and group or organizational benefits. However, few studies other than the pioneering research by Allen (1977) have sought to make the links from space to behaviour to organizational value. Will the linkages continue to hold as different types of knowledge work are assessed? At present, the research focuses on scientific R&D, software development and design.

- Link between collaborative behaviours and collaborative corporate culture. Can changes in the workplace produce changes in collaborative behaviours that, in turn, influence cultural norms and values? Identifying the tradeoffs between individual and collaborative work for different contexts. Under what circumstances does collaboration become too costly to the individual – for instance, the time needed to maintain relationships and networks may detract sufficiently from individual accomplishment to make further investments inappropriate? Does this point differ for different kinds of work?

REFERENCES

Adams, L., Toomey, L., et al. (1999). *Distributed research teams: Meeting asynchronously in virtual space.* International Conference on System Sciences, Hawaii, FX Palo Alto Laboratory

Agarwal, S. S. (2004). *Supporting collaborative computing and interaction.* Office of Advanced Computing Research, U.S. Department of Energy.

Anderson, B., Button, G., et al. (1993). *Supporting the design process within an organisational context.* Third European Conference on Computer-Supported Cooperative Work, Milan, Italy. Kluwer.

Angehrn, A. (2001). C-VIBE: A virtual interactive business environment addressing change management learning. *Proceedings of ICALT'2001* Madison. Retrieved from http://www.insead.fr/calt/

Bannon, J. L. (1986). Computer mediated communication. In Norman, D. A., & Draper, S. W. (Eds.), *User centered system design, new perspectives on human-computer interaction* (pp. 433–452). Hillsdale, NJ: Lawrence Erlbaum Associates.

Bardram, J. E. (1998). Designing for the dynamics of cooperative work activities. *Proceedings of the ACM 1996 Conference on Computer Supported Cooperative Work (CSCW '98)*. New York, NY: ACM Press.

Bayles, D. (1998). *Version control within a collaborative extranet*. Prentice-Hall PTR.

Boland, R. J., Schwartz, D. G., et al. (1992). Sharing perspectives in distributed decision making. *Proceedings of the Conference on Computer Supported Cooperative Work CSCW 92*, Toronto, Canada. ACM Press.

Bondi, A. B. (2000). Characteristics of scalability and their impact on performance. *Proceedings of the 2nd International Workshop on Software and Performance*, ACM.

Borghoff, U. M., & Schlichter, J. H. (2000). *Computer supported cooperative work: Introduction to distributed applications*. Munich, Germany: Springer.

Chen, W., & You, M. (2003). A framework for the development of online design learning environment. In *Proceedings of the 6th Asian Design Conference: Integration of Knowledge, Kansei, and Industrial Power,* October 14-17, Tsukuba, Japan.

Coleman, D., & Furey, D. (1996). *Collaborative infrastructures for knowledge management*. Collaborative Strategies LLC.

Cross, N. (1997). Descriptive models of creative design: Application to an example. *Design Studies*, *18*(4), 427–455. doi:10.1016/S0142-694X(97)00010-0

Cross, N., & Christiaans, H. (1996). *Analyzing design activity*. Chichester, UK: Wiley.

Curtis, B., & Krasner, H. (1988). A field study of the software design process for large systems. *Communications of the ACM*, *31*(11), 1268–1287. doi:10.1145/50087.50089

Dray, S. M. (1997). *Structured observation: Practical methods for understanding users and their work in context*. CHI'97.

Eppinger, S. D. (1997). Generalized models of design iteration using signal flow graphs. *Research in Engineering Design*, *9*(2), 112–123. doi:10.1007/BF01596486

ESA. (2004). *Glossary of terms*. ESA Publications Division, (ECSS-P-001B). ISSN: 1028-396X

ESA. (2008). *Space management – Organisation and conduct of reviews*. ECSS Secretariat, ESA-ESTEC Requirements & Standards Division, (ECSS-M-ST-10-01C).

ESA. (2011). *Collaborative environment for space systems engineering - Statement of work*. (CDF-SOW-004-RB).

Fan, J., Gao, Y., et al. (2007). Hierarchical classification for automatic image annotation. *Proceedings of the 30th Annual International ACM SIGIR Conference on Research and Development in Information Retrieval - SIGIR '07* (p. 111).

Fan, Z., & Oliveira, M. M. (2004). *A sketch-based interface for collaborative design* (p. 8).

Forbes, S. (1997). *Software configuration management*. Sydney, Australia: OzmoSys.

Gaver, W. W., & Sellen, A. (1993). *One is not enough: Multiple views in a media space. ACM INTERCHI '93*. ACM Press.

Greenberg, S., & Marwood, D. (1994). Real time groupware as a distributed system: Concurrency control and its effect on the interface. *Proceedings of the ACM Conference on Computer Supported Cooperative Work*.

Greenberg, S., & Roseman, M. (1997). *Groupware toolkits for synchronous work, trends in CSCW*. New York, NY: John Wiley & Sons.

Grinter, R. (1996). Supporting articulation work using software configuration management systems. *The Journal of Collaborative Computing, 5*, 447–465. doi:10.1007/BF00136714

Günther, J., & Frankenberger, E. (1996). Investigation of individual and team design processes. In Cross, N., Christiaans, H., & Dorst, K. (Eds.), *Analysing design activity* (pp. 117–132). Chichester, UK: Wiley Press.

Gutwin, C. (1997). *Workspace awareness in real-time distributed groupware*. The University of Calgary, PhD Thesis.

Henry, J. (2001). *Creative management*. London, UK: Sage.

Herlea, D., & Greenberg, S. (1998). Using a groupware space for distributed requirements engineering. *Proceedings of the 7th Workshop on Enabling Technologies: Infrastructure for Collaborative Enterprises*, (pp. 57-62).

Hix, D., & Gabbard, J. L. (1999). *Usercentered design and evaluation of a realtime battlefield visualization virtual environment* (pp. 96–103). IEEE.

Hix, D., & Hartson, H. R. (1993). *User interface development: Ensuring usability through product and process*. New York, NY: John Wiley and Sons.

Hymes, C. M., & Olson, G. M. (1992). Unblocking brainstorming through the use of a simple group editor. *ACM Conference on Computer-Supported Cooperative Work (CSCW'92)*. ACM Press.

Integrated Design Model. (n.d.). Retrieved January 10, 2012, from http://atlas.estec.esa.int/uci_wiki/Integrated%20Design%20Model

Ivashkov, M., Souchkov, V., et al. (2000). *A Triz based method for intelligent design decisions*. ETRIA European TRIZ association.

Jordan, J. (2001). *Collaboration in a mediated haptic environment*. Department of Computer Science, University College London.

Klein, M. (2002). A complex systems perspective on how agents can support collaborative design. In Gero, J. S., & Brazier, F. M. T. (Eds.), *Agents in Design 2002* (pp. 95–111).

Klein, M., & Sayama, H. (2001). What complex systems research can teach us about collaborative design. *Communications of the ACM, 38*(8), 1–8.

Lawrence, W. G. (1964). Creativity and the design process. *Journal of Architectural Education, 19*, 3–4.

Leevers, D. (1999). *Collaboration and shared virtual environments - From metaphor to reality*. Virtual Environments and Human-Centred Computing. Retrieved November 20, 2005, from http://www.vers.co.uk/dleevers/PAPERS/bonas%20html/C%20and%20SVE%20fro%20book%20word%202000.htm

Liapis, A. (2007). The designer's toolkit: A collaborative design environment to support virtual teams. In *Proceedings of the International Association for the Scientific Knowledge Conference, IASK 2007*, Oporto, Portugal.

Liapis, A. (2008). Synergy: A prototype collaborative environment to support the conceptual stages of the design process. *International Conference on Digital Interactive Media in Entertainment and Arts*, DIMEA 2008, Athens, Greece. Springer, ACM.

Maclean, A., Bellotti, V., et al. (1990). What rationale is there in design? *IFIP TC 13 Third International Conference on Human Computer Interaction - INTERACT'90*. Cambridge, UK: Elsevier.

Mayhew, J. D. (1997). Managing the design of the user interface. *CHI Proceedings, 13*(3), 4.

Metros, S. E., & Hedberg, J. G. (1997). *Multimedia visual interface design*. CHI'97.

Millen, D. R. (2000). Rapid ethnography: Time deepening strategies for HCI field research. *Proceedings of DIS 2000*. New York, NY: ACM.

Mitchell, W. J. (2004). *Challenges and opportunities for remote collaborative design*. Massachusetts Institute of Technology.

Mørch, A., & Stiemerlieng, O. (1998). Tailorable groupware. Issues, methods, and architectures. *ACM SIGCHI Bulletin Archive*, *30*(2), 40–42.

Mulder, I., & Swaak, J. (2003). ICT innovation: Starting with the team: A collaborative design workshop on selecting technology for collaboration. *Journal of Educational Technology & Society*.

Muller, M. J. (1992). Retrospective on a year of participatory design using the PICTIVE technique. *In Proceedings CHI '92: Striking a Balance - ACM Conference on Human Factors in Computing Systems*, Monterey, CA: Addison-Wesley.

Nam, T. J., & Wright, D. (2000). *Computer support for collaborative design: Analysis of tools for an integrated collaborative design environment*. 5th Asian Design Conference.

Neale, J. M., & Rosson, M. B. (2004). *Evaluating computer-supported cooperative work: Models and frameworks*. Conference on Computer Supported Collaborative Work, 2004. Chicago, IL: ACM.

Neumann, L. (2007). *An analysis of e-identity organisational and technological solutions within a single European information space*. Knowledge Creation Diffusion Utilization.

OCDS. (n.d.). *User Community Portal*. Retrieved January 10, 2012, from http://atlas.estec.esa.int/uci_wiki/tiki-index.php

Perlman, G. (1997). *Practical usability evaluation*. CHI'97.

Pinelle, D., & Gutwin, C. (2003). Task analysis for groupware usability evaluation: Modeling shared-workspace tasks with the mechanics of collaboration. *Transactions on Computer-Human Interaction*, *10*(4), 281–311. doi:10.1145/966930.966932

Pinsonneault, A., & Kraemer, K. L. (1989). The impact of technological support on groups: An assessment of the empirical research. *Decision Support Systems*, *5*(2), 197–211. doi:10.1016/0167-9236(89)90007-9

Plowman, L., Rogers, Y., et al. (1995). What are workplace studies for? In *Proceedings of ECSCW '95 European Conference on Computer-Supported Cooperative Work*. Dordrecht, The Netherlands: Kluwer.

Popovic, V. (1996). Design activity structural categories. In Cross, N., Christiaans, H., & Dorst, K. (Eds.), *Analysing design activity* (pp. 211–224). Chichester, UK: Wiley.

Rodden, T., & Mariana, J. A. (1992). Supporting cooperative applications. *Computer Supported Cooperative Work*, *1*, 41–67. doi:10.1007/BF00752450

Sahin, C., Weihrauch, C., Dimov, I. T., & Alexandrov, V. N. (2008) *A collaborative working environment for a large scale environmental model*. In 6th International Conference on Large-Scale Scientific Computing (LSSC 2007), Sozopol, Bulgaria.

Smith, R. P., & Eppinger, S. D. (1997). Identifying controlling features of engineering design iteration. *Management Science*, *43*(3), 276–293. doi:10.1287/mnsc.43.3.276

Sommerville, I., & Rodden, T. (1994). *Requirements engineering for cooperative systems*. Retrieved September 26, 2006, from http://citeseer.ist.psu.edu/sommerville94requirements.html

Spool, J. M., Scanlon, T., et al. (1997). *Product usability: Survival techniques*. CHI'97.

Wikipedia. (2011). *Concurrent design facility*. Retrieved January 10, 2012, from http://en.wikipedia.org/wiki/Concurrent_Design_Facility

Wolf, J. (2002). *Thinkcycle@home: Asynchronous interface for online collaboration.*

Yingfei, W., & Mingxi, T. (2002). *A collaborative platform supporting graphic pattern design and reuse of design knowledge*. Design Technology Research Centre.

KEY TERMS AND DEFINITIONS

Brainstorming: Brainstorming is a group or individual creativity technique by which efforts are made to find a conclusion for a specific problem by gathering a list of ideas spontaneously contributed by its member(s).

Computer Supported Collaborative Work (CSCW): CSCW is a generic term, which combines the understanding of the way people work in groups with the enabling technologies of computer networking, and associated hardware, software, services and techniques.

Concurrent Engineering: Concurrent engineering is a work methodology based on the parallelization of tasks (i.e. performing tasks concurrently). It refers to an approach used in product development in which functions of design engineering, manufacturing engineering and other functions are integrated to reduce the elapsed time required to bring a new product to the market.

Decision Support Systems: A decision support system (DSS) is a computer-based information system that supports business or organizational decision-making activities. DSSs serve the management, operations, and planning levels of an organization and help to make decisions, which may be rapidly changing and not easily specified in advance. DSSs include knowledge-based systems. A properly designed DSS is an interactive software-based system intended to help decision makers compile useful information from a combination of raw data, documents, and personal knowledge, or business models to identify and solve problems and make decisions.

Distributed Collaborative Design: A design (of physical artifacts such as cars and planes as well as behavioral ones such as plans, schedules, production processes or software) can be represented as a set of *issues* (sometimes also known as *parameters*) each with a unique value. A complete design for an artifact includes issues that capture the *requirements* for the artifact, the *specification* of the artifact itself (e.g. the geometry and materials), the *process* for creating the artifact (e.g. the manufacturing process) and so on through the artifacts' entire life cycle. If we imagine that the possible values for every issue are each laid along their own orthogonal axis, then the resulting multi-dimensional space can be called the *design space*, wherein every point represents a distinct (though not necessarily good or even physically possible) design. The choices for each design issue are typically highly *interdependent*. Typical sources of inter-dependency include shared resource (e.g. weight, cost) limits, geometric fit, spatial separation requirements, I/O interface conventions, timing constraints etc. *Collaborative* design is performed by multiple participants representing individuals, teams or even entire organizations), each potentially capable of proposing values for design issues and/or evaluating these choices from their own particular perspective (e.g. manufacturability).

Graphical User Interface: A graphical user interface (GUI, commonly pronounced *gooey*) is a type of user interface that allows users to interact with electronic devices using images rather than text commands. *GUI*s can be used in computers, hand-held devices such as MP3 players, portable media players or gaming devices, household appliances and office equipment. A *GUI* represents the information and actions available to a user through graphical icons and visual indicators such as secondary notation, as opposed to text-based interfaces, typed command labels or text navigation. The actions are usually performed through direct manipulation of the graphical elements.

Semantics: Semantics (from Greek: sēmantiká, neuter plural of sēmantikós) is the study of meaning. It focuses on the relation between signifiers, such as words, phrases, signs and symbols, and what they stand for, their denotata. Linguistic semantics is the study of meaning that is used to understand human expression through language. Other forms of semantics include the semantics of programming languages, formal logics, and semiotics.

Synchronous and Asynchronous Tools: Synchronous and asynchronous communication tools are used to facilitate collaboration between individuals and groups of people, and are particularly useful for collaborative environments. Synchronous communication occurs in real time and can take place face-to-face, and as technology has evolved, can take place irrespective of distance (e.g. telephone conversations and instant messaging). Asynchronous communication is not immediately received or responded to by those involved (e.g. emails and message board forums which allow people to communicate on different schedules). To enhance collaboration between people, many software applications offer a blend of synchronous and asynchronous technology.

Chapter 16
Case Study:
Version Control in Component–Based Systems

Nisha Ratti
Rayat Institute of Engineering and Technology, India

Parminder Kaur
Guru Nanak Dev University, India

ABSTRACT

As software is developed and deployed, it is extremely common for multiple versions of the same software to be deployed in different sites, and for the software's developers to be working privately on updates. Bugs and other issues with software are often only present in certain versions (because of the fixing of some problems and the introduction of others the program evolves). Therefore, for the purposes of locating and fixing bugs, it is vitally important for the debugger to be able to retrieve and run different versions of the software to determine in which version(s) the problem occurs. All these tasks are related with version control. This case study makes an attempt to show that how Subversion, an open source version control tool, is helpful in tracing the changes processed at different time. This case study also shows the comparison between open source and commercial version control tools.

INTRODUCTION

Component-based software technology has become an increasingly popular approach to facilitate the development of software systems, as it suggested the solutions to some of the problems of object – oriented development technologies. The aim of component-based software development is to develop new software by widely reusing prefabricated software components. One of the basic problems when developing component-based systems is that it is difficult to keep track of components and their interrelationships as component development evolves in small steps or versions.

DOI: 10.4018/978-1-4666-2958-5.ch016

Version control is used to keep track of the changing states of files over time and merge the contributions of multiple developers. It is most commonly used in engineering and software development to mange ongoing development of digital documents like application source code, art resource such as blueprints or electronic models and other critical information that may be worked on by a team of people. Changes to these documents are identified by incrementing an associated no. or letter code, termed the revision no. or simply revision and associated historically with the person making the change. If more than one developer handles the project, then there is need of mechanism which makes sure that no developer can overwrite other's versions/revision. It is just as important to be able to merge the contributions of those many developers into a single whole. To handle these problems, various software tools are increasingly recognized as being necessary for almost all software development projects. A good version control system helps to protect the integrity of your data. Having a central project repository can also help with data backup. If a group of developers don't want to do the integration of work by hand, then a version control system (VCS) can greatly increase productivity.

A version control system also protects again productivity lost to re-implemented work, not only by avoiding losses of data that was incorrectly deemed to be unnecessary but also by making each developer's work readily available to other developers on the project. In the development process, it is important to know exactly who added each bit of code to a project, when those additions are done and who is responsible for it. A version control system will help to enforce policies that can ensure a project keeps quality records for later use. Version control can make dealing with distributed development easier, by automating much of the workload of exchanging and merging the work of different developers (Spinellis, 2005), (Louridas, 2006).

BASIC CONCEPTS OF VERSION CONTROL SYSTEM

A version control system helps to enforce policies that can ensure a project keeps quality records for later use. Version control can make dealing with distributed development easier, by automating much of the workload of exchanging and merging the work of different developers. A version control system (VCS) is a tool for managing a collection of program code that provides you with three important capabilities: reversibility, concurrency, and annotation. When a file is under version control, it is registered in the version control system. The system has a repository, which stores both the file's present state and its change history— enough to reconstruct the current version or any earlier version. The repository also contains other information, such as log entries that describe the changes made to each file.

Following are the basic concepts related to version control:

1. **Tracking Changes:** A version control system is mostly based around one concept, tracking changes that happen within directories or files. Depending on the version control system, this could vary from knowing a file changed to knowing specific characters or bytes in a file have changed. In most cases, user specifies a directory or set of files that should have their changes tracked by version control. This can happen by checking out a repository from a host, or by telling the software which of the files user wishes to have under version control.

2. **Committing:** As the files are under version control, each change is tracked automatically. This can include modifying a file, deleting a directory, adding a new file, moving files or just about anything else that might alter the state of the file. Instead of recording each change individually, the version control system will wait for the user to submit the

changes as a single collection of actions. In version control, this collection of actions is known as a "commit".

3. **Revisions and Change Sets:** When a commit is made, the changes are recorded as a change set and given a unique revision. This revision could be in the form of an incremented number or a unique hash depending on the system.

4. **Getting Updates:** As members of the team commit changes, it is important that every user have the latest version. Having the latest version reduces the chance of a conflict. When an update or pull is requested, only the changes since user's last request are downloaded.

5. **Conflicts:** Latest updates may result in a conflict. That is, if the changes are so similar to the changes that another team member made that the version control system can't determine which is the correct and authoritative change? In most cases, the version control system will provide a way to view the difference between the conflicting versions, allowing the user to make a choice.

6. **Branching and Merging:** There are some cases when user wants to experiment or commit changes to the repo that could break things elsewhere in the code. Instead of committing this code directly to the main set of files, referred to as trunk or master, user can create something called a branch. A branch allows to create a copy (or snapshot) of the repository that can be modified in parallel without altering the main set. Since the version control system has recorded every change so far, it knows how each file has been altered. By merging the branch with the trunk or master, the version control tool will attempt to seamlessly merge each file and line of code automatically. Once a branch is merged it then updates the trunk or master with the latest files.

In some cases, the version control system might not be able to figure out which change to apply between two revisions when doing a merge. If this happens a conflict will arise. A conflict in this scenario is the same as the conflict mentioned above and requires manual intervention to decide which files or lines of code should remain.

METHODS OF VERSION CONTROL

Now the question arises: why there is a need of version control & how it can be performed? As software is developed and deployed, it is extremely common for multiple versions of the same software to be deployed in different sites, and for the software's developers to be working privately on updates. Bugs and other issues with software are often only present in certain versions (because of the fixing of some problems and the introduction of others as the program evolves). Therefore, for the purposes of locating and fixing bugs, it is vitally important for the debugger to be able to retrieve and run different versions of the software to determine in which version(s) the problem occurs. It may also be necessary to develop two versions of the software concurrently, where one version has bugs fixed, but no new features, while the other version is where new features are worked on.

At the simplest level, developers can simply retain multiple copies of the different versions of the program, and number them appropriately. This simple approach has been used on many large software projects. But this method requires a lot of self-discipline on the part of developers, and often leads to mistakes. Consequently, systems to automate some or all of the revision control process have been developed.

In most software development projects, multiple developers work on the program at the same time. If two developers try to change the same file at the same time, without some method of managing access the developers may well end up overwriting each other's work. Most revision control systems solve this in one of two ways. This is only a problem for centralized revision control systems, since distributed systems inherently allow multiple simultaneous editing.

Some systems prevent concurrent access problems, by simply locking files so that only one developer at a time has write access to the central repository copies of those files. Others, such as Subversion, allow multiple developers to be editing the same file at the same time, and provide facilities to merge changes later. There are two techniques through which one can perform version control i.e. version control by hand and automated version control.

Manual Version Control

The most primitive but very common method is hand-hacking. One can snapshot the project periodically by manually copying everything in it to a backup. Also history comments can be included in source files. Verbal or email arrangements can be made with other developers to keep their hands off certain files while hacking them. The hidden costs of this hand-hacking method are high, especially when it breaks down. The procedures take time and concentration, they're prone to error, and tend to get slipped under pressure. As with most hand-hacking, this method does not scale well and also it is very time consuming. It restricts the granularity of change tracking, and tends to lose metadata details such as the order of changes, who did them, and why.

Automated Version Control

To avoid these problems, a version-control system (VCS) which is a set of programs that automates away most of the steps involved in keeping an annotated history of project and avoid modification conflicts, can be used. Most VCSs share the same basic logic. To start with, one has to register a collection of source files, that is, telling VCS to start archive files describing their change histories.

Thereafter, when a user wants to edit one of these files, he/she has to check out the file by creating it's working copy. When changes are done, check in the file, add changes to the archive, releasing the lock, and entering a change comment explaining what he/she did.

VCSs have their problems. The biggest one is that using a VCS involves extra steps every time we want to edit a file. Another problem is that some kinds of natural operations tend to confuse VCSs. For example, renaming files is a notorious trouble spot; also, it's not easy to ensure that a file's version history will be carried automatically along with it when it is renamed. Renaming problems are particularly difficult to resolve when the VCS support branching.

Despite these difficulties, VCSs are a huge boon to productivity and code quality in many ways, even for small single-developer projects. They help a lot in recovering from mistakes. They make programmers free to experiment by guaranteeing that reversion to a known-good state will always be easy.

TOOLS FOR AUTOMATED VERSION CONTROL

Automated version control tools are available in two categories: non-commercial tools and commercial tools. Some prominent non-commercial tools are: CVS, PRCS, Aegis, RCS, Subversion, TortoiseCVS, WinCVS whereas BitKeeper, ClearCase, Perforce, Synergy, QVCS, SourceSafe are some commercial tools.

- **CVS:** Concurrent Version System (CVS) provides multiple user checkouts & merge, and a client-server model. It is available on most Linux distributions. There are a variety of graphical front-ends to CVS which are compatible on Win95/NT (CVS).
- **Subversion:** It is a newer open source version control system, designed to be a better

system than CVS. It has most of the features of CVS and a similar interface, but also several improved features such as true atomic commits, faster and simpler branching and directory versioning. It is compatible with GNU/UNIX/Linux/Windows/MacOS/X (SVN).

- **Aegis:** It is a transaction-based software configuration management system, or, more simply, a source-code control system with configuration management features like enforced testing and auditing (AGS).
- **PRCS:** Project Revision Control System (PRCS), is the front end to a set of tools that (like CVS) provide a way to deal with sets of files and directories as an entity, preserving coherent versions of the entire set. It is easier to use than CVS and higher performance too. But currently, it lacks network features, although these are being developed (PRC).
- **RCS:** Revision Control System (RCS), is an industry standard collection of tools providing basic file locking and version control mechanisms. Its strength and durability are indicated by the fact that almost all other version control tools use RCS as their low-level interface. It is not client-server. It is available on all Linux distributions (Louridas, 2006), (RCS).
- **SCCS:** Source Code Control System (SCCS), is considered by many to be obsolete, but still has many active fans, and is in active development, in the form of GNU CSSC. The SCCS command line is standardized in the Single UNIX Specification, Version 2 (Rochkind, 1975).
- **Tortoise CVS:** This tool integrates with Windows explorer to be able to check in and check out files to a CVS system (TVS).
- **WINCVS:** It provides a GUI for the CVS system that allows clients on Windows, MAC and Unix/Linux to easily make use of a CVS system on remote systems (WVS).

- **BitKeeper:** It is a scalable configuration management system, supporting globally distributed development, disconnected operation, compressed repositories and change sets (BIT).
- **ClearCase:** It is an enterprise version control system from Rational Corporation. It is integrated with their ClearQuest tool for defect and change tracking (CLC).
- **Perforce:** It supports client-server architecture and optimized for fast and easy configuration and use. It can also be integrated with graphical clients like Photoshop, Maya and 3ds max (PER).

SELECTION OF VERSION CONTROL SYSTEM

The selection of version control system depends on various factors which also include the operating environment. It might be the case that one is already installed and ready to run—probably CVS (Concurrent Versions System) or RCS (Revision Control System). If not, there is a variety of VCS available. One can safely pick a suitable free, open source system, as many multimillion-line projects have relied on such systems for more than a decade. If someone can spend some cash, then there are several commercial systems in the market, which offer additional features and a more polished interface.

Since a significant number of different version control tools are available, it is probably worth mentioning why we selected subversion. The subversion project was started by a team of developers who had extensive experience with the Concurrent Version System (CVS). Subversion is a relatively new open source version control system designed to be the successor to CVS. The designers set out to win the hearts of CVS users in two ways: by creating an system with a design similar to CVS, and by attempting to fix most of CVS's noticeable flaws. While the result isn't necessarily the next great evolution in version control design, but, Subversion is proving to be very powerful, very usable, and very flexible.

Installing a VCS typically involves setting up a repository, the location where the definitive version of source code and its changes will reside (Spinellis, 2005) Subversion is a free/open-source version control system. It manages files and directories over time. A tree of files is placed into a central repository. The repository is much like an ordinary file server, except that it remembers every change ever made to files and directories. This allows us to recover older versions of data, or examine the history of how data changed. In this regard, many people think of a version control system as a sort of "time machine".

Subversion can access its repository across networks, which allows it to be used by people on different computers. Different people can make the modifications and manage the same set of data from their respective locations. Progress can occur more quickly without a single conduit through which all modifications must occur. As the work is versioned, there is no need to fear that quality is the trade-off for losing that standard—if some incorrect change is made to the data, just undo that change.

Some version control systems are also software configuration management (SCM) systems. These systems are specifically tailored to manage trees of source code, and have many features that are specific to software development—such as natively understanding programming languages, or supplying tools for building software. Subversion, however, is not one of these systems. It is a general system that can be used to manage any collection of files, which could be a source code or anything from grocery shopping lists to banks data base or digital video mixdowns and beyond (Collins, 2004).

WHY SUBVERSION?

Subversion is a successor of CVS. CVS was a version control tool used by majority of users who want to work on shared data. So Subversion took the same path and tried to win the hearts of CVS users in two ways: by creating an Open-Source system with a design similar to CVS and by attempting to fix most of CVS's Noticeable flaws.

What is Subversion?

Subversion is a free/open source version Control system (Nagel, 2005), (Collins, 2004). It manages files and directories over time. Subversion can access its repository across networks, which allows it to be used by people on different computers. Different people can make the modifications and manage the same set of data from their respective locations. Progress can occur more quickly without a single conduit through which all modifications must occur. As the work is versioned, there is no need to fear that quality is the trade-off for losing that standard if some incorrect change is made to the data, just undo that change. It manages files & directories over time.

The main characteristics of automated version control system using Subversion are:

- **Directory Versioning:** Subversion implements a "virtual" versioned file system that tracks changes to whole directory trees over time. Files and directories are versioned and history is preserved correctly.
- **True Version History:** With Subversion, one can add, delete, copy, and rename both files and directories, and every newly added file begins with a fresh, clean history.
- **Atomic Commits:** Subversion allows developers to construct and commit changes as logical chunks, and prevents problems that can occur when only a portion of a set of changes is successfully sent to the repository.

- **Versioned Metadata:** Files and directories can also have metadata associated with them. One can create and store any arbitrary key/value pairs. Properties are versioned over time, just like file contents and can be merged with newer revisions.
- **Choice of Network Layers:** Automated version control tools have an abstracted notion of repository access, making it easy for people to implement new network mechanisms. As an instance, Subversion can be plugged into the Apache HTTP Server as an extension module.
- **Efficient Branching and Tagging:** The cost of branching and tagging need not be proportional to the project size. Subversion creates branches and tags by simply copying the project, using a mechanism similar to a hard-link.
- **True Cross-Platform Support:** Mostly version control tools have cross-platform support. Subversion is also available for a wide variety of platforms. The server also works well on Windows. This makes easy for users that don't have a UNIX server available and makes it much easier to get started.

Working with Subversion

The basic Version Control (VC) idea is to separate the files that programmers work on, called working copies, from the master copies of the same files, which are stored in a repository. The programmers never work on the repository. They check out their working copies from the repository, make changes, and then check in (commit) their changes. Every time a programmer commits a file, the VC system creates a new version in the repository. In this way, the repository contains all versions of a file.

This doesn't waste: VC systems are cautious, storing only the differences between successive versions. Because "version" also refers to a spe-cific software product release, VC systems often use "revision" to refer to the successive versions of a VC file.

When two or more programmers want to use the same version, the potential for conflicts arises. There are two approaches through which these conflicts can handle. First is: lock-modify-unlock model, in which, developers can get a lock on any file they wish to change. For as long as a developer has the file's lock, no one else can change the file, although it's possible to check it out (say, for viewing or compilation). When the developer with the lock finishes working on the file, he or she commits the changes to the repository and unlocks the file.

The second approach is: copy-modify-merge model, in which, developers are always free to modify their working copies. If conflicting modifications appear, the VC system alerts the developers of the conflict, and they must resolve it by merging the modifications.

The lock-modify-unlock model is simple but restrictive. It's especially cumbersome in distributed development, when different people in different geographic locations and possibly different time zones work on the same project. The copy-modify-merge model is more open, but it requires developers to work around conflicts cordially. Subversion employs the copy-modify-merge model (Collins, 2004), (Louridas, 2006).

DOS Prompt Working with Subversion

To start work with subversion, first thing to be done is a need to create a repository. Create an empty directory for the repository and then tell subversion to create a new repository in the directory. One can use following commands (for Windows) to create a repository:

```
mkdir c:\ svn-repos
svnadmin create c:\svn-repos
```

After creating repository, import project files into the repository using following command:

```
svn import path URL
```

The import keyword tells Subversion that some files are going to import in repository. The parameter URL describes the fact where files are to be imported. Subversion responds by displaying a message that it has added files from a given path and has committed the change into the repository.

To start working with the project files stored in the repository, a working copy of the project files must be prepared. Suppose the project is called newproject. One can get a working copy by using the svn checkout command:

```
svn checkout  url...path
```

For example:

```
C:\work>svn co file:///c:/svn-repos/
project newproject
```

This command creates a new directory called newproject in the current directory and populates it with working copies of all the project files in the repository.

All Subversion commands start with svn, followed by the svn operation's name and target, usually a set of files or directories. After making changes, save the latest version in the repository with the command svn commit. For example: you are working on the file named day.txt. The command would be:

```
svn commit  day.txt
```

A log message can also be added describing the changes here by using the syntax:

```
svn commit -m "conflict removed" day.
txt
```

With the execution of this command, Subversion adds a new version of the file to the repository. Actually, it stores the current version of the file and the differences between the current version and the previous one. It does this process at each and every commit, thus maintaining a complete history of the file.

Suppose one of our colleagues has committed a newer version in the meantime. Subversion then alerts us that commit is not possible, and we must reconcile the differences between the latest repository version and our working copy. To bring the working copy up to date with respect to the repository, update command can be used:

```
svn update day.txt
```

If Subversion can reconcile the differences without conflict, it will do so automatically, and then commit can be done. Otherwise, it will change our working copy, demarcating the changes between it and the repository. It's up to our colleague and us to edit the file, fix the conflicts, and then proceed to commit. One can find the differences between any two versions with the svn diff command. svn diff command shows the changes between the repository version of the file and local file.

At any point in a file's history, one can start a parallel development. Suppose you have shipped your software and are now actively working on the next version. And suppose there is a bug in the shipped version. In this situation, you can go back to that version and create a branch on which you can incorporate the bug fix. Figure 1 shows the evolution of a file that has two branches and one main line (known as trunk). As the figure shows, changes in the branch can be merged with the trunk.

Branches aren't only used for bug fixes. These can be used for other purposes like you can put each release of a project onto a separate branch. The release branch can contain one or more releases i.e. points at which the project is shipped.

Figure 1. A subversion branching example

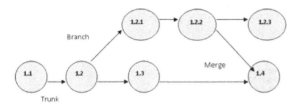

You can use tags here to define these points. The facility of using tag is of great use. Actually, a tag refers to a symbolic name for a set of files, each with a particular revision number. Tags are helpful when you want to pick and choose a particular version of project components to be packaged together during a release.

Subversion has many more features, including Subversion commands to add new project files and directories (svn add), to remove a file from a project (svn delete), and to import a directory structure into Subversion and start a new project (svn import). For tracking purposes, Subversion keeps a complete log history for each file and offers commands to examine the log for who did what and when at different levels of detail (svn log). To print the status of working copy files and directories, it offers svn status command (Collins, 2004).

CASE STUDY

A case study has been made on Subversion version control tool. Basically firstly, a text file is created and then some modifications are made to its content and it is saved. Now this new file's contents are different from older one. The changes are committed. So the user cannot view the older contents. But with the help of Subversion version control tool, the user can view the differences between the two files as well as the user can merge these two files also. Merging of the two files are important because many a times two persons may unknowingly change the contents of the file atomically but one after the other and changes of first user may be not retained after the changes of the second one. So in order to keep both users changes, merging can be used.

Similar operations can be performed on Word document also. Figure 2 shows the content of the file originally and Figure 3 shows the contents of the file after some contents are removed. So if any user wants to view the original contents as they are not there in modified version of that file, that user may user svn diff tool for this purpose. This is shown in Figure 4. Now if a user wants to merge the contents of the two files then svn merge tool can be used as shown in Figure 5. Figure 6 shows the log maintained by Subversion. In the log window, it shows the special sign that show file modified, newly created, file deleted. Other columns for the author, date and time of creation/modification/deletion and the last column for the message attached with it.

Each revision graph node represents a revision in the repository where something changed in the tree (Figure 7). Different types of node can be distinguished by shape and colour. Items which have been added or created by copying another

Figure 2. First.docx original file

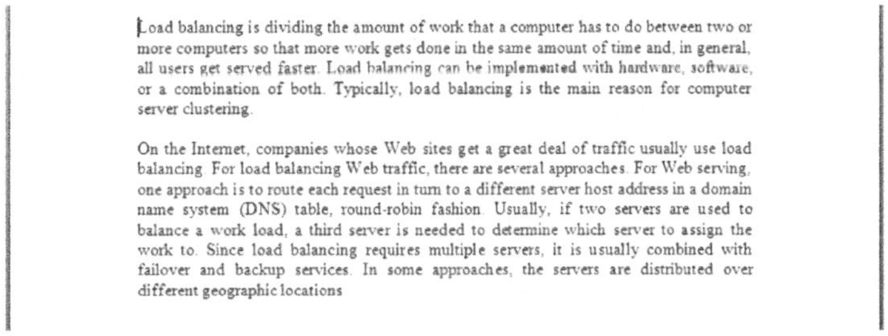

Load balancing is dividing the amount of work that a computer has to do between two or more computers so that more work gets done in the same amount of time and, in general, all users get served faster. Load balancing can be implemented with hardware, software, or a combination of both. Typically, load balancing is the main reason for computer server clustering.

On the Internet, companies whose Web sites get a great deal of traffic usually use load balancing. For load balancing Web traffic, there are several approaches. For Web serving, one approach is to route each request in turn to a different server host address in a domain name system (DNS) table, round-robin fashion. Usually, if two servers are used to balance a work load, a third server is needed to determine which server to assign the work to. Since load balancing requires multiple servers, it is usually combined with failover and backup services. In some approaches, the servers are distributed over different geographic locations.

Figure 3. First.docx file modified and saved

Load balancing is dividing the amount of work that a computer has to do between two or more computers so that more work gets done in the same amount of time and, in general, all users get served faster. Load balancing can be implemented with hardware, software, or a combination of both. Typically, load balancing is the main reason for computer server clustering.

Figure 4. The svn diff tool showing the difference between the two files

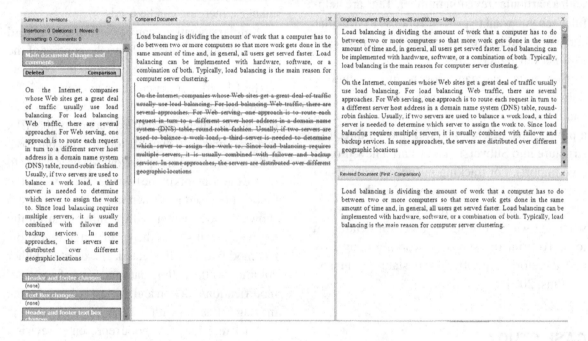

Figure 5. The merged file done with svn merge tool

Load balancing is dividing the amount of work that a computer has to do between two or more computers so that more work gets done in the same amount of time and, in general, all users get served faster. Load balancing can be implemented with hardware, software, or a combination of both. Typically, load balancing is the main reason for computer server clustering.

On the Internet, companies whose Web sites get a great deal of traffic usually use load balancing. For load balancing Web traffic, there are several approaches. For Web serving, one approach is to route each request in turn to a different server host address in a domain name system (DNS) table, round-robin fashion. Usually, if two servers are used to balance a work load, a third server is needed to determine which server to assign the work to. Since load balancing requires multiple servers, it is usually combined with failover and backup services. In some approaches, the servers are distributed over different geographic locations

Figure 6. The log maintained by the svn tool

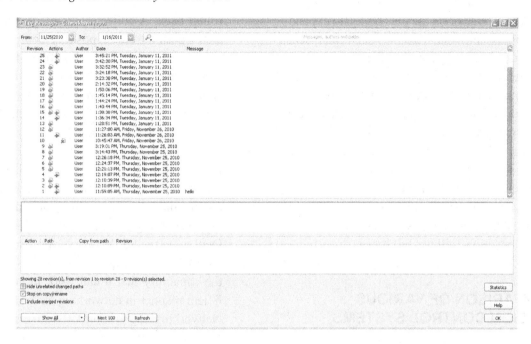

Figure 7. The revision graph by the svn tool

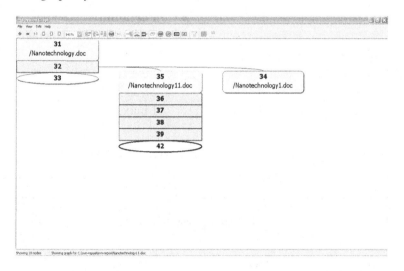

file/folder are shown using a rounded rectangle. The default colour is green. Deleted items e.g. a branch which is no longer required, are shown using an octagon (rectangle with corners cut off). The default colour is red. All other items are shown using a plain rectangle. If two revisions are selected (Use Ctrl-left click), use the context menu to show the differences between these revisions. To show differences as at the branch creation points can be chosen, but usually the differences are shown at the branch end points, i.e. at the HEAD revision. A large tree can be difficult to navigate and sometimes parts of it can be hidden, or break it down into a forest of smaller trees. A user can click on the minus button to collapse the attached sub-tree or on the plus button to expand a collapsed tree. When a tree has been collapsed, this button remains visible to indicate the hidden sub-tree. User can click on the cross button to split the attached sub-tree and show it as a separate tree on the graph. If a user click on the circle button, a split tree can be reattached. When a tree has been split away, this button remains visible to indicate that there is a separate sub-tree. If a user clicks on the graph background for the main context menu, it offers options to expand all and Join all. If no branch has been collapsed or split, the context menu will not be shown.

COMPARISON OF VARIOUS VERSION CONTROL SYSTEMS

Various version control systems are taken to compare with Subversion on the basis of following parameters (Table 1):

- **Atomic Commit:** Subversion uses a database trisection analogy when a user commits a change to the repository, making sure that either the entire change is successfully committed or it's aborted and rolled back. A collection of modifications either goes into the repository completely, or not at all. This allows developers to construct and commit changes as logical chunks, and prevents problems that can occur when only a portion of a set of changes is successfully sent to the repository.

- **Ease of Deployment:** Software may have a number of dependencies. So while deploying the software, one of the major concerns are that the software can be deployed easily after satisfying all the dependencies. And Deploying the Subversion is very easy.

- **Networking Support:** Subversion has the capability that it can work in very efficient manner in networking environment. Networking integration of Subversion is very good. A number of users on a network can work on the same file with the help of Subversion.

- **Portability:** Another point that is considered is that whether a version control system can work on various platforms. Subversion can work on different types of operating systems like Windows, Unix/Linux.

Table 1. Comparative analysis of various version control systems (CMPa), (CMPb)

NAME OF VCS	FEATURES								
	Repository Model	License	Cost	Programming Language	Atomic Commit	Networking support	Ease of Deployment	Intelligent Merging after Moves or Renames	Portability
Bazaar	Distributed	GPL	Free	Python, C	Yes	Excellent	Very Easy	Yes	Python port
Bit-Keeper	Distributed	Proprietary	Non-free	C	Yes	Good	Good	Yes	Very Good
CVS	Client-server	GPL	Free	C	No	Good	Good	No	Good
Git	Distributed	GPL	Free	C, Shell Scripts	Yes	Excellent	Good	No	Not Good
Mercurial	Distributed	GPL	Free	Python, C	Yes	Excellent	Excellent	Yes	Excellent
Subversion	Client-server	Apache/BSD Style	Free	C	Yes	Very Good	Average	No	Excellent

- **Repository Model:** Centralized VCS systems are designed with the intent that there is One True Source that is Blessed, and therefore Good. All developers work (checkout) from that source, and then add (commit) their changes, which then become similarly Blessed. The only real difference between CVS, Subversion, ClearCase, Perforce, VisualSourceSafe and all the other CVCSes is in the workflow, performance, and integration that each product offers. Distributed VCS systems are designed with the intent that one repository is as good as any other, and that merges from one repository to another are just another form of communication. Any semantic value as to which repository should be trusted is imposed from the outside by process, not by the software itself.
- **License:** Some version control systems are propriety, that is, that have to be purchased before usage and some are available under General Public License (GPL). Subversion is available under GPL.

FUTURE WORK

As has been mentioned, version control is a very important activity to assess and monitor the evolution of a particular product. It becomes very essential to keep track of various versions over a period of time. This not only helps to gauge the speed of development but can also help to monitor and control the quality of the intended product. The future work will consist the working of Subversion with different available formats of files e.g. document, text, database, bitmap image etc. on a large volume of data.

CONCLUSION

In this case study, an effort has been made to understand a version control system. Among various version control systems available, Subversion has been selected on the basis of various parameters. A case study of subversion has been performed on Ms-Word Document to understand its working. It is proved that Subversion can be used for working on the same file by different users at different instances of time and still maintaining the concurrency. With the help of version control system like Subversion, changes made over a period of time can be tracked also. In order to understand the working of other available version control systems, a comparison chart has been drafted on the basis of parameters like networking support, repository model, programming language, concurrency model and ease of deployment.

REFERENCES

Aegis. (n.d.). *Version control system*. Retrieved from http://aegis.sourceforge.net

Bitkeeper. (n.d.). *Version control system*. Retrieved from http://www.bitkeeper.com

CLC. (n.d.). *ClearCase version control system*. Retrieved from http://www.clearcase.com

CMPa. (n.d.). *Better SCM Initiative Comparison (Version Control System Comparison)*. Retrieved from http://better-scm.shlomifish.org/comparison/comparison.html

CMPb. (n.d.).*Comparison between centralized and distributed version control systems*. Retrieved from http://stackoverflow.com/questions/111031/comparison-between-centralized-and-distributed-version-control-systems

Collins, B. S., Fitzpatrick, W. B., & Pilato, C. M. (2004). *Control with subversion for subversion 1.7*. O'Reilly Media.

CVS. (n.d.). *Concurrent version control systems.* Retrieved from http://www.cvshome.org

Glassy, L. (2006). Using version control to observe student software development processes. *Journal of Computing Sciences in Colleges, 21*(3), 99–106.

Haw, N. K. (2006). *Comparison of version control systems for software maintenance.* Retrieved from http://kevinhaw.com/Documents/ConfigMgt_Licenced.pdf

Louridas, P. (2006). Version control. *IEEE Software, 23*(1), 104–107. doi:10.1109/MS.2006.32

Nagel, W. (2005). *Subversion version control: Using the subversion version control system in development projects.* Prentice Hall Professional Technical Reference.

PER. (n.d.). *Perforce version control system.* Retrieved from http:// www.perforce.com

PRC. (n.d.). *Project revision control system.* Retrieved from http;//prcs.sourceforge.net

RCS. (n.d.). *Revision control system.* Retrieved from www.gnu.org/software/rcs

Rochkind, M. J. (1975). The source code control system. In *Proceedings of IEEE Transactions on Software Engineering,* (pp. 364-370).

Spinellis, D. (2005). Version control systems. *IEEE Software, 22*(5), 108–109. doi:10.1109/MS.2005.140

SVN. (n.d.). *Subversion version control system.* Retrieved from http://subversion.tigris.org

Tichy, W. F. (1985). RCS- A system for version control. *Software, Practice & Experience, 15*(7), 637–654. doi:10.1002/spe.4380150703

TVS. (n.d.). *Tortoise version control system.* Retrieved from http://www.tortoisecvs.org

Version Control System Comparison Matrix. (n.d.). *Comparing Plastic SCM with some popular version control systems.* Retrieved from http://www.plasticscm.com/infocenter/comparisons.aspx

WVS. (n.d.). *Windows concurrent version control system.* Retrieved from http://www.wincvs.org

ADDITIONAL READING

Candrlic, S., Pavlic, M., & Poscic, P. (2007). A comparison and the desirable features of version control tools. In *Proceedings of the ITI 2007 29th International Conference on Information Technology Interfaces,* Cavtat, Crotia, (pp. 121-126).

CCP. (n.d.). *Cope co-op, peer-to-peer version control for distributed development.* Reliable Software. Retrieved from http://www.relisoft.com/Co_op/

Conardi, R., & Westfechtel, B. (1998). Version models for software configuration management. *ACM Computing Surveys, 30*(2).

DCV. (n.d.). *Distributed concurrent version system.* Retrieved from http://en.wikipedia.org/wiki/Distributed_Concurrent_Versions_System

Dittrich, K., & Lorie, R. (1988). Version support for engineering database systems. *IEEE Transactions on Software Engineering, 14*(4), 429–437. doi:10.1109/32.4664

Gardler, R., & Mehandjiev, N. (2002). Supporting component-based software evolution. In *International Conference NetObjectDays on Objects, Components, Architectures, Services, and Applications for a Networked World,* (pp. 103–120).

Gergic, J. (2003). Towards a versioning model for component-based software assembly. In *Proceedings of the International Conference on Software Maintenance* (September 22 - 26, 2003), (p. 138). Washington, DC: IEEE Computer Society.

Green, R. (2000). *Documentation meets version control: An automated backup system for HTML-Based help* (pp. 541–548). IEEE.

Janaki Ram, D., Sreekanth, M., & Ananda Rao, A. (2000). Version management in unified modeling language. *Proceedings of 6th International Conference on Object Oriented Information Systems (OOIS 2000)*, London, (pp. 238-252).

Kaiser, G. E., & Habermann, N. (1983). An environment for system version control. In *Proceedings of 26th IEEE Computer Society Conference*. San Francisco, CA: IEEE Computer Society Press.

Katz, R. (1990). Toward a unified framework for version modelling in engineering databases. *ACM Computing Surveys, 22*(4), 375–408. doi:10.1145/98163.98172

Katz, R., Chang, E., & Bhateja, R. (1986). Version modelling concepts for computer-aided design databases. *Proceedings of the ACM-SIGMOD Conference*, Washington DC, (pp. 379-386). DOI: http://doi.acm.org/10.1145/16856.16891

Katz, R., & Lehman, T. (1984). Database support for versions and alternatives of large design files. *Proceedings of the IEEE Transactions on Software Engineering, 10*(2), 191–200. doi:10.1109/TSE.1984.5010222

Kaur, P., & Singh, H. (2008). Automated versioning mechanism in component-based systems. *CSI Communications, 32*(6), 21–28.

Kaur, P., & Singh, H. (2010). Metrics suite for component versioning control mechanism in component-based systems. *Journal of Software Engineering, 4*(3), 231-243. ISSN 1819-4311

Kaur, P., Singh, H., & Ratti, N. (2011). Document control through automated version control tools. *Apeejay Journal of Computer Science & Applications, 2011,* 159-164. ISSN:09745742

MCV. (N.D.). *Microsoft, MSDN library, component versioning.* Retrieved from http://msdn.microsoft.com/enus/library/aa309506(VS.71).aspx

Mukherjee, P., Leng, C., Terpstra, W. W., & Schurr, A. (2008). Peer-to-peer based version control. In *14th IEEE International Conference on Parallel and Distributed Systems, ICPADS '08*, 8-10 Dec. 2008, (pp. 829–834). Melbourne, VIC.

Nagel, W. (2005). *Subversion version control: Using the subversion version control system in development projectS*. Prentice Hall. ISBN 0-13-185518-2

Compilation of References

Aaen, I., Arent, J., Mathiassen, L., & Ngwenyama, O. (2001). A conceptual map of software process improvement. *Scandinavian Journal of Information Systems, 13,* 81–101.

Abadi, D. J. (2009). Data management in the cloud: Limitations and opportunities. *A Quarterly Bulletin of the Computer Society of the IEEE Technical Committee on Data Engineering, 32*(1), 3–12.

Abi-Antoun, M., Aldrich, J., Nahas, N., Schmerl, B., & Garlan, D. (2008). Differencing and merging of architectural views. *Automated Software Engineering Journal, 15*(1), 35–74. doi:10.1007/s10515-007-0023-3

Abiteboul, S., Buneman, P., & Suciu, D. (1999). *Data on the web: From relations to semistructured data and XML.* Morgan Kaufman.

Abiteboul, S., Quass, D., Mchugh, J., Widom, J., & Wiener, J. (1997). The Lorel query language for semistructured data. *International Journal on Digital Libraries, 1,* 68–88.

Adams, B., Schutter, K., Tromp, H., & Meuter, W. (2007). The evolution of the Linux build system. *ERCIM Symposium on Software Evolution,* Vol. 8.

Adams, L., Toomey, L., et al. (1999). *Distributed research teams: Meeting asynchronously in virtual space.* International Conference on System Sciences, Hawaii, FX Palo Alto Laboratory

Adomavicius, G., Sankaranarayanan, R., Sen, S., & Tuzhilin, A. (2005). Incorporating contextual information in recommender systems using a multidimensional approach. *ACM Transactions on Information Systems, 23*(1), 103–145. doi:10.1145/1055709.1055714

Adomavicius, G., & Tuzhilin, A. (2005). Toward the next generation of recommender systems: A survey of the state-of-the-art and possible extensions. *IEEE Transactions on Knowledge and Data Engineering, 17*(6), 734–749. doi:10.1109/TKDE.2005.99

Aegis. (n.d.). *Version control system.* Retrieved from http://aegis.sourceforge.net

Agarwal, S. S. (2004). *Supporting collaborative computing and interaction.* Office of Advanced Computing Research, U.S. Department of Energy.

Alexander, I. (2003). Misuse cases help to elicit non-functional requirements. *Computing & Control Engineering Journal, 14*(1), 40–45. doi:10.1049/cce:20030108

Alshayeb, M., & Li, W. (2005). An empirical study of system design instability metric and design evolution in an agile software process. *Journal of Systems and Software, 74*(3). doi:10.1016/j.jss.2004.02.002

Althoff, K., Decker, B., Hartkopf, S., Jedlitschka, A., Nick, M., & Rech, J. (2001). Experience management: The Fraunhofer IESE experience factory. In P. Perner, (Ed.), *Industrial Conference on Data Mining.* Leipzig, Germany: Institute for Computer Vision and applied Computer Sciences.

Althoff, K., Birk, A., Hartkopf, S., Muller, W., Nick, M., Surmann, D., & Tautz, C. (2000). Systematic population, utilization, and maintenance of a repository for comprehensive reuse. In Ruhe, G., & Bomarius, F. (Eds.), *SEKE 1999, LNCS* (Vol. 1756, pp. 25–50). Heidelberg, Germany: Springer.

Altmanninger, K., Seidl, M., & Wimmer, M. (2009). A survey on model versioning approaches. *International Journal of Web Information Systems*, 5(3), 271–304. doi:10.1108/17440080910983556

Alvaro, A., Santana de Almeida, E., & Lemos Meira, S. (2007). Towards a software component certification framework. In *Proceedings of Seventh International Conference on Quality Software* (QSIC 2007). ISBN 0-7695-3035-4/07

Alvaro, A., Santana de Almeida, E., & Romero de Lemos Meira, E. (2010). A software component quality framework. *SIGSOFT Software Engineering Notes, 35*, 1-18. DOI=10.1145/1668862.1668863

Anderson, B., Button, G., et al. (1993). *Supporting the design process within an organisational context.* Third European Conference on Computer-Supported Cooperative Work, Milan, Italy. Kluwer.

Angehrn, A. (2001). C-VIBE: A virtual interactive business environment addressing change management learning. *Proceedings of ICALT'2001* Madison. Retrieved from http://www.insead.fr/calt/

Antón, A., & Potts, C. (2003). Functional paleontology: The evolution of user-visible system services. *IEEE Transactions on Software Engineering*, 29(2), 151–166. doi:10.1109/TSE.2003.1178053

Apple Computer Inc. (1995). *Open doc: User manual.* Retrieved from http://opendoc.apple.com

Arlat, J. (1990). Fault injection for dependability validation: A methodology and some applications. *IEEE Transactions on Software Engineering*, 16(2), 166–182. doi:10.1109/32.44380

Armando, A., Carbone, R., Compagna, L., Li, K., & Pellegrino, G. (2010). Model-checking driven security testing of web-based applications. In *Proceedings of the 2010 Third International Conference on Software Testing, Verification, and Validation Workshops, ICSTW'10.* IEEE Computer Society Press.

Arora, M., Sarangdevot, S. S., Rathore, V. S., Deegwal, J., & Arora, S. (2011). Refactoring, way for software maintenance. *International Journal of Computer Science Issues, 8*(2). ISSN: 1694-0814

Aurum, A., Jeffery, R., Wohlin, C., & Handzic, M. (2003). *Managing software engineering knowledge.* Berlin, Germany: Springer-Verlag.

Badia, A. (2002). Conceptual modeling for semistructured data. *3rd International Conference on Web Information Systems Engineering*, (pp. 170–177).

Baker, B. S. (1995). On finding duplication and near-duplication in large software systems. In L. Wills, P. Newcomb, & E. Chikofsky (Eds.), *Second Working Conference on Reverse Engineering.* Los Alamitos, CA: IEEE Computer Society Press.

Baker, J., et al. (2011). Megastore: Providing scalable, highly available storage for interactive services. *Conference on Innovative Database Research* (CIDR 11), ACM (pp. 223-234).

Balazinska, M., Merlo, E., Dagenais, M., Lague, B., & Kontogiannis, K. (2000). Advanced clone-analysis to support object-oriented system refactoring. In *Working Conference on Reverse Engineering*, (pp. 98–107). IEEE Computer Society Press.

Banerjee, J., & Kim, W. (1987). Semantics and implementation of schema evolution in object-oriented databases. In *Proceedings of the ACM SIGMOD Conference*, 1987.

Bannon, J. L. (1986). Computer mediated communication. In Norman, D. A., & Draper, S. W. (Eds.), *User centered system design, new perspectives on human-computer interaction* (pp. 433–452). Hillsdale, NJ: Lawrence Erlbaum Associates.

Bardram, J. E. (1998). Designing for the dynamics of cooperative work activities. *Proceedings of the ACM 1996 Conference on Computer Supported Cooperative Work (CSCW '98).* New York, NY: ACM Press.

Bar-Gad, I., & Klein, A. (2002). *Developing secure web applications.* Sanctum Inc. Retrieved from http://www.cgisecurity.com/lib/WhitePaper_DevelopingSecureWebApps.pdf

Basili, V., Caldiera, G., Mcgarry, F., Pajerski, R., Page, G., & Waligora, S. (1992). *The software engineering laboratory - An operational software experience factory.* Paper presented at the 14th International Conference on Software Engineering.

Basili, V., Costa, P., Lindvall, M., Mendonca, M., & Seaman, C. (2001). *An experience management system for a software engineering research organisation*. Paper presented at the 26th Annual NASA Goddard Software Engineering Workshop.

Basili, V. R., Briand, L. C., & Melo, W. L. (1996). A validation of object-oriented design metrics as quality indicators. *IEEE Transactions on Software Engineering, 22*, 751–761. doi:10.1109/32.544352

Basili, V. R., Caldiera, G., & Rombach, H. D. (1994). The experience factory. In Marciniak, J. J. (Ed.), *Encyclopedia of software engineering (Vol. 1*, pp. 469–476). New York, NY: John Wiley & Sons.

Basili, V., & Rombach, H. D. (1991). Support for comprehensive reuse. *IEEE Software Engineering Journal, 22*(4), 303–316.

Bass, L., Buhman, C., Dorda, S., Long, F., Robert, J., Seacord, R., & Wallnau, K. (2000). *Market assessment of component-based software engineering*. Software Engineering Institute (SEI). *Technical Report, I*, 2000.

Bayles, D. (1998). *Version control within a collaborative extranet*. Prentice-Hall PTR.

Be'ery, T. N., Shulman, A., & Rachwald, R. (2011). *Imperva's Web application attack report -2011*. Retrieved from http://www.imperva.com

Beck, J. E., Stern, M., & Woolf, B. P. (1997). Using the student model to control problem difficulty. In A. Bednarik, R. (2005). *Potentials of eye-movement tracking in adaptive systems*. In the 10th International Conference on User Modeling UM2005, Edinburgh, (pp. 1-8).

Beck, K. (2000). *Extreme programming explained: Embrace change*. Reading, MA: Addison-Wesley.

Bedi, P., & Agarwal, S. (2011). Aspect-oriented mobility-aware recommender system. In *Proceedings of International Conference on World Congress on Information and Communication Technologies,* December 11-14, Mumbai, India, (pp. 191-196). IEEE Xplore.

Bedi, P., & Agarwal, S. (2011). Preference learning in aspect oriented recommender system. In *Proceedings of International Conference on Computational Intelligence and Communication Systems,* October 7-7, Gwalior, India, (pp. 611-615). IEEE Xplore.

Bedi, P., & Agarwal, S. (2011). Managing security in aspect-oriented recommender system. In *Proceedings of International Conference on Communication Systems and Network Technologies,* June 03- 05, Jammu, India, (pp. 709-713). IEEE Computer Society.

Bedi, P., Sinha, A., Agarwal, S., Awasthi, A., Prasad, G., & Saini, D. (2010). Influence of terrain on modern tactical combat: Trust-based recommender system. *Defence Science Journal, 60*(4), 405–411.

Begg, C., Cho, M., Eastwood, S., Horton, R., Moher, D., & Olkin, I. (1996). Improving the quality of reporting randomized trials (the ONSORT Statement). *Journal of the American Medical Association, 276*(8), 637–639. doi:10.1001/jama.1996.03540080059030

Bellotti, V., & MacLean, A. (n.d.). *Design space analysis (DSA)*. Retrieved from http://www.mrccbu.am.ac.uk/amodeus/summaries/DSAsummary.html

BENEVOL. (2008). *The 7th Belgian- Netherlands Software Evolution Workshop,* Eindhoven, December 11-12, 2008.

Bental, D., Cawsey, A., Pearson, J., & Jones, R. (2003). Does adapted information help patients with cancer? In Brusilovsky, P., Corbett, A., & De Rosis, F. (Eds.), *User Modeling 2003 (Vol. 2702*, pp. 288–291). Lecture Notes in Computer ScienceBerlin, Germany: Springer. doi:10.1007/3-540-44963-9_38

Benyon, D. (1993). Adaptive systems: A solution to usability problems. *User Modeling and User-Adapted Interaction, 3*, 65–87. doi:10.1007/BF01099425

Bergmann, R. (2002). *Experience management: Foundations, development methodology and internet-based applications. Lecture Notes in Artificial Intelligence (Vol. 2432)*. Berlin, Germany: Springer.

Berkovsky, S., Coombe, M., Freyne, J., Bhandari, D., & Baghaei, N. (2010). Physical activity motivating games: Virtual rewards for real activity. *Proceedings of, CHI2010*, 243–252.

Berns, G. M. (1984). Assessing software maintainability. *ACM Communications, 27*(1), 14–23. doi:10.1145/69605.357965

Bernstein, P. A. (2011). Adapting Microsoft SQL server for cloud computing. *IEEE 27th International Conference on Data Engineering* (ICDE 11) (pp. 1255-1263).

Bertolino, A., Inverardi, P., & Muccini, H. (2001). *An explorative journey from architectural tests definition down to code tests execution.* Software Engineering, 23rd International Conference on Software Engineering (ICSE'01). IEEE Computer Society Press.

Bevan, N. (1995). Measuring usability as quality of use. *Software Quality Journal, 4*, 115–130. doi:10.1007/BF00402715

Beyer, H., & Holtzblatt, K. (1998). *Contextual design: Defining customer- centered systems.* San Francisco, CA: Morgan Kaufmann Publishers, Inc.

Billsus, D., & Pazzani, M. (1998). Learning collaborative information filters. In *Proceedings of the International Conference on Machine Learning*, Madison, Wisconsin, (pp. 116-118). Morgan Kaufmann Publishers.

Binkley, A. B., & Schach, S. R. (1998). Validation of the coupling dependency metric as a predictor of run-time failures and maintenance measures. In *International Conference on Software Engineering*, (pp. 452-455).

Birk, A., Surmann, D., & Althoff, K.-D. (1999). Applications of knowledge acquisition in experimental software engineering. *International Conference on Knowledge Acquisition, Modeling and Management, LNCS, vol. 1621*, (pp. 67-84), Springer Verlag, Germany.

Bitkeeper. (n.d.). *Version control system.* Retrieved from http://www.bitkeeper.com

Boag, S., Chamberlin, D., Fernández, M. F., Florescu, D., Robie, J., & Siméon, J. (2010). *XQuery 1.0: An XML query language.* Object Management Group. Retrieved from http://www.w3.org/TR/xquery/

Boegh, J. (2006). Certifying software component attributes. *IEEE Software, 23*(3), 74–81. doi:10.1109/MS.2006.69

Boehm, B. W., Brown, J. R., Kaspar, H., Lipow, M., McLeod, G., & Merritt, M. (1978). *Characteristics of software quality.* Amsterdam, The Netherlands: North Holland.

Boger, M., Sturm, T., & Fragemann, P. (2002). Refactoring browser for UML. In *Proceedings of International Conference on eXtreme Programming and Flexible Processes in Software Engineering*, (pp. 77–81). Sardinia, Italy: Alghero.

Boland, R. J., Schwartz, D. G., et al. (1992). Sharing perspectives in distributed decision making. *Proceedings of the Conference on Computer Supported Cooperative Work CSCW 92*, Toronto, Canada. ACM Press.

Bondi, A. B. (2000). Characteristics of scalability and their impact on performance. *Proceedings of the 2nd International Workshop on Software and Performance*, ACM.

Borghoff, U. M., & Schlichter, J. H. (2000). *Computer supported cooperative work: Introduction to distributed applications.* Munich, Germany: Springer.

Boronat, A., Carsi, J. A., Ramos, I., & Letelier, P. (2007). Formal model merging applied to class diagram integration. *Electronic Notes in Theoretical Computer Science, 166*(1), 5–26. doi:10.1016/j.entcs.2006.06.013

Bose, R. P. J. C., & Srinivasan, S. H. (2005). Data mining approaches to software fault diagnoses. *Proceedings in the 15th International Workshop on Research Issues in Data Engineering.* IEEE.

Bosert, J. L. (1991). *Quality functional deployment: A practitioner's approach.* New York, NY: ASQC Quality Press.

Braa, K., & Ogrim, L. (1994). Critical view of the ISO standard for quality assurance. *Information Systems Journal, 5*, 253–269.

Brajnik, G. (2003). Comparing accessibility evaluation tools: results for a case study. *Proceedings of Symposium on Human-Computer Interaction HCITALY' 2003.*

Breivold, H. P., Chauhan, M. A., & Ali Babar, M. (2010). A systematic review of studies of open source software evolution. *Asia-Pacific Software Engineering Conference*, (pp. 356-365). 2010 Asia Pacific Software Engineering Conference, 2010.

Brereton, P., Linkman, S., Thomas, N., Begh, J., & Panfilis, S. D. (2002). Software components—Enabling a mass market. *Proceedings of the International Workshop Software Technology, & Engineering Practice* (STEP) 2002, (p. 169). IEEE CS Press.

Brooks, F. P. (1995). *The mythical man-month: Essays on software engineering* (2nd ed.). Pearson Education.

Brossler, P. (1999). Knowledge management at a software house: An experience report. In Ruhe, G., & Bomarius, F. (Eds.), *Learning Software Organizations: Methodology and Applications, SEKE '99* (pp. 163–170). Berlin, Germany: Springer-Verlag.

Brun, M., Delatour, J., & Trinquet, Y. (2008). Code generation from AADL to a real-time operating system: An experimentation feedback on the use of model transformation. In *Proceedings of the 13th IEEE International Conference on on Engineering of Complex Computer Systems* (ICECCS '08). IEEE Computer Society.

Brunil, D., Haddad, H. M., & Romero, M. (2009). Security vulnerabilities and mitigation strategies for application development. In *Sixth International Conference on Information Technology: New Generations* (pp. 235-240). Las Vegas, NV: IEEE Press.

Brunstein, A., Jacqueline, W., Naumann, A., & Krems, J. F. (2002). Learning grammar with adaptive hypertexts: Reading or searching? In P. De Bra, P. Brusilovsky, & R. Conejo (Eds.), *Proceedings of the Second International Conference, AH 2002*, Málaga, Spain, May 29-31, 2002.

Brusilovsky, P., & Millan, E. (2006). *User models for adaptive hypermedia and adaptive educational systems*. Springer.

Bucchiarone, A., Muccini, H., & Pelliccione, P. (2007). *Architecting fault-tolerant component-based systems: From requirements to testing. Electronic Notes in Theoretical Computer Science*. Elsevier.

Bunt, A. (2005). User modeling to support user customization. In *Proceedings of UM 2005, LNAI 3538*, (pp. 499-501).

Burigat, S., Chittaro, L., & Marco, L. (2005). Lecture Notes in Computer Science: *Vol. 3585. Bringing dynamic queries to mobile devices: A visual preference-based search tool for tourist decision support* (pp. 213–226). Springer. doi:10.1007/11555261_20

Burke, R., Mobasher, B., Williams, C., & Bhaumik, R. (2006). *Detecting profile injection attacks in collaborative recommender systems*. IEEE Join Conference on E-Commerce Technology and Enterprise Computing, E-Commerce and E-Services.

Burke, R., Mobasher, B., Zabicki, R., & Bhaumik, R. (2005). *Identifying attack models for secure recommendation in beyond personalization*. A Workshop on the Next Generation of Recommender systems, San Diego, CA.

Burke, R. (2002). Hybrid recommender systems: Survey and experiments. *User Modeling and User-Adaptation Interaction, 12*, 331–370. doi:10.1023/A:1021240730564

Burke, R. (2002). Hybrid recommender systems: Survey and experiments. *User Modeling and User-Adapted Interaction, 12*(4), 331–370. doi:10.1023/A:1021240730564

Burns, A., & Davies, G. (1993). *Concurrent programming*. Reading, MA: Addison Wesley.

Cardelli, L., & Ghelli, G. (2004). TQL: A query language for semistructured data based on the ambient logic. *Journal of Mathematical Structures in Computer Science, 14*(3), 285–327. doi:10.1017/S0960129504004141

Card, S. K., Moran, T. P., & Newell, A. (1986). *The psychology of human- computer interaction*. Hillsdale, NJ: Erlbaum.

Carroll, J. M. (2000). *Making use: Scenario-based design of human-computer interactions*. Cambridge, MA: MIT Press.

Carroll, J. M. (2007). *Making use is more than a matter of task analysis*. Hershey, PA: Idea Group Inc.

Carvalho, F. (2009). Towards an embedded software component quality verification framework. In *Proceedings of 14th IEEE International Conference on Engineering of Complex Computer Systems*, (pp 248-257).

Cena, F., Gena, C., & Modeo, S. (2005). How to communicate commendations: Evaluation of an adaptive annotation technique. In the *Proceedings of the Tenth IFIP TC13 International Conference on Human-Computer Interaction* (INTERACT 2005), (pp. 1030-1033).

Chang, F. (2008). Bigtable: A distributed storage system for structured data. *ACM Transactions on Computers, 26*(2). doi:doi:10.1145/1365815.1365816

Chaves, A. C. F., Vellasco, M. M. B. R., & Tanscheit, R. (2005). *Fuzzy rule extraction from support vector machines*. In Fifth International Conference on Hybrid Intelligent Systems.

Chen, M., Mishra, P., & Kalita, D. (2008). Coverage-driven automatic test generation for UML activity diagrams. In *Proceedings of the 18th ACM Great Lakes Symposium on VLSI* (GLSVLSI '08). ACM.

Chen, W., & You, M. (2003). A framework for the development of online design learning environment. In *Proceedings of the 6th Asian Design Conference: Integration of Knowledge, Kansei, and Industrial Power,* October 14-17, Tsukuba, Japan.

Cheng, B. H. C., & Atlee, J. M. (2007). Research directions in requirement engineering. In *Future of Software Engineering* (pp. 285–303). Minneapolis, MN: IEEE Press. doi:10.1109/FOSE.2007.17

Chirinos, L., Losavio, L., & Boegh, J. (2005). Characterizing a data model for software measurement. *Journal of Systems and Software, 74*(2), 207–226. doi:10.1016/j.jss.2004.01.019

Chirita, P., Nejdl, W., & Zamfir, C. (2005) Preventing shilling attacks in online recommender systems. In 7th Annual ACM International Workshop on Web Information and Data Management, New York, (pp. 67-74).

Choi, Y., Lee, S., Song, H., Park, J., & Kim, S. (2008). Practical S/W component quality evaluation model. *International Conference on Advanced Computer Technology,* (pp. 259-264).

Choudhury, S., Chaki, N., & Bhattacharya, S. (2006). GDM: A new graph based data model using functional abstraction. *Journal of Computer Science and Technology, 21*(3), 430–438. doi:10.1007/s11390-006-0430-0

Chunguang, K., Qing, M., & Hua, C. (2006). Analysis of software vulnerability. In N. Mastorakis & A. Cecchi (Eds.). Proceedings of the 5th WSEAS International Conference on Information Security and Privacy (ISP'06), (pp. 218-223). Stevens Point, WI: World Scientific and Engineering Academy and Society (WSEAS).

Chwala, N., Kevin, W., Hall, L., & Kegelmeyer, W. (2002). SMOTE: Synthetic minority over-sampling technique. *Journal of Artificial Intelligence Research, 16*, 321–357.

Ciapessoni, E., Mirandola, P., Coen-Porisini, A., Mandrioli, D., & Morzenti, A. (1999). From formal models to formally based methods: An industrial experience. *ACM Transactions on Software Engineering and Methodology, 8*(1), 79–113. doi:10.1145/295558.295566

Cichos, H., Oster, S., Lochau, M., & Schürr, A. (2011). Model-based coverage-driven test suite generation for software product lines. In J. Whittle, T. Clark, & T. Kühne (Eds.), *Proceedings of the 14th International Conference on Model Driven Engineering Languages and Systems* (MODELS'11). Springer-Verlag

Cimitile, A., & Fasolino, A. R. (1999). *A software model for impact analysis: A validation experiment.* In Sixth Working Conference on Reverse Engineering.

Clark, A., & Pradhan, D. K. (1995). Fault injection: A method for validating computer-system dependability. *Computer, 28*(6), 47–56. doi:10.1109/2.386985

Clark, K. A. (2011). Human interaction and collaborative innovation human centered design. *Lecture Notes in Computer Science, 2011*, 13–21. doi:10.1007/978-3-642-21753-1_2

CLC. (n.d.). *ClearCase version control system.* Retrieved from http://www.clearcase.com

CMPa. (n.d.). *Better SCM Initiative: Comparison (Version Control System Comparison).* Retrieved from http://better-scm.shlomifish.org/comparison/comparison.html

CMPb. (n.d.). *Comparison between centralized and distributed version control systems.* Retrieved from http://stackoverflow.com/questions/111031/comparison-between-centralized-and-distributed-version-control-systems

Cobena, G., Abiteboul, S., & Marian, A. (2002). Detecting changes in XML documents. *Proceedings of 18th International Conference on Data Engineering,* San Jose, USA, (pp. 41-52).

Coleman, D. M., Ash, D., Lowther, B., & Oman, P. W. (1994). Using metrics to evaluate software system maintainability. *IEEE Computer, 27*(8), 44–49. doi:10.1109/2.303623

Coleman, D., & Furey, D. (1996). *Collaborative infrastructures for knowledge management.* Collaborative Strategies LLC.

Collins, B. S., Fitzpatrick, W. B., & Pilato, C. M. (2004). *Control with subversion for subversion 1.7.* O'Reilly Media.

Combi, C., & Oliboni, B. (2006). Conceptual modeling of XML data. *ACM Symposium on Applied Computing*, (pp. 467 – 473).

Common Criteria Implementation Board. (1999). *Common criteria for information technology security evaluation, Part 2: Security Functional Requirements*. CCIB.

Conrad, R., Scheffner, D., & Freytag, J. C. (2000). XML conceptual modeling using UML. *19th International Conference on Conceptual Modeling*, (pp. 558-574).

Conradi, R., & Fuggetta, A. (2002). Improving software process improvement. *IEEE Software, 19*(4), 92–99.

Cooper, B. F., et al. (2008). PNUTS: Yahoo!'s hosted data serving platform. *Proceedings of the VLDB Endowment* (VLDB 08), ACM (pp. 1277-1288).

Councill, B. (2001). Third-party certification and its required elements. In *Proceedings of the 4th Workshop on Component-Based Software Engineering* (CBSE), Canada, May, 2001.

Crnkovic, I., et al. (Eds.). (2001). 4th ICSE Workshop on Component-Based Software Engineering: Component Certification and System Prediction. *Software Engineering Notes, 26*(6).

Crnkovic, I. (2001). Component-based software engineering – New challenges in software development. *Software Focus, 2*(4), 27–33. doi:10.1002/swf.45

Cross, N. (1997). Descriptive models of creative design: Application to an example. *Design Studies, 18*(4), 427–455. doi:10.1016/S0142-694X(97)00010-0

Cross, N., & Christiaans, H. (1996). *Analyzing design activity*. Chichester, UK: Wiley.

Curtis, B., & Krasner, H. (1988). A field study of the software design process for large systems. *Communications of the ACM, 31*(11), 1268–1287. doi:10.1145/50087.50089

CUS. (2010, March). *Web app security- Managing web app security risks*. CUSIP (Web App Security Working Group). Retrieved from http://www.cusip.com/cusip

CVS. (n.d.). *Concurrent version control systems*. Retrieved from http://www.cvshome.org

D'Ambros, M., Lanza, M., & Lungu, M. (2009). Visualizing co-change information with the evolution radar. *IEEE Transactions on Software Engineering, 35*(5), 720–735. doi:10.1109/TSE.2009.17

Daniel, B., et al. (2007). Automated testing of refactoring engines. *ACM SIGSOFT Symposium on Foundations of Software Engineering*, (pp. 185–194). ACM Press.

Darken, R. P., & Siebert, J. L. (1993). A tool set for navigation in virtual environments. *UIST Proceedings*, (p. 157).

Davenport, T. H., & Prusak, L. (1998). *Working knowledge: How organizations manage what they know*. Boston, MA: Harvard Business School Press.

Davis, N. (2005). *Secure software development life cycle processes: A technology scouting report*. December 2005.

DeCandia, G., et al. (2007). Dynamo: Amazon's highly available key-value store. *21st ACM SIGOPS Symposium of Operating Systems Principles* (SOSP 07), ACM (pp. 205-220).

Deissenboeck, F., Juergens, E., Lochmann, K., & Wagner, S. (2009). *Software quality models: Purposes, usage scenarios and requirements*. In 7th International Workshop on Software Quality (WoSQ '09), IEEE Computer Society.

Deissenboeck, F., Wagner, S., Pizka, M., Teuchert, S., & Girard, J.-F. (2007). An activity-based quality model for maintainability. In *International Conference on Software Maintenance, ICSM 2007* (pp. 184-193).

Demillo, R. A., Lipton, R. J., & Sayward, F. G. (1978). Hints on test data selection: Help for the practicing programmer. *Computer, 11*(4), 34–41. doi:10.1109/C-M.1978.218136

Deming, E. W. (2000). *Out of the crisis*. Cambridge, MA: The MIT Press.

Deshpande, A., & Riehle, D. (2004). The total growth of open source. *Proceedings of the Fourth conference on Open Source Systems*, (pp. 197–209). Springer Verlag.

Diallo, M. H., Romero-Mariona, J., Sim, S. E., Alspaugh, T. A., & Richardson, D. J. (2006). *A comparative evaluation of three approaches to specifying security requirements*. In 12th Working Conference on Requirements Engineering: Foundation for Software Quality (REFSQ'06). Luxembourg: Springer.

Diaz, M., & Sligo, J. (1997). How software process improvement helped Motorola. *IEEE Software, 14*, 75–81.

Dillon, A. (2000). *Group dynamics meet cognition: Combining socio-technical concepts and usability engineering in the design of information systems*. Retrieved from http://dlist.sir.arizona.edu/1282/01/Ad2000.pdf

Dong, X., Hua, W., Qiming, T., & Xiangqun, C. (2007). *Towards a software framework for building highly flexible component-based embedded operating systems*. In IFIP International Federation For Information Processing (2007).

Dray, S. M. (1997). *Structured observation: Practical methods for understanding users and their work in context*. CHI'97.

Dromey, R. G. (1996). Concerning the Chimera. *IEEE Software, 13*(1), 33–43. doi:10.1109/52.476284

Ducasse, S., Rieger, M., & Demeyer, S. (1999). A language independent approach for detecting duplicated code. In *International Conference on Software Maintenance*, (pp. 109–118).

Duggan, E. W., & Reichgelt, H. (Eds.). (2006). *Measuring information systems delivery quality*. Idea Group. doi:10.4018/978-1-59140-857-4

Dunn, M. F., & Knight, J. C. (1993). *Certification of reusable software parts*. Technical Report CS-93-41, University of Virginia, August 31, 1993.

Elmasri, R., Navathe, S. B., Somayajulu, V. L. N. D., & Gupta, K. S. (2006). *Fundamentals of database systems. Dorling Kindersley*. India: Pvt. Ltd., Licensees of Pearson Education in South Asia.

Emam, K. E. (2005). *The ROI from software quality*. Auerbach Publications, Taylor and Francis Group, LLC.

Embedded, C. M. M. I. (2001). *Controller style guidelines for production intent using Matlab, Simulink and Stateflow*. Retrieved from http://www.embeddedcmmi.at/fileadmin/docs/reports/MAAB_v1p00.pdf

Eppinger, S. D. (1991). Model-based approaches to managing concurrent engineering. *Journal of Engineering Design, 2*(4), 283–290. doi:10.1080/09544829108901686

Eppinger, S. D. (1997). Generalized models of design iteration using signal flow graphs. *Research in Engineering Design, 9*(2), 112–123. doi:10.1007/BF01596486

ESA. (2004). *Glossary of terms*. ESA Publications Division, (ECSS-P-001B). ISSN: 1028-396X

ESA. (2008). *Space management – Organisation and conduct of reviews*. ECSS Secretariat, ESA-ESTEC Requirements & Standards Division, (ECSS-M-ST-10-01C).

ESA. (2011). *Collaborative environment for space systems engineering - Statement of work*. (CDF-SOW-004-RB).

Essafi, M., Labed, L., & Ghezala, H. B. (2006). Addressing software application security issues. In *10th WSEAS International Conference on Computers* (pp. 361-366). Athens, Greece: ACM Digital Library.

Essafi, M., Labed, L., & Ghezala, H. B. (2007). S2D-Prom: A strategy oriented process model for secure software development. In *International Conference on Software Engineering Advances* (p. 24). France: IEEE Computer Society.

Fagan, M. (1976). Design and code inspections to reduce errors in program development. *IBM Systems Journal, 15*(3). doi:10.1147/sj.153.0182

Fan, J., Gao, Y., et al. (2007). Hierarchical classification for automatic image annotation. *Proceedings of the 30th Annual International ACM SIGIR Conference on Research and Development in Information Retrieval - SIGIR '07* (p. 111).

Fan, Z., & Oliveira, M. M. (2004). *A sketch-based interface for collaborative design* (p. 8).

Fenton, N., & Neil, M. (1999). A critique of software defect prediction models. *IEEE Transactions on Software Engineering, 25*(5), 675–689. doi:10.1109/32.815326

Fenton, N., & Pfleeger, S. L. (1996). *Software metrics: A rigorous and practical approach* (2nd ed.). London, UK: International Thomson Computer Press.

Fischer, M., & Gall, H. C. (2006). Evograph: A lightweight approach to evolutionary and structural analysis of large software systems. In *Proceedings of the 13th Working Conference on Reverse Engineering* (WCRE), (pp. 179–188). IEEE Computer Society.

Fitzgerald, J., & Larsen, P. G. (2006). Triumphs and challenges for model-oriented formal methods: The VDM++ experience. *Proceedings of the 2nd International Symposium on Leveraging Applications of Formal Methods, Verification and Validation*, Paphos, Cyprus, (pp. 1-4).

Fitzgerald, J., Larsen, P. G., & Sahara, S. (2008). VD-MTools: Advances in support for formal modeling in VDM. *ACM SIGPLAN Notices, 43*(2), 3–11.

Fluri, B., Wursch, M., Pinzger, M., & Gall, H. C. (2007). Change distilling: Tree differencing for fine-grained source code change extraction. *IEEE Transactions on Software Engineering, 33*(11), 725–743. doi:10.1109/TSE.2007.70731

FOR. (2010). *Optimizing the Microsoft SDL for secure development.* Whitepaper, Fortify Solutions to Strengthen and Streamline a Microsoft Security Development Lifecycle Implementation. Retrieved from http://www.fortify.com/servlet/download/public/Optimizing_the_Microsoft_SDL_for_Secure_Development.pdf

Forbes, S. (1997). *Software configuration management.* Sydney, Australia: OzmoSys.

Fowler, M. (2003). *Refactorings in alphabetical order.* Retrieved from http://www.refactoring.com/

Fowler, M., Beck, K., Brant, J., Opdyke, W., & Roberts, D. (1999). *Refactoring: Improving the design of existing code.* Addison-Wesley.

Franca, R. B., Bodeveix, J., Filali, M., Rolland, J., Chemouil, D., & Thomas, D. (2007). The AADL behaviour annex -- Experiments and roadmap. In *Proceedings of the 12th IEEE international Conference on Engineering Complex Computer Systems* (ICECCS). IEEE Computer Society.

Frost, R. (2007). Jazz and the eclipse way of collaboration. *IEEE Software, 24*(6), 114–117. doi:10.1109/MS.2007.170

Gabbard, J. L., Brown, D., & Livingston, M. A. (2011). *Usability engineering for complex adaptive systems* (pp. 513–525).

Gandotra, V., Singhal, A., & Bedi, P. (2009). Identifying security requirements hybrid technique. In *4th International Conference on Software Engineering Advances* (pp. 407-412). Porto, Portugal: IEEE Computer Society and ACM Digital Library.

Gandotra, V., Singhal, A., & Bedi, P. (2010). A step towards secure software system using fuzzy logic. In *IEEE 2nd International Conference on Computer Engineering and Technology* (pp. 417-422). China: IEEE Press.

Gandotra, V., Singhal, A., & Bedi, P. (2012). Threat-oriented security framework: A proactive approach in threat management. In *Second International Conference on Computer, Communication, Control and Information Technology.* West Bengal, India: Elsevier.

Gandotra, V., Singhal, A., & Bedi, P. (2011). Layered security architecture for threat management using multi-agent system. *ACM SIGSOFT Software Engineering Notes, 36*(5), 1–11. doi:10.1145/2020976.2020984

Garcia, A., Kulesza, U., & Lucena, C. (2005). Aspectizing multi-agent systems: From architecture to implementation. In *Software Engineering for Multi-Agent Systems III* (Vol. 3390, pp. 121–143). Lecture Notes in Computer Science Berlin, Germany: Springer-Verlag. doi:10.1007/978-3-540-31846-0_8

Garcia, A., Sant'Anna, C., Chavez, C., Silva, V., Lucena, C., & Von, S. A. (2004). Separation of concerns in multi-agent systems: An empirical study. In *Software Engineering for Multi-Agent Systems II, LNCS* (Vol. 2940, pp. 49–72). Berlin, Germany: Springer-Verlag. doi:10.1007/978-3-540-24625-1_4

Garvin, D. A. (1984). What does product quality really mean? *Sloan Management Review, 26,* 25–45.

Gaver, W. W., & Sellen, A. (1993). *One is not enough: Multiple views in a media space. ACM INTERCHI '93.* ACM Press.

GeNIe & SMILE. (n.d.). Retrieved from http://genie.sis.pitt.edu

Giesecke, S. (2003). *Clonebased Reengineering fÄur Java auf der EclipsePlattform.* Master's thesis, Carl von Ossietzky UniversitÄat Oldenburg, Germany.

Giesecke, S. (2006). Generic modelling of code clones. In *Proceedings of Duplication, Re-dundancy, and Similarity in Software,* Dagstuhl, Germany. ISSN 16824405

Girba, T. (2005). *Modeling history to understand software evolution.* PhD thesis, University of Berne.

Glass, R. L. (1996). The relationship between theory and practice in software engineering. *Communications of the ACM, 39*(11), 11–13.

Glass, R. L. (1999). The realities of software technology payoffs. *Communications of the ACM, 42,* 74–79.

Glass, R. L., Ramesh, V., & Iris, V. (2004). An analysis of research in computing disciplines. *Communications of the ACM, 47*(6), 89–94.

Glassy, L. (2006). Using version control to observe student software development processes. *Journal of Computing Sciences in Colleges, 21*(3), 99–106.

Godfrey, M. W., & German, D. M. (2008). The past, present, and future of software evolution. *Proceedings of Frontiers of Software Maintenance*, (pp. 129-138). Beijing.

Godfrey, M., & Tu, Q. (2000). Evolution in open source software: A case study. *Proceedings of the International Conference on Software Maintenance*, (pp. 131–142).

Godfrey, M., & Tu, Q. (2001). Growth, evolution, and structural change in open source software. In *Proceedings of the 4th International Workshop on Principles of Software Evolution* (IWPSE '01), (pp. 103–106). Vienna, Austria: ACM Press.

Good, N., Schafer, B., Konstan, J., Borchers, A., Sarwar, B., Herlocker, J., & Riedl, J. (1999). Combining collaborative filtering with personal agents for better recommendations. In *Conference of the American Association of Artificial Intelligence*, (pp. 186-191).

Górski, J., Rydzak, F., Breistrand, l., Sveen, F., Qian, Y., & Gonzalez, J. (2006). Exploring resilience towards risks in eoperations in the oil and gas industry. *Computer Safety, Reliability, and Security. LNCS.*

Grady, R. B. (1992). *Practical software metrics for project management and process improvement.* New Jersey, USA: Prentice Hall.

Greenberg, S., & Marwood, D. (1994). Real time groupware as a distributed system: Concurrency control and its effect on the interface. *Proceedings of the ACM Conference on Computer Supported Cooperative Work.*

Greenberg, S., & Roseman, M. (1997). *Groupware toolkits for synchronous work, trends in CSCW.* New York, NY: John Wiley & Sons.

Grinter, R. (1996). Supporting articulation work using software configuration management systems. *The Journal of Collaborative Computing, 5*, 447–465. doi:10.1007/BF00136714

Guelfi, N. (2011). A formal framework for dependability and resilience from a software engineering perspective. *Central European Journal of Computer Science, 1*(3), 294–328. doi:10.2478/s13537-011-0025-x

Günther, J., & Frankenberger, E. (1996). Investigation of individual and team design processes. In Cross, N., Christiaans, H., & Dorst, K. (Eds.), *Analysing design activity* (pp. 117–132). Chichester, UK: Wiley Press.

Gutwin, C. (1997). *Workspace awareness in real-time distributed groupware.* The University of Calgary, PhD Thesis.

Hajar, M. J., & Salama, A. M. (2011). Implementing case-based reasoning technique to software requirements specifications quality analysis. *International Journal of Advancements in Computing Technology, 3*(1), 23–31. doi:10.4156/ijact.vol3.issue1.3

Haley, C. B., Laney, R. C., Moffett, J. D., & Nuseibeh, B. (2004). The effect of trust assumptions on the elaboration of security requirements. In *12th IEEE International Conference on Requirements Engineering* (pp. 102-111). Kyoto, Japan: IEEE Computer Society Press.

Halkidis, S. T., Tsantalis, N., Chatzigeorgiou, A., & Stephanides, G. (2008). Architectural risk analysis of software systems based on security patterns. *IEEE Transactions on Dependable and Secure Computing, 5*(3), 129-142. DOI=10.1109/TDSC.2007.70240

Halstead, M. (1977). *Elements of software science.* New York, NY: Elsevier Science.

Han, J., & Kamber, M. (2006). Data mining: Concepts and techniques, 2nd ed. Elsevier publication.

Hansen, B., Rose, J., & Tjornhoj, G. (2004). Prescription, description, reflection: The shape of the software process improvement field. *International Journal of Information Management, 24*(6), 457–472.

Haw, N. K. (2006). *Comparison of version control systems for software maintenance.* Retrieved from http://kevinhaw.com/Documents/ConfigMgt_Licenced.pdf

Heineman, G. T., Councill, W. T., et al. (2000). Component-based software engineering and the issue of trust. In *Proceedings of the 22nd International Conference on Software Engineering* (ICSE), Canada, 2000, (pp. 661-664).

Heineman, G. T., & Councill, W. T. (2001). *Component-based software engineering: Putting the pieces together.* Reading, MA: Addison-Wesley.

Henninger, S., & Schlabach, J. (2001). A tool for managing software development knowledge. In Bomarius, F., & Komi-Sirvio, S. (Eds.), *PROFES 2001, LNCS (Vol. 2188,* pp. 182–195). Heidelberg, Germany: Springer.

Henry, J. (2001). *Creative management.* London, UK: Sage.

Herlea, D., & Greenberg, S. (1998). Using a groupware space for distributed requirements engineering. *Proceedings of the 7ᵗʰ Workshop on Enabling Technologies: Infrastructure for Collaborative Enterprises,* (pp. 57-62).

Herrera-Viedama, E., Pasi, G., Lopez-Herrera, A. G., & Porcel, C. (2006). Evaluating the information quality of web sites: A methodology based on fuzzy computing with words. *Journal of the American Society for Information Science and Technology, 57*(4), 538–549. doi:10.1002/asi.20308

Hessel, A., Larsen, K. G., Mikucionis, M., Nielsen, B., Pettersson, P., & Skou, A. (2008). Testing real-time systems using UPPAAL. In Hierons, R. M., Bowen, J. P., & Harman, M. (Eds.), *Formal Methods and Testing (Vol. 4949).* Lecture Notes In Computer ScienceBerlin, Germany: Springer-Verlag. doi:10.1007/978-3-540-78917-8_3

Hinchey, M. G. (2008). *Industrial-strength formal methods in practice.* Springer.

Hissam, S. A., Moreno, G. A., Stafford, J., & Wallnau, K. C. (2003). Enabling predictable assembly. *Journal of Systems and Software, 65,* 185–198. doi:10.1016/S0164-1212(02)00038-9

Hix, D., & Gabbard, J. L. (1999). *User centered design and evaluation of a realtime battlefield visualization virtual environment* (pp. 96–103). IEEE.

Hix, D., & Hartson, H. R. (1993). *User interface development: Ensuring usability through product and process.* New York, NY: John Wiley and Sons.

Holzinger, A. (2004). Application of rapid prototyping to the user interface development for a virtual medical campus. In *Proceedings of the IEEE VR'03 Conference,* (pp. 92-99). Los Angeles, CA: IEEE Computer Society Press.

Holzinger, A. (2000). Usability engineering methods for software developers. *Communications of the ACM, 48*(1), 71–74. doi:10.1145/1039539.1039541

Houdek, F., Schneider, K., & Wieser, E. (1998). *Establishing experience factories at Daimler-Benz: An experience report.* Paper presented at the 20th International Conference on Software Engineering.

Hoyle, D. (2001). *ISO 9000 quality systems handbook.* London, UK: Butterworth-Heinemann.

Humphrey, W. S. (1989). *Managing the software process.* Reading, MA, USA: Addison-Wesley.

Hussein, G. (2010). Enhanced k-means-based mobile recommender system. *International Journal of Information Studies, 2*(2).

Hymes, C. M., & Olson, G. M. (1992). Unblocking brainstorming through the use of a simple group editor. *ACM Conference on Computer-Supported Cooperative Work (CSCW'92).* ACM Press.

IBM. (2008, January). *Understanding web application security challenges.* Web Application Security Management whitepaper by IBM.

IEC 61508. (1998). Functional Safety of Electrical/Electronic/ Programmable Electronic Safety Related Systems, Int'l Electrotechnical Commission, 1998.

IEEE. (1987). *Software engineering standards.* IEEE Press.

Ignat, C. L., & Norrie, M. C. (2006). Customizable collaborative editing supporting the work processes of organizations. *Computers in Industry, 57*(8), 758–767. doi:10.1016/j.compind.2006.04.005

Inside Risks. (2007). *Communications of the ACM, 50*(8). Retrieved December 22, 2011, from http://www.csl.sri.com/users/neumann/insiderisks.html

Integrated Design Model. (n.d.). Retrieved January 10, 2012, from http://atlas.estec.esa.int/uci_wiki/ Integrated%20Design%20Model

Inzunza, S., Juarez-Ramirez, R., & Mejia, A. (2011). *Implementing user oriented interface: From user analysis to framework's components* (pp. 107–112). IEEE Computer Society Press. doi:10.1109/URKE.2011.6007858

ISO International Standard ISO/WD121199. ISO/WD121199-V4. (2001). *Software engineering –Software product evaluation- Requirements for quality of commercial off-the shelf software products (COTS) and instructions for testing*. Geneva, Switzerland: ISO.

ISO. IEC 12119. (1994). International Organization for Standardization ISO/IEC 12119, Information Technology – Software Packages – Quality Requirements and Testing, p. 16, Geneve ISO.

ISO. IEC 14598-1. (1999). *International organization for standardization ISO/IEC 14598 -1 Information technology- Software product evaluation- Part 1: General overview*. Geneva, Switzerland: ISO.

ISO. IEC 15408. (1999). *Information technology—Security techniques—Evaluation criteria for IT security*. Geneva, Switzerland: ISO.

ISO. IEC 17011. (2004). *Conformity assessment—General requirements for accreditation bodies accrediting conformity assessment bodies*. Geneva, Switzerland: ISO.

ISO. IEC 17025. (1999). *General requirements for the competence of testing and calibration laboratories*. Geneva, Switzerland: ISO.

ISO. IEC 25000. (2005). *Software engineering – Software product quality requirements and evaluation (SQuaRE): Guide to SQuaRE*. Geneva, Switzerland: ISO.

ISO. IEC 25051. (2006). *Software engineering—Software product quality requirements and evaluation (SQUARE) — Requirements for quality of commercial off-the-shelf (COTS) software product and instructions for testing*. Geneva, Switzerland: ISO.

ISO. IEC 9126-1. (2001). *Software engineering - Product quality - Part 1: Quality model*. International Standard Organization.

ISO. IEC 9126-1. (2001). *Software engineering—Software product quality—Part 1: Quality model*. Geneva, Switzerland: ISO.

Ivashkov, M., Souchkov, V., et al. (2000). *A Triz based method for intelligent design decisions*. ETRIA European TRIZ association.

Izurieta, C., & Bieman, J. (2006). The evolution of Free-BSD and Linux. *Proceedings of International Symposium on Empirical Software Engineering* (pp. 204–211).

Jacko, J. A. (2000). *The human-computer interaction handbook: Fundamentals, evolving technologies* (pp. 247–257). New York, NY: Springer.

Jacobson, I., Griss, M., & Jonsson, P. (1997). *Software reuse: Architecture, process and organization for business success*. Reading, MA: Addison-Wesley, Longman.

Jalote, P. (1994). *Fault tolerance in distributed systems*. Englewood Cliffs, NJ: Prentice Hall.

Jameson, C. Paris, & C. Tasso (Eds.), *User Modeling: Proceedings of the Sixth International Conference, UM97*, Vienna, (pp. 277-288). New York, NY: Springer.

Jang, S. R., Sun, T., & Mizutani, E. (2007). *Neuro-fuzzy and soft computing*. Pearson Education.

Jia, Y., Harman, M., & Krinke, J. (2009). *KClone: A proposed approach to fast precise code clone detection*. Workshop on Detection.

Jiang, Y., Cukic, B., & Menzies, T. (2007). Fault prediction using early lifecycle data. In *Proceedings of ISSRE 2007*, TBF.

Jiang, Y., Cukic, B., Menzies, T., & Bartlow, N. (2008). Comparing design and code metrics for software quality prediction. In *PROMISE 2008*. New York, NY: ACM. doi:10.1145/1370788.1370793

Jin, Z. (2000). *A software architecture-based testing technique*. PhD thesis, George Mason University.

Jin, Z., & Offutt, J. (2001). Deriving tests from software architectures. In *Proceedings of the 12th International Symposium on Software Reliability Engineering (ISSRE '01)*. IEEE Computer Society.

Jin, L., Zhu, H., & Hall, P. (1997). Adequate testing of hypertext. *Information and Software Technology*, *39*, 225–234. doi:10.1016/S0950-5849(96)01141-X

John, R. (1994). OpenDoc, IBM and Apple's pitfall for mega-applications. *Scientific American*, 130–131.

Jordan, J. (2001). *Collaboration in a mediated haptic environment*. Department of Computer Science, University College London.

Jung, H.-W., Kim, S.-G., & Chung, C.-S. (2004). Measuring software product quality: a survey of ISO/IEC 9126. *IEEE Software*, *21*(5), 88–92. doi:10.1109/MS.2004.1331309

Juriens, J. (2003). Lecture Notes in Computer Science: *Vol. 2863. Developing safety-critical systems development with UML* (pp. 360–372).

Jurjens, J. (2005). *Secure systems development with UML.* Springer-Verlag.

Jurjens, J. (2008). *Model-based security testing using UMLsec. Electronic Notes in Theoretical Computer Science.* Springer.

Kamiya, T., Kusumoto, S., & Inoue, K. (2002, July). CCFinder: A multilinguistic token-based code clone detection system for large scale source code. *Transactions on Software Engineering*, 28(7), 654–670. doi:10.1109/TSE.2002.1019480

Kapser, C., & Godfrey, M. (2003). *A taxonomy of clones in source code: The reengineers most wanted list.* In Working Conference on Reverse Engineering. IEEE Computer Society Press.

Kapser, C., & Godfrey, M. W. (2006). *Clones considered harmful.* In Working Conference on Reverse Engineering.

Kass, R., & Finin, T. (1988). Modeling the user in natural language systems. *Computer Linguistic Journal*, 14(3), 5–22.

Kataoka, T., Ernst, M. D., Griswold, W. G., & Notkin, D. (2001). Automated support for program refactoring using invariants. In *Proceedings of International Conference on Software Maintenance*, (pp. 736–743). IEEE Computer Society.

Kaynar, D. K., Lynch, N., Segala, R., & Vaandrager, F. (2003). Timed I/O automata: A mathematical framework for modeling and analyzing real-time systems. In *Proceedings of the 24th IEEE International Real-Time Systems Symposium* (RTSS '03). Washington, DC: IEEE Computer Society.

Khan, K. M., & Han, J. (2002). Composing security-aware software. *IEEE Software*, 19(1). doi:10.1109/52.976939

Khosgoftaar, T. M., & Munson, J. C. (1990). Predicting software development errors using software complexity metrics. *IEEE Journal on Selected Areas in Communications*, 8(2).

Khoshgoftaar, T. M., Allen, E. B., Kalaichelvan, K. S., & Goel, N. (1996). Early quality prediction: A case study in telecommunications. *IEEE Software*, 13(1). doi:10.1109/52.476287

Kiczales, G., Lamping, J., Mendhekar, A., Maeda, C., Lopes, C., Loingtier, J., & Irwin, J. (1997). *Aspect-oriented programming* (pp. 220–242). ECOOP.

Kim, B., & Li, Q. (2004). Probabilistic model estimation for collaborative filtering based on items attributes. *IEEE/WIC/ACM International Conference on Web Intelligence*, Beijing, China, (pp. 185–191).

Kim, H., & Boldyreff, C. (1996). Lecture Notes in Computer Science: *Vol. 1088. An approach to increasing software component reusability in Ada. Reliable Software Technologies –Ada-Europe'96* (pp. 89–100). Berlin, Germany: Springer.

Kitchenham, B., Linkman, S. G., Pasquini, A., & Nanni, V. (1997). The SQUID approach to defining a quality model. *Software Quality Control*, 6(3), 211–233.

Kitchenham, B., & Pfleeger, S. L. (1996). Software quality: The elusive target. *IEEE Software*, 13(1), 12–21. doi:10.1109/52.476281

Klein, M. (2002). A complex systems perspective on how agents can support collaborative design. In Gero, J. S., & Brazier, F. M. T. (Eds.), *Agents in Design 2002* (pp. 95–111).

Klein, M., & Sayama, H. (2001). What complex systems research can teach us about collaborative design. *Communications of the ACM*, 38(8), 1–8.

Kontogiannis, K., Mori, R. D., Merlo, E., Galler, M., & Bernstein, M. (1996). Pattern matching for clone and concept detection. *Automated Software Engineering*, 3(1/2), 79–108.

Koo, H.-M., & Mishra, P. (2009). Functional test generation using design and property decomposition techniques. *ACM Transactions in Embedded Computing Systems, 8*(4).

Koru, A. G., & Liu, H. (2005). An investigation of the effect of module size on defect prediction using static measures. *Proceedings of the Workshop Predictor Models in Software Engineering.*

Koza, J., & Poli, R. (2002). *A genetic programming tutorial.* Retrieved from http://www.genetic-programming.com/johnkoza.html

Krug, S. (2006). *Don't make me think! A common sense approach to web usability* (2nd ed.). Indianapolis, IN: New Riders Publishing.

Kumar, B. (2002). *Component security*. White paper.

Laguae, B., Proulx, D., Mayrand, J., Ettore, M., & Hudepohl, J. (1997). Assessing the benefits of incorporating function clone detection in a development process. In *Proceedings of the 13th International Conference on Software Maintenance (ICSM'97)*, (pp. 314-321). Bari, Italy.

Lam, S., & Riedl, J. (2004). Shilling recommender systems for fun and profit. In *13th International WWW Conference*, New York, (pp. 345-350).

Lamsweerde, A., Brohez, S., De Landtsheer, R., & Janssens, D. (2003). From system goals to intruder antigoals: Attack generation and resolution for security requirements engineering. *In Workshop on Requirements for High Assurance Systems (RHAS'03), Pre-Workshop on the 11th IEEE International Conference on Requirements Engineering* (pp. 49-56). Monterey, CA: IEEE Computer Society Press.

Land, L., Aurum, A., & Handzic, M. (2001). *Capturing implicit software engineering knowledge*. Paper presented at the 2001 Australian Software Engineering Conference.

Langelier, G., Sahraoui, H. A., & Poulin, P. (2005). Visualization based analysis of quality for large-scale software systems. In *Proceedings of 20th IEEE/ACM International Conference on Automated Software Engineering* (ASE 2005), (pp. 214–223). ACM Press.

Lanza, M. (2001). The evolution matrix: Recovering software evolution using software visualization techniques. In *Proceedings of IWPSE 2001, 4th International Workshop on Principles of Software Evolution*, (pp. 37–42). ACM Press.

Lanza, M., & Ducasse, S. (2002). Understanding software evolution using a combination of software visualization and software metrics. In *Proceedings of Langages et Modèles à Objets* (LMO'02), (pp. 135–149). Paris, France: Lavoisier.

Laprie, J., & Kanoon, K. (1996). Software reliability and system reliability. In Lyu, M. R. (Ed.), *Handbook of software reliability engineering* (Vol. 1, pp. 27–69). IEEE CS Press-McGraw Hill.

Latour, L., Wheeler, T., & Frakes, B. (1991). Descriptive and Prescriptive Aspects of the 3 C's Model: SETA1 Working Group Summary. *Ada Letters*, *XI*(3), 9–17. doi:10.1145/112630.112632

Lawrence, W. G. (1964). Creativity and the design process. *Journal of Architectural Education*, *19*, 3–4.

Leavens, G. T., & Sitaraman, M. (2000). *Foundations of component-based systems*. Cambridge, UK: Cambridge University Press.

Lédeczi, Á., Bakay, A., Maroti, M., Volgyesi, P., Nordstrom, G., Sprinkle, J., & Karsai, G. (2001). Composing domain-specific design environments. *IEEE Computer*, *34*(11), 44–51. doi:10.1109/2.963443

Lee, Y., Yang, J., & Chang, K. (2007). Metrics and Evolution in Open Source Software, Proceedings of Seventh International Conference on Quality Software (QSIC 2007), pp 191-197.

Leevers, D. (1999). *Collaboration and shared virtual environments - From metaphor to reality*. Virtual Environments and Human-Centred Computing. Retrieved November 20, 2005, from http://www.vers.co.uk/dleevers/PAPERS/bonas%20html/C%20and%20SVE%20fro%20book%20word%202000.htm

Lehman, M., Ramil, J., Wernick, P., Perry, D., & Turski, W. (1997) Metrics and laws of software evolution—The nineties view. In *Proceedings of the 4th International Software Metrics Symposium* (METRICS).

Lehman, M. (1980). On understanding laws, evolution and conservation in the large program life cycle. *Journal of Systems and Software*, *1*(3), 213–221.

Lehman, M., & Belady, L. A. (1985). *Program evolution. Processes of software change*. San Diego, CA, USA: Academic Press Professional, Inc.

Lemantia, M., Cai, Y., & MacCormack, A. (2007). Analyzing the evolution of large-scale software systems using design structure matrices and design rule theory: Two Exploratory Cases. *WICSA '08: Proceedings of the Seventh Working IEEE/IFIP Conference on Software Architecture* (WICSA 2008).

Lettnin, D., Winterholer, M., Braun, A., Gerlach, J., Ruf, J., Kropf, T., & Rosenstiel, W. (2007). Coverage driven verification applied to embedded software. In *Proceedings of the IEEE Computer Society Annual Symposium on VLSI* (ISVLSI '07). IEEE Computer Society.

Leventhal, L. M., & Barnes, J. (2008). *Usability engineering: Process, products, and examples*. Pearson/Prentice Hall.

Lewis, C., & Wharton, C. (1997). Cognitive walkthroughs. In Helander, M. (Ed.), *Handbook of human-computer interaction* (2nd ed., pp. 717–732). Amsterdam, The Netherlands: Elsevier.

Liapis, A. (2007). The designer's toolkit: A collaborative design environment to support virtual teams. In *Proceedings of the International Association for the Scientific Knowledge Conference, IASK 2007,* Oporto, Portugal.

Liapis, A. (2008). Synergy: A prototype collaborative environment to support the conceptual stages of the design process. *International Conference on Digital Interactive Media in Entertainment and Arts*, DIMEA 2008, Athens, Greece. Springer, ACM.

Lim, H., Kaynar, D., Lynch, N., & Mitra, S. (2005). Translating timed I/O automata specifications for theorem proving in PVS. In P. Pettersson & W. Yi (Eds.), *Proceedings of the Third international conference on Formal Modeling and Analysis of Timed Systems* (FORMATS'05). Springer-Verlag

Lindqvist, U., & Jonsson, E. (1998). A map of security risks associated with using COTS. *IEEE Computer, 31*(6).

Lindvall, M., Frey, M., Costa, P., & Tesoriero, R. (2001). *Lessons learned about structuring and describing experience for three experience bases.* Paper presented at the 3rd International Workshop on Advances in Learning Software Organisations.

Lipner, S. (2004). The trustworthy computing security development lifecycle. In *20th Annual Computer Security Applications Conference* (pp. 2-13). Arizona: IEEE Computer Society Press.

Liu, H., Lu, Y., & Yang, Q. (2006). XML conceptual modeling with XUML. *28th International Conference on Software Engineering*, (pp. 973–976).

Liu, H., Li, G., Ma, Z. Y., & Shao, W. Z. (2008). Conflict-aware schedule of software refactorings. *IET Software, 2*(5), 446–460. doi:10.1049/iet-sen:20070033

Li, W., Shim, J., & Candan, K. S. (2002). WebDB: A system for querying semi-structured data on the web. *Journal of Visual Languages and Computing, 13*, 3–33. doi:10.1006/jvlc.2001.0225

Li, Z., Lu, S., Myagmar, S., & Zhou, Y. (2006). CP-miner: Finding copy-paste and related bugs in large-scale software code. *IEEE Transactions on Software Engineering, 32*(3), 176–192. doi:10.1109/TSE.2006.28

Losavio, F., Chirinos, L., Lévy, N., & Ramdane-Cherif, A. (2003). Quality Characteristics for software architecture. *Journal of Object Technology, 2*, 133–150. doi:10.5381/jot.2003.2.2.a2

Lósio, B. F., Salgado, A. C., & GalvĐo, L. R. (2003). Conceptual modeling of XML schemas. *5th ACM International Workshop on Web Information and Data Management*, (pp. 102–105).

Louridas, P. (2006). Version control. *IEEE Software, 23*(1), 104–107. doi:10.1109/MS.2006.32

Lynch, N., & Tuttle, M. R. (1989). An introduction to input/output automata. *CWI Quarterly, 2*(3).

Maclean, A., Bellotti, V., et al. (1990). What rationale is there in design? *IFIP TC 13 Third International Conference on Human Computer Interaction - INTERACT'90.* Cambridge, UK: Elsevier.

Madan, B. B., Popsotojanova, K. G., Vaidyanathan, K., & Trivedi, K. S. (2002). Modeling and quantification of security attributes of software system. In *International Conference on Dependable Systems and Networks* (pp. 505-514). Bethesda, MD: IEEE Computer Society Press.

MAFTIA Consortium. (2003). *Conceptual model and architecture of MAFTIA (Malicious- and Accidental-Fault Tolerance for Internet Applications).* Public Deliverable, EU MAFTIA Project. Retrieved from http://spiderman-2.laas.fr/TSF/cabernet/maftia/deliverables/D21.pdf

Malek, M. (2004). Security management of Web services. *Network Operations and Management Symposium, NOMS 2004,* IEEE/IFIP, Vol. 2, (pp. 175–189).

Mamdani, E. H., & Assilian, S. (1975). An experiment in linguistics synthesis with a fuzzy logic controller. *International Journal of Man-Machine Studies, 7*(1), 2–15. doi:10.1016/S0020-7373(75)80002-2

Mani, M. (2004). EReX: A conceptual model for XML. *2nd International XML Database Symposium*, (pp. 128-142).

Marca, D. A. (2012). *SADT/IDEF0 for augmenting UML, agile and usability engineering methods.* (SADT/IDEF01-11).

Marciniak, J. J. (2002). *Encyclopaedia of software engineering* (Vol. 2). Chichester, UK: Wiley. doi:10.1002/0471028959

Marcus, A. (2002). Dare we define user-interface design? In *Proceedings of the IEEE VR'04 Conference*, (pp. 19–24). Los Angeles, CA: IEEE Computer Society Press.

Marcus, A., Sergeyev, A., Rajlich, A., & Maletic, J. I. (2004). *An information retrieval approach to concept location in source code*. In 11th Working Conference on Reverse Engineering. Washington, DC: IEEE Computer Society.

Marquis, S., Dean, T. R., & Knight, S. (2005). SCL: A language for security testing of network applications. In *Proceedings of the 2005 Conference of the Centre for Advanced Studies on Collaborative Research* (CASCON '05).

Martinez, P., Amescua, A., Garcia, J., Cuadra, D., Llorens, J., & Fuentes, J. M. … Feliu, T. S. (2005). Requirements for a knowledge management framework to be used in software intensive organizations. *IEEE International Conference on Information Reuse and Integration*, (pp. 554-559).

MathWorks. (n.d.). *Fuzzy logic toolbox for MATLAB and Simulink*. Retrieved from http://www.mathworks.com/products/fuzzylogic

Mayhew, J. D. (1997). Managing the design of the user interface. *CHI Proceedings, 13*(3), 4.

Mc Cabe, T. J. (1976). A complexity measure. *IEEE Transactions on Software Engineering, SE, 2*(4), 308–320. doi:10.1109/TSE.1976.233837

McCall, J. A., Richards, P. K., & Walters, G. F. (1977). *Factors in software quality*. Springfield, VA: National Technical Information Service.

McDermott, J., & Fox, C. (1999). Using abuse case models for security requirements analysis. In *15ᵗʰ Annual Computer Security Applications Conference* (p. 55). Arizona: IEEE Computer Society.

McGraw, G. (2006). *Software security: Building security in.* Boston, MA: Addison Wesley Software Security Series.

McHugh, J., Abiteboul, S., Goldman, R., Quass, D., & Widom, J. (1997). Lore: A database management system for semistructured data. *SIGMOD Record, 26*(3), 54–66. doi:10.1145/262762.262770

McIlroy, D. (1968). Mass-produced software components. *Proceedings of the 1st International Conference on Software Engineering*, (pp. 138–155). Garmisch, Germany.

Mead, N. R., & Mcgraw, G. (2005). A portal for software security. *IEEE Security & Privacy, 3*(4), 75–79. doi:10.1109/MSP.2005.88

Mehmood, T., Ashraf, N., Rasheed, K., & Rehman, S. (2005). Framework for modeling performance in multi agent systems (MAS) using aspect oriented programming (AOP). In the *Sixth Australasian Workshop on Software and System Architectures*, Brisbane Australia, (pp. 40-45).

Melo, W. L., Briand, L., & Basili, V. R. (1995). Measuring the impact of reuse on quality and productivity in object-oriented systems. Technical Report CS-TR-3395, University of Maryland, 1995.

Mendonca, M., Seaman, C., Basili, V., & Kim, Y. (2001). *A prototype experience management system for a software consulting organization*. Paper presented at the International Conference on Software Engineering and Knowledge Engineering.

Mens, T. (2002). A state of the art survey on software merging. *IEEE Transactions on Software Engineering, 28*(5), 449–462. doi:10.1109/TSE.2002.1000449

Mens, T., & Demeyer, S. (2001). *Future trends in software evolution metrics*. Vienna, Austria: IWPSE.

Mens, T., & Demeyer, S. (Eds.). (2008). *Software evolution*. Springer Verlag.

Mens, T., Taentzer, G., & Runge, O. (2005). Detecting structural refactoring conflicts using critical pair analysis. *Electronic Notes in Theoretical Computer Science, 127*(3), 113–128. doi:10.1016/j.entcs.2004.08.038

Mens, T., Taentzer, G., & Runge, O. (2007). Analysing refactoring dependencies using graph transformation. *Software & Systems Modeling, 6*, 269–285. doi:10.1007/s10270-006-0044-6

Mens, T., & Tourwe, T. (2004). A survey of software refactoring. *IEEE Transactions on Software Engineering, 30*, 126–139. doi:10.1109/TSE.2004.1265817

Menzies, T., Dekhtyar, A., Distefano, J., & Greenwald, J. (2007). Problems with precision: A response to comments on data mining static code attributes to learn defect predictors. *IEEE Transactions on Software Engineering, 33*(9), 637–640. doi:10.1109/TSE.2007.70721

Metros, S. E., & Hedberg, J. G. (1997). *Multimedia visual interface design*. CHI'97.

Metula, E. (2012). *Web application attacks*. NET Security User Group, from 2B Secure. Retrieved May 9, 2012, from http://www.microsoft.com/download/7/7/b/77b7a327.../m1-1p.pdf

Meyer, B. (2003). The grand challenge of trusted components. In *Proceedings of 25th International Conference on Software Engineering* (ICSE), USA, (pp. 660–667).

Michal, H., David, L., & John, V. (2009). *19 deadly sins of software security, programming flaws and how to fix them* (1st ed.). McGraw-Hill Osborne Media.

Microsoft, A. C. E. Team. (n.d.). *Microsoft threat analysis and modeling* [EB/OL]. Retrieved January 1, 2012, from http://www.microsoft.com/en-us/download/details.aspx?id=14719

Millen, D. R. (2000). Rapid ethnography: Time deepening strategies for HCI field research. *Proceedings of DIS 2000*. New York, NY: ACM.

Mishra, B., & Shukla, K. K. (2011, December). Support vector machine based fuzzy classification model for software fault prediction. *Proceeding in IICAI 2011*.

Mishra, B., & Shukla, K. K. (Sep 2011). Impact of attribute selection on defect proneness prediction in OO software. In *Proceedings of International Conference on Computer & Communication Technology* (ICCCT).

Mishra, B., & Shukla, K. K. (2011). Genetic programming based prediction of defects using static code attributes. *International Journal of Data Analysis and Information Systems, 3*(1).

Mitchell, W. J. (2004). *Challenges and opportunities for remote collaborative design*. Massachusetts Institute of Technology.

Mohagheghi, P., Conradi, R., Killi, M., & Schwarz, H. (2004). An empirical study of software reuse vs. defect-density and stability. In *ICSE '04: Proceedings of the 26th International Conference on Software Engineering*, (pp. 282–292). Washington, DC: IEEE Computer Society.

Mohagheghi, P., & Conradi, R. (2007). Quality, productivity and economic benefits of software reuse: A review of industrial studies. *Empirical Software Engineering, 12*, 471–516. doi:10.1007/s10664-007-9040-x

Montaner, M., López, B., & Rosa, J. (2003). A taxonomy of recommender agents on the internet. *Artificial Intelligence Review, 19*(4), 285–330. doi:10.1023/A:1022850703159

Mørch, A., & Stiemerlieng, O. (1998). Tailorable groupware. Issues, methods, and architectures. *ACM SIGCHI Bulletin Archive, 30*(2), 40–42.

Morris, J., Lee, G., Parker, K., Bundell, G. A., & Lam, C. P. (2001). Software component certification. *IEEE Computer, 34*.

Moses, J. (2009). Should we try to measure software quality attributes directly? *Software Quality Journal, 17*, 203–213. doi:10.1007/s11219-008-9071-6

Mouelhi, T., Fleurey, F., Baudry, B., & Traon, Y. (2008). A model-based framework for security policy specification, deployment and testing. In *Proceedings of the 11th International Conference on Model Driven Engineering Languages and Systems* (MoDELS '08).

Mouratidis, H., & Giorgini, P. (2007). Security attack testing (SAT)-Testing the security of information systems at design time. *Information Systems Journal, 32*(8).

MSD. (2010). *The Microsoft security development lifecycle* (SDL). Microsoft, Version 5.0, 2010. Retrieved from http://msdn.microsoft.com/en-us/security/cc448177.aspx

Muccini, H. (2002). *Software architecture for testing, coordination and views model checking*. PhD Thesis, University La Sapienza, Rome.

Mulder, I., & Swaak, J. (2003). ICT innovation: Starting with the team: A collaborative design workshop on selecting technology for collaboration. *Journal of Educational Technology & Society*.

Muller, M. J. (1992). Retrospective on a year of participatory design using the PICTIVE technique. *In Proceedings CHI '92: Striking a Balance - ACM Conference on Human Factors in Computing Systems,* Monterey, CA: Addison-Wesley.

Murphy-Hill, E., & Black, A. P. (2008). Refactoring tools: Fitness for purpose. *IEEE Software, 25*, 38–44. doi:10.1109/MS.2008.123

Musa, J. D., Iannino, A., & Okumoto, K. (1987). *Software reliability measurement prediction application*. New York, NY: McGraw-Hill.

Myagmar, S., Lee, A. J., & Yurcik, W. (2005). *Threat modeling as a basis for security requirements*. In IEEE Symposium on Requirement Engineering for Information Security (SREIS). Paris, France.

Nagappan, N., & Ball, T. (2006). *Explaining failures using software dependences and churn metrics*. Redmond, WA: Microsoft Research.

Nagel, W. (2005). *Subversion version control: Using the subversion version control system in development projects*. Prentice Hall Professional Technical Reference.

Najjar, R., Counsell, S., Loizou, G., & Mannock, K. (2003). The role of constructors in the context of refactoring object-oriented systems. In *Proceedings of the European Conference on Software Maintenance and Reengineering*, (pp. 111–120).

Nam, T. J., & Wright, D. (2000). *Computer support for collaborative design: Analysis of tools for an integrated collaborative design environment*. 5th Asian Design Conference.

NASA IV&V Facility. (n.d.). *Metrics data program*. Retrieved from http://promisedata.org/repository/data/cm1/cm1_bn.arff

Nat'l, I. of Standards and Technology. (May 2002). *The economic impacts of inadequate infrastructure for software testing*. Technical Report 02-3.

Natali, A. C. C., & Falbo, R. A. (2002). *Knowledge management in software engineering environments*. Paper presented at the 14th International Conference on Software Engineering and Knowledge Engineering, Ischia, Italy.

Navarro, G. (2001). A guided tour to approximate string matching. *ACM Computing Surveys*, *33*(1), 31–88. doi:10.1145/375360.375365

Neale, J. M., & Rosson, M. B. (2004). *Evaluating computer-supported cooperative work: Models and frameworks*. Conference on Computer Supported Collaborative Work, 2004. Chicago, IL: ACM.

Necasky, M. (2006). *Conceptual modeling for XML: A survey*. Tech. Report No. 2006-3, Dep. of Software Engineering, Faculty of Mathematics and Physics, Charles University, Prague.

Necasky, M. (2007). XSEM: A conceptual model for XML. *4th ACM International Asia-Pacific Conference on Conceptual Modeling*, Vol. 67, (pp. 37–48).

Neumann, L. (2007). *An analysis of e-identity organisational and technological solutions within a single European information space*. Knowledge Creation Diffusion Utilization.

Ni, W., & Ling, T. W. (2003). GLASS: A graphical query language for semi-structured data. *8th International Conference on Database Systems for Advanced Applications*, (pp. 363–370).

Nielsen, J. (1996). *The alert box*. Retrieved from http://www.useit.com/alertbox

Nielsen, J. (1998). *Using link titles to help users predict where they are going*. Retrieved from www.useit.com/altertbox/990530.html

Nielsen, J. (1998). *Content usability. NPL: Usability forum-Making webs work*. Middlesex, UK: NPL.

Nielsen, J. (1998). *Usability engineering*. Boston, MA: Academic Press.

Nielsen, J. (1999). *Designing web usability: The practice of simplicity*. Indianapolis, IN: New Riders Publishing.

Nilsson, N. J. (1998). *Artificial intelligence: A new synthesis*. San Francisco, CA: Morgan Kaufmann Inc.

Nonaka, I. (1994). A dynamic theory of organizational knowledge creation. *Organization Science*, *5*(1), 14–37.

Nuseibeh, B., & Easterbrook, S. (2000). Requirements engineering: A roadmap. *Proceedings of the Conference on the Future of Software Engineering*, Limerick, Ireland, (pp. 35-46).

O'Mahony, M., Hurley, N., Kushmerick, N., & Silvestre, G. (2004). Collaborative recommendation: A robustness analysis. *ACM Transactions on Internet Technology*, *4*(4), 344–350.

OCDS. (n.d.). *User Community Portal*. Retrieved January 10, 2012, from http://atlas.estec.esa.int/uci_wiki/tiki-index.php

Olthoff, K. G. (2001). *Observations on security requirements engineering*. In Symposium on Requirements Engineering for Information Security.

Opdahl, A. L., & Sindre, G. (2009). Experimental comparison of attack trees and misuse cases for security threat identification. *Journal of Information and Software Technology*, *51*(5). doi:10.1016/j.infsof.2008.05.013

Opdyke, W. F. (1992). *Refactoring: A program restructuring aid in designing object-oriented application frameworks*. Ph.D. thesis, University of Illinois at Urbana-Champaign.

Oracle. (1999). *Code conventions for the Java programming language*. Retrieved from http://www.oracle.com/technetwork/java/codeconv-138413.html

OWA. *The open web application security project (OWASP): Top ten project theme page*. Retrieved from http://www.owasp.org/index.php/

Pan, K., Kim, S., & Whitehead, E. (2006). Bug classification using program slicing metrics. *Proceedings of the Sixth IEEE International Workshop on Source Code Analysis and Manipulation.*

Patel, S., Stein, A., Cohen, P., Baxter, R., & Sherman, S. (1992). *Certification of reusable software components.* In WISR 5 [WIS92].

Paulk, M. C., Weber, C. V., Curtis, B., & Chrissis, M. B. (1995). *The capability maturity model for software: Guidelines for improving the software process*. Reading, MA: Addison-Wesley.

Pearson, K. (1901). On lines and planes of closest fit to systems of points in space. *Philosophical Magazine, 2*(6), 559–572.

Penichet, V. M. R., Marin, I., Gallud, J. A., Lozano, M. D., & Tesoricro, R. (2007). A classification method for CSCW systems. *Electronic Notes in Theoretical Computer Science, 168*(1), 237–247. doi:10.1016/j.entcs.2006.12.007

PER. (n.d.). *Perforce version control system*. Retrieved from http:// www.perforce.com

Perez, J. M., Berlanga, R., Aramburu, M. J., & Pedersen, T. B. (2008). Integrating data warehouses with web data: A survey. *IEEE Transactions on Knowledge and Data Engineering, 20*(7), 940–955. doi:10.1109/TKDE.2007.190746

Pérez, J., Crespo, Y., Hoffmann, B., & Mens, T. (2010). A case study to evaluate the suitability of graph transformation tools for program refactoring. *International Journal of Software Tools and Technology Transfer, 12*, 183–199. doi:10.1007/s10009-010-0153-y

Perlman, G. (1997). *Practical usability evaluation.* CHI'97.

Petrenko, A., Yevtushenko, N., & Huo, J. L. (2003). Testing transition systems with input and output testers. In D. Hogrefe & A. Wiles (Eds.), *Proceedings of the 15th IFIP International Conference on Testing of Communicating Systems* (TestCom'03), (pp. 129-145). Berlin, Germany: Springer-Verlag.

Pettorossi, A., & Proietti, M. (1996). Rules and strategies for transforming functional and logic programs. *Computing Surveys, 28*(2).

Pigoski, T. M. (1996). *Practical software maintenance: Best practices for managing your software investment.* New York, NY: Wiley Computer Publishing.

Pinelle, D., & Gutwin, C. (2003). Task analysis for groupware usability evaluation: Modeling shared-workspace tasks with the mechanics of collaboration. *Transactions on Computer-Human Interaction, 10*(4), 281–311. doi:10.1145/966930.966932

Pinsonneault, A., & Kraemer, K. L. (1989). The impact of technological support on groups: An assessment of the empirical research. *Decision Support Systems, 5*(2), 197–211. doi:10.1016/0167-9236(89)90007-9

Plowman, L., Rogers, Y., et al. (1995). What are workplace studies for? In *Proceedings of ECSCW '95 European Conference on Computer-Supported Cooperative Work.* Dordrecht, The Netherlands: Kluwer.

Popovic, V. (1996). Design activity structural categories. In Cross, N., Christiaans, H., & Dorst, K. (Eds.), *Analysing design activity* (pp. 211–224). Chichester, UK: Wiley.

Powermapper. (n.d.). *Home page*. Retrieved from www.powermapper.com

PRC. (n.d.). *Project revision control system*. Retrieved from http;//prcs.sourceforge.net

Pressman, R. S. (2001). *Software engineering*. McGraw Hill. ISBN-0-07-365578-3

Pressman, R. S. (1992). *Software engineering: A practitioner's approach*. New York, NY: McGraw-Hill.

Pretschner, A., Mouelhi, T., & Le Traon, Y. (2008). Model-based tests for access control policies. In *Proceedings of the 2008 International Conference on Software Testing, Verification, and Validation* (ICST '08). IEEE Computer Society Press

Proyova, R., Peach, B., Wicht, A., & Wetter, T. (2010). Lecture Notes in Computer Science: *Vol. 6182. Use of personal values in requirements engineering-A research preview* (pp. 17–22). Berlin, Germany: Springer.

Psaila, G. (2000). ERX: A conceptual model for XML documents. *ACM Symposium on Applied Computing*, (pp. 898-903).

Quarterman, J. S., & Wilhelm, S. (1993). *UNIX, POSIX, and open system*. Reading, MA: Addison-Wesley.

Ratzinger, J., Fischer, M., & Gall, H. (2005). Evolens: Lens-view visualizations of evolution data. In *Eighth International Workshop on Principles of Software Evolution*, (pp. 103–112).

Ravichandran, T., & Rothenberger, M. (2003). Software reuse strategies and component markets. *Communications of the ACM, 46*(8), 109–114. doi:10.1145/859670.859678

Raz, R. (2012). *Web application security: Cyber fraud & hacktivism*. Retrieved from http://chaptersinwebsecurity.blogspot.com/

RCS. (n.d.). *Revision control system*. Retrieved from www.gnu.org/software/rcs

Richardson, D. J., & Wolf, A. L. (1996). Software testing at the architectural level. In *Joint Proceedings of the Second International Software Architecture Workshop (ISAW-2) and International Workshop on Multiple Perspectives in Software Development (Viewpoints '96) on SIGSOFT '96 Workshops (ISAW '96)*

Ries, B. (2009). *SESAME - A model-driven process for the test selection of small-size safety-related embedded software*. PhD thesis, Laboratory for Advanced Software Systems, University of Luxembourg.

Rizzi, S., Abelló, A., Lechtenbörger, J., & Trujillo, J. (2006). Research in data warehouse modeling and design: Dead or alive? *9th ACM International Workshop on Data Warehousing and OLAP (DOLAP'06)*, (pp. 3–10).

Robles, G., Gonzalez-Barahona, J., & Merelo, J. (2006). Beyond source code: The importance of other artifacts in software development (A case study). *Journal of Systems and Software, 79*(9), 1233–1248. doi:10.1016/j.jss.2006.02.048

Robson, C. M. (2004). *TIOA and UPPAAL*. MIT Master thesis. Retrieved from http://dspace.mit.edu/bitstream/handle/1721.1/17979/57188153.pdf?sequence=1

Rochkind, M. J. (1975). The source code control system. In *Proceedings of IEEE Transactions on Software Engineering*, (pp. 364-370).

Rodden, T., & Mariana, J. A. (1992). Supporting cooperative applications. *Computer Supported Cooperative Work, 1*, 41–67. doi:10.1007/BF00752450

Rodriguez-Dapena, P. (1999). Software safety certification: A multidomain problem. *IEEE Software, 16*(4), 31–38. doi:10.1109/52.776946

Rojanavasu, P., Srinil, P., & Pinngern, O. (2005). New recommendation system using reinforcement learning. *Special Issue of the International Journal of the Computer, the Internet and Management, 13*.

Roshanak, R., Somo, B., Leslie, C., Nenad, M., & Leana, G. (2006). *Estimating software component reliability by leveraging architectural models*. ICSE'06. Retrieved from http://www.irisa.fr/lande/lande/icse-proceedings/icse/p853.pdf

Rosson, M. B., & Carroll, J. M. (2001). *Usability engineering: Scenario-based development of human-computer interaction*. San Francisco, CA: Morgan Kaufmann Publishers Inc.

Rus, I., & Lindvall, M. (2002). Knowledge management in software engineering. *IEEE Software, 19*(3), 26–38.

Russell, S., Binder, J., Koller, D., & Kanazawa, K. (1995). Local learning in probabilistic networks with hidden variables. In *Proceedings of the 1995 Joint International Artificial Intelligence (IJCAI'95)*, (pp. 1146–1152). Montreal, Canada.

Sahin, C., Weihrauch, C., Dimov, I. T., & Alexandrov, V. N. (2008) *A collaborative working environment for a large scale environmental model*. In 6th International Conference on Large-Scale Scientific Computing (LSSC 2007), Sozopol, Bulgaria.

Saidane, A., & Guelfi, N. (2011). Towards improving security testability of AADL architecture models. In *Proceedings of the International Conference on Network and System Security*. IEEE. Milano, 2011.

Saidane, A., & Guelfi, N. (2012). Seter: Towards architecture model based security engineering. *International Journal of Secure Software Engineering, 3*(3), 23–49. doi:10.4018/jsse.2012070102

Sametinger, J. (1997). *Software engineering with reusable components*. New York, NY: Springer-Verlag.

Sarkar, A., & Roy, S. S. (2011, July). Graph semantic based conceptual model of semi-structured data: An object oriented approach. *11th International Conference on Software Engineering Research and Practice (SERP 11, WORLDCOMP 2011)*, Vol. 1, (pp. 24–30).

Sarkar, A. (2011, November). Conceptual level design of semi-structured database system: Graph-semantic based approach. *International Journal of Advanced Computer Science and Applications, 2*(10), 112–121.

Sarkar, A., Choudhury, S., Chaki, N., & Bhattacharya, S. (2009). Conceptual level design of object oriented data warehouse: Graph semantic based model. *International Journal of Computer Science, 8*(4), 60–70.

Schafer, J. B., Konstan, J., & Riedl, J. (1999). Recommender systems in e-commerce. *Proceedings of 1st ACM Conference on Electronic Commerce*, Denver, USA, (pp. 43-51).

Schneider, K. (2000). LIDs: A light-weight approach to experience elicitation and reuse. In Bomarius, F., & Oivo, M. (Eds.), *PROFES 2000, LNCS (Vol. 1840*, pp. 407–424). Heidelberg, Germany: Springer.

Schneier, B. (2000). *Secrets and lies: Digital security in a networked world*. John Wiley & Sons.

Schulz, S., Honkola, J., & Huima, A. (2007). Towards model-based testing with architecture models. In *Proceedings of the 14th Annual IEEE International Conference and Workshops on the Engineering of Computer-Based Systems* (ECBS '07).

Sedro, N. (2001). *Experience design 1*. Indianapolis, IN: New Riders Publishing.

Seffah, A., & Metzker, E. (2009). On usability and usability engineering. *Adoption Centric Usability Engineering*, 3-13. Springerlink.

Seffah, A., & Metzger, E. (2009). *Adoption-centric usability engineering: Systematic deployment, assessment*. San Francisco, CA: Morgan Kaufmann, Inc.doi:10.1007/978-1-84800-019-3

Sengupta, A., Mohan, S., & Doshi, R. (2003). XER - Extensible entity relationship modeling. *XML 2003 Conference*, (pp. 140-154).

Shaikh, S. A., & Cerone, A. (2007). *Towards a quality model for open source software (OSS)*. Elsevier Science B.V.

Sharma, N., Singh, K., & Goyal, D. P. (2009). Knowledge management in software engineering environment: Empirical evidence from Indian software engineering firms. *Atti Della Fondazione Giorgio Ronchi, 3*, 397–406.

Sharma, N., Singh, K., & Goyal, D. P. (2009). Knowledge management in software engineering: Improving software process through managing experience. In Batra, S., & Carrillo, F. J. (Eds.), *Knowledge management and intellectual capital: Emerging perspectives* (pp. 223–235). New Delhi, India: Allied Publishers Pvt. Ltd.

Sharp, H., Robinson, H., & Segal, J. (2009). Integrating user centered design and software engineering: A role for extreme programming. *BCS-HCI Group's 7th Educators Workshop: Effective Teaching and Training in HCI, Learning and Teaching Support Network's Subject Centre for Information and Computer Science,* (pp. 98-107).

Shirazi, H. M. (2009). A new model for secure software development. *Proceedings of International Journal of Intelligent Information Technology Application, 2*, 136–143.

Shull, F. ad b., V. B., Boehm, B., Brown, A., Costa,P., M. Lindvall, Port, D., Rus, I., Tesoriero, R., and Zelkowitz, M. (2002). What we have learned about fighting defects. *Proceedings of 8th International Software Metrics Symposium,* Ottawa, Canada, (pp. 249–258). Retrieved from http: //fc-md.umd.edu/fcmd/Papers/shull defects.ps

Simon, F., Steinbruckner, F., & Lewerentz, C. (2001). Metrics based refactoring. In *Proceedings of European Conference on Software Maintenance and Reengineering*, (pp. 30–38). IEEE Computer Society.

Sindre, G., & Opdahl, A. L. (2000). Eliciting security requirements by misuse cases. In *37th International Conference on Technology of Object-Oriented Languages and Systems* (pp. 120-131). Sydney, Australia: IEEE Computer Society.

Sindre, G., & Opdahl, A. L. (2005). Eliciting security requirements with misuse cases. *Requirements Engineering*, *10*(1), 34–44. doi:10.1007/s00766-004-0194-4

Smith, G. (2000). *The object-Z specification language.* Kluwer Academic Publishers. doi:10.1007/978-1-4615-5265-9

Smith, N., Capiluppi, A., & Ramil, J. (2005). A study of open source software evolution data using qualitative simulation. *Software Process Improvement and Practice*, *10*, 287–300. doi:10.1002/spip.230

Smith, R. P., & Eppinger, S. D. (1997). Identifying controlling features of engineering design iteration. *Management Science*, *43*(3), 276–293. doi:10.1287/mnsc.43.3.276

Sodiya, A. S., Longe, H. O. D., & Fasan, O. M. (2007). Software security risk analysis using fuzzy expert system. *Journal of INFOCOMP: Journal of Computer Science*, *7*(3), 70–77.

Sohaib, O., & Khan, K. (2010). Integrating usability engineering and agile software development: A literature review. *2010 International Conference on Computer Design and Applications*, Vol. 2, (pp. 32-38).

Sommerville, I., & Rodden, T. (1994). *Requirements engineering for cooperative systems.* Retrieved September 26, 2006, from http://citeseer.ist.psu.edu/sommerville94requirements.html

SPICE. (2009). *Website.* Retrieved December 22, 2011, from http://www.sqi.gu.edu.au/Spice

Spinellis, D. (2005). Version control systems. *IEEE Software*, *22*(5), 108–109. doi:10.1109/MS.2005.140

Spool, J. M., Scanlon, T., et al. (1997). *Product usability: Survival techniques.* CHI'97.

Stafford, J., & Wallnau, K. (2001). Is third-party certification necessary? In *Proceedings of the 4th ICSE Workshop on Component-Based Software Engineering*, Toronto, Canada, (pp. 13-17).

Steve, L., & Michael, H. (2005). The trustworthy computing security development lifecycle. Retrieved from http://msdn.microsoft.com/security/default.aspx?pull=/library/en-us/dnsecure/html/sdl.asp

Steward, D. V. (1981). The design structure system: A method for managing the design of complex systems. *IEEE Transactions on Engineering Management*, *28*(3), 71–74.

Stoneburner, G., Hayden, C., & Feringa, A. (2004). *Engineering principles for information technology security. Recommendations of the National Institute of Standards and Technology, Computer Security Division.* Gaithersburg, MD: Information Technology Laboratory, National Institute of Standards and Technology.

Subramaniam, M., Xiao, L., Guo, B., & Pap, A. (2009). An approach for test selection for EFSMs using a theorem prover. In *Proceedings of the 21st IFIP WG 6.1 International Conference on Testing of Software and Communication Systems and 9th International FATES Workshop* (TESTCOM '09/FATES '09).

Subramanyam, R., & Krishnan, M. S. (2003). Empirical analysis of ck metrics for object-oriented design complexity: Implications for software defects. *IEEE Transactions on Software Engineering*, *29*, 297–310. doi:10.1109/TSE.2003.1191795

Sun, C., & Chen, D. (2002). Consistency maintenance in real-time collaborative graphics editing systems. *ACM Transactions on Computer-Human Interaction*, *9*(1), 1–41. doi:10.1145/505151.505152

Sun, Z., & Finnie, G. (2004). *Intelligent techniques in e-commerce: A case-based reasoning perspective.* Heidelberg, Germany: Springer-Verlag.

Sutherland, J. (1995). Business objects in corporate information systems. *ACM Computing Surveys*, *27*(2), 274–276. doi:10.1145/210376.210394

SVN. (n.d.). *Subversion version control system.* Retrieved from http://subversion.tigris.org

Swan, J. E., Gabbard, J. L., Hix, D., Schulman, R. S., & Kim, K. P. (2003). A comparative study of user performance in a map-based virtual environment. In *Proceedings of the IEEE VR'03 Conference*, (pp. 259-266). Los Angeles, CA: IEEE Computer Society Press.

Swiderski, F., & Snyder, W. (2004). *Threat modeling.* Redmond, WA: Microsoft Press.

SYM. (2009). *Threat activity trends- Web based attack report 2009-10.* Retrieved from http://www.symantec.com/business/threat-report/

Szyperski, C. (1999). *Component software - Beyond object-oriented programming* (2nd ed.). Addison-Wesley.

Szyperski, C. (2002). *Component software: Beyond object-oriented programming*. Reading, MA: Addison-Wesley.

Tarr, P., Ossher, H., Harrison, W., & Sutton, S. (1999). N degrees of separation: Multi dimensional separation of concerns. In *21st International Conference on Software Engineering*, (pp. 107-119).

Terveen, L. G., Sefridge, P. G., & Long, M. D. (1993). *From 'folklore' to 'living design memory'*. Paper presented at the ACM Conference on Human Factors in Computing Systems.

Tevis, J.-E. J., & Hamilton, J. A. (2004). Methods for the prevention, detection and removal of software security vulnerabilities. In *Proceedings of the 42nd Annual Southeast Regional Conference* (ACM-SE 42), (pp. 197-202). New York, NY: ACM. DOI=10.1145/986537.986583http://doi.acm.org/10.1145/986537.986583

Thomas, C., & Bevan, N. (Eds.). (1996). *Usability context analysis: A practical guide*. Teddington, UK: National Physical Laboratory.

Tian, J. (2005). *Software quality engineering: Testing, quality assurance, and quantifiable improvement*. New York, NY: John Wiley & Sons. doi:10.1002/0471722324

Tichelaar, S., Ducasse, S., Demeyer, S., & Nierstrasz, O. (2000). A meta-model for language-independent refactoring. In *Proceedings of Symposium on Principles of Software Evolution*, (pp. 157–169). IEEE Computer Society.

Tichy, W. F. (1985). RCS- A system for version control. *Software, Practice & Experience, 15*(7), 637–654. doi:10.1002/spe.4380150703

Tokuda, T., & Batory, D. S. (1995). Automated software evolution via design pattern transformations. In *Proceedings of International Symposium on Applied Corporate Computing*, 1995.

Trass, V., & Hillegersberg, J. (2000). The software component market on the Internet, current status and conditions for growth. *ACM Sigsoft Software Engineering Notes, 25*(1), 114–117. doi:10.1145/340855.341145

Tsantalis, N., & Chatzigeorgiou, A. (2009). Identification of move method refactoring opportunities. *IEEE Transactions on Software Engineering, 35*(3), 347–367. doi:10.1109/TSE.2009.1

Tumas, G., & Ricci, F. (2009). Personalized mobile city transport advisory system. In Fuchs, M., Ricci, F., & Cantoni, L. (Eds.), *Information and communication technologies in tourism* (pp. 173–184).

TVS. (n.d.). *Tortoise version control system*. Retrieved from http://www.tortoisecvs.org

Upadhyay, N., Despande, B. M., & Agrawal, V. P. (2011). Towards a software component quality model. *Journal of Advances in Computer Science and Information Technology. Communications in Computer and Information Science, 131*(3), 398–412. doi:10.1007/978-3-642-17857-3_40

Uzi Ben-Artzi, L., & Donald, S. (2003). *Web application security: A survey of prevention techniques against SQL injection*. Thesis Stockholm University/Royal Institute of Technology, June 2003.

Valerio, A., Cardino, G., & Leo, V. (2001). Improving software development practices through components. *Proceedings of the 27th Euromicro Conference 2001: A Net Odyssey* (Euromicro01), (pp. 97-103). Warsaw, Poland.

Vasa, R., Lumpe, M., & Jones, A. (2001). *Helix - Software evolution data set*. Swinburne University of Technology, 2010.

Vashisth, P., Agarwal, S., Wadhwa, B., & Bedi, P. (2011). Capturing user preferences through interactive visualization to improve recommendations. In *Proceedings of International Conference on World Conference on Information Technology*, November 23-27, Antalya, Turkey, Procedia Journal of Technology, Elsevier (Accepted).

Version Control System Comparison Matrix. (n.d.). *Comparing Plastic SCM with some popular version control systems*. Retrieved from http://www.plasticscm.com/infocenter/comparisons.aspx

Vetterling, M., Wimmel, G., & Wisspeintner, A. (2002). Secure systems development based on the common criteria: The PalME Project. In *10th ACM SIGSOFT Symposium on Foundations of Software Engineering* (pp.129-138). Charleston, SC. New York, NY: Association for Computing Machinery.

Voas, J., & Payne, J. (2000). Dependability certification of software components. *Journal of Software Systems, 52*, 165–172. doi:10.1016/S0164-1212(99)00143-0

Voas, M. J. (1998). Certifying off-the-shelf software components. *IEEE Computer, 31*(6), 53–59. doi:10.1109/2.683008

Voas, M. J. (1999). Certifying software for high-assurance environments. *IEEE Software, 16*(4), 48–54. doi:10.1109/52.776948

Voas, M. J. (2000). Developing a usage-based software certification process. *Computer, 33*(8), 32–37. doi:10.1109/2.863965

von Krogh, G., Ichijo, K., & Nonaka, I. (2000). *Enabling knowledge creation.* New York, NY: Oxford University Press.

von Oheimb, D., & Lotz, V. (2002). Formal security analysis with interacting state machines. In *Proceedings of the 7th European Symposium on Research in Computer Security* (ESORICS '02). Springer-Verlag

Wagner, S. (2009). *A Bayesian network approach to assess and predict software quality using activity-based quality models.* In International Conference on Predictor Models in Software Engineering (PROMISE '09). New York, NY: ACM.

Walker, J. (2012). *Web application security--Keeping your application safe.* Retrieved May 9. 2012, from http://ajaxexperience.techtarget.com/images/Presentations/Walker_Joe_WebAppSecurity.pdf

Wallnau, K. (2004). *Software component certification: 10 useful distinctions* (CMU/SEI-2004-TN-031). Retrieved May 2, 2012, from the http://www.sei.cmu.edu/library/abstracts/reports/04tn031.cfm

Wallnau, K. C. (2003). *Volume III: A technology for predictable assembly from certifiable components.* Software Engineering Institute (SEI), Technical Report, Vol. 03.

Wallnau, W. (2000). *Technical concepts of component-based software engineering,* 2nd ed. (Technical Report CMU/SEI-2000-TR-008, ESC-TR-2000-007).

Wang, F., Wang, S., & Ji, Y. (2009). An automatic generation method of executable test case using model-driven architecture. In *Proceedings of the 2009 Fourth International Conference on Innovative Computing, Information and Control* (ICICIC '09). IEEE Computer Society

Wang, L., Dobbie, G., Sun, J., & Groves, L. (2006). *Validating ORA-SS data models using alloy.* Australian Software Engineering Conference, 2006.

Ward, J., & Aurum, A. (2004). *Knowledge management in software engineering - Describing the process.* Paper presented at the Australian Software Engineering Conference, IEEE Computer Society, Los Alamitos.

WAS. (n.d.). *Web app security—How to minimize prevalent risk of attacks.* Retrieved from www.qualys.com

Wettel, R., & Lanza, M. (2008). *Visual exploration of large-scale system evolution.* 2008 15th Working Conference on Reverse Engineering, IEEE Computer Society Press.

Weykuer, E. J. (1988). Evaluating software complexity measures. *IEEE Transactions on Software Engineering, 14*(9), 1357–1365. doi:10.1109/32.6178

WHW. (2010). *White Hat Website security statistic report,* 10th edition. Retrieved from www.whitehatsec.com

Wikipedia. (2011). *Concurrent design facility.* Retrieved January 10, 2012, from http://en.wikipedia.org/wiki/Concurrent_Design_Facility

Wohlin, C., & Runeson, P. (1994). Certification of software components. *IEEE Transactions on Software Engineering, 20*(6), 494–499. doi:10.1109/32.295896

Wolf, J. (2002). *Thinkcycle@home: Asynchronous interface for online collaboration.*

Woodcock, J., Larsen, P. G., Bicarregui, J., & Fitzgerald, J. (2009). Formal methods: Practice and experience. *ACM Computing Surveys, 41*(4), 1–36. doi:10.1145/1592434.1592436

Wu, J., Holt, R. C., & Hassan, A. E. (2004). Exploring software evolution using spectrographs. In *Proceedings of the 11th WCRE,* (pp. 80-89).

Wu, X., Ling, T. W., Lee, M. L., & Dobbie, G. (2001). Designing semistructured databases using ORA-SS model. *2nd International Conference on Web Information Systems Engineering,* Vol. 1, (pp. 171–180).

WVR. (2009, January). Webapps vulnerability report. *Core Impact Professional.* Retrieved from http://www.coresecurity.com/files/attachments/core_impact_webapps_vulnerabilities_report.pdf

WVS. (n.d.). *Windows concurrent version control system.* Retrieved from http://www.wincvs.org

Xie, G., Chen, J., & Neamtiu, I. (2009). Towards a better understanding of software evolution: An empirical study on software evolution. *Proceedings of the International Conference on Software Maintenance.* Edmonton, Canada: IEEE Computer Society Press.

Xing, F., Guo, P., & Lyu, M. R. (2005). A novel method for early software quality prediction based on support vector machine. In *Proceedings of the 16th IEEE International Symposium on Software Reliability Engineering.*

Xiong, P., Stepien, B., & Peyton, L. (2009). *Model-based penetration test framework for web applications using TTCN-3. E-Technologies: Innovation in an Open World, Lecture Notes in Business Information Processing* (*Vol. 21*). Springer.

Xu, D., & Nygard, K. (2006). Threat-driven modeling and verification of secure software using aspect-oriented petri nets. *IEEE Transactions on Software Engineering, 32*(4), 265–278. doi:10.1109/TSE.2006.40

Yang, B., Yao, L., & Huang, H. Z. (2007). Early software quality prediction based on a fuzzy neural network model. In *Proceedings of Third International Conference on Natural Computation.*

Yang, Y., Jiao, J., Wang, H., & Xia, C. (2009). A task-deployment model for the simulation of computer network attack and defense exercises. In *Proceedings of the 2009 First IEEE International Conference on Information Science and Engineering* (ICISE '09). IEEE Computer Society.

Yasar, A. U. H., Preuveneers, D., Berbers, Y., & Bhatti, G. (2008). Best practices for software security: An overview. In *12th IEEE International Multitopic Conference* (pp. 169-173). Karachi, Pakistan: IEEE Press.

Yingfei, W., & Mingxi, T. (2002). *A collaborative platform supporting graphic pattern design and reuse of design knowledge.* Design Technology Research Centre.

Younan, Y. (2003). *An overview of common programming security vulnerabilities and possible solutions.* Master's thesis, Vrije University Brussel.

Yuan, X., Khoshgoftaar, T. M., Allen, E. B., & Ganesan, K. (2000). An application of fuzzy clustering to software quality prediction. In *Proceedings of The 3rd IEEE Symposium on Application-Specific Systems and Software Engineering Technology.*

Yu, L., Chen, K., & Ramaswamy, S. (2009). Multiple-parameter coupling metrics for layered component-based software. [Springer.]. *Software Quality Journal, 17*, 5–24. doi:10.1007/s11219-008-9052-9

Zadeh, L. A. (1965). Fuzzy sets. *Information and Control, 8*, 338–353. doi:10.1016/S0019-9958(65)90241-X

Zadeh, L. A., Klir, J. G., & Yuan, B. B. (1996). *Fuzzy sets, fuzzy logic, and fuzzy systems: Selected papers by Lofti A. Zadeh* (*Vol. 6*). London, UK: World Scientific Publishing Co Pte Ltd.

Zaphris, P., & Mtei, L. (1997). *Depth vs. breadth in the arrangement of Web links.* Retrieved from http://www.otal.umd.edu/SHORE97

Zhang, Y., Huo Zhang, L., Zhu, H., & Greenwood, S. (2001). Structure and page complexity metrics for web applications. *Proceedings of 4th Workshop on Web Engineering at 1oth WWW Conference,* Hong Kong, (pp. 72-81).

Zhang, J., Jones, N., & Pu, P. (2008). A visual interface for critiquing-based recommender systems. *EACM C, 08*, 230–239.

Zhou, C., & Kumar, R. (2009). Modeling simulink diagrams using input/output extended finite automata. In *Proceedings of the 2009 33rd Annual IEEE International Computer Software and Applications Conference* (COMPSAC '09), Vol. 2. IEEE

Zimmermann, T., Premraj, R., & Zeller, A. (2007). Predicting defects for Eclipse. *PROMISE '07: Proceedings of the Third International Workshop on Predictor Models in Software Engineering.*

Zulkernine, M. F. R., & Uddin, M. G. (2009). Towards model-based automatic testing of attack scenarios. In *Proceedings of the 28th International Conference on Computer Safety, Reliability, and Security* (SAFECOMP '09)

About the Contributors

Hardeep Singh is presently Professor, Department of Computer Science and Engineering; Director, Placement Cell and Dean, Alumni Guru Nanak Dev University, Amritsar. Having throughout first class academic career, Dr. Singh is an MS (Software Systems) from Birla Institute of Technology and Science (BITS), Pilani and has received his PhD from Guru Nanak Dev University, Amritsar, India. His career spans more than two decades' of research, research guidance at doctoral, MTech, MCA, & BTech and university teaching in field of Computer Science and Engineering. During his this professional career, he has also been visiting faculty to different universities, institutes and corporate, apart from associating as member of UGC teams, AICTE panels, governing boards of various educational institutions and member of academic bodies like Board of Studies, RDCs and Academic Councils of different universities viz. H.P. University, Shimla; Kurukshetra University, Kurukshetra; Punjab Technical University, Jalandhar; HNB Gharwal University, Srinagar, Uttrakhand; Panjab University, Chandigarh; etc. An active researcher and a prolific writer, Dr. Singh has authored five books and has contributed around 100 papers to several journals. He is also an active member many of professional societies: he is Fellow, British Computer Society (FBCS); Member, Association for Computing Machinery (ACM); Member, International Association of Engineers (IAENG); Global Member, Internet Society; Life Member, Punjab Science Congress and Computer Society of India etc. He is a frequent reviewer, discussant, and session chair for several seminars and conferences.

Kulwant Kaur is Dean, School of Information Technology, Apeejay Institute of Management Technical Campus, Jalandhar. She received Master's degree from M.B.M. Engineering College, Jai Narian Vyas University, Jodhpur. She is pursuing her PhD in Software Engineering in the Faculty of Engineering & Technology, Guru Nanak Dev University, Amritsar, India. Her career spans about two decades' of research guidance, and teaching in field of Computer Science/ Applications at Bachelor's and Master's level courses. Her expertise areas include artificial intelligence and software engineering. As a researcher, she has presented several research papers in national conferences and seminars. She has also organised national conferences and seminars. Ms. Kaur has edited two books and has contributed numerous papers to several journals and chapters to edited books. She is Life Member of Computer Society of India and Punjab Academy Sciences, Patiala.

* * *

Sumit Kr. Agarwal received his MTech degree in Information Technology from USIT, Guru Gobind Singh Indraprasth University Delhi, India in 2007 and his MSc in Information Science from Dr. Bhim Rao Ambedkar University, Agra in 2002. He is a Doctorate student in Department of Computer Science, University of Delhi. Mr. Agarwal is an Associate Member of IETE, Loadhi Road, New Delhi. His research interests include web intelligence, multi-agent systems, trust, recommender systems, and aspect-oriented programming.

Evangelos Argyzoudis holds a Master's Degree in Network Systems with Distinction and a Bachelor's degree in Computer Systems Engineering from the University of Sunderland. His employment record includes positions such as IT Specialist in the Production Support Group of the Continuous Linked Settlement project in IBM UK, System Administrator in a retail chain in Cyprus, IT Manager in Invoke SA, an IT services provider in Greece and R&D Consultant in the University of Brussels (Vrije Universiteit Brussel). Recently, Mr. Argyzoudis joined European Dynamics as an R&D Consultant where he will focus on the areas of system interoperability, Web 2.0, ambient intelligence, semantics, and e-government.

Punam Bedi received her Ph.D. in Computer Science from the Department of Computer Science, University of Delhi, India in 1999 and her MTech in Computer Science from IIT Delhi, India in 1986. She is an Associate Professor in the Department of Computer Science, University of Delhi. She has about 25 years of teaching and research experience and has published more than 140 research papers in national/international journals/conferences. Dr. Bedi is a member of AAAI, ACM, senior member of IEEE, and life member of Computer Society of India. Her research interests include web intelligence, soft computing, semantic web, multi-agent systems, intelligent information systems, intelligent software engineering, software security, intelligent user interfaces, requirement engineering, human computer interaction (HCI), trust, information retrieval, personalization, steganography, and steganalysis.

Nitin Bhatia received his Graduate degree in Science in 1998 and Master's degree in Computer Applications in 2001, from Guru Nanak Dev University, Amritsar, India. He is working as Assistant Professor in the Department of Computer Science, DAV College, India. He is also pursuing his PhD from Punjabi University, Patiala, India. He has 20 research papers to his credit. His areas of interest are pattern recognition, computer vision, and fuzzy logic. He is associated with various international journals as reviewer and has edited a book entitled, "Cross-Disciplinary Applications of Artificial Intelligence and Pattern Recognition: Advancing Technologies" for IGI Global, USA.

Renu Dhir received her degree in Doctor of Philosophy (PhD) in Computer Science and Engineering from Punjabi University, Patiala in 2008. She received her Master's degree in Technology in Computer Science and Engineering from TIET Patiala in 1997. She did her B.Sc. in Electrical Engineering from Panjab University in 1983. She has ten papers published in international journals and thirty-four in national/international conferences. She acted as research supervisor of twelve MTech theses. Presently, she is supervising three PhD scholars.

Vandana Gandotra received her Master's degree in Computer Applications from Punjab University, Chandigarh, India in 1996. She is working as an Associate Professor in the Department of Computer Science, Delhi University and has some 15 years of teaching experience in this field. She is also pursuing her PhD in the area of secure Software Engineering. She has number of research publications in national and international journals / conferences to her credit. Her research is primarily focused on security issues concerning present day threat perceptions. In her research, she has evolved threat-oriented security model which integrates various proactive steps in risk management for securing software systems.

D. P. Goyal is Professor of Management Information Systems at Management Development Institute (MDI), Gurgaon. Earlier he has been Professor and Dean of Academics at Institute of Management Technology (IMT), Ghaziabad. A post graduate in Business Management and Doctorate in Management Information Systems, Prof. Goyal is a recipient of merit scholarship and merit certificate for having secured third rank in the university. He has participated in a number of faculty enhancement programmes organized by the top business schools including IIM Ahmedabad; IIM Calcutta; IIT Mumbai; and Thapar University Patiala. He has more than 25 years of industry; teaching; training; research; and academic administration experience. Prof Goyal is a member of various professional bodies and associated with many B-Schools and universities in the capacity of member, Board of Governors; member, Board of Studies; and member, Advisory committees. He has also been on the expert / assessment committees of various bodies including AICTE. His teaching and research interest areas include Management Information Systems, Strategic Information Systems, IS Solutions for Business; Knowledge Management; and Business Process Management. Prof. Goyal has successfully supervised 12 PhD scholars and currently supervising four PhD scholars. He has published over 50 research papers in refereed international/national journals of repute; has been principal investigator of sponsored research projects; has organized several conferences both at national and international level; has presented his research findings in more than 40 national/international conferences; and published a number of research, edited, and textbooks including two textbooks one each on Management Information Systems: Managerial Perspectives published by Macmillan; and on Enterprise Resource Planning: A Managerial Perspective published by Tata McGraw Hill. He has also been the Editor of a couple of research journals; and is on the editorial board of many national/ international journals. Currently, Dr. Goyal is involved in supervising research projects in the areas of business value of IT, business process management, ERP systems, and knowledge management.

Nicolas Guelfi is Professor at the Faculty of Sciences, Technologies, and Communications of the University of Luxembourg since March 1999, where he teaches, directs PhD students, and makes research in collaboration with national and international partners. Currently, he is a leading member of Laboratory for Advanced Software Systems. His main research and development activities concern the engineering and the evolution of dependable systems based on semi-formal methods and model driven engineering. He is the author of around 90 publications in books, journals, conferences, and workshops and has been editor of several books in his expertise domains.

Ashu Gupta is Sr. Faculty Member of Simulation Modeling in School of Information Technology, Apeejay Institute of Management Technical Campus, Jalandhar, India. His expertise areas include system simulations & modeling, data structure, and business process re-engineering, etc. Presently he is actively involved in research on application of simulation tools in manufacturing industry and developing a framework for evaluation of simulation software in Indian automobile Industry. An active researcher and a prolific writer, he has contributed numerous papers to several seminars and conferences and published research papers in various journals also.

Kawal Jeet received her B.Tech degree in Computer Science from B.C.E.T Gurdaspur in 2001. She is pursuing her MTech degree in Computer Science from NIT, Jalandhar. Her area of interest includes software engineering especially risk management and quality management of the software, wireless sensor networks and fuzzy logic. She has two papers published in international journals, five in international conferences, and three in international newsletter, two in national journals and two in national conferences. She also received grant from University Grants Commission, India for the project titled "A Fuzzy Inference Approach to Access and Predict Software Quality Using Activity-Based Quality Models".

Amandeep Kaur obtained her Gold Medal in Master's of Computer Applications from Punjab Technical University, India in 2004. Currently, she is Assistant Professor, School of Information Technology, Apeejay Institute of Management Technical Campus, Jalandhar, India. She has over seven years of teaching experience. Her research areas include usability engineering, cloud engineering, etc.

Daljit Kaur received her BCA and MSc degree in Network and Protocol Designing from Guru Nanak Dev University, Amritsar in 2004 and 2006, respectively. She worked as Software Engineer for three years in an IT company. She is currently working as an Assistant Professor in Department of Computer Science and Information Technology at Lyallpur Khalsa College, Jalandhar. Her research interests include security in software systems, security in software development life cycle, web security, and cyber attacks.

Kuljit Kaur is a faculty member in the Department of Computer Science & Engineering, Guru Nanak Dev University, Amritsar, Punjab, India. She has 15 years of teaching and research experience. She completed her PhD in Software Engineering in the Faculty of Engineering & Technology, Guru Nanak Dev University, Amritsar (Punjab) in 2011. Her research interests lie in software metrics, object oriented programming, software evolution, and service oriented architecture. She has been awarded a research project by the University Grants Commission (UGC), New Delhi, India to analyze evolution of open source software. Her research work has been published in international peer-reviewed journals and conferences. She is a member of ACM, and Punjab Academy of Sciences (Punjab, India).

Lakhwinder Kaur is a Sr. Faculty Member School of Information Technology, Apeejay Institute of Management Technical Campus, Jalandhar,Punjab,India. She is an MCA and is pursuing her PhD from Punjab Technical University, Kapurthala. Her current area of research is Software refactoring. She has 15 years of teaching experience and taught the subjects of Software Engineering, Data Structures, Object Oriented Programming in C++/Java, System Software, DBMS and Oracle, Computer Networks and Data Communications, etc. She has various publications in national/ international conferences/seminars/journals to her credit. She has organized a faculty development programme, has been a member of editorial board for edited books of seminars/ conferences, is an active member of various organizing committees for organizing different events at the Institute and is Editor-in-Chief of Institute's annual magazine.

Parminder Kaur is working as an Assistant Professor, Department of Computer Science & Engineering, Guru Nanak Dev University, Amritsar. She has done her post graduation in Mathematics as well as System Software and Doctorate in the field of Component-Based Systems, a branch of Software Engineering. She has around 45 international/national publications related to component certification, component versioning, version-control tools, software architecture, and software security. She is an editorial review committee member, *The International Arab Journal of Information Technology* (IAJIT), Zarqa University, Jordan. She is a life member of Punjab Science Congress and Computer Society of India.

Aggelos Liapis holds a PhD in Computer Mediated Collaborative Design Environments from the Robert Gordon University in Aberdeen, two Master's Degrees from the Universities of Sunderland and Hull in Network Systems and Computer Graphics and Virtual Environments and a Bachelor's degree from Lincoln University in Hull. Dr. Liapis worked in the Semantic Technologies and Applications Laboratory (STARLab) as a Research and Development coordinator at the University of Brussels (Vrije Universiteit Brussel). In 2009 Dr. Liapis was honoured with the position of Associate Professor from the Robert Gordon University in Aberdeen, and also joined the Defence Logistics Laboratory at Evelpidon Military University in Athens as a Research and Development coordinator. In 2010 Dr. Liapis joined European Dynamics SA as Head of Research and Development focusing in the areas of CSCW, semantics, Web 2.0, e-government, cloud computing, logistics, enterprise and system interoperability.

Bharavi Mishra is a PhD student in the Department of Computer Engineering, Institute of Technology, Banaras Hindu University, India under the supervision of Prof. K.K. Shukla. He received his MTech degree from Indian Institute of Information Technology, Allahabad in 2009. His research interest includes software engineering, machine learning, and data mining.

Nisha Ratti is presently working as an Assistant Professor in Rayat Institute of Engineering and Information Technology. She has three research papers in various journals and 04 in various national and international conferences. Her area of specialization is component -based systems. She is in editorial board of *International Journal of New Practices in Management and Engineering*.

Ayda Saidane has PhD in Computer Systems from INSA Toulouse (France) and MEng in Computer Science from ENSI Tunisia. She prepared her PhD thesis at LAAS-CNRS on intrusion tolerant architectures for Internet servers in the context of collaboration with SRI International. In 2005, she worked as expert Engineer on the DADDi project (Dependable Anomaly Detection with Diagnosis) with SSI team at Supelec Rennes (France). Between 2006 and 2009, she has been research fellow at University of Trento (Italy) working in the EU project SERENITY (System Engineering for Security and Dependability). She has been visiting Scholar at Ryerson University (Canada) in 2010. From 2010 to 2012, she has been a Research Associate at University of Luxembourg, working on SETER project (Security Testing for Resilient Systems).

Anirban Sarkar is presently a faculty member in the Department of Computer Applications, National Institute of Technology, Durgapur, India. He received his PhD degree from National Institute of Technology, Durgapur, India in 2010. His areas of research interests are database systems and software engineering. His total numbers of publications in various international platforms are about 35. He is actively involved in collaborative research with several Institutes in USA and has also served in the committees of several international conferences in the area of software engineering and computer applications.

Neeraj Sharma is Associate Professor in the Department of Computer Science. He holds Master's degree in Computer Applications as well as Master's degree in Business Administration. He is a Doctorate in the area of Software Experience Bases. Dr. Sharma has authored five books in the area of Information Systems, Computerized Accounting and Business Systems. He has presented his research findings in more than 20 national and international conferences and published papers in international journals of repute.

He has chaired several sessions at international conferences outside India. He is a consistent reviewer for many international research journals and is also contributing as a member of the Editorial Board. He is actively involved in writing, teaching and research for the last seventeen years in the diverse areas of software process improvement, experience bases and software modelling. He is currently supervising four Ph.D. candidates in the area of Agile Software Engineering and Software Experience management. Dr. Sharma is an active member of IEEE, Senior Member of ACM, and Computer Society of India.

K. K. Shukla is Professor of Computer Engineering, Institute of Technology, BHU, India. He has 30 years of research and teaching experience. Professor Shukla has published more than 100 research papers in reputed journals and conferences and has more than 90 citations. 10 PhDs have been awarded under his supervision so far. Professor Shukla has to his credit, many projects of national importance at BHU, Hindustan Aeronautics and Smiths Aerospace U.K. Presently he has research collaboration with Space Applications Center, ISRO, Tata Consultancy Services and INRIA, France. He has written four books on neuro-computers, real time task scheduling, fuzzy modeling, image compression, and has contributed chapters to two books published in the U.S. Professor Shukla is a Fellow of the Institution of Engineers, Fellow of the Institution of Electronics and Telecommunications Engineers, Senior Member, ISTE, and the Senior Member, Computer Society of India.

Kawaljeet Singh is Director of University Computer Centre (UCC) of Punjabi University, Patiala and Chairman, Board of Studies (Honorary), Faculty of Computer Applications, Punjab Technical University, Jalandhar. He has earned his degree of Master of Computer Applications (MCA) in year 1988 and Doctorate of Philosophy (Ph.D.) in year 2001 in Computer Science from Thapar Institute of Engineering & Technology, Patiala. He is having nearly two decades of professional, administrative and academic career. He had started his career as Lecturer from Punjabi University, Patiala and then afterwards has served for more than a decade at various positions such as Reader & Head of Department of Computer Science and Engineering in Guru Nanak Dev University, Amritsar. He has also headed many responsible positions such as Dean & Chairman of RDC Committee of Faculty of Engineering & Technology of G.N.D.U. and guided a number of research scholars for doctorate and MPhil in Computer Science. He has also co- authored three text books and published more than 32 research papers and articles in national and international journals, conferences, seminars, and workshops. His subjects of interest are simulation modeling and intelligent databases.

Archana Singhal received her PhD in Computer Science from the School of Computer and Systems Sciences (SC&SS), Jawaharlal Nehru University, Delhi, India in 1998. She is an Associate Professor in the Department of Computer Science, IP College, University of Delhi, Delhi. She has some 14 years of teaching and research experience and has number of research papers published in national/international journals / conferences. Her areas of research include agile software development, cloud computing, web intelligence, soft computing, semantic web, multi-agent systems, intelligent information systems, information retrieval, and ontologies.

G. Sreedhar is awarded with PhD in Computer Science and Technology from Sri Krishnadevaraya University, Anantapur in the year 2011 and he also awarded with MPhil (Computer Science) from Alagappa University, Karaikudi 2005, respectively. He passed MTech (CSE) in first division from Acharya

Nagarjuna University, Nagarjuna Nagar in the year 2010 and passed M.C.A in first division from Sri Krishnadevaraya University, Anantapur, India in the year 1998, respectively. He is working as Assistant Professor in Dept. of Computer Science at Rashtriya Sanskrit Vidyapeetha, Tirupati since 2001. His research articles were published in number of national and international journals. He has over 14 years of teaching and research experience in the field of Computer Science.

Fathi Taibi is an academician with research and professional interests in software engineering. He holds a B.Sc. (Hons) degree, a Master's degree, and PhD degree all in Computer Science. Dr. Taibi has more than 13 years of combined teaching and research experience. Currently, he is an Assistant Professor at the University of Management and Technology, Malaysia. He has published extensively in refereed journals and conference proceedings. His research interests include software analysis, software quality and metrics, software reuse, formal, and object-oriented methods.

Index